Relationship marketing

Visit the *Relationship Marketing, third edition* Companion Website at **www.pearsoned.co.uk/egan** to find valuable **student** learning material including:

- An online glossary to explain key terms
- Annotated links to relevant sites on the web

Relationship marketing

Exploring relational strategies in marketing

THIRD EDITION

JOHN EGAN
Middlesex University

FT Prentice Hall
FINANCIAL TIMES

An imprint of **Pearson Education**
Harlow, England • London • New York • Boston • San Francisco • Toronto • Sydney • Singapore • Hong Kong
Tokyo • Seoul • Taipei • New Delhi • Cape Town • Madrid • Mexico City • Amsterdam • Munich • Paris • Milan

Pearson Education Limited

Edinburgh Gate
Harlow
Essex CM20 2JE
England

and Associated Companies throughout the world

Visit us on the World Wide Web at:
www.pearsoned.co.uk

First published 2001
Second edition published 2004
Third edition published 2008

© Pearson Education Limited 2008

ISBN: 978-0-273-71319-7

British Library Cataloguing-in-Publication Data
A catalogue record for this book is available from the British Library

Library of Congress Cataloging-in-Publication Data
Egan, John, 1952–
    Relationship marketing : exploring relational strategies in marketing / John Egan.--
3rd ed.
        p. cm.
    Includes bibliographical refereneces and index.
    ISBN-13: 978-0-273-71319-7 (pbk. : alk. paper)   1. Relationship marketing.   I.
Title.
    HF5415.55.E34 2008
    658.8'12--dc22

                                                    2007052391

10 9 8 7 6 5 4 3 2 1
11 10 09 08

Typeset in 9pt Stone Serif by 30
Printed by Ashford Colour Press Ltd., Gosport

The publisher's policy is to use paper manufactured from sustainable forests.

For Alison, Thomas and Alice

Contents

Part I Relationships

Part II The core firm and its relationships

Part III Managing and controlling the relationship

Supporting resources

Visit **www.pearsoned.co.uk/egan** to find valuable online resources

Companion Website for students
- An online glossary to explain key terms
- Annotated links to relevant sites on the web

For instructors
- Complete, downloadable Instructor's Manual
- PowerPoint slides that can be downloaded and used for presentations

For more information please contact your local Pearson Education sales representative or visit **www.pearsoned.co.uk/egan**

Preface

As I noted in the first edition, although the main title *Relationship Marketing* sets out the parameters of this text, it is the subtitle that may prove more enlightening. Exploring relational strategies in marketing continues to acknowledge the role that relationship marketing (RM) plays in modern management and establishes the contexts in which RM is most beneficially exercised. This is not, however, a 'how-to' text on relationship marketing, customer relationship management or any of the various relational business subject areas (complete with prescriptive solutions). Rather, this book seeks to generate questions and debate and encourage individual responses to particular marketing situations.

The book is not without bias. It is most definitely written from the viewpoint of marketing as an art rather than a science, and my concerns regarding the mathematical manipulation of sometimes spurious data no doubt resonate in the text. I concur with that body of opinion that views marketing as a 'messy set of rules, tools and guidelines that produce (results) according to the expertise and sensitivity of the craftsman (or craftswoman), not the empirical accuracy of the rules, tools and guidelines' (Damarest, 1997, p. 375). This may understandably annoy some of my more mathematically and statistically minded colleagues.

Despite this one fundamental bias, I have attempted to be objective. This does not negate, however, the responsibility of the reader to make up his or her own mind as to whether to accept or refute any of the positions taken in the text. While reading this book, maintain a healthy scepticism and question conclusions and research findings in whatever way you see fit.

RM has recently experienced a perhaps justified backlash. This text should *not* be regarded as a fight-back by relational marketers but rather as a contribution to the ongoing debate. I do, however, take the view that just because a concept may be flawed (and which one is not?) it does not necessarily mean it should be wholly abandoned. This potential for 'throwing the baby out with the bath water' incidentally, in my view, applies to *both* relationship and traditional marketing.

Although RM is usually associated with services marketing I would like to think that many of the ideas hold resonance for product manufacturers. In the same way I trust that it will be of interest to both consumer and business-to-business marketers. Indeed, I hope that the text may offer help in establishing how these areas of business are associated with one another within a relational context.

Although not strictly necessary, I have continued the tradition of past editions and fully referenced each author or authors as several research colleagues have indicated that it is useful to them.

Book structure

The book is divided into three parts. Part I discusses ideas surrounding relational strategies in general and, in particular, relationship marketing. Part II analyses over several chapters the central RM tenet of the 'core firm and its partnerships'. Part III explores the place of technology in relational strategy management and the management process itself.

New to this edition!

As RM is an evolving discipline, this latest edition references the latest developments in the field. There are also 12 new case studies referencing and highlighting issues discussed in the text. Having introduced a completely new chapter (Back to the future) at the end of the second edition, I have introduced another (100 years of marketing) at the beginning to further contextualise RM's position in the history of marketing development. As a result, all the remaining chapters have been renumbered. A Glossary has also been added to this edition.

Comprehensive web resources

A complete package of supplements is available to assist students and instructors in using this book. Visit <www.booksites.net/Egan> to find an Instructor's manual, PowerPoint slides, and links to other useful sites.

Acknowledgements

The first edition would never have seen the light of day without the help of a number of people whose input I gratefully acknowledge. In particular I would also like to thank the following reviewers for their pre-revision review comments:

Roger Baty, University of Central England
David Gilbert, University of Surrey
Caroline Tynan, Nottingham University Business School
Cleopatra Veloutsou, University of Glasgow
Peter Verhoef, Erasmus University

I am grateful to the publishers, and in particular to David Cox, Andrew Harrison and Chris Shaw, for their support on this latest edition of *Relationship marketing*.

Last, but very definitely not least, I continue to be grateful to my family for putting up with me locking myself away and to whom this book is dedicated.

I welcome any comments or suggestions regarding this third edition. I take this opportunity to thank those readers (students and lecturers in the main) who have made comments and suggestions in the past some of which I have incorporated in this latest edition. As Brown (2002) notes, the ongoing debate over definitions, domains and the nature of the discipline itself is a sign of a healthy and imaginative marketing environment. So let's get healthy!

John Egan
April 2008
j.egan@mdx.ac.uk

References

Damerest, M. (1997) 'Understanding knowledge management', *Long Range Planning* 30(3), 374–84.

Brown, S. (2002) 'Vote, vote, vote for Philip Kotler', *European Journal of Marketing*, 36(3), 313–24.

Acknowledgements

We are grateful to the following for permission to reproduce copyright material:

Figure 3.5 reprinted by permission of Harvard Business School Press, from *The Loyalty Effect: The Hidden Force Behind Growth, Profits and Lasting Value* by F.F. Reichheld, Boston, MA 1996, p.43, copyright © 1996 Harvard Business School Publishing Corporation; Figure 11.2 from *Stages in the Planning Process* by Brassington and Pettitt, Copyright Elsevier (1987); the Telegraph for an extract from 'No room for loyalty at United' by Jim White from *The Daily Telegraph* 16th June 2007; Haymarket Direct for the articles 'Is personal touch worth it' by Ed Kemp from *Marketing* 24th January 2007, 'Why should we trust you?' by Melanie Godsell and 'Complaints are there to be heard' by Gemma Charles from *Marketing* 10th January 2007, 'Why firms must listen and learn from complaints' by Laura Mazur from *Marketing* July 2000, 'Look out for the bastardization of buzz phrases' by Julian Dodds from *Marketing* 29th June 2000, 'Bouncing ideas around' by Trevor Davis and Ian Bradbury from *Management Today* September 2007, 'A Decisive Edge' by Rebecca Alexander from *Management Today* May 2007, and 'Keep Your Customers Cool' by Horacio Falão from *World Business* November – December 2006; The Chartered Institute of Marketing, Don Peppers and Martha Rogers for the article 'Return on Customer' by Don Peppers and Martha Rogers first published in *The Marketer* June 2006 by The Chartered Institute of Marketing; The Chartered Institute of Marketing and Susan M. Drake for the article 'Who are your most ardent fans?' by Susan M. Drake first published in *The Marketer* November 2006 by The Chartered Institute of Marketing; The Chartered Institute of Marketing for the articles 'Building Bridges' by Chris Ellery first published in *The Marketer* June 2007 by The Chartered Institute of Marketing, 'Technology is no substitute for thought when it comes to customer care' by John Edmund first published in *Marketing Business* May 1999 by The Chartered Institute of Marketing and 'Reclaiming the customer high ground' by Holly Wright first published in *The Marketer* July/August 2007 by The Chartered Institute of Marketing; and Penton Media for the article 'Understanding and Addressing Your Client's Needs' by Michael Greenberg taken from the Chiefmarketer.com website http://chiefmarketer.com.

We are grateful to the Financial Times Limited for permission to reprint the following material:

Chapter 18 Case Study: What the Willy Wonka of BSkyB knows about customers, © FT Business Life, Financial Times, 17 April 2007.

List of figures

List of abbreviations

B2B	business-to-business/industrial marketing
B2C	business-to-consumer marketing or consumer marketing
CIM	Chartered Institute of Marketing
CPT	cost-per-thousand (media audience measurement)
CRM	customer relationship management
DbM	database marketing
DM	direct marketing
DMA	Direct Marketing Association
EDI	electronic data interchange
ERP	enterprise resource planning
FMCG	fast moving consumer goods
IDM	Institute of Direct Marketing
IMP	Industrial Marketing & Purchasing Group
ISP	Institute of Sales Promotion
IT	information technology
NPD	new product development
PMP	process management perspective
PTM	part-time marketers
R&D	research and development
RFV	recency, frequency, monetary value model
RM	relationship marketing
ROI	return on investment
ROR	return on relationships
SME	small/medium-sized enterprises
SRC	supplier/retailer collaboration
TM	transactional (or transaction-based) marketing
TQM	total quality management
WWW	World Wide Web

Part I
Relationships

This first part describes and analyses the market phenomenon that has become generally known as **relationship marketing (RM)**. RM is itself 'shorthand' for quite a wide range of 'relationship-type' strategies that have developed over the past few decades in product as well as service markets and in consumer as well as business-to-business sectors although not necessarily with the same intensity or success.

In this new edition a 'prequel' has been added (Chapter 1) detailing the progression of marketing to the point when writers began to question the validity of the traditional marketing paradigm in every circumstance. Chapter 2 continues the development of relationship marketing itself from this point. As Chapter 2 develops it may become apparent that agreement on a definition of RM is far from generally accepted. The chapter does, however, build up (or construct) a working definition that may be a starting point for analysis. Those readers who prefer to 'deconstruct' are invited to jump ahead to page 37 where they will find the definition upon which the second half of this chapter is based.

Chapter 3 investigates the concept of relationships, both actual and metaphoric. It examines whether relationships with constructs as nebulous as 'organisations' are possible and whether they are a result, a prelude to and/or a mediating factor in the establishment of interpersonal and non-personal relationships. It examines various forms and types of relationship (including so-called customer loyalty) and examines these from the perspective of the RM debate.

Chapter 4 looks at the economic arguments that are seen to underpin RM. In a commercial world RM strategies must be based on the perceived profitability of relationship retention and longevity. The acceptance of relationship strategy profitability as a 'given' is, however, questionable in certain industry situations.

Chapter 5 investigates the potential for a 'marketing strategy continuum'. This suggests the need to develop a portfolio of strategies not only across industries but within individual organisations.

Chapter 6 follows up on the strategy portfolio by looking at those drivers to relational strategies that are perceived to exist and tests whether these are apparent in different industries or along the continuum.

1 100 years of marketing

Key issues

- Historical development of marketing during the twentieth century
- Development and progression of marketing theory

Introduction

Although we see **marketing** as a twentieth-century phenomena, much of what we would today recognise as marketing practice existed long before its formal beginnings as a field of study. From the time of the ancient Greeks through the great economists of the 1700s and 1800s (including Smith, Malthus, Jevons, Ricardo, Mill and Marshall), concepts such as markets, marginal analysis, value, production, humans as social and economic entities, competition and the role of governments had already been raised and extensively debated (Wilkie and Moore, 2003). Ambler (2004), for example, traces marketing thought to the Middle Ages with the first formal analysis of buyer motivation by St Thomas Aquinas (1225–74) and St Bernardino of Siena's (1380–1444) recognition of function, **market price** (i.e. economic benefit) and **psychological benefits**. In the nearer term it is also possible to track marketing's direct economic origins back through to the 'Physiocrats' of the eighteenth century and the 'Austrian School of Economics' at the end of the nineteenth century (Broeckelmann, 2004) and its mercantile origins to eighteenth-century English entrepreneurs such as Josiah Wedgwood (1730–95). Marketing, therefore, is as old as commerce and has been practised for centuries. What the twentieth century brought that was new was an independent discipline and what might be called the specialist marketer (Ambler, 2004).

One undisputed fact about the birth of modern marketing and its formative years is that it was largely North America-dominated. Unlike its precursor, economics, which was largely of European origin and was to retain its internationalism, modern marketing began, developed and flourished in the USA. Not that recognisable concepts did not exist internationally, but it was in the USA that marketing was recognised early on as a subject worthy of academic endeavour. This young discipline benefited from that country's powerful sense of individualism and entrepreneurship, its exuberance and fierce competition (Witowski, 2005). That the USA subsequently became the world's largest economy strengthened and consolidated its position. This heritage is the reason why, even in the current global commercial and academic marketplace, American marketing journals, and indeed American academics, still, rightly or wrongly, dominate the discipline.

The early days

It was commercial pressures that brought the marketing debate to the fore in the USA. By the end of the nineteenth century the Industrial Revolution had created such quantities of products (at substantially lower prices) as to completely change the nature of US consumer markets from sellers' markets where choice was limited (and expensive) to buyers' markets where competitors vied for the patronage of the consumer. In Europe, and notably the UK, somewhat different dynamics existed early in the century. 'Job and batch' production continued here long after North American manufacturers adopted 'flow production' methods. One reason for this was that the UK was a very unequal society with much of the country's wealth in a very few hands, the majority of the population poor and little between those two extremes. A large market for consumer indulgences simply did not yet exist. In the USA, meanwhile, there was a growing middle-class at whom moderately priced consumer goods could be targeted. Under these conditions, for example, the cost of buying a motor vehicle fell 60 per cent with the advent of production line techniques enabling a growing number of people to afford them. By 1923 Ford Motor Company had sold over two million Model Ts largely to an aspiring middle-class.

Modern marketing in the eyes of many observers (e.g. Bartels, 1976) began at the turn of the twentieth century, when more structured academic attention started to be given to the area of market distribution, a topic that was evolving and assuming great prominence in the marketplace (Wilkie and Moore, 2003). Although it is acknowledged that marketing grew out of the field of economics, modern marketing owed much of its independence to its challenge of accepted economic tenets. Economic theorists had long held the view that value was created by production. Say's Law (Jean-Baptiste Say, 1767–1832) stated that there could be no demand without supply and that no sooner was a product produced than it afforded a market for other products to the full extent of its value (Say, 1803). Mass production capabilities required mass consumption which in turn required more complex and varied distribution systems and a more sophisticated understanding of tools to influence mass consumer demand (Wilkie and Moore, 2003). By 1900 marketers were proposing that demand consisted of more than just the ability to purchase and that it also required desire on the part of the consumer. The suggestion was that desire could be increased and manipulated by factors (e.g. distribution, advertising) other than the mere existence of supply (Bartels, 1976) and value added beyond that of production (Wilkie and Moore, 1999).

Earliest writings on marketing concentrated on the agricultural industry where the added-value of the distribution process was evident. Other discussions were in the field of advertising covering such subjects as advertising copy, layout, campaigns, principles and practice, economics and psychology (Bartels, 1976) and in 1908 Scott wrote *The Theory of Advertising*. Concepts such as **elasticity of demand** (developed by Alfred Marshall 1842–1924) were being used by marketing writers as a theoretical basis for developments in selling, advertising and promotions as well as marketing in general. **Value theory** was another area of economic (and philosophical) thought built upon by early marketers. Value theorists investigated how people value things (positively or negatively), the reasons why they make such evaluations and use consumer choice as evidence of intrinsic value. By 1910 literature relating to marketing research began to appear. The emergence of marketing research was itself the result of growing pressure to produce and apply accurate knowledge to the field and to bring the methods of science to the field of marketing (Bartels, 1976).

The decade between 1910 and 1920 has been called the 'period of conceptualization' for marketing (Bartels, 1976). In this phase marketing authors built upon distribution theory to develop their understanding of marketing. Weld (1916, p. 6) wrote 'At each step an increment of value is added by those who handle or transform the product' emphasising further that value was no longer regarded as wholly created in the production process. It was also around this time that the term 'marketing' itself was added to the commercial lexicon. Although the concept of marketing had always existed it was at this time that the word was first used as a noun as opposed to its earlier use as a verb (Petrof, 1997). Until this time what marketing now described had always been referred to as 'trade', 'distribution', or 'commerce'. Among highly influential writers of the period Ralph Starr Butler and Arch W. Shaw are considered important to the development of the new marketing discipline. Ralph Starr Butler (1882–1971), believed marketing was all about coordination, planning and the management of complex relationships. Shaw (1876–1962) distinguished three basic business operations: production, distribution and facilitating functions or administration. Given the changing forms involved between production and distribution, the latter conceived marketing as 'matter in motion' (Bartels, 1976). It was Shaw (1912, p. 708) who also first proposed the centrality of the customer when he wrote that 'the more progressive business man is searching out the unconscious needs of the consumer, and is then producing the goods to gratify them.' It was also in this period that concepts developed that were later to become known as the **commodity approach** (focusing on all marketing actions involved in a particular product category), the **institutional approach** (focusing on describing the operations of a specialised type of marketing agency, such as a wholesaler or a broker) and the **functional approach** (focusing on the purposes served by various marketing activities) (Wilkie and Moore, 2003). The functional approach in particular was to gain wide acceptance among marketing thinkers and was valued as a means of defining and rationalising the field of marketing and its numerous activities and for its usefulness in analysing marketing problems (Fullbrook, 1940). The marketing field also began to take on its own distinct academic identity when a number of US universities independently began to develop new courses to examine various aspects of the marketing system. Academic programmes including 'distributive and regulative industries', 'the marketing of products', 'methods of marketing farm products' and 'mercantile institutions' were early examples (Bartels, 1951a, 1988; Wilkie and Moore, 2003).

By the second decade of the twentieth century ideas were starting to coalesce around a number of tentative generalisations. In 1923 Fred Emerson Clark (1890-1948) produced *Principles of Marketing* (Clark, 1923) in which he defined marketing as 'those efforts which effect transfer in the ownership of goods'. Paul Dulaney Converse (1889–1968) in his book *Marketing Methods and Policies* (Converse, 1922) distinguished between the functions of middlemen and the marketing functions. Cherington (1920) added an important basis for future thought by asking whether marketing performance and societal welfare might be enhanced by focusing on the underlying functions of marketing; probably the first mention of social marketing. The ubiquitous AIDA (attention, interest, desire, action) model appeared in a publication by Strong (1925), albeit based on an idea of St Elmo Lewis writing towards the end of the previous century. The first doubts about the dangers of consumerism were also being discussed at this time largely in terms of moral degeneration (Fitchett, 2005). There was debate too about whether non-essential services could be eliminated and whether there were too many middlemen adding to costs (Wilkie and Moore, 2003). Advertising was particularly singled out for criticism regarding its '**economic value**' (e.g., Moriarty 1923; Vaughan, 1928) and whether it essentially caused prices to rise. There were also certain 'unorthodox' studies going on that were to become the bases for the further evolution of marketing such as White's (1927) very managerial proposal of a '**scientific marketing management**', offering guidance to the companies who wish to understand marketing (Skålén *et al.*, 2005).

The period 1930–40 was characterised more by the development of existing concepts rather than the production of new ideas. Exceptions included Charles F. Phillips whose book *Marketing* (Phillips, 1938) was published towards the end of the decade. His text showed an interest in the consumer that went well beyond the study of buying motives to consider consumers as the driving force of the economy. There were also developments in theory designed to embrace what was called oligopolistic competition (Chamberlain, 1933; Sheth *et al.*, 1988; Waterschoot and Van den Bulte, 1992). In an **oligopoly**, firms operate under imperfect conditions and with a kinked demand curve. Following the fierce price competitiveness created by the **sticky** (i.e. inelastic) **demand curve** firms utilise **non-price competition** in order to achieve greater revenue and market share. This theoretical insight later led marketing theoreticians (e.g. McGarry, 1950; McKitterick, 1957; Alderson, 1957) to create 'lists' of marketing variables deduced from econometric, profit optimising equations. In 1936 the *Journal of Marketing* was launched and began to attract articles that had previously found limited favour in economic journals. Interest in marketing was also starting to develop in Europe albeit tentatively. In September 1931 the magazine *Marketing* first appeared in the UK but it took another 37 years for the magazine's publisher, the Incorporated Sales Managers' Association, to change its name to the Institute of Marketing, the predecessor of today's Chartered Institute of Marketing.

In the 1940s an increasing number of different approaches were being considered. New emphasis was given to the management of marketing and more attention paid to the consumer viewpoint. Whereas early marketing had frequently centred on rural agriculture (e.g. Weld, 1916), after 1945 topics such as the growth of the mass market, employment, consumer savings and industrial development (e.g. Hahn, 1946; Vance, 1947; Grether, 1948) started to be discussed. The field of modern demographics developed around the explosion of births and migration patterns after the Second World War. William Lloyd Warner, an anthropologist, for example, researched American society and its class system. He divided social classes by three distinct groups, which he labelled lower, middle and upper, with each class sub-divided further into two parts. This was to become the basis of **demographic profiling**. The role of marketing theory as a science began to be seriously discussed. Leading articles such as Converse's (1945) 'The development of the science of marketing', Alderson and Cox's (1948) 'Towards a theory of marketing', and slightly later Bartels' (1951b) 'Can marketing be a science?' exemplified the call from scholars for more theoretical frameworks and began to explore new parameters for this body of thought (Wilkie and Moore, 2003). An important economic distinction should once again be made between what was happening in the US and Europe at this time. While USA consumerism was buoyant, Europeans were still suffering from shortages that would last into the 1950s. In the UK, for example, rationing did not end until 3 July 1954. European marketing at this time was less directed at stimulating wants than restricting needs.

Modern marketing

The 1950s represented a watershed for marketing thought as the mainstream debate became steeped in science. This science-led revolution reflected a conscious movement in US business thinking. In the early 1950s the Ford Foundation started an initiative to infuse scientific theory into US business systems and marketers were quick to get involved. US business schools responded by raising admission standards and including more mathematics, statistics, economics and other sciences to the curriculum (Mentzer and Schumann, 2006). But not everyone agreed that this was the right way forward. Hutchinson (1952, p. 290) noted that the forebears of marketers were merchants not scientists and that it was a 'travesty to relate the scientist's search for knowledge to the market research man's seeking after customers'. Marketing textbooks continued to disseminate new ideas. In *Theory in Marketing*, Cox and Alderson (1950) contributed ideas such as heterogeneous markets, the uniqueness of organisational positioning and competition based on differential advantage. In the early 1950s, Borden (1954) introduced the concept of the marketing mix, a list of 12 variables (product, price, branding, distribution, personal selling, advertising, promotions, packaging, display, servicing, physical handling, fact finding and analysis) from which the marketer could blend the ingredients or variables of the mix into an integrated marketing programme.

From the mid-1950s, interest in the topic of marketing management grew rapidly effectively replacing the functionalist school of thought. From the marketing management perspective, marketers were viewing the field from the standpoint of marketing practitioners in order to help them develop successful marketing programmes. Relative to what had gone before, marketing management theory suggested that it was less important to study and explain how marketing as a practice functions rather than how marketing should function (Skålén *et al.*, 2005). The theory implied the integration of marketing activities and the downward delegation of authority. The literature at the time particularly emphasised problem-solving and decision-making. This move towards marketing management was, incidentally, to further increase the professional and vocational appeal of university marketing programmes (Wilkie and Moore, 2003).

In a seminal work, McCarthy (1960) presented the 'marketing mix', reconstructing Borden's original 12 variables into the **'4Ps' model of marketing** (price, product, promotion and placement). Although this concept retained many of the key elements of the functional school it did shift the perspective firmly toward the marketing management approach. Ironically, McCarthy specifically denied that his list of variables were intended as a definition of the scope of marketing (Payne, 1995; Duncan and Moriarty, 1998); rather he presented the 4Ps as an aid to instruction and a starting point from which to construct a marketing strategy (Grönroos, 1994a, 1994b). The 'mix' was not the only 'list' model proposed during this period, but its inherent simplicity ensured the rise of both the model and its attendant marketing management theory.

In addition to the 4Ps marketing mix a number of concepts still prominent today were developed at this time including **market segmentation** (Smith, 1956) and **brand image** (Gardner and Levy, 1955). In time these were to become the basis of what would later be called 'modern' **transactional marketing (TM)** (Kotler, 1992; Takala and Uusitalo, 1996; Aijo, 1996). Kotler (1967) summed up how the thinking of the period was applied when he characterised marketing as a decision-making activity designed to satisfy the customer, at a profit, by targeting and making optimal decisions on the various elements of the mix.

Economic conditions in the 1950s and 1960s were to conspire to reinforce the perceived superiority of the marketing mix paradigm. Infrastructure development aided distribution, there was a decided shift to urban living and television was to offer opportunities to advertise to vast audiences. In the large, rapidly expanding (76 million new consumers were born in the period 1946–65), domestic, post-Second World War US consumer market of relatively homogeneous and insatiable customers there were rapid increases in the demand for standardised consumer goods. Despite this demand the prevailing economic thinking was to ensure that consumption kept up with output (Packard, 1957). Marketing was seen as a way of achieving this but there was a perceived need to formalise it to ensure that it was guaranteed to work every time (O'Malley and Patterson, 1998). The simplicity and communicability of the marketing mix paradigm, together with its apparent success, combined to turn marketing into 'a highly effective impact machine' (Grönroos, 1996, p. 16). In this time (and place) of high consumer trust, effective mass marketing, growing prosperity, homogeneous demand and dominant manufacturers (O'Driscoll and Murray, 1998) modern transactional marketing theory appeared to be working very effectively indeed.

In Europe, economies were recovering from their post-war gloom and the growth in consumer spending (albeit from a lower base) was beginning to mirror that of the US economy of a decade earlier. Advertising spending grew rapidly in this period largely on the back of commercial television. In the UK, Independent Television (ITV) was launched on 22 September 1955. This greater interest in marketing created a need for marketing education and the obvious source of inspiration was the USA. As marketing education sped around the globe, from its US birthplace, transactional marketing rapidly became the overwhelmingly dominant marketing paradigm (Dixon and Blois, 1983; Kent, 1986).

The 1960s saw the emergence of new conceptual and methodological perspectives on managerial decision-making, social and behavioural patterns, qualitative analysis, systems structure and behaviour, environmental constraints, comparative analysis, international markets and physical distribution (Bartels, 1976). A major external factor that was to have an immense affect on marketing was the rapid development of computer technology. This tool enabled researchers to undertake sophisticated modelling of complex marketing problems. Reflecting this development Bass *et al.* (1961) published *Mathematical Models and Methods in Marketing* which was quickly followed by other texts on this subject matter (e.g. Frank *et al.*, 1962; Buzzell, 1964; Kotler, 1971). The scientific analysis approach to marketing was greatly advanced by Professor Paul Green, who developed **conjoint analysis** in the late 1960s. This tool allowed companies to analyse consumer preferences and buying intentions, as well as measure how they might react to changes in existing products and services or product introductions. Computing power was also to have an effect on the practice of marketing from a research and sales perspective. Marketing theorist, Lester Wunderman is regarded as the first to have coined the term '**direct marketing (DM)**' in the 1960s, an industry that was to develop rapidly in the latter part of the century.

The topic of consumer behaviour was developing during this period and there were texts by Zaltman (1965), Engel *et al.* (1968) and Howard and Sheth (1969) devoted to this area of research. However, not all of this consumer behaviour research necessarily fitted comfortably with the now dominant managerial approach (Wilkie and Moore, 2003). The FMCG consumer markets, where relatively low-valued products were sold to mass markets using mass media, still dominated marketing thinking. In the late 1960s, Kotler (1967) published *Marketing Management: Analysis, Planning, and Control*. This text was to influence many young academics and researchers and went some way to directing future research by explicitly incorporating the quantitative and behavioural sciences as part of the thrust in marketing thought (Wilkie and Moore, 2003).

As the leading marketing author of the 1970s, Kotler (1972) further entrenched the existing paradigm when he determined the mantra underlying thinking during this period. This was that marketing management sought to adapt the settings of the company's marketing decision variables such that they maximised company objectives in the light of the expected behaviour of non-controllable demand variables (Vargo and Lusch, 2004). Two schools of thought became influential during the period. The **macromarketing school** examined the impact of marketing practices on society and society on marketing whereas the **strategic planning school** explored the relationship between environmental change and change within the organisation. The 1970s also saw debate concerning the breadth of marketing thought as marketing thinking was applied to ideas, places and people in addition to products and services. **Not-for-profit** and **societal marketing** came to the fore. Other topics which developed at this time were in the areas of '**demarketing**' (i.e. marketing designed to change behaviour) and '**network marketing**'. While marketing boundaries continued to expand so apparently did the gap between academics and practitioners. In 1977 the American Marketing Association and the Marketing Science Institute convened a commission to evaluate the effect of research on marketing practice (Mentzer and Schumann, 2006). The conclusion of the Commission was that academic marketing had very little impact on improving marketing management practice (Myers *et al.*, 1980). The academic/practitioner divide debate was to continue into the next decade with very little evidence of a satisfactory outcome (see Brennan and Ankers, 2004).

Despite the apparent supremacy of marketing in the period doubts were starting to be raised about the all-embracing nature of the traditional marketing paradigm. These doubts largely originated from those operating within businesses and socio-political environments very different from those of the United States, for example Europe (Hammarkvist *et al.*, 1982; Elg and Johansson, 1996) and from marketers working within the industrial (business-to-business) and service sectors. Marketing had always had an uncomfortable relationship with those sectors which operated outside of mainstream consumer goods.

Some attempts were made to accommodate the evident anomalies. However, rather than start again by challenging the conceptual basis of transactional marketing, the quickest and most convenient 'solution' to the problem was to paper over the cracks. The standard method of 'overcoming' deficiencies in the 4P 'tablet of faith' (Grönroos, 1994b) was to expand on the same approach – abstracting the market relationship into a list of decision-making variables (Grönroos, 1994b; Brodie *et al.*, 1997). An unintentional legacy of McCarthy's 4P model was that most of these lists used words beginning with the same letter (e.g. Lipson and Darling 1971; Kelly and Lazer, 1973: see Grönroos, 1994b) often the letter P. From the late 1970s, this pedantry became more extreme: 'after the four P's were definitely canonised . . . new items to the list [were] almost exclusively put in the form of P's' (Grönroos, 1994a, p. 5). The guilty were many, Kotler (1986), public relations and politics; Booms and Bitner (1981), people, physical evidence and process; Judd (1987), people; Le Doux (1991), preservation.

The perceived orthodoxy did not, however, go wholly unchallenged. The Fall 1983 edition of the *Journal of Marketing* provided a platform with articles by Arndt (1983), Day and Wensley (1983), Deshpande (1983), Howard (1983) and Hunt (1983) much of which suggested that the traditional microeconomic view of marketing was increasingly inadequate (Ambler, 2004). The issue contained several articles which attacked the perception of marketing as a science and raised concerns about marketing's reliance on the logical positivism/empiricism perspective that now dominated research. Criticisms of transactional marketing were also generated based on the difficulties in applying it outside its original context.

Many weaknesses of the transactional paradigm were initially hidden in the context of a buoyant post-Second World War US economy. These defects were revealed as the competitive environment in which firms operated evolved beyond recognition in the 1980s (Turnbull and Wilson, 1989; Blattberg and Deighton, 1991; Aijo, 1996). In the USA intra-market competition intensified considerably as the number of firms – both local and foreign – increased (Jackson, 1985; Gummesson, 1987). This spread to most developed consumer goods markets changing them from growth to mature markets (Hammarkvist *et al.*, 1982). Firms had to compete for a static number of customers within markets that were becoming increasingly saturated with products (Berry, 1983; Morgan and Hunt, 1994), a development which has been termed hyper-competition (Ohmae, 1990; Kotler, 1991). This exposed transactional marketing as a theory developed out of growth, not stagnation (Grönroos, 1991; Gummesson, 1991) or super-competitiveness, and that it was proving unsuitable in many circumstances.

New frames of reference not directly associated with the marketing mix did start to appear. Sheth *et al.* (1988) saw what they called a paradigm shift in the development of strategic marketing theory. The objective here was competitive advantage and market share became its primary indicator of performance (Ambler 2004). Porter (1979, 1985) warned against being 'stuck in the middle' between price competitiveness and distinctiveness and to establish competitive advantage through the five-forces analysis (Porter, 1979). PIMS research in Cambridge sought to link market share to profitability as did the Boston Consulting Group matrix and other 'big is beautiful' models of the period. Despite these developments, however, most research topics published in the period still relied heavily on the 4Ps model (Gundlach and Wilkie, 1990).

The 1990s were seen as a sea-change in the attitudes of business within the Anglo-American sphere of financial influence. Short-term profits and their impact on the share price put marketers on the defensive from which many would suggest they have not emerged. Marketers were called to account and required to measure the success of their output. That they were not necessarily measuring the right things appeared to be of secondary importance. Marketers from around the world, and in particular in Scandinavia, were recognising that the traditional marketing approach had diverted marketers away from their original customer-orientated perspective. From this point on our history continues through the lens of relationship marketing research. The 'rise and rise of relationship marketing' (Saren, 2007, p. 12) does not mean, however, that thinking has not developed since the first edition of this book in 2001: indeed, quite the contrary. Several authors have contributed interesting perspectives which this edition seeks to represent. One lesson that this review of history has taught this author is that, although ideas develop, what has gone before rarely goes away. Rather, theory builds on theory. This makes for a complexity which may be uncomfortable for some but which adds to the value of the discipline.

References

Aijo, T. (1996) 'The theoretical and philosophical underpinnings of relationship marketing', *European Journal of Marketing*, **30** (2) 8–18.

Alderson, W. (1957) *Marketing Behaviour and Executive Action*, Homewood, IL: Irwin.

Alderson, W. and Cox, R. (1948) 'Towards a theory of marketing', *Journal of Marketing* **13** (Oct), 137–52.

Ambler, T. (2004) 'The new dominant logic of marketing: views of the elephant', Centre for Marketing Working Paper No. 04–903, London Business School.

Arndt, J. (1983) 'The political economy paradigm: foundation for theory building in marketing', *Journal of Marketing*, Fall, **47** (4), 44–54.

Bartels, R. (1951a) 'Influences on the development of marketing thought 1900–1923', *Journal of Marketing* **16** (July), 1–17.

Bartels, R. (1951b), 'Can marketing be a science?', *Journal of Marketing*, **16** (January), 319–28.

Bartels, R. (1976) *The History of Marketing Thought*, 2nd edn, Columbus, OH: Grid Publishing.

Bass, F.M., Buzzel, R.D., Greene, M.R., Lazer, W., Pessimier, E.A., Shawver, D., Schuchman, A. and Wilson, G.W. (1961) *Mathematical Models and Methods in Marketing*, Homewood, IL: Richard D. Irwin.

Berry, L.L. (1983) 'Relationship marketing', in Berry, L.L., Shostack, G.L. and Upah, G.D. (eds) *Emerging Perspectives on Services Marketing*, Chicago: American Marketing Association, pp. 25–8.

Blattberg, R.C. and Deighton, J. (1991) 'Interactive marketing: exploring the age of addressability', *Sloan Management Review*, Fall, 5–14.

Booms, B.H. and Bitner, M.J. (1981) 'Marketing strategies and organisational structures for service firms', in Donnelly, J. and George, W.R. (eds) *Marketing of Services*, Chicago, IL: American Marketing Association, pp. 47–51.

Borden, N.H. (1954) 'The concept of the marketing mix', *Journal of Advertising Research*, **4** (June) 2–7.

Brennan, R. and Ankers, P. (2004) 'In search of relevence: is there an academic–practitioner divide in business-to-business marketing?, *Marketing Intelligence & Planning*, **22** (5), 511–19.

Brodie, R.J., Coviello, N.E., Brookes, R.W and Little, V. (1997) 'Towards a paradigm shift in marketing: an examination of current marketing practices', *Journal of Marketing Management*, **13** (5), July, 383–406.

Broeckelmann, P. (2004) 'Austrian economics as a basis for a general marketing theory: potentials and limitations', *Humboldt-Universität zu Berlin*, <http://edoc.hu-berlin.de/master/broeckelmann-philipp-2004-11-26/HTML/front.html> (accessed 16 November 2007).

Buzzell, R.D. (1964), *Mathematical Models and Marketing Management*, Boston, MA: Harvard Graduate School of Business.

Chamberlain, E.H. (1933) *The Theory of Monopolistic Competition*, Cambridge, MA: Harvard University Press, pp. 99–113.

Clark, F.E. (1923) *Principles of Marketing*, New York: Macmillan.

Converse, P.D. (1922) *Marketing Methods and Policies*, New York: Prentice Hall.

Converse, P.D. (1945) 'The development of the science of marketing: an exploratory survey', *Journal of Marketing*, **10** (July), 14–23.

Cox, R. and Alderson, W. (1950) (eds), *Theory in Marketing*, Homewood, IL: Irwin.

Day, G.S. and Wensley, R. (1983) 'Marketing theory with strategic orientation', *Journal of Marketing*, Fall, **47** (4), 79–89.

Deshpande, R. (1983) 'Paradigms lost: on theory and method in research in marketing', *Journal of Marketing*, Fall, **47** (4), 101–10.

Dixon, D.F. and Blois, K.J (1983) 'Some limitations of the 4Ps as a paradigm for marketing', Marketing Education Group Annual Conference, Cranfield Institute of Technology, Cranfield, UK, July.

Duncan, T. and Moriarty, S.E. (1998) 'A communication-based marketing model for managing relationships', *Journal of Marketing*, **62** (April), 11–21.

Elg, U. and Johansson, U. (1996) 'Networking when national boundaries dissolve', *European Journal of Marketing*, **30** (2), 61–74, 132–41.

Engel, J.F., Blackwell, R.D. and Kollat, D.T. (1968) *Consumer Behavior*, Hillsdale IL: The Dryden Press.

Fitchett, J. (2005) 'The twenty-first century consumer society', in Kimmel, A.J. (ed.) *Marketing Communication: New Approaches, Technologies and Styles*, Oxford: Oxford University Press, pp. 42–62.

Frank, R.E., Kuehn, A.A. and Massy, W.F. (1962) *Quantitative Techniques in Marketing Analysis*, Homewood, IL: Richard D. Irwin.

Gardner, B.B. and Levy, S.J. (1955), 'The product and the brand', *Harvard Business Review*, March/April, 33–9.

Green, P.E. and Rao, V. (1971) 'Conjoint measurement for quantifying judgmental data', *Journal of Marketing Research*, 8 (August), 355–63

Grether, E.T. (1948) 'The postwar market and industrialization in California', *Journal of Marketing*, **12** (Jan), 311–16.

Grönroos, C. (1991) 'The marketing strategy continuum: towards a marketing concept for the 1990s', *Management Decision*, **29** (1) 7–13.

Grönroos, C. (1994a) 'From marketing mix to relationship marketing: towards a paradigm shift in marketing', *Management Decision*, **32** (2) 4–20.

Grönroos, C. (1994b) 'Quo vadis, marketing? toward a relationship marketing paradigm', *Journal of Marketing Management*, **10**, 347–60.

Grönroos, C. (1996) 'Relationship marketing logic', *Asia–Australia Marketing Journal*, **4** (1), 7–18.

Gummesson, E. (1987) 'The new marketing: developing long-term interactive relationships', *Long Range Planning*, **20** (4), 10–20.

Gummesson, E. (1991) 'Marketing orientation revisited: the crucial role of the part-time marketer', *European Journal of Marketing*, **25** (2), 60–75.

Gundlach, G.T. and Wilkie, W.L. (1990) 'The marketing literature in public policy: 1970–1988', in Murphy, P.E. and Wilkie, W.L. (eds) *Marketing and Advertising Regulation: The Federal Trade Commission in the 1990s*, Notre Dame, IL: University of Notre Dame Press, pp. 329–44.

Hahn, L.A. (1946) 'The effects of saving on employment and consumption', *Journal of Marketing*, **11** (July), 35–43.

Hammarkvist, K.O., Hakansson, H. and Mattsson, L. (1982) *Marketing for Competitiveness*, Lund: Liber.

Howard, J.A. (1983) 'Marketing theory of the firm', *Journal of Marketing*, Fall, **47** (4), 90–100.

Howard, J.A. and Sheth, J.N. (1969) *The Theory of Buyer Behavior*, New York: John Wiley & Sons.

Hunt, S.D. (1983) 'General theories and the fundamental explananda of marketing', *Journal of Marketing*, Fall, **47** (4), 9–17.

Hutchinson, K.D. (1952) 'Marketing as a science: an appraisal', *Journal of Marketing*, **16** (January), 286–93.

Jackson, B.B. (1985) 'Build customer relationships that last', *Harvard Business Review*, November/December, 120–28.

Judd, V.C. (1987) 'Differentiate with the 5th P: People', *Industrial Marketing Management*, **16** (November), 241–7.

Kelly, E.J. and Lazer, W. (1973) *Managerial Marketing*, Homewood, IL: Irwin.

Kent, R.A. (1986) 'Faith in the 4Ps: an alternative', *Journal of Marketing Management*, **2** (2), 145–54.

Kotler, P. (1967) *Marketing Management: Analysis, Planning and Control*, Englewood Cliffs, NJ: Prentice Hall.

Kotler, P. (1971) *Marketing Decision Making: A Model Building Approach'*, New York: Holt, Rinehart and Winston.

Kotler, P. (1972) *Marketing Management: Analysis, Planning and Control'*, 2nd edn, Englewood Cliffs, NJ: Prentice Hall.

Kotler, P. (1986) 'Megamarketing', *Harvard Business Review*, March/April, 117–24.

Kotler, P. (1991) *Marketing Management: Analysis, Planning and Control*, 7th edn, Englewood Cliffs, NJ: Prentice Hall.

Kotler, P. (1992) 'Total marketing', *Business Week Advance Executive Brief No. 2*, Columbus, OH: McGraw Hill.

Le Doux, L. (1991) 'Is preservation the fifth "P" or just another microenvironmental factor?', in McKinnon, G.F. and Kelley, C.A. (eds) *Challenges of New Decade in Marketing Education*, Northridge, CA: Western Marketing Educators' Association.

Lipson, H.A. and Darling, J.R. (1971) *Introduction to Marketing: An Administration Approach*, New York: Wiley.

McCarthy, E.J. (1960) *Basic Marketing*, Homewood, IL: Irwin.

McGarry, E.D. (1950) 'Some functions of marketing reconsidered', in Cox, R. and Alderson, W. (eds) *Theory of Marketing*, Chicago, IL: Irwin.

McKitterick, J.B. (1957) 'What is the marketing management concept?', in Bass, F. (ed.) *The Frontiers of Marketing Thought in Action*, Chicago, IL: AMA.

Mentzer, J.T. and Schumann, D.W. (2006) 'The theoretical and practical implications of marketing scholarship', *Journal of Marketing Theory and Practice*, **14** (3), 179–90.

Morgan, R.M. and Hunt, S.D (1994) 'The commitment–trust theory of relationship marketing', *Journal of Marketing*, **58**, 20–38.

Moriarty, W.D. (1923) *The Economics of Marketing and Advertising*, New York: Harper & Brothers.

Myers, J.G., Massey, W.F. and Greyster, S.A. (1980) *Marketing Research and Knowledge Development*, Englewood Cliffs, NJ: Prentice Hall.

O'Driscoll, A. and Murray, J.A. (1998) 'The changing nature of theory and practice in marketing: on the value of synchrony', *Journal of Marketing Management*, **14** (5), 391–416.

Ohmae, K. (1990) *The Borderless World*, London: Collins.

O'Malley, L. and Patterson, M. (1998) 'Vanishing point: the mix management paradigm re-viewed', *Journal of Marketing Management*, **14**, 829–51.

Packard, V. (1957) *The Hidden Persuaders*, Harmondsworth: Penguin.

Payne, A. (ed.) (1995) *Advances in Relationship Marketing*, The Cranfield Management Series, London: Kogan Page.

Petrof, J.V. (1997) 'Relationship marketing: the wheel reinvented?', *Business Horizons*, (Nov–Dec).

Phillips, C.F. (1938) *Marketing*, New York: Houghton Mifflin.

Porter, Michael E. (1979) 'How competitive forces shape strategy', *Harvard Business Review*, (March/April), 137.

Porter, Michael E. (1985) *Competitive Advantage*, New York: The Free Press.

Saren, M. (2007) 'Marketing is everything: the view from the street', *Marketing Intelligence and Planning*, **25** (1), 11–16.

Say, J.-B. (1803) 'A Treatise on Political Economy, or the Production, Distribution and Consumption of Wealth' (English translation).

Scott, W.D. (1908) *The Theory of Advertising*, Boston, MA: Small, Maynard & Company.

Shaw, A. (1912), 'Some problems in market distribution', *Quarterly Journal of Economics*, **26**, 700–760.

Sheth, J.N., Garner, D.M. and Garrett, D.E. (1988) *Marketing Theory: Evolution and Evaluation*, New York: Wiley.

Skålén, P., Fellesson, M. and Fougère, M. (2005) 'Marketing, government and governmentality', Proceedings of the CMS Conference 2005, University of Waikato <http://www.mngt.waikato.ac.nz/ejrot/criticalmarketing/Skalen.pdf> (accessed 6 May 2007).

Smith, W. (1956) 'Product differentiation and marketing segmentation as alternative marketing strategies', *Journal of Marketing*, **20** (July), 3–8.

Strong, E.K. (1925) *'The Psychology of Selling'*, New York: McGraw-Hill.

Takala, T. and Uusitalo, O. (1996) 'An alternative view of relationship marketing: a framework for ethical analysis', *European Journal of Marketing*, **30** (2), 45–60.

Turnbull, P.W. and Wilson D.T. (1989) 'Developing and protecting profitable customer relationships', *Industrial Marketing Management*, **18**, 233–8.

Vance, L.L. (1947) 'The interpretation of consumer dis-saving', *Journal of Marketing*, **11** (Jan), 243–9.

Vargo, S. and Lusch, R. (2004) 'Evolving to a new dominant logic for marketing', *Journal of Marketing*, **67**(1) 1–17.

Vaughan, F.L. (1928) *Marketing and Advertising*, Princeton, NJ: Princeton University Press.

Waterschoot, W. and Van den Bulte, C. (1992) 'The 4P classification of the marketing mix revisited', *Journal of Marketing*, **56** (Oct), 83–93.

Weld, L.D.H. (1916) *The Marketing of Farm Products*, New York: The Macmillan Company.

White, P. (1927) *Scientific Marketing Management: Its Principles and Methods*, New York: Harper & Bros.

Wilkie, W.L. and Moore, E.S. (1999) 'Marketing's contribution to society', *Journal of Marketing*, **63** (Special Issue), 198–218.

Wilkie, W.L. and Moore, E.S. (2003) 'Scholarly research in marketing: exploring the "4 eras" of thought development', *Journal of Public Policy & Marketing*, **22** (2) Fall, 116–46.

Witkowski, T.H. (2005) 'Sources of immoderation and proportion in marketing thought', *Marketing Theory*, **5** (2), 221–31.

Zaltman, G. (1965) *Marketing: Contributions from the Behavioral Sciences*, New York: Harcourt, Brace & World.

2 Relationships in marketing

Key issues

- Current state of marketing
- Antecedents to relationship marketing (RM)
- Development of RM
- Defining RM

Introduction

The preceding chapter sought to chronicle the history of marketing during the twentieth century. Its inclusion in this edition was as a backdrop to the development of relationship marketing (RM) in the latter part of this century. In many respects RM cannot be fully discussed without reference to marketing paradigms of previous generations. This chapter takes up the story from the perspective of RM research and its subsequent influence on marketing thought.

Relationship marketing

Relationship marketing (RM) has been a topic of serious discussion among academics and marketing practitioners for the best part of 20 years. It was, however, during the last decade of the twentieth century that relational strategies gained a wider following and that debate on RM began to dominate the marketing agenda. During this period RM was probably *the* major trend in marketing and certainly the major (and arguably the most controversial) talking point in business management. RM in the 1990s became the leading topic of discussion at academic conferences in Europe, North America, Australia and elsewhere around the globe. RM was frequently the subject of dedicated practitioner conferences, academic journal articles (as a general topic), in

RM editions of major publications as well as in at least one dedicated RM journal (the *International Journal of Consumer Relationship Management*) and specialist marketing magazines. RM was the basis of academic and practitioner texts by major marketing writers (e.g. McKenna, 1991; Christopher *et al.*, 1991; Payne *et al.*, 1995; Buttle, 1996; Gordon, 1998; Gummesson, 1999), and such was RM's perceived importance that few, if any, marketing books failed to include at least one section dedicated to the concept.

RM's rise to prominence was rapid. As the last decade of the twentieth century passed into history, the number of devotees to the concept continued to grow fast. Indeed, RM had, according to one prominent marketing writer, managed to get up a real 'head of steam', with academics seemingly leaping aboard with 'lemming like abandon' (Brown, 1998, p. 171). If this was true of marketing academics then market-ing practitioners were just as (if not more) enthusiastic. Indeed, practitioner interest became the driving force behind RM's growth (O'Malley and Tynan, 2000, p. 809), with innumerable case studies reported at conferences, in magazines and in texts sup-porting and justifying the relational approach.

Claims for the benefits of relational strategies abounded, not least that RM was becoming a unifying force within marketing. Mattsson (1997a, p. 448) suggested that here at last there was a concept within marketing research that served as the generic context for all marketing transactions, whether products or services, consumer or industrial. This viewpoint is supported by Sheth and Parvatiyar (2000, p. 121) who suggest that the scope of RM is wide enough to cover the entire spectrum of market-ing's sub-disciplines including 'channels, business-to-business marketing, services marketing, marketing research, customer behaviour, marketing communications, marketing strategy, international marketing and direct marketing'! Grönroos (1996, pp. 12–13) believed that RM represented the biggest change in 50 years, in effect 'taking marketing back to its roots'. RM, it was being suggested, was a (or *the*) 'new marketing paradigm' (e.g. Kotler, 1992; Grönroos, 1994a; Gummesson, 1999, 2001) and a 'paradigm shift' (e.g. Sheth and Parvatiyar, 1993; Grönroos, 1994a; Morgan and Hunt, 1994; Gummesson, 1997; Buttle, 1997) was taking place in marketing practice and thought. Major companies (e.g. British Airways, Boots, Tesco) were confident enough about RM's capabilities to appoint RM managers and directors whose princi-pal function was to operationalise the concept. At around the same time Safeway became the first UK supermarket chain to set up a dedicated RM team (Whalley, 1999). According to Sheth and Parvatiyar (2000, p. 119) the emergence of an RM 'school of thought' was imminent given the interest of marketing scholars in the rela-tional paradigm. RM was in vogue among contemporary marketing academics and practitioners, not only in service and inter-organisational contexts, from where it had developed, but even in consumer markets, where it had initially been overtly shunned (O'Malley and Tynan, 1999, p. 587). By the end of the century it was claimed that, in both practice and research, RM was beyond the introduction stage and on a growth curve toward becoming a mature concept (Berry, 2000, p. 151).

While most marketers approached the concept with some level of rationality, there were some claims that were almost messianic in nature. Reichheld (1996, p. 24) sug-gested that the relational concept[1] represented a 'shift in business thinking as fundamental as the shift to a Copernican sun-centred system was for astronomers'. Elsewhere (p. 33) he suggested that the benefits of loyalty-based marketing represented 'a kind of miracle of loaves and fishes'. According to Mattsson (1997b, p. 37) relationship marketing was the 'battle cry' of the 1990s. The 'marketing mix' and other aspects of 'traditional marketing' were, it was suggested, dying: 'Long live Relationship Marketing'.

Influences on relational strategy development

The assumption is sometimes made that RM was the first major new development in marketing for many years. As the previous chapter emphasised this was not the case. During the twentieth century there were a number of major developments, often associated with differences in research emphasis. According to Christopher *et al.* (1991, pp. 8–9) the 1950s were the age of consumer marketing when corporate manufacturers and brand marketing concepts dominated the marketing agenda. In the 1960s marketing was characterised by industrial marketing research. The 1970s were a decade when attention started to be paid to the non-profit sector and the 1980s the period where the service sector came to prominence for the first time. Each of these research concentrations (see Figure 2.1) led to new ideas being developed and a general expansion of marketing's influence in the commercial world.

Figure 2.1
Development in marketing

(*Source*: Adapted from Christopher *et al.*, 1991)

All of these prior developments were to have an influence on 'relational research' in the 1990s and beyond. In addition, RM mirrored (and to a certain extent borrowed from) events taking place in other areas of business research, including trends in organisational structures (Gummesson, 1999, p. 7), **distribution management** and total quality concepts and, more recently, **knowledge management**.

This diversity of influences was to lead to several different academic perspectives from which RM theory (or, more correctly, theories) was to develop (Figure 2.2). Grönroos and Strandvik (1997, p. 342) note that these perspectives included contributions from the Nordic school of service management, the network approach to industrial (or business-to-business) marketing, the Anglo-Australian approach to integrating quality, customer service and marketing, 'strategic alliances and partnerships' research and, more generally, investigation into the nature of relationships in marketing. One factor which may be noted was that, although North American researchers made a significant contribution to the development of RM, their influence over this area of research was not as dominant as had been the case in the past (see Chapter 1). It should also be noted that many North American researchers have led, and are leading, relationship marketing in directions other than those that are defined in this text (see Chapter 13). Regardless of domain variabilities, however, RM, in its widest sense, was undoubtedly becoming a global concept.

Figure 2.2
Influences on relationship marketing

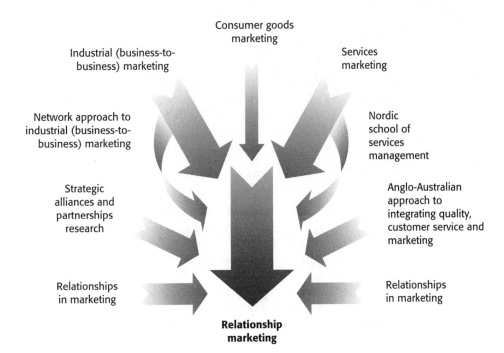

Consumer goods marketing

Industrial (business-to-business) marketing

Services marketing

Network approach to industrial (business-to-business) marketing

Nordic school of services management

Strategic alliances and partnerships research

Anglo-Australian approach to integrating quality, customer service and marketing

Relationships in marketing

Relationships in marketing

Relationship marketing

Claims for the origins of 'relationship marketing' are numerous (see page 31). Among the various centres of research, the Nordic school in particular was to be highly influential in European[2] RM development. According to Gummesson (1996, p. 32), this school was originally conceived for services marketing research in the early 1980s and was characterised by a shift in focus from those ideas associated with traditional marketing concepts. These included:

■ stressing the importance and relevance of services marketing and industrial marketing more than consumer goods marketing;

■ a gradual shift away from an emphasis on goods and services to an emphasis on customer value;

■ the integration of the marketing department function with other organisational functions and with general management;

■ less emphasis on quantitative research than that suggested by management research traditions in other countries;

■ more theory generation than theory testing and, consequently, more **inductive** and **abductive** than **deductive research** (see Box 2.1).

■ research output that was empirical, theoretical and holistic.

Box 2.1   Research terms defined

Deductive: Argument from general principles to particular conclusions, thus analytical and certain. Deduced, or capable of being deduced, from premises. Deductive research is associated with a 'scientific' view of research.

Inductive: Making empirical (i.e. founded on experience and observation and not theory) generalisations by observing particular instances. The conclusions go beyond the facts so they can never be more than strong possibilities. Inductive research is associated with qualitative research methods.

Abductive: Reasoning for the purposes of discovery as opposed to the justification of scientific hypotheses or theories.

According to the Nordic school approach, managing services was at the core of relationship building and maintenance although also supported by other factors such as the building of networks, the establishment of strategic alliances, the development of customer databases and the management of relationship-orientated marketing communications (Grönroos, 2000, p. 97). Another characteristic of the Nordic school's approach was that marketing was seen more as '**market-orientated management**' than as tasks for marketing specialists. In other words marketing was viewed as an overall process rather than as a separate (i.e. marketing department) function (ibid., p. 98).[3]

It is probably not surprising that, with these various inputs from different countries and research traditions, different approaches to what had generally become known as 'relationship marketing' appeared to be developing. By the middle of the 1990s Palmer (1996, p. 19) was suggesting that research into RM could be classified in three broad ways:

- at a tactical level where RM is used principally as a sales promotion tool (e.g. loyalty schemes);
- at a strategic level where long-term relationships with customers are created by 'detention rather than retention' with the aid of legal, economic, technological, geographical and other 'barriers to exit' (see page 86);
- At a philosophical level where RM was seen to go to the heart of marketing philosophy, refocusing marketing strategy away from products and their life cycles towards customer relationship life cycles and the integration of customer orientation and inter-functional coordination.

The suggestion made in Palmer's research was that some marketers, rather than embracing the philosophy, were using the term 'relationship marketing' as a smokescreen for largely traditional (if updated) 'transactional' strategies and tactics. This rhetoric versus reality argument reappears regularly in the discussion of relationship marketing (see Chapters 3 and 13).

Brodie *et al.* (1997) and Coviello *et al.* (1997), in their review of relationship marketing, also noted multiple uses of the term (see Figure 2.3). They suggested that RM was being applied at four levels. At the first level it was seen as an elaborate form of database marketing. This represented RM as a technology-based tool (not unlike those associated with direct marketing and customer relationship management) used by firms to facilitate the acquisition and management of customers. Again, the implication was that, rather than employing ideas and concepts new to marketing, this form of RM was simply utilising new and updated 'tools' to manage largely traditional customer transactions, albeit in a more efficient way, a charge that has been levelled against some direct marketers (see Chapter 12) and the processes collectively called **customer relationship management (CRM)** (see Chapter 11).

Figure 2.3
Relationship marketing definitions

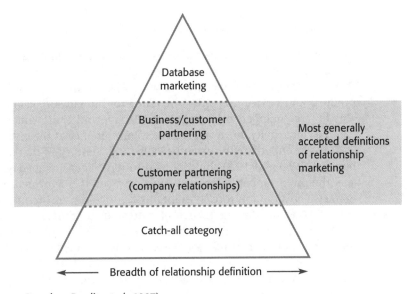

(*Source*: Based on Brodie *et al.*, 1997)

At a second, broader, level Brodie *et al.* saw RM as a focus on actual or potential relationships between the business and its customer base with a concentration on customer retention. On a third (even broader) level, RM was seen as a form of 'customer partnering' with buyers cooperatively involved in the design of the product or service offering. Working relationships on this level implied true interaction between the buyer and seller. At a fourth (and broadest) level RM was seen as incorporating 'everything from databases to personalised service, loyalty programmes, brand loyalty, internal marketing, personal/social relationships and strategic alliances'. When used in this way the term becomes a 'catch-all' phrase for a variety of relational (and perhaps some strictly non-relational) concepts.

This last, very broad, definition could be said to have helped create difficulties in establishing the parameters of RM from more traditional marketing approaches. As O'Malley and Tynan (2000, p. 809) note, with 'the diversity in operational approaches employed, and the lack of accepted definitions', it became 'impossible to delimit the [RM] domain'. The boundaries, they noted, were 'completely permeable and elastic' and this resulted in 'difficulties in identifying appropriate contexts for empirical research and exacerbated conceptual problems within the emerging discipline'.

RM development

Although RM undoubtedly emerged as a strong concept on the back of prior research, its dramatic growth has been strongly associated with the perceived crises in marketing that took place during the latter part of the twentieth century. To get a fuller picture of the drivers to relational strategy development, a brief examination of the history and perceived weaknesses of traditional marketing may be appropriate.

The golden age of marketing

As Chapter 1 illustrated, marketing as a distinct discipline was born out of economics around the beginning of the twentieth century (Sheth and Parvatiyar, 2000, p. 119). The turn of that century coincided with a period in history when, for the first time, products and services not strictly required for human survival became generally available to large numbers of consumers in Europe and North America. As a recognisable commercial activity, however, it came to prominence as the century developed.

If the twentieth century can be called the 'century of marketing' then the period between 1950 and 1970 could be said to have been its heyday. During this 'golden age' the public appetite for new goods and services appeared insatiable. In western markets consumption rose substantially as prices, in real terms, fell. The period coincided in the UK with the launch of independent commercial television, which was, ultimately, to become the marketer's most powerful mass-market communications medium. Consumer spending (conservatively) doubled during this time and much of this increase was attributed to the power and influence of marketing. Marketing was hailed as amongst the most powerful forces for cultural stability at work in the world (Sherry, 2000, p. 328). Modern marketing, it appeared, could do no wrong.

As the contribution of marketing came to be regarded as more and more important so the demand for marketing education and research grew. It was during this period that many of the marketing concepts still taught in business schools around Europe, North America and the rest of the world today were first developed. In the 1960s Borden (1964) produced his 12 elements of a marketing programme (see Figure 2.4), which were later simplified further to what became known as the '4Ps of marketing' (see Figure 2.5) or the 'marketing mix' (McCarthy, 1978). The traditional marketing framework that developed during this period viewed marketing as a strategic and managerial matching process. This matching process sought to ensure that the marketing mix and internal policies of the company were appropriate to the market forces (opportunities and threats) operating within the company's competitive environment.

Figure 2.4
Borden's 12 elements of a marketing programme and McCarthy's marketing mix

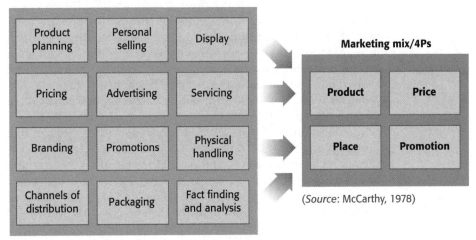

(*Source*: Borden, 1964)

(*Source*: McCarthy, 1978)

Figure 2.5
Marketing mix

New product development, brand management, features, benefits, packaging, after-sales service

Product

Costs, profits, liquidity, competitiveness, value, incentives

Price

Place

Channel management, retail location and retail image, logistics

Promotion

Marketing communications mix, integrated communications

This traditional marketing framework was quickly adopted, by students, teachers and practitioners alike, as a straightforward, easy to remember and intuitively rational marketing model. In this era of high consumer trust, effective mass advertising, growing prosperity, homogeneous demand, poorly developed distribution channels and, above all, dominant manufacturing power (O'Driscoll and Murray, 1998, p. 396), the **'brand management model'** and the 'toolbox' approach (Grönroos, 1994b, p. 5) of the marketing mix appeared to be working very effectively indeed.

Market changes

In the 1960s the favourable conditions that had seen the growth of marketing began to change dramatically. During this decade the UK, USA and other developed consumer markets became saturated. Population growth, a feature and major driver behind the rise in consumer purchasing, was declining. Most brands showed very little growth and markets became dominated by oligopolies. **Branding**, originally conceived to provide customers with quality assurance and little else, had, over time, evolved into a segmentation tool with different brands for each segment. As segments proliferated so did brands, contributing further to marketing's productivity problems (Sheth and Sisodia, 1999, p. 78).

As Christopher (1996, p. 55) notes, 'mature markets', such as those that developed in the UK and the USA in the 1960s, exhibit certain characteristics that differentiate them from 'growth markets' and these characteristics were to contribute significantly to marketing's perceived decline in effectiveness. In particular, consumers, faced with a surfeit of goods and services, were becoming much more demanding. In this 'buyer's market' customers began to realise the attractiveness of their spending power and began taking advantage of it. Customers were also growing more sophisticated and less easily persuaded by marketing messages.

At the same time as this greater consumer power and sophistication became evident, the perceived benefits (relative to costs) of advertising were seen to be in decline as the media market fragmented and the **'cost-per-thousand'**[4] targets rose substantially. In addition 'premium brand' dominance was declining as consumers perceived little difference between rival products, leading to a decline in market share and profitability for manufacturers' brands largely in favour of retail store equivalents ('own brands'). Many of the top fast-moving consumer goods (FMCG) brands were, by now, over 40 years old and the failure rate for new brands was reaching very high levels despite often substantial marketing support. There was an erosion of margins caused by a decline in brand premiums as manufacturers' brands fought for market share. There was a subsequent increase in 'below the line' expenditure as brand owners vied for shelf space from increasingly powerful retailers. The combined effect of these changes was the downward pressure on pricing and ultimately profitability.

Despite the growing complexity and competitiveness of the marketplace at the end of the 1980s, marketers were still persevering with the tools and concepts of the more predictable 'golden age' that had evidently now passed. Both academics and practitioners were still working with theory and practice developed and first promulgated in a bygone age (Christopher and Baker, 2000, p. 284). According to McKenna (1991, p. viii), the homogeneity marketers continued to seek was a myth advanced by those who were still using the American market model *circa* 1950–1960. By this time consumers, politics and even religions were growing more diverse as each year passed. The world was changing but marketing appeared stuck in a rut.

Marketing in crisis

As marketing entered the 1990s things appeared to be going from bad to worse. Companies were beginning to question the large expenditure on marketing without a measurable return on investment that had been assumed in past decades. Accountants, looking to reduce costs and increase rates of return, asked for justification of expenditure and were not pleased with the vague responses they were receiving from marketing departments. Brand-building exercises with largely immeasurable outcomes were no longer seen as justifiable.

The last decade of the twentieth century was also to see the marketing function being marginalised in many organisations (Sheth and Sisodia, 1999, p. 84). Even marketing pioneers such as Procter & Gamble and Unilever were abolishing the position of marketing director (Doyle, 1995, p. 23) to concentrate on other functional activities. Marketing was being openly criticised for lack of innovation in the face of hostile markets and for largely adopting defensive strategies to cope. As Doyle (ibid., p. 24) noted, marketers of the period generally made the mistake of seeing marketing as a functional discipline rather than an integrated business process. This led to the belief that 'the discipline was about tactical and generally superficial segmentation and positioning rather than real innovation and the creation of sustainable competitive advantage'. This functional defensiveness was to further harden attitudes against marketers.

Marketing education

Despite the obvious problems that existed, little was changing in marketing education. Marketing theory remained mired in a futile search for laws, regularities and predictability (Brown, 1995, p. 159). The marketing mix approach was still (and arguably still is) the dominant marketing model although it was beginning to be seen as offering a too 'seductive sense of simplicity' (Christopher *et al.*, 1991, p. 8) which, despite its pedagogical virtues, was prone to misguide academic and practitioner alike (Grönroos, 1990, p. 3). The 'toolbox' approach (Grönroos, 1994b, p. 5) of science-orientated marketing was criticised as a 'neglect of process in favour of structure', leading to a consequent 'lack of study into other key variables' (Christopher *et al.*, 1991, p. 8) not suggested by the marketing mix concept. Marketers were suffering from difficulties of their own creation by applying, unmodified, the principles they had learned in past decades (Gordon, 1998, p. 1) despite the fact that the commercial world was changing all around them. Whereas the marketing mix paradigm had served a function at one time in the development of marketing theory, once it had established itself as the 'universal truth' in marketing it began to cause more harm than good (Grönroos, 1994c). It had dominated marketing for over 40 years, downplaying the relational aspects of exchange and obscuring the role of relationships in marketing (Harris *et al.*, 2003, p. 10). It seemed that the problem was no longer 'marketing myopia'[5] but the myopia of marketing (Brown, 1995, p. 179).

So it appeared that marketing, the leading department of the first three-quarters of the century, was losing its primacy to other organisational disciplines (Doyle, 1995, p. 23) and doing little to resolve the problem. According to Gordon (1998, p. 1), marketers were so busy attending to the practice of marketing they may not have noticed that it was, for all practical purposes, dead. If not dead, it certainly was in crisis.

Antecedents of RM

As Chapter 1 illustrated, the marketing discipline had, from its very beginning, been dominated by consumer goods marketing and in particular US consumer goods practice of the 1950s (O'Driscoll and Murray, 1998, p. 409). In most marketing texts prior to 1990, concepts, models and strategies concentrated primarily on corporate manufacturers and their consumer brands. Services and industrial (business-to-business) marketing, despite their growing recognition as important components of the overall business environment, continued to be largely treated as separate disciplines. To many marketers of the period the traditional principles of marketing did not quite 'fit' these different marketing types. Rather than question the validity of the existing model, non-consumer goods (i.e. services and business-to-business) were treated as anomalies or afterthoughts usually found in separate chapters invariably towards the end of marketing texts.

A number of marketers were, however, beginning to recognise that 'gaps' existed between marketing textbooks and analysis, on the one hand, and practical implementation on the other (Gummesson, 1998, p. 242). They hypothesised that the disparity suggested by researchers into industrial (business-to-business) and services marketing, rather than being an argument for continued separation of the disciplines, should be considered as a basis for inclusive research. It was these researchers who were to begin the search for a more holistic view of marketing and whose radical ideas were to revolutionise marketing thought.

Industrial marketing research

Industrial marketing had always been treated as mainstream marketing's unglamorous 'poor relation', a disciplinary sub-field long overshadowed by consumer goods marketing (Brown, 1998, p. 173). The emphasis in this business seemed to be on raw materials, bulk shipments, pricing mechanisms and rational buying models where marketing played only a marginal role. What part it did play relied on extending the prevailing view of consumer marketing while acknowledging certain perceived differences (e.g. order size and frequency).

It was becoming apparent, however, largely through the work of the Industrial Marketing and Purchasing Group (IMP), that this approach did not reflect the complexities of how industrial markets operated (Naudé and Holland, 1996, p. 40). Empirical research showed that many inter-firm transactions are conducted within enduring business relationships where mutual trust and adaptation are commonplace rather than the then prevailing view of inter-firm transactions conducted largely on a contractual basis (Brennan and Turnbull, 2001, p. 1). As Baker (1999, p. 211) notes, industrial marketers had learnt that if you could not offer a 'better' product at the same price or an equivalent product at a lower price then the only way to stay in business was to foster relationships and add value through important, but usually intangible, service elements. Research suggested industrial marketing involved not just managing exchanges between companies but much more complex human inter-actions. This theory of **network-interaction marketing** was to be defined as all activities undertaken by the firm to build, maintain and develop customer relations (Christopher *et al.*, 1991, p. 10). The IMP literature argued that it was the ongoing nature of exchange episodes that led to the formalisation of relationships between buying and selling firms (Naudé and Holland, 1996, p. 40).

It is interesting to note that this industrial or 'business-to-business' research into interaction, relationships and networks predated RM research by at least a decade and maybe two (Mattsson, 1997a, p. 37). It stressed the importance of the understanding of the complex relationships that exist within and between industries (Naudé and Holland, 1996, p. 44) and served as a platform upon which relationship marketers were to develop their ideas.

Services marketing

If industrial (or business-to-business) marketing was the poor relation then '**services marketing**' was the black sheep. This second-class view of services *vis-à-vis* consumer goods was despite the fact that the importance of services was growing rapidly. Indeed, development in most western countries was such that they were becoming largely **service-led** as opposed to **production-led economies**. In the early 1990s, for example, the UK became the first country to export more services than physical goods and they were rapidly followed by many other economies previously distin-guished as 'industrialised nations'. By the middle of the decade over 75 per cent of the working populations of the UK and the USA were employed in service industries and this movement has continued into the new millennium. This rapidly changing situation both emphasised the importance of services and underlined the require-ment for further research.

The intangible nature of service industries had always posed a problem to tradi-tional marketers whose models (e.g. the **BCG matrix**, the **product life cycle**) had always proved to be an ineffectual fit. Pure service characteristics, often described as intangibility, inseparability, variability, perishability and inability to 'own' the service (Palmer, 1998, p. 11), coupled with the importance of people and processes, was pro-viding challenges that traditional marketing concepts were having difficulty rationalising. Above all, it was in industries where the potential advantages associated with the building of relationships was recognisable, and where service differential was low, that research was most required.

Impetus for RM research

It was, therefore, to be the relationship issues surfacing in industrial and service marketing that exposed the problems of the traditional marketing model in a more explicit way than with consumer goods (Christopher *et al.*, 1991, p. 10). The stimulation for this research into industrial and service marketing was to prove key in bringing 'relationships' onto the marketing agenda.

The development of RM

With the difficulties that marketers were experiencing and the ideas emanating from industrial and service research, questions were being asked. In particular, could marketing theories and practice, designed for a bygone era, be developed to cope with the multiplicity and complexity of products and services now available, or did the whole structure require rebuilding?

The marketing mix

Research was beginning to show that the 4Ps model of marketing was evidently too restrictive for business-to-business and services marketing. Gummesson (1987) went so far as to suggest that application of the marketing mix to areas other than consumer goods could be destructive as it failed to recognise the unique features of these areas. To a growing extent the marketing mix was also becoming an outdated concept for consumer goods marketing as the importance of intangible service characteristics and customer service considerations became a prime differentiation factor between products.

The first attempts to extend beyond the restrictive nature of marketing were, however, through the adaptation of the marketing mix model. According to Grönroos (1996, p. 8) the marketing mix could still be useful but other elements, not normally regarded as part of the marketing function, needed to be added (e.g. delivering, installing, repairing, servicing and maintenance, billing, complaints, customer education). Gummesson (1994a, p. 9), too, believed that the marketing mix would always be needed, but that it had become peripheral in comparison to relationships. Other authors tried to retain the 'mix' as an easy-to-remember framework that incorporated the new marketing ideas coming through. Further Ps were added such as People, Physical evidence, Processes (Booms and Bitner, 1981), Political power and Public opinion. Other adaptations (see Gummesson, 1994a, p. 8; Little and Marandi, 2003, p. 11) were suggested to fill the credibility gap. Indeed, early models of RM (e.g. Christopher *et al.*, 1991, p. 13) adopted this approach by incorporating the notion of 'customer service' (and by implication an endless list of sub-functions) as additional and central to the 'updated' marketing mix (see Figure 2.6).

Kotler *et al.* (1999, p. 110) took a marginally different approach. They suggested that the marketing mix represented the seller's view of marketing and proposed that marketers should view the 4Ps from a customer-orientated perspective. Thus the 4Ps became **4Cs** (see Figure 2.7) where companies met customer needs economically, conveniently and with effective communication. Thus price became the cost to the customer, place was substituted with convenience, products and services become customer needs and wants and promotion was transformed into communication.

Figure 2.6
Customer
service and the
marketing mix

(*Source*: Adapted from Christopher *et al.*, 1991, p. 13)

Figure 2.7
From 4Ps to 4Cs

(*Source*: Based on Kotler *et al.*, 1999, p. 110)

Valuable as these contributions were for some marketers, they were not radical enough for others. This latter group saw the attempts to update the marketing mix as failing to see the underlying problems in marketing. They suggested that the 'tool-box' approach to education had, for too long, restricted discussion of the meaning and consequences of the marketing concept. In catering for the real needs and desires of the consumers, marketing had become, in effect, the sterile management of this toolbox (Grönroos, 1994b, p. 5) and was philosophically and operationally incompatible with RM (O'Malley and Tynan, 2000, p. 11). To these marketers the marketing mix concept theoretically had no foundation, pedagogically no longer served a useful purpose and practically was being surpassed by more dynamic approaches (O'Malley and Patterson 1998, p. 840). Rather than tinkering with the 'mix', they believed a more fundamental change was required.

Customer supremacy

The marketing mix was not the only traditional marketing practice being challenged. It was frequently acknowledged that 'customer supremacy', the central tenet of marketing, although rational in principle was flawed in practice. What in effect was happening was that marketers attributed 'need' to individuals as a *post hoc* rationalisation to account for, and render rationality and meaning to, some recurrent behaviour observed rather than as a 'driver' (Knights *et al.*, 1994, p. 48). Despite the claims to the contrary the actual needs, wants and expectations of the customer were not perceived in reality as of paramount importance (Buttle, 1996, p. 7).

Thus, while lip-service was paid to customer supremacy in principle, in practice marketers all too frequently ignored it. Indeed marketers appeared to view their customers in one (or both) of two ways: the first as near-passive recipients of messages and prompts from marketers, and the second as one half of a confrontational or adversarial relationship (ibid., p. 8) where the language of warfare (e.g. mission, strategy, tactics, intelligence) was regularly used (O'Malley and Tynan, 1999, p. 591). Neither perception sat comfortably with the traditional marketing doctrine of 'customer supremacy' yet they largely dictated strategy development.

Market segmentation, positioning, market share and marketing research

A number of other established marketing concepts were under attack. Market segmentation and positioning strategies were proving particularly vulnerable (Doyle, 1995, p. 27). Market segmentation, a central marketing concept, no longer appeared to be operating effectively. While markets were still being presented demographically, psychologically, attitudinally or by lifestyle, the realisation was beginning to dawn on marketers that the only category that was really meaningful was 'actual', as opposed to 'speculative', buyer behaviour (Gordon, 1998, p. 3). Relationship-based strategies revolve around real customers, as distinct from traditional marketing which was concerned with imaginary or illusory relationships with statistical consumers (Sisodia and Wolfe, 2000, p. 549).

Market share, widely regarded as a principal performance measure, was also under fire. It was becoming apparent that it was ambiguous and subjective (Doyle, 1995, p. 27) and largely manipulated by marketers to serve whatever arguments they sought to promote. Market (or marketing) research too was showing its limitations. It was being used by marketers to identify issues and assess customer responses to hypothetical solutions (Gordon, 1998, p. 6) based on a frequently outdated historical basis. It was also, in fast-changing markets, taking more time than marketers generally had available and was proving a barrier to swift competitive response.

The eclipse of TM

The traditional transactional marketing (TM) model was, it appeared, unsuited to complex modern marketing reality and rapidly becoming outdated. TM was seen as overly scientific, relying heavily on quantitative research, and based solely on short-term economic transactions. Vividly described by one author as 'hit and run' marketing (Buttle, 1996, p. vii), it looked to each transaction as an opportunity to 'get one over' on the gullible customer without any consideration of future contact. At the extreme it was regarded as manipulative and exploitative of the customer's ignorance (Gummesson, 1994a, p. 9).

The recognition of the problems associated with the TM model suggested a functional and theoretical 'mid-life crisis' in marketing which demanded attention. Under siege from all sides, not only were specific components of marketing being challenged but so also was the validity of the whole. It was openly debated that a 'paradigm shift' was needed if marketing was going to survive as a discipline (Grönroos, 1994b, p. 4). The apparent success of a relational approach in the service and business-to-business sectors (which were themselves beginning to receive proper recognition) began to attract the attention of other marketers, who hypothesised the emergence of a new generic marketing paradigm to possibly replace, but certainly augment, the transactional model.

The early days of RM

It was into this growing theoretical void that the concept of RM began to take shape across all areas of marketing and to excite the marketing fraternity. There are various claims as to who to invest with the 'discovery' of RM. Fred Webster in his seminal article 'The changing nature of marketing' (Webster, 1992) has been credited by at least one major writer as the first to 'discover RM' (Baker, 2000), while others (e.g. Buttle, 1996) suggest that Berry (1983) was the first to publish substantive work on the subject. Evans (2002) notes that definitions of marketing in the 1950s by prominent writers such as Borch and Alderson implied the development of relationships and that the well-established 'adoption' construct within 'diffusion/adoption theory' was concerned with regular, committed, purchasing. Varey (2002) credits direct marketing pioneer Lester Wunderman, who, he claims, used the term 'relationship marketing' with a client in 1949. Gummesson (1999) directs us to Dale Carnegie's 1936 book *How to Win Friends and Influence People* to find relationship marketing's bible, while Parvatiyar and Sheth (2000) would claim RM's roots were in the pre-industrial age.

Whatever its heritage, RM found ready acceptance in a marketing world where it had become patently obvious that strategic competitive advantage could no longer be delivered on the basis of product characteristics alone and where corporate profitability was beginning to become associated with satisfying existing customers (Barnes, 1994, pp. 651–2). In industrial marketing, services marketing, managing distribution channels and even packaged goods marketing itself, a shift was clearly taking place from marketing to anonymous masses of customers to developing and managing relationships with more or less well known, or at least somehow identifiable, customers (Grönroos, 1994b, p. 14).

The need for market-driven business was as strong as ever but was now perceived, more realistically, as an iterative process in which marketing strategy shapes as well as responds to buyer behaviour (Sheth and Sisodia, 1999, p. 81). It became evident that there was a need to transform marketing from a narrow set of functional skills based on the conventional marketing mix to a broader business orientation where delivery of 'superior customer value' was a key objective (Christopher, 1996, p. 64). What was needed was a form of marketing that was orientated to creating rather than controlling a market and based on developmental education, incremental improvement and ongoing process rather than simple market share tactics and raw sales data (McKenna, 1991, pp. 2–3). A clear shift would also be needed away from the adversarial mind-set implied by the bargaining power perspective towards a cooperative stance focused on mutual gain.

Towards a definition of RM

Although a clearer picture of RM may be becoming evident it may be beneficial to determine, more specifically, what is meant by the term 'relationship marketing'. One thing that will become clear very early on is that RM is not an easy concept to define in a form which is acceptable to even a majority of 'relational marketers'. Nowhere is this more evident than in the current debate concerning RM and CRM (see Chapter 13).

Despite considerable academic research and practitioner interest, RM may still be regarded more as a general 'umbrella philosophy' with numerous relational variations rather than as a wholly unified concept with strongly developed objectives and strategies. Dann and Dann (2001, p. 347) suggest there are nearly 50 published definitions on the subject. Harker (1999) estimated, at the time of writing, 28 substantial RM definitions. To confuse matters further other terms have been frequently used either as substitutes for relationship marketing, or to describe similar concepts (Buttle, 1996, p. 2). These include direct marketing, database marketing, customer relationship management, data-driven marketing, micromarketing, one-to-one marketing, loyalty (or loyalty-based) marketing, 'segment-of-one' marketing, wraparound marketing, customer partnering, symbiotic marketing, individual marketing, relevance marketing, bonding, frequency marketing, integrated marketing, dialogue marketing and interactive marketing (Vavra, 1992; Buttle, 1996; Tapp, 1998), to name but a few. Many of these relational variations describe a particular or closely associated aspect of RM philosophy rather than necessarily a holistic concept and can (arguably) rarely be said to 'stand alone' in any true sense. Others are associate concepts that may be seen to overlap with RM in some way. What is generally described as 'direct marketing' or 'database marketing', for example, while not fully mirroring RM concepts, may nevertheless include a number of recognisable relational strategies and tactics. In general, however, the major characteristics of these techniques are more transactional than relational in nature. Customer relationship management (CRM), a concept to which we will return in Chapters 11 and 13, is another 'relational approach' that has grown in popularity particularly among direct marketers. CRM's definition is as hazy as the rest but seems to relate to management of the 'lifetime relationship with the customer' usually through the use of information technology (Ryals, 2000, p. 259), and is, as such, more tactical than strategic. As the definition of RM becomes clearer these differences may become more evident (see Chapters 11 and 13).

Broad church?

RM has been used to reflect a variety of themes and perspectives. Some take a narrow functional marketing perspective, others a view that is broad and somewhat paradigmatic in approach and orientation[6] (Parvatiyar and Sheth, 2000, p. 4). As RM is used to cover a fragmented set of ideas and theoretical frameworks it has been accused of being characterised more by rhetoric than vigorous examination of what the concept actually means (Möller and Halinen, 2000, p. 30). According to Dann and Dann (2001, p. 347), asking any two relationship marketers for a definition of RM and its core principles will result in at least four definitions and five 'must have' variables. Perhaps, however, differences of emphasis are to be expected as the theory (or theories) associated with RM continue to develop. One view may be to suggest that no purist definition of RM is possible or even practical. It may be wholly valid to recognise that a term such as relationship marketing, involving as it does such a vague notion as 'relationships', is bound to generate multiple definitions. Relationships are after all 'fuzzy' entities with 'fuzzy' borders and many overlapping properties (Gummesson, 1994b, p. 18).

A potentially defendable position may be to suggest that RM should continue to remain a flexible series of concepts and ideas rather than a fixed and inflexible theory if for no other reason than its application may differ considerably from industry to industry. In effect, RM should remain a 'broad church' (see Chapter 13). It may indeed be beneficial to RM development not to become 'straight-jacketed' by one position or the other (Grönroos, 1994b, p. 10). Indeed, it may be possible, within a general relational management position, for companies to develop strategies that appear contradictory to one another yet are relevant to specific industries or even individual customer types. After all, isn't differentiation at the heart of marketing? In this way RM can make a major contribution to marketing thought and practice by challenging the embedded strategies of the past and by encouraging marketers to constantly review their business strategies in the light of changing relationships.

Common ground?

Despite the undoubted problems in coming to a consensus on the meaning and application of RM, the marketing literature on the subject can be examined to establish whether research suggests some common ground. What is clear is that the current divergence of views suggests no agreement as to a single definition of RM (one of a number of reasons[7] why its claim to 'paradigm status' may be premature).

Indeed, concerns relating to the delineation of the appropriate domain has been one of the causes of a more recent criticism of RM (O'Malley and Tynan, 2000, p. 2). It is, however, equally evident that many definitions have common denominators. As such, and despite the evident difficulties, we can try to establish a 'best fit' definition from where RM can be further investigated.

RM's roots

RM, according to Gordon (1998, p. 9), is not a wholly independent philosophy but draws on traditional marketing principles. This view suggests that the basic focus upon customer needs still applies but that it is the way marketing is practised that requires changing fundamentally (Christopher, 1996, p. 55). If RM is indeed a descendant of traditional marketing then a good starting point in developing a definition of RM would be to look at how marketing has traditionally been perceived. This traditional view might be summed up succinctly using the Chartered Institute of Marketing's (CIM, 2005) definition of marketing as:

> the management process of identifying, anticipating and satisfying customer requirements profitably.[8]

This definition includes a number of assumptions that are important in the discussion of relational strategy development. 'Process' assumes that traditional marketing is a series of activities carried out as part (only) of a company's other functions. It implies a functional marketing department responsible for a fixed number of responsibilities presumably closely associated with the 'marketing mix'. It also implicitly suggests that 'identifying, anticipating and satisfying customer requirements' is the singular responsibility of the marketing department. 'Profitably' is assumed to mean that these responsibilities are carried out in a competitively superior manner (Gordon, 1998, p. 9), although there is no indication of the time scale over which this profitability should be measured.

This description of traditional marketing and others of a similar nature emphasise, above all, the functional and process nature of traditional marketing and make no explicit recognition of the long-term value of the customer (Buttle, 1996, p. 2). One particular axiom of transactional marketing is the belief that competition and self-interest are the drivers of value creation. This is challenged by the proponents of RM who believe that mutual cooperation, as opposed to competition and conflict, leads to value creation (Sheth and Parvatiyar, 1995, p. 399).

Early definition

Berry (1983, p. 25), as has been noted, was among the first to introduce the term 'relationship marketing' as a modern concept in marketing. He suggested that this 'new' approach should be defined as:

> attracting, maintaining and . . . enhancing customer relationships.

While recognising that customer acquisition was, and would remain, part of a marketer's responsibilities, this viewpoint emphasised that a 'relationship view of marketing' implied that retention and development were of equal (or perhaps even greater) importance to the company in the longer term than customer acquisition. It further implied, by differentiating between customer types, that not all customers or potential customers should be treated in the same way. The focus of traditional or mass marketing implied that whatever the status of the customer (non-customers, current customers and past customers) they were all treated in the same way and were of comparable worth and status to the organisation. RM, in contrast, saw the need to communicate in different (perhaps even contradictory) ways dependent on that customer's status and worth.

Cooperative marketing

The concept was taken a stage further by, among others, Grönroos (1996, p. 6), who challenged the traditional notion that marketing to be profitable needs to be an adversarial contest between the company and the customer. Certainly in the past markets had been frequently conceived as 'battlefields' and marketing practice dominated by combative battle metaphors (fight, competition, capture, take-over, etc.). The general view of the traditional marketing model was of businesses vying to be winners over not only their competition, but their customers as well. RM, in contrast, implied a focus on building 'value-laden relationships' and 'marketing networks' (Grönroos, 1994b, p. 9) rather than confrontation.

A change in attitude away from the traditional 'winner and loser' philosophy was also promulgated. Sheth and Sisodia (1999, p. 82) noted the clear evidence of a shift from the adversarial mind-set implied by the 'bargaining power' perspective towards a cooperative stance focused on mutual gain. Gummesson (1997, p. 56) suggested that the RM approach resulted in both parties deriving value from the transaction, and Voss and Voss (1997, p. 293) identified shared value as a key objective in the design and implementation of an RM programme. In effect 'relational marketers' were seeking strategies that produced 'win–win' situations (Gummesson, 1997, p. 56) with both parties gaining value from the buyer–seller partnership. The result was to be achieved through mutual exchange and fulfilment of promises (Grönroos, 1994b, p. 9) by *both parties* in a series of interactions over the lifetime of their relationship.

This view of marketing also implied that suppliers were not alone in creating or benefiting from the value created by the company. Rather RM was seen as an ongoing process of identifying and *creating new value* with individual customers and then *sharing the value benefits* with them over the lifetime of the association (Gordon, 1998, p. 9). A 'relationship', in these terms, was definable as the sum total of 'meaning-filled episodes' where relational partners co-produce value (Buttle, 1997, p. 148).

Relationship burdens

One important aspect of the original Berry definition required attention. The seemingly altruistic sentiments implied by RM might be seen to contradict the fact that the profit motive was still a principal business driver. The difference between RM and traditional marketing was that RM was seen to achieve this profitability through co-production and cooperation rather than through manipulation. RM would, it was suggested, potentially benefit both parties: the buyer through reduced transaction costs, and the seller through better understanding of customers' circumstances and requirements (Tynan, 1997, p. 992).

Not all relationships, however, are (or have the potential to be) profitable. Berry (2000, p. 154) notes that some customers, typically, are more profitable than others and that some are unprofitable to serve. Although, as a rule of thumb, customer retention was seen as the path to prosperity, some buyer–seller relationships were definite 'burdens' to a company (Håkansson and Snohota, 1995, p. 522). Indeed, situations can develop where a small number of highly profitable customers, in essence, subsidise a larger number of customers where the company actually loses money (Sheth and Sisodia, 1999, p. 83).

Such is the likely scale of this problem that Storbacka et al. (1994, pp. 31–2) suggest that it is not uncommon for 50 per cent of a retail bank's customers to be unprofitable. In later research concentrating on the Scandinavian banking system, Storbacka (1997, p. 488) reported that approximately 1 per cent of customers were responsible for the erosion of the profits from the top 25 per cent of the bank's customer base. Other researchers have made similar observations. In certain industrial markets, for example, Cooper and Kaplan (1991, p. 134) reported that 20 per cent of customers represented 225 per cent of total customer base profitability. Around 70 per cent of these customers hovered around the break-even point while 10 per cent of the customer base represented a loss equivalent to 125 per cent of the firm's eventual profit! Allowing this situation to continue over any length of time is particularly dangerous for larger companies that may be vulnerable to entry into the market of smaller companies that systematically target their most profitable customers (Sheth and Sisodia, 1999, p. 83).

This recognition of the potential loss-making capability of some relationships suggested that marketing management from a relationship perspective must pay attention to three key objectives rather than the two areas originally suggested (Strandvik and Storbacka, 1996, p. 72):

■ management of the initiation of customer relationships;

■ maintenance and enhancement of existing relationships;

■ handling of the termination of relationships.

This termination may be interpreted in two ways. In the first, marketing may be seen to be moving towards accepting 'customer de-selection' or 'adverse selection' (Smith, 1998, p. 4) as part of the marketing process. This might be operationalised, according to Smith, by 'dumping unprofitable customers while selectively seeking and keeping the more profitable ones'. The implication here is that cost–benefit ratios needed to be constantly monitored (Tynan, 1997, p. 992) to minimise, and where possible remove, the effect of loss-making customers. Although this perspective appears intuitively counter to a relationship philosophy, it represents a commercial realism that required incorporation into the RM definition.

A second interpretation of the requirement to manage the 'burden of relationships' (Håkansson and Snohota, 1995, p. 552) is to regard loss-making customers as part and parcel of the business. In this respect marketing needs to develop a theory of subsidisation (Sheth and Sisodia, 1999, p. 83): in effect, a strategic understanding of when and how to subsidise. This view suggests that subsidies are not always bad for business and that if used strategically can turn competitive vulnerability into competitive advantage. It also challenges marketers to accept the burden of loss making in the short term in the hope of long-term profitability.

Relationships, networks and interactions

A further feature of 'older' definitions and writings on the subject of relationship marketing was that they focused wholly on the supplier–customer relationship (the '**supplier–customer dyad**'). Later contributions, however, were seen to widen RM's scope (Buttle, 1996, p. 3). The logic behind this reasoning was that you could not serve your customer well without attention to these important internal and external relationships. According to Gummesson (1999, p. 1), marketing is more than just the dyadic relationship between the buyer and the seller; rather, it represents the whole series of 'relationships, networks and interactions' which the company (or more strictly the company's employees or representatives) undertakes as part of its commercial dealings. As marketing activities are subsets or properties of society, it is suggested (ibid., p. 6) that these relationships, networks and interactions have been at the core of business since time immemorial.

As will become apparent in later chapters, RM thinking was developing away from the strictly 'two-way dialogue' between the supplier and the customer towards the synonymous development of other company relationships.[9] Among the relationships (the simple dyad as well as the complex networks) the parties enter into active contact with each other. This Gummesson (1999, p. 1) calls 'interaction'. Thus RM was seen to represent 'all marketing activities directed towards establishing, developing and maintaining successful relational exchanges' (Morgan and Hunt, 1994, p. 22).[10]

RM definition

Most of the concepts, ideas and developments discussed above are present in Grönroos's (1994b, p. 9) refined definition of RM, in which he described the objectives of RM as to:

> identify and establish, maintain and enhance and, when necessary, terminate relationships with customers and other stakeholders, at a profit so that the objectives of all parties involved are met; and this is done by mutual exchange and fulfillment of promises.

No definition will ever be perfect and it may well be that other ideas and concepts may in time also require inclusion, but, as Harker (1999, p. 15) concluded, this definition seemed most elegant and succinct and represented what most researchers believed was the essence of RM. In later chapters we will investigate more closely how these concepts were translated into strategies and tactics and their perceived benefits.

In particular we will look at the claims that are implicit in this definition. These include six dimensions that differ significantly from the historical definition of marketing (Gordon, 1998, p. 9):

- RM seeks to create new value for customers and then share it with these customers.
- RM recognises the key role that customers have both as purchasers *and* in defining the value they wish to achieve.
- RM businesses are seen to design and align processes, communication, technology and people in support of customer value.
- RM represents continuous cooperative effort between buyers and sellers.
- RM recognises the value of customers' purchasing lifetimes (i.e. lifetime value).
- RM seeks to build a chain of relationships within the organisation, to create the value customers want, and between the organisation and its main stakeholders, including suppliers, distribution channels, intermediaries and shareholders.

The growing interest in RM suggests a shift in the nature of marketplace transactions from discrete to relational exchanges, from exchanges between parties with no past history and no future to interactions between parties with a history and plans for future interaction (Weitz and Jap, 2000, p. 209). Interaction is an important concept in this new thinking as it had previously been assumed that buyers were passive; indeed this remains an implicit assumption of the mix-management paradigm (O'Malley, 2003, p. 127).

On the tactical side comparisons have been suggested (Payne *et al.*, 1995, p. viii) between the different approaches to customers that TM and RM take (see Box 2.2). These elements too will be expanded upon in later chapters.

As Sheth and Sisodia (1999, p. 84) note, we should always bear in mind that marketing is context driven, and that the context has changed, is changing and will no doubt change in the future. Marketers need to question and challenge what these authors call the well-accepted 'law-like generalisations' (or in-bedded concepts) that have grown up around marketing. In many ways whether or not RM represents a true paradigm shift in marketing is less important than its ongoing ability to shed light on important marketing phenomena (Ambler and Styles, 2000, p. 505). Over the following chapters RM ideas, concepts, claims and perceptions will be tested as we try to establish the importance of relationship marketing.

Box 2.2 TM and RM compared

Transactional marketing	Relationship marketing
■ Orientation to single sales	■ Orientation to customer retention
■ Discontinuous customer contact	■ Continuous customer contact
■ Focus on product features	■ Focus on customer value
■ Short time scale	■ Long time scale
■ Little emphasis on customer service	■ High emphasis on customer service
■ Limited commitment to meeting customer expectations	■ High commitment to meeting customer expectations
■ Quality as the concern of production staff	■ Quality as the concern of all staff

(*Source*: Adapted from Payne *et al.*, 1995)

Summary

This chapter has looked at the development of relationship marketing (RM) and the considerable interest it has created among academics, consultants and practitioners alike. Although there are different perspectives evident there are also a number of common denominators beginning to develop. It looked at the roots of RM. It reviewed the perceived problems with traditional marketing in the light of fast-changing and complex markets. It examined RM's growth in popularity, acknowledging that there is no generally accepted definition. In an attempt to clarify thinking on RM, different perceptions (from simple to catch-all) were explored.

The earliest definitions of RM were analysed and found somewhat wanting. Not only was customer acquisition and retention important but ways had to be found to eliminate (or otherwise accommodate) loss-making customers. In addition RM theory was developing to include other relationships with key stakeholders. A broad definition of RM was, therefore, presented that, it is suggested, could act as a reference point from where to begin our investigation. It will not all be plain sailing, however. We should not, for example, expect anything as inherently complicated as 'relationships' to be anything other than complex and paradoxical. Indeed, marketing reality requires that we learn to live with this complexity, these paradoxes and the uncertainty, ambiguity and instability generated (Gummesson, 1997, p. 58) if we are to develop further the marketing discipline.

Discussion questions

1 What were recognised, towards the end of the twentieth century, as the perceived weaknesses of traditional marketing?
2 What were the influences that led to the development of relationship marketing?
3 What part did (a) business-to-business and (b) services marketing play in this development?
4 What are the major differences between traditional and relationship marketing?

Case study What the Willy Wonka of BSkyB knows about customers

You might have thought that James Murdoch would have had better things to do with his time than to sit in a not particularly distinguished conference suite on London's Edgware Road, listening to 60-second 'elevator pitches' from a roomful of enthusiastic amateurs.

On a grey Wednesday afternoon last month, the 34-year-old chief executive of satellite broadcaster BSkyB gave up a few precious hours that could have been spent hammering out tactics for his battle with Sir Richard Branson's Virgin Media, or preparing for the ordeal of further scrutiny from Ofcom, the UK's media regulator.

Instead, he sat and listened carefully as BSkyB customers attempted to win his backing for various community-based or environmental initiatives, such as powering satellite dishes and digi-boxes with solar energy, or hooking up every school in the country to broadband.

The customers had been divided into teams and each had to select a brave spokesperson to make a brief submission to the chief executive. A big blue clock projected on a screen showed how much time the speaker had left and, as the minute ran out, a loud buzz signalled that it was time to shut up. A roaming camera crew came up close to make sure every moment of each pitch was recorded.

Mr Murdoch concentrated, took notes and nodded – and very occasionally smiled. And after sitting through 20 – yes, 20 – presentations, he declared his favourite to be table 10's brain wave, 'Sky's bigger picture' – a new loyalty card for BSkyB customers that would reward green and socially responsible behaviour. The boss's verdict on the idea? 'Dynamite!'

As the energy levels in the room grew, and an atmosphere more akin to some kind of television game show developed, I was reminded of the excitement experienced by lucky holders of one of Willy Wonka's golden tickets – you know, the ones that entitled you to a once-in-a-lifetime tour of his world-famous chocolate factory. In his sober blue suit, Mr Murdoch cut a more understated and businesslike figure than Roald Dahl's extraordinary hero – who wore, you may remember, 'a black top hat on his head', 'a tail coat made of beautiful plum-coloured velvet', bottle-green trousers, pearly grey gloves, all set off by a fine gold-topped walking cane. The clean-cut Mr Murdoch did not, like Mr Wonka, sport 'a small, neat, pointed black beard'. While Mr Wonka's face was 'alight with fun and laughter', Mr Murdoch's emotions remained pretty firmly in check.

But what the two business leaders had in common was an understanding that there is no substitute for getting really close to your customers. Mr Murdoch wants his customers to know he cares about the same things they care about. BSkyB has been 'carbon neutral' since last year and its chief executive is a proud owner of a hybrid car – they are 'dynamite' too, apparently. At the end of the session he said, 'It is so incredibly important for us to have this dialogue with you.' He was palpably sincere. He was also exactly right.

Had the Edgware Road Hilton's conference suite been filled with hardened business leaders rather than enthusiastic amateurs, it is unlikely the same amount of energy and creativity would have been generated.

And had you been unwise enough to suggest to those business leaders that what they were engaged in was an example of '**corporate social responsibility**' (**CSR**), the groans would have been audible at both ends of that long and busy road.

But the idea that young Mr Murdoch is some kind of softy would clearly be misplaced. His company controls almost 70 per cent of the UK pay-TV market. Last November, BSkyB coughed up £1bn ($2bn) to grab 17.9 per cent of rival broadcaster ITV, a move that has attracted the attention of the regulator. He rarely misses an opportunity to condemn the

BBC's 'unfair' UK market position. He is now toe to toe with Virgin Media, a dispute that is heading for the High Court.

In other words, Mr Murdoch is emulating that other powerful businessman who once observed that 'monopoly is a terrible thing – until you have one' – a quotation attributed, of course, to a certain Keith Rupert Murdoch.

Smart businesses in the 21st century are going to find more and more ingenious ways of tuning in to their customers' legitimate concerns, deepening the relationship they have with them and extending their customers' appreciation of their business and their brand. You don't have to call it CSR (or even CSR 2.0) if you don't want to. But virtue is increasingly going to build competitive advantage, and inactive sneerers will be left further and further behind. Responsibility is not incompatible with aggressive competition. On the contrary, it can form a key part of a competitive strategy.

James Murdoch is a talented and hard-working young man and, if I were Virgin Media, I would be very, very worried. But, however capable he is, I'm not sure BSkyB will ever be able to match one of Willy Wonka's greatest achievements – television chocolate. This genuine technological innovation allows the broadcaster to beam real chocolate bars through the television screen into the viewers' living rooms, taking the 'customer experience' to a new level.

'Just imagine,' cried Mr Wonka, 'when I start using this across the country . . . you'll be sitting at home watching television and suddenly a commercial will flash on to the screen and a voice will say: 'EAT WONKA'S CHOCOLATES! THEY'RE THE BEST IN THE WORLD! IF YOU DON'T BELIEVE US, TRY ONE FOR YOURSELF – NOW!' And you simply reach out and take one! How about that, eh?'

(*Source*: *Financial Times* FT.Com, 16 April 2007)

Case study questions

1 Why was James Murdoch prepared to spend time considering various community-based or environmental initiatives?
2 Is this CRS or philanthropy, or are there other motives?
3 How might smart businesses tune in to their customers' legitimate concerns, deepening the relationship they have with them and extending their customers' appreciation of their business and their brand?

References

Ambler, T. and Styles, C. (2000) 'Viewpoint: the future of international research in international marketing: constructs and conduits', *International Marketing Review*, **17** (6), 492–508.

Baker, M.J. (1999) 'Editorial', *Journal of Marketing Management*, **15**, 211–14.

Baker, M.J. (2000) 'Writing a literature review', *The Marketing Review*, **1**, 219–47.

Barnes, J.G. (1994) 'Close to the customer: but is it really a relationship?', *Journal of Marketing Management*, **10**, 561–70.

Berry, L.L. (1983) 'Relationship marketing', in Berry, L.L., Shostack, G.L. and Upsay, G.D. (eds) *Emerging Perspectives on Service Marketing*, Chicago, IL: American Marketing Association, pp. 25–8.

Berry, L.L. (2000) 'Relationship marketing of services: growing interest, emerging perspectives', in Sheth, J.N. and Parvatiyar, A. (eds) *Handbook of Relationship Marketing*, Thousand Oaks, CA: Sage, pp. 149–70.

Booms, B.H. and Bitner, M.J. (1981) 'Marketing strategies and organisational structures for service firms', in Donnelly, J. and George, W.R. (eds) *Marketing of Services*, Chicago, IL: American Marketing Association.

Borden, N. (1964) 'The concept of the marketing mix', *Journal of Advertising Research*, **4** (June), 2–7.

Brennan, R. and Turnbull, P.W. (2001) 'Sophistry, relevance and technology transfer in management research: an IMP perspective', Middlesex University Business School, unpublished.

Brodie, R.J., Coviello, N.E., Brookes, R.W. and Little, V. (1997) 'Towards a paradigm shift in marketing: an examination of current marketing practices', *Journal of Marketing Management*, **13** (5), 383–406.

Brown, S. (1995) *Postmodern Marketing*, London: Routledge.

Brown, S. (1998) *Postmodern Marketing II*, London: International Thomson Business Press.

Buttle, F.B. (1996) *Relationship Marketing Theory and Practice*, London: Paul Chapman.

Buttle, F.B. (1997) 'Exploring relationship quality', paper presented at the Academy of Marketing Conference, Manchester, UK.

Christopher, M. (1996) 'From brand values to customer values', *Journal of Marketing Practice*, **2** (1), 55–66.

Christopher, M. and Baker, S. (2000) 'Relationship marketing: tapping the power of marketing' in Cranfield School of Management, *Marketing Management: A Relationship Marketing Perspective*, Basingstoke: Macmillan, pp. 283–90.

Christopher, M., Payne, A. and Ballantyne, D. (1991) *Relationship Marketing*, London: Butterworth Heinemann.

CIM (2005) *Marketing and the 7Ps*, Cookham: Chartered Institute of Marketing.

Cooper, R. and Kaplan, R.S. (1991) 'Profit priorities from activity-based costing', *Harvard Business Review*, May/June, 130–35.

Coviello, N., Brodie, R.J. and Munro, H.J. (1997) 'Understanding contemporary marketing: development of a classification scheme', *Journal of Marketing Management*, **13** (6), 501–22.

Dann, S.J. and Dann, S.M. (2001) *Strategic Internet Marketing*, Milton, Queensland: John Wiley & Sons.

Doyle, P. (1995) 'Marketing in the new millennium', *European Journal of Marketing*, **29** (12), 23–41.

Evans, M. (2002) 'The unreliable marketing route map and the road to hell (?)', Competitive Paper, Academy of Marketing Conference, Nottingham University.

Gordon, I.H. (1998) *Relationship Marketing*, Etobicoke, Ontario: John Wiley & Sons.

Grönroos, C. (1990) 'Relationship approach to the marketing function in service contexts: the marketing and organization behaviour interface', *Journal of Business Research*, **20**, 3–11.

Grönroos, C. (1994a) 'From marketing mix to relationship marketing: towards a paradigm shift in marketing', *Asia–Australia Marketing Journal*, **2** (1), 9–29.

Grönroos, C. (1994b) 'From marketing mix to relationship marketing: towards a paradigm shift in marketing', *Management Decisions*, **32** (2), 4–20.

Grönroos, C. (1994c) 'Quo vadis, marketing? Towards a relationship marketing paradigm', *Journal of Marketing Management*, **10**, 347–360.

Grönroos, C. (1996) 'Relationship marketing: strategic and tactical implications', *Management Decisions*, **34** (3), 5–14.

Grönroos, C. (2000) 'Relationship marketing: the Nordic school perspective', in Sheth, J.N. and Parvatiyar, A. (eds) *Handbook of Relationship Marketing*, Thousand Oaks, CA: Sage, pp. 95–117.

Grönroos, C. and Strandvik, T. (1997) 'Editorial', *Journal of Marketing Management*, 13 (5), 342.

Gummesson, E. (1987) 'The new marketing: developing long-term interactive relationships', *Long-Range Planning*, 20 (4), 10–20.

Gummesson, E. (1994a) 'Making relationship marketing operational', *International Journal of Service Industry Management*, 5, 5–20.

Gummesson, E. (1994b) 'Broadening and specifying relationship marketing', *Asia–Australia Marketing Journal*, 2 (1), 31–43.

Gummesson, E. (1996) 'Relationship marketing and imaginary organisations: a synthesis', *European Journal of Marketing*, 30 (2), 31–44.

Gummesson, E. (1997) 'Relationship marketing: the emperor's new clothes or a paradigm shift?', *Marketing and Research Today*, February, 53–60.

Gummesson, E. (1998) 'Implementation requires a relationship marketing paradigm', *Journal of the Academy of Marketing Science*, 26 (3), 242–9.

Gummesson, E. (1999) *Total Relationship Marketing: Rethinking Marketing Management from 4Ps to 30Rs*, Oxford: Butterworth Heinemann.

Gummesson, E. (2001) 'Are current research approaches in marketing leading us astray?' *Marketing Theory*, 1 (1), 27–48.

Håkansson, H. and Snohota, I. (1995) 'The burden of relationships or who next?', in *Proceedings of the 11th IMP International Conference,* Manchester, UK, pp. 522–36.

Harker, M.J. (1999) 'Relationship marketing defined? An examination of current relationship marketing definitions', *Marketing Intelligence and Planning*, 17 (1), 13–20.

Harris, L.C., O'Malley, L. and Patterson, M. (2003) 'Professional interaction: exploring the concept of attraction', *Marketing Theory*, 5 (1), 9–36.

Knights, D., Sturdy, A. and Morgan, R.M. (1994) 'The consumer rules? An examination of the rhetoric and "reality" of marketing in financial services', *European Journal of Marketing*, 28 (3), 42–54.

Kotler, P. (1992) 'Marketing's new paradigm: what's really happening out there?', *Planning Review*, 20 (5), 50–2.

Kotler, P., Armstrong, G., Saunders, J. and Wing, V. (1999) *Principles of Marketing*, 2nd European edn, New York: Prentice Hall.

Levitt, T. (1960) 'Marketing Myopia', *Harvard Business Review*, July/August, 45–56.

Little, E. and Marandi, E. (2003) *Relationship Marketing Management*, London: International Thomson Business Press.

McCarthy, E.J. (1978) *Basic Marketing: A Managerial Approach*, 6th edn, Homewood, IL: Richard D. Irwin.

McKenna, R. (1991) *Relationship Marketing*, London: Addison Wesley.

Mattsson, L.G. (1997a) "Relationship marketing" and the "markets as networks approach": a comparative analysis of two evolving streams of research', *Journal of Marketing Management*, 13 (5), 447–61.

Mattsson, L.G. (1997b) 'Relationships in a network perspective', in Gemünden, H.G., Rittert, T. and Walter, A. (eds) *Relationships and Networks in International Markets*, Oxford: Elsevier, pp. 37–47.

Möller, K. and Halinen, A. (2000) 'Relationship marketing theory: its roots and direction', *Journal of Marketing Management*, 16, 29–54.

Morgan, R.M. and Hunt, S.D. (1994) 'The commitment–trust theory of relationship marketing', *Journal of Marketing*, 58 (3), 20–38.

Naudé, P. and Holland, C. (1996) 'Business-to-business marketing', in Buttle, F. (ed.) *Relationship Marketing Theory and Practice*, London: Paul Chapman.

O'Driscoll, A. and Murray, J.A. (1998) 'The changing nature of theory and practice in marketing: on the value of synchrony', *Journal of Marketing Management*, **14** (5), 391–416.

O'Malley, L. (2003) 'Relationship marketing', in Hart, S. (ed.) *Marketing Changes*, London: International Thomson Business Press, pp. 125–45.

O'Malley, L. and Patterson, M. (1998) 'Vanishing point: the mix management paradigm reviewed', *Journal of Marketing Management*, **14**, 829–51.

O'Malley, L. and Tynan, C. (1999) 'The utility of the relationship metaphor in consumer markets: a critical evaluation', *Journal of Marketing Management*, **15**, 587–602.

O'Malley, L. and Tynan, C. (2000) 'Relationship marketing in consumer markets: rhetoric or reality?', *European Journal of Marketing*, **34** (7), 797–815.

Palmer, A.J. (1996) 'Relationship marketing: a universal paradigm or management fad?', *The Learning Organisation*, **3** (3), 18–25.

Palmer, A.J. (1998) *Principles of Services Marketing*, London: Kogan Page.

Parvatiyar, A. and Sheth, J.N. (2000) 'The domain and conceptual foundations of relationship marketing', in Sheth, J.N. and Parvatiyar, A. (eds) *Handbook of Relationship Marketing*, Thousand Oaks, CA: Sage, pp. 3–38.

Payne, A., Christopher, M. and Peck, H. (eds) (1995) *Relationship Marketing for Competitive Advantage: Winning and Keeping Customers*, Oxford: Butterworth Heinemann.

Reichheld, F.F. (1996) *The Loyalty Effect: The Hidden Force behind Growth, Profits and Lasting Value*, Boston, MA: Harvard Business School Press.

Ryals, L. (2000) 'Organising for Relationship Marketing' in Cranfield School of Management', *Marketing Management: A Relationship Marketing Perspective*', Basingstoke: Macmillan, pp. 249–64.

Sherry, J.F. Jr (2000) 'Distraction, destruction, deliverance: the presence of mindscape in marketing's new millennium', *Marketing Intelligence and Planning*, **18** (6/7), 328–36.

Sheth, J.N. and Parvatiyar, A. (1993) *Relationship Marketing: Theory, Methods and Application*, Atlanta, GA: Atlanta Centre for Relationship Marketing.

Sheth, J.N. and Parvatiyar, A. (1995) 'The evolution of relationship marketing', *International Business Review*, **4** (4), 397–418.

Sheth, J.N. and Parvatiyar, A. (2000) 'The evolution of relationship marketing', in Sheth, J.N. and Parvatiyar, A. (eds) *Handbook of Relationship Marketing*, Thousand Oaks, CA: Sage, pp. 119–45.

Sheth, J.N. and Sisodia, R.S. (1999) 'Revisiting marketing's lawlike generalizations', *Journal of the Academy of Marketing Sciences*, **17** (1), 71–87.

Sisodia, R.S. and Wolfe, D.B. (2000) 'Information technology', in Sheth, J.N. and Parvatiyar, A. (eds) *Handbook of Relationship Marketing*, Thousand Oaks, CA: Sage, pp. 525–63.

Smith, P.R. (1998) *Marketing Communications: An Integrated Approach*, 2nd edn, London: Kogan Page.

Storbacka, K. (1997) 'Segmentation based on customer profitability: retrospective analysis of retail bank customer bases', *Journal of Marketing Management*, **13** (5), 479–92.

Storbacka, K., Strandvik, T. and Grönroos, C. (1994) 'Managing customer relations for profit: the dynamics of relationship quality', *International Journal of Service Industry Management*, **5**, 21–38.

Strandvik, T. and Storbacka, K. (1996) 'Managing relationship quality', in Edvardsson, B., Brown, S.W., Johnston, R. and Scheuing, E.E. (eds) *Advancing Service Quality: A Global Perspective*, New York: ISQA, 67–76.

Tapp, A. (1998) *Principles of Direct and Database Marketing*, London: Financial Times Management/Pitman Publishing.

Tynan, C. (1997) 'A review of the marriage analogy in relationship marketing', *Journal of Marketing Management*, **13** (7), 695–704.

Varey, R.J. (2002) *Relationship Marketing: Dialogue and Networks in the e-Commerce Era*, Chichester: John Wiley & Sons.

Vargo, S. and Lusch, R. (2004) 'Evolving to a new dominant logic for marketing', *Journal of Marketing*, **67** (1), 1–17.

Vavra, T.G. (1992) *Aftermarketing*, Homewood, IL: Richard D. Irwin.

Voss, G.B. and Voss, Z.G. (1997) 'Implementing a relationship marketing programme: a case study and managerial implications', *Journal of Services Marketing*, **11** (4), 278–98.

Webster Jr, F.E. (1992) 'The changing role of marketing in the corporation', *Journal of Marketing*, **56** (October), 1–17.

Weitz, B.A. and Jap, S.D. (2000) 'Relationship marketing and distribution channels', in Sheth, J. N. and Parvatiyar, A. (eds) *Handbook of Relationship Marketing*. Thousand Oaks, CA: Sage, pp. 209–44.

Whalley, S. (1999) 'ABC of relationship marketing', *SuperMarketing*, 12 March, 12–13.

Notes

1 Reichheld uses the term 'loyalty-based management' although the term embodies what most scholars would recognise as relationship marketing concepts.

2 According to Baker (2000), Berry and Webster may have been working on RM without being aware of the Nordic school.

3 In hindsight many of the ideas emerging from the Nordic school were the basis for Vargo and Lusch's (2004) concept of a new dominant logic discussed later in this edition (see page 151).

4 Cost-per-thousand (CPT) is a frequently used comparative ratio of cost to audience or circulation.

5 A term coined by Levitt (1960) in his seminal article of the same title.

6 The narrow and broad perspectives are discussed further in Chapter 13.

7 For other reasons see Chapter 13.

8 In 2007 this still appears to be the definition preferred by the CIM and which appears in their website learning materials. In contrast, in 2004, the American Marketing Association (AMA) announced a new, more relationship-friendly definition of marketing: 'Marketing is an organizational function and a set of processes for creating, communicating and delivering value to customers and for managing customer relationships in ways that benefit the organization and its stakeholders.'

9 Research into business-to-business marketing RM was particularly influential in the development of these external relationship theories.

10 As noted in Chapter 13 there is some opposition to this viewpoint.

3 Relationships

Key issues

- Relationship terminology
- Organisational relationships
- Motivational investment
- Relationship loyalty
- Unrealistic relationship development

Introduction

This chapter looks in more depth at what is meant by the term **'relationship'** and how the various definitions and concepts contribute to (and sometimes confuse) the relationship marketing debate.

Relationships

RM theory suggests that relationships add quality to marketing transactions. As Mitchell (2001, p. 33) puts it:

> Traditional markets are extremely powerful but they have huge limitations. Real human exchange is much richer than market exchange. Whenever people deal with people in 'relationships' or communities (rather than markets) they not only exchange money for goods, they share ideas, opinions, information and insights. They have a say. They also tend to form affections, bonds, ties of loyalty, feelings of obligation and so on. They begin to share and exchange values as well as value. And the people whose values are most in tune with those around them tend to form the strongest, most supportive bonds with other people.

So relationships are important. Despite this, as with so many marketing concepts, there is no definite agreement as to what is meant by the term 'relationship' within 'relationship marketing'. RM critics suggest that this lack of clarity has provided researchers with the luxury of being able to choose whatever relationship definition best suits their research agendas at any given time (O'Malley and Tynan, 1999, p. 589). A further criticism is that relationships are invariably discussed and defined from the company perspective. That consumers should be equally interested in building and sustaining relationships is often taken for granted (Carlell, 1999, p. 1). This chapter will attempt to go beyond the rhetoric and clarify what marketers mean when they talk about relationships.

Relationship terminology

The relationship metaphor dominates contemporary marketing thought and practice (Fournier, 1998, p. 343). The very word 'relationship', however, appears to many as the basis for some concern. The use of a highly emotive term to describe a commercial strategy is open to some justifiable criticism. Such language is not, however, new to marketing. Levitt (1983, p. 111) used the language of love when he declared over two decades ago that the sale merely consummated the relationship with the customer and after that the marriage began. These human relationship analogies are used frequently (see Tynan, 1997; Smith and Higgins, 2000). The RM vocabulary abounds with terms such as 'stages of a love affair', 'one night stands', 'extra marital dalliances', 'comparisons with a Mills and Boon novel' (see Brown, 1998, pp. 174–5), polygamy and seduction (Tynan, 1997, p. 987). Seduction, according to Smith and Higgins (2000, p. 87), is used so often that even the seducers cannot remember why or what they are seducing. There have even been terms seen to represent the darker side of relationships, such as stalking, prostitution and rape, used to describe certain, less than ethical business practices (Tynan, 1997, p. 987). Even the most innocent of consumers runs the risk of being described as 'flirting' with the competition or of being a 'promiscuous' shopper.

In relationship marketing, therefore, metaphors abound. The difficulties begin, however, when marketers start to believe their own rhetoric. As O'Malley and Tynan (1999, p. 593) note:

> As a conceptual tool a metaphor must be literally false whilst simultaneously offering creative possibilities. Thus in the case of RM, it is important to understand that exchange between consumers and organisations are not interpersonal relationships *per se* but that the attributes of interpersonal relationships might be usefully employed when describing or attempting to understand that exchange.

It is evident that the language of RM misleads some organisations into assuming that all customer–supplier contacts in particular are capable of closeness when many (if not most) are not much more than impersonal exchanges. What these marketers call intimacy some customers see as intrusion (Smith and Higgins, 2000, p. 82) and justifiably resent it. When marketing-speak becomes hopelessly hyperbolic it is recognised, and discounted as such, by increasingly sceptical customers (Brown and Patterson,

2000, p. 658). When all types of repeat behaviour, including spurious loyalty, is seen as relationship maintenance, then the use of relationship as a metaphor in this context must be examined (Carlell, 1999, p. 8).

Two key questions must, therefore, be asked regarding relationships (Buttle, 1996, p. 11):

■ Can customer–supplier interactions ever be called 'relationships'?

■ Can customers ever develop relationships with companies or must relationships always be interpersonal?

Needless to say, there are no straightforward answers. Over the next few pages we will look at what evidence there is to support either or both concepts and whether and in what way they may require qualification.

Relationship forming

It would seem initially safe to assume that social relationship activity per se can only take place between individuals. In business-to-business markets in particular, relationships between the personnel of companies are explicitly recognised by both the buyer and the seller organisations and individuals within those organisations (Blois, 1997, p. 53). As we will see later, these bilateral and network relationships can, at times, develop into deep friendships that may even supersede an individual's loyalty to his or her own company.

In consumer markets, the premise is that by building strong relationships this will have a positive influence on exchange outcomes (Palmatier et al., 2006, p. 140). However, many attempts to develop RM programmes give the appearance of something 'done' to the customer (Palmer, 2000, p. 699) rather than a cooperative arrangement. It is frequently taken for granted that consumers are equally interested in building and sustaining relationships (Carlell, 1999, p. 1). In contrast, Barnes and Howlett (1998, p. 16) express the view that two characteristics must be present for an exchange situation to be described as a relationship:

■ The relationship is mutually perceived to exist and is acknowledged as such by both parties.

■ The relationship goes beyond occasional contact and is recognised as having some special status.

While acknowledging that relationships involve more than these characteristics, Barnes and Howlett suggest a 'true relationship' cannot exist if these factors are absent. The one-sided and emotionless nature of most everyday commercial (and in particular consumer goods) exchanges would suggest that they would have difficulty fulfilling such criteria. Certainly if we were to further stipulate that 'relationships' must include 'status recognition', then it is doubtful that this level of relationship could ever be developed with, for example, a local supermarket. In consumer markets, therefore, the existence of personal relationships is less obvious. Indeed as Brown (1998, p. 177) notes with some feeling: 'what consumer in their right mind would ever want to establish a relationship with a commercial organisation?'

There is empirical evidence to suggest that, regardless of what marketing strategies are implemented by the supplier, buyers frequently have no wish to enter into a relationship with a company (Palmer, 1996, p. 20). Even in service industries many customers simply do not want a relationship. In research into the US banking industry 70 per cent of consumers were unreceptive to the idea of a relationship with their bank (McAdam, 2005). It is probable that situations exist where the seller may want to develop a 'relationship' whereas the customer is happier with a transactional approach (Bund-Jackson, 1985, p. 34). This may be particularly evident in the case of certain industries (see page 61). An interesting dichotomy, it is suggested, may even be developing where, according to Sisodia and Wolfe (2000, p. 545):

> Today's customers appear to have lower expectations for a 'one and done' transaction orientated purchase (e.g. McDonald's) and higher expectations for long-term (longitudinal) purchases (e.g. from dentists). Ironically many companies offering the former tend to practise RM, whereas too many of the firms offering the latter fail to do so.

This domain extension, often under the mantle of customer relationship management (CRM), is no longer questioned, indeed as O'Malley and Tynan (1999, p. 589) note, 'researchers now treat exchange in consumer markets as though it is (or should be) relational and deliberately search for evidence of inter-personal relationship attributes.'

Despite the perceived difficulties and complications with defining the level of relationship, particularly in the consumer goods area, marketers perceive (either metaphorically or in reality) that relationships of some sort exist in commercial exchange situations.

Categorising relationships

There would appear to be a considerable number of variations in the types of relationship that are perceived to exist between a buyer and seller dependent on the industry, the company, the customer and numerous other factors. Research by Palmatier *et al.* (2006, p. 147) further suggests that customer relationships do not equally influence all exchange outcomes. Gummesson (1999) makes a valiant attempt to classify many of them in his 30Rs model. No attempt is made here to list the innumerable types (see Box II.1, p. 146 for a comprehensive list). Instead we will look at the various relationship criteria and how these impact upon relationship strategy development.

Organisational relationships

The question was raised earlier as to whether or not individual customers can have relationships with organisations or whether relationships must always be interpersonal. Research suggests that relationships have a greater impact on customer loyalty when the target of the relationship is an individual person (Palmatier *et al.*, 2006, p. 147) and that consumers perceive greater relational benefits when engaged in a relationship with high personal contact (Kinard and Capella, 2006, p. 365). However, although social relationships are always between individuals, it is interesting to observe that customer–supplier relationships (of whatever level or closeness) frequently continue despite the loss of personnel previously involved in the relationship. This suggests that a bonding of sorts must exist, independent of company employees, between the customer (individual or company) and that organisation. Gummesson (2000, p. 6) calls this 'embedded knowledge'. He explains that if an employee leaves then 'human capital' is lost. Embedded knowledge, however, is part of the structural capital that does not disappear with the employee and is, in effect, 'owned' by the company.

From an RM perspective structural capital consists of relationships that have been made with the company, as an entity, in addition to (and perhaps parallel with) the relationship with the employees. As Gummesson (ibid.) notes, 'the more successful a company [is in tying] relationships to its structure, the less dependent it is on individual employees and the higher the value of its structural capital'. Clubs or charities may be particularly clear examples of where organisational loyalty is not necessarily directly associated with the personnel who work for it. Relationships with these organisations may last for years without, necessarily, any close bond developing with that organisation's employees. In the case of football clubs individual fans may be deeply attached to a particular player until they leave for another club!

It is also observable that reputation matters when dealing for the first time or subsequently with an organisation. The historical trustworthiness of parties in previous interactions make reputational effects possible (Rousseau *et al.*, 1998, p. 397) that may again supersede individual relationships. Thus a customer will continue to frequent a supplier for reputational reasons as well as (or even in spite of) their personal relationship with that company's employees.

Based on the recognition of embedded knowledge and reputational effects it may be suggested that organisational relationships are possible as a prelude to and/or as a mediating factor in, the establishment of interpersonal or non-personal business relationships. That relationships can exist with organisations, albeit at varying emotional levels, is supported by Blois (1997, p. 53), who suggests that, unless a counter-intuitive definition of 'relationship' is used, it is difficult, if not impossible, to suggest that firms do not have relationships. O'Malley and Tynan (1999, p. 594), too, suggest that when viewed as an association between two or more variables then it is clear a relationship exists between consumers and organisations.

Learning relationships

Relationships are part of a knowledge-generating process (Håkansson and Johanson, 2001, p. 9). Peppers and Rogers (2000, p. 244) have suggested that relationships are built on knowledge and propose that, when customers tell a company something about themselves, then it is the responsibility of the company to customise its offering to that customer. From that point the relationship has started. The more the customer tells the company, the more valuable they become *provided* the company continues to adapt its product or service to meet the more and more specific customer needs. As customers interact more frequently with sellers they appear to gain more information which reduces uncertainty and improves trust (Palmatier *et al.*, 2006, p. 149). This learning relationship gets 'smarter and smarter' with every interaction. The relational view of developing competitive advantage identifies relationship learning as an important way to create differential advantage (Selnes and Sallis, 2003, p. 80).

Motivational investments

Dwyer *et al.* (1987, p. 14) suggest that the type of relationship that develops between a supplier and a customer is determined by the different amounts of motivational investment that buyers and sellers are prepared to commit to the relationship. They hypothesise that there are four types of active relationships in addition to 'no exchange' (see Figure 3.1):

Figure 3.1
Hypothesised realm of buyer–seller relationships

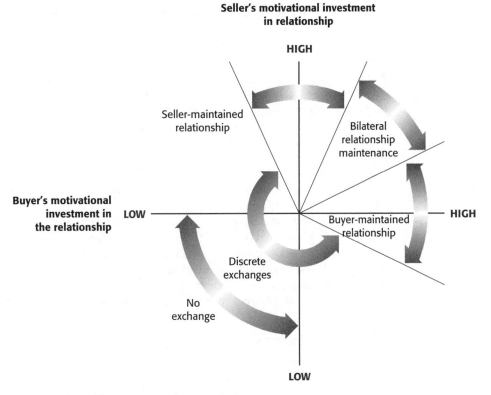

(*Source*: Adapted from Dwyer *et al.*, 1987, p. 14)

- **bilateral relationships**;
- **seller-maintained relationships**;
- **buyer-maintained relationships**;
- **discrete exchanges**.

Bilateral relationships are those in which both parties are motivated highly enough to invest in a relationship. This situation reflects many of the relationship definitions and criteria discussed in Chapter 2. These bilateral relationships are particularly relevant to business-to-business markets, although some relationships of this type may be seen to exist in some consumer markets (e.g. financial services). At the other end of the scale, **discrete exchanges** are low-involvement, purely transactional relationships (see Chapter 5).

That relationships might exist other than bilateral (i.e. with the active involvement of both parties) or discrete (i.e. transactional) does not, according to Dwyer *et al.* (1987, p. 15), denigrate the significance of this type of relationship, albeit that it is one-sided. In Dwyer *et al.*'s conception just because one or other party has a low motivational investment does not mean it is not a relationship – rather that it is a relationship of a different type.

Examples of **buyer-maintained relationships** may be seen in the automobile market where Toyota, Ford and other manufacturers regularly share their production information with their suppliers. Retail stores such as Tesco and Sainsbury also allow suppliers access to 'point of sale' data to facilitate distribution. It is noticeable that buyer-maintained relationships are more likely to exist when the buyer is the more dominant partner. It is, however, a significant change in attitude from past decades when such information was regarded as commercially confidential and was used to maintain an element of control over suppliers.

In consumer markets, although it is possible that customers may actively seek a relationship, the likelihood is that suppliers will largely manage the interaction. Relationships between buyers and sellers in these markets are generally considered to be much looser, with the bonds that tie the partners together being weaker and fewer (Möller and Halinen, 2000, p. 41). In mass-produced consumer goods markets, for example, where a large gap exists between the manufacturer and the consumer, 'relationships' are often restricted to service 'hotlines' and personalised mailings (Hennig-Thurau, 2000, p. 56). In these markets, many companies are using tactics that have more in common with traditional marketing techniques (e.g. mass mailings) than RM. In these situations, according to McDonald (2000, p. 31), supplier delusions about the state of their customer relationships have reached alarming proportions.

Higher-level relationships

Although higher-level and closer relationships may be more common in business-to-business environments (see Chapters 9 and 10), it seems possible for some consumer organisations to develop relationships that appear to be higher up the 'relationship ladder' (see Figure 4.3, p. 80). The higher the level at which RM is practised, it is suggested, the greater the potential for sustained competitive advantage (Berry, 2000, p. 158).

Attachment or affinity to local football teams or voluntary organisations (e.g. a favourite charity or a political party) can result in behaviour that suggests a deep and frequently emotional relationship. When an individual joins such an organisation as a member they make a visible statement that they wish to be in a relationship with that organisation and its membership (Gruen, 2000, p. 356). This may be despite the fact that many of the activities (from the perspective of the outsider) reflect commercial considerations. Thus the blatant commercialism of the football club that changes its kit design frequently in the knowledge that its fans will buy the new version or continues to increase season ticket prices *may* have no apparent effect on that supporter's loyalty to the club (see Box 3.1). In the not-for-profit sector a high level of relationship may mean not only subscribing regularly but may involve participating in fund-raising, volunteering or even governance of the organisation (Garbarino and Johnson, 1999, p. 9).

Box 3.1   No room for loyalty at United

For the past fortnight, my inbox has been filled with tales of long-standing Manchester United fans who cannot afford to renew their season tickets, following the 26 per cent rise in prices in the past two years.

These people have supported the club spiritually and financially for decades; now they are priced out. And what really upsets them is that the rises are to underwrite the new owners' takeover costs.

This week, those contemplating life without United learned what the club feels about them. A spokesperson observed that the defection of large numbers of committed customers wasn't a problem since there are 14,000 people on the season-ticket waiting list, happy to pick up any stack from the departures.

Perhaps we should be grateful for such honesty. Now we have it officially: for the English champions, loyalty is not a commodity of any value. All that concerns the Glazer-driven board is maximising revenues as quickly as possible.

As a model for the football business, however, the approach of the Old Trafford organisation might prove to be fundamentally wrong-headed. Logic suggests this summer is not the end of double digit ticket price rises. So what will happen next season when many of the incoming 14,000 also find they cannot afford their renewals? Will churn-over continue until we reach a point when everyone in the country has become an ex-season holder?

Perhaps only then will the administration appreciate that there is a financial value in loyalty. When that time arrives, sadly, for those who have found their long-term dedication so scandalously spurned by the administration, there will be no pleasure in saying 'I told you so'.

(*Source*: Jim White, *Daily Telegraph*, 16 June 2007)

Some organisations with higher-level relationships may raise funds with the assistance of other, more commercial operators. Affinity partnering is a strategy in which the primary goal is to 'leverage the felt affinity, goodwill or brand name strength of a partner so as to enhance relational market behaviour' (Swaminathan and Reddy, 2000, p. 382). The programmes are known variously as **affinity packages**, **cause-related marketing**,

co-branding, dual signature and other terms. Affinity packages (e.g. university credit cards, society or group insurance or assurance policies) are often arranged through companies such as MBNA, Royal Bank of Scotland and Membership Services Direct and are prompted by the consumer's close relationship with the affiliated organisation. Whether the consumer sees this as a close relationship with the actual (as opposed to the nominal) supplier is, however, doubtful. What is more realistic is that the member sees this 'relationship' as a relatively cost-efficient way of contributing to the sponsor organisation's coffers. From the actual supplier's perspective it may be a means of targeting customers with specific needs or particular profiles associated with the membership of certain organisations.

Some affinity groups may be made up of like-minded people who share a common interest and actively want a relationship not only with the supplier/organiser but also with each other (see Chapter 11). Examples of this include specialist societies (often encouraged and supported by producers), such as the Harley Davidson and Jaguar clubs. The Internet has not only accelerated this movement but has led to the development of what may be called 'community sites' (MySpace, Facebook, etc.). Although commercially sponsored sites, the content is largely dominated by the patrons.

Other affinity-type relationships include those that Foxall *et al.* (1998, p. 17) call 'frequency marketing'. Frequency marketing describes those interconnected programmes designed to link customers with brands by engaging them into clubs entitling members to special discounts, newsletters, tie-in purchases, credit cards, promotions and other privileges. Examples include collectors' clubs such as those for Swatch watches and Royal Doulton bone china figurines.

Relationship loyalty

It is almost impossible to discuss relationships without discussing the concept of loyalty as customer loyalty is frequently seen as an expected outcome of RM (Palmatier *et al.*, 2006, p. 140). Indeed the phrase '**loyalty marketing**' is frequently used interchangeably with relationship marketing.

Loyalty is a state of mind (Dick and Basu, 1994, p. 99). Such is its perceived importance that it has been claimed that customer loyalty 'is emerging as the marketplace currency for the twenty-first century' (Singh and Sirdeshmukh, 2000, p. 150) and that it represents an important basis for developing sustainable competitive advantage (Dick and Basu, 1994, p. 99).

Loyalty is, however, a much used and abused term. Although it is widely utilised, most authors fail to define what they mean by the term, resulting in a lack of consistency in the marketing literature. The frequent assumption is that loyalty translates into an unspecified number of repeat purchases from the same supplier over a specified period (Kendrick, 1998). It is, however, more complex a term than this suggests. At its most profound, the term loyalty suggests the highest possible level of relationship impinging upon the emotional, not to say the irrational. Its use in commercial situations has, however, debased this higher-level meaning, although some suppliers would have us believe differently. Although loyalty itself is an important concept, its nuances have been lost in traditional brand loyalty debate (Fournier, 1998, p. 343). The idea that loyalty has some special magical powers that marketers can invoke that are 'different' or 'in addition to' their normal marketing activities has been growing (Mitchell, 1998, p. 16) despite considerable evidence to the contrary.

Defining loyalty

There appear to be two main strands of thought on the essence of commercial loyalty (Javalgi and Moberg, 1997, p. 165):

■ A definition of loyalty in *behavioural* terms, usually based on the number of purchases and measured by monitoring the frequency of such purchases and any brand switching.

■ A definition of loyalty in *attitudinal* terms, incorporating consumer preferences and disposition towards brands to determine levels of loyalty.

The frequent assumption is that, from whatever sources the loyalty is derived, it translates into an unspecified number of repeat purchases from the same supplier over a specified period. Neal (1999, p. 21), for example, defines customer loyalty as:

> the proportion of time a purchaser chooses the same product or service in a category compared with his or her total number of purchases in the category, assuming that acceptable competitive products or services are conveniently available.

The problem with relying on this behavioural definition is that there may be many reasons for repeat patronage other than loyalty, among them lack of other choices, habit, low income, convenience etc. (Hart *et al.*, 1999, p. 545). Equating loyalty wholly with relationship longevity, therefore, tells us little about relationship strength (Storbacka *et al.*, 1994, p. 30).

A more comprehensive definition of loyalty[1] may be:

> The biased (i.e. non-random) behavioural response (i.e. re-visit), expressed over time, by some decision-making unit with respect to one [supplier] out of a set of [suppliers], which is a function of psychological (decision making and evaluative) processes resulting in brand commitment.

(Bloemer and de Ruyter, 1998, p. 500)

Simple repatronage, therefore, is not enough. Loyalty, if it is to have any credence, must be seen as 'biased repeat purchase behaviour' or 'repeat patronage accompanied by a favourable attitude' (Dick and Basu, 1994, p. 99; O'Malley, 1998, p. 50; Hart *et al.*, 1999, p. 545). The strongest conceptualisation of customer loyalty, therefore, views it as a multi-faceted construct which takes into account both the psychological and behavioural components (Too *et al.*, 2001, p. 292). Loyalty can originate from factors extrinsic to the relationship such as the market structure in which the relationship exists (and the possible geographic limitations) but also in intrinsic factors such as relationship strength and the handling of critical episodes during the relationship (Storbacka *et al.*, 1994, p. 29).

Antecedents to loyalty

There are two distinct viewpoints as to the antecedents to loyalty. In the first, loyalty is seen as more often built on 'hard' dimensions, such as value for money, convenience, reliability, safety and functionality, and that these are the prime drivers for product or service choice (Christopher, 1996, p. 60). Fredericks and Salter's (1998, p. 64) model (Figure 3.2) shows this graphically and encompasses some of the areas that will be discussed more fully in later chapters.

Figure 3.2
Customer loyalty: an integrated model

(*Source*: Adapted from Fredericks and Salter, 1998, p. 64)

This viewpoint suggests that, while a customer's positive experiences with products or services may enhance a type of temporal loyalty, it is essential to remember that 'money talks' and 'everyone has a price' (Hassan, 1996, p. 7). Such is the level and scope of price-based competition in some consumer markets (e.g. FMCG retailing) that some would even suggest that fostering 'real' loyalty in such markets is an almost impossible task (Pressey and Mathews, 1998, p. 39).

An alternative to this view is expressed by Dick and Basu (1994, p. 99). In this model, 'softer', more intangible factors such as emotion and satisfaction are seen to affect attitude in a decisive way. This viewpoint suggests that customer loyalty is viewed principally as a result of the bond between an individual's relative attitude and repeat patronage, again mediated by social norms and situational influences or experiences (Figure 3.3).

What both models implicitly suggest is that customer satisfaction sustains loyalty. The presumption is that loyalty is built upon satisfaction derived from a positive differentiation achieved by providing superior customer service (Javalgi and Moberg, 1997, p. 165). Research (Hassan, 1996, p. 9), however, suggests that loyalty should not be con-

Figure 3.3
Framework for
customer loyalty

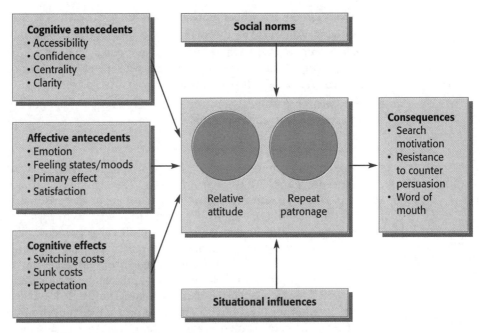

(*Source*: Adapted from Dick and Basu, 1994, p. 100)

fused with satisfaction (though creating more satisfaction *may* reduce the likelihood of disloyalty). Satisfaction does not always result in retention (loyalty) and it is equally apparent that dissatisfaction does not necessarily result in defection (Buttle, 1997, p. 145; O'Malley, 1998, p. 48). Not only is there not a simple linear effect but there appears to be no consistency across industries (Singh and Sirdeshmukh, 2000, p. 161). Dick and Basu's (1994, p. 101) 'relative attitude/behaviour matrix' (see Figure 6.3, p. 134) graphically shows that 'spurious loyalty' may be caused by the lack of alternatives and numerous other variables. As Storbacka *et al.* (1994, p. 28) note:

> Customer loyalty is not always based on positive attitude, and long-term relationships do not necessarily require positive commitment from customers. The distinction is important because it challenges the idea that customer satisfaction (the attitude) leads to long-lasting relationships (the behaviour).

Indeed, research suggests that neither loyalty and satisfaction (Hassan, 1996, p. 9) nor loyalty and profitability (East, 2000, p. 7) necessarily go hand in hand.

Loyalty-type behaviour

There are many ways of describing loyalty-type and non-loyal customer behaviour. For example, Uncles (1994, p. 342) proposes three ways of considering customer repatronising behaviour:

- *Switching behaviour*: where purchasing is seen as an 'either/or' decision – either the customer stays with you (loyalty) or turns against you (switching).
- *Promiscuous behaviour*: where customers are seen as making a 'stream of purchases' but still within the context of an either/or decision – either the customer is always with you (loyalty) or flits among an array of alternatives (promiscuous).
- *Polygamous behaviour*: again, the customer makes a stream of purchases but their loyalty is divided among a number of products. They may be more or less loyal to your brand than any other.

Evidence from consumer research tends to support the view that patterns of promiscuity and polygamy are the norm (Uncles, 1994, p. 344). Barnard and Ehrenberg (1997, p. 23), for example, suggest that many or most consumers are multi-brand buyers and that only one-tenth of buyers are 100 per cent loyal. In the UK and the USA for example the average number of credit cards exceeds four per person. This may be because a customer's holistic requirements frequently extend beyond those capable of being effectively fulfilled by a single firm's products and services.

Consumers are, therefore, prone to 'mix and match' products and services according to their specific needs (Kandampully and Duddy, 1999, p. 316). There is also doubt over whether loyal buyers are more profitable than promiscuous or polygamous buyers. Research evidence suggests that loyalists are more often light buyers of products or services in various categories whereas multi-brand (or broad repertoire) buyers are heavier users (East, 2000, p. 7). It is not difficult to perceive a situation where the less loyal 'heavy' buyer is a more frequent purchaser of a company's products or services (and is consequently more attractive) than a buyer who is 100 per cent loyal (Uncles, 1994, pp. 346–7).

Loyalty schemes

There can be little doubt that we are living in the age of the loyalty scheme (Hart *et al.*, 1999, p. 544). Indeed, the perceived significance of such schemes, if claims at 'loyalty' conferences and in 'loyalty' magazines are to be believed, has reached heroic proportions. Many authors are pointing to the use of store loyalty cards in particular as evidence of the uptake of relationship marketing in the retail sector (Pressey and Mathews, 1998, p. 39). According to Uncles (1994, p. 341), the espoused view is that customers actively seek an involving relationship with 'their' brand (product manufacturer, service supplier, brand owner or retailer), which in turn offers psychological reassurances to the buyer and creates a sense of belonging. The proposed benefit of **loyalty schemes**, for loyal and heavy or frequent customers, is having this sense of belonging reinforced. According to Bolton *et al.* (2000, p. 95) the goal of such programmes is to establish a higher level of customer retention in profitable segments by providing increased satisfaction and value to certain customers.

Hart *et al.* (1999, p. 546) offers a wider range of motives for setting up loyalty schemes:

- building lasting relationships with customers by rewarding them for their patronage;
- gaining higher profits through extended product usage and **cross-selling**;

- gathering customer data (and development into information);
- **de-commodifying** brands (i.e. differentiating from the crowd);
- defending market position (against a competitor's loyalty schemes);
- pre-empting competitive activity.

As noted above, one of the increasingly important objectives of loyalty programmes is the collection and qualification of customer data. There is little doubt that this data has the potential to be valuable and it is frequently suggested that this offsets the costs of loyalty schemes (see Chapter 11). Views differ on customers' motives and expectations for providing this data. According to Kelly (2000, p. 263), when you hand a customer a loyalty card you immediately create the expectation in the mind of the consumer that you are now going to study their behaviour and that, in return, they expect the supplier to do something intelligent with that information. This 'cooperation' may be the basis of a future relationship. Evidence on both customer expectations and competitive advantage is, however, patchy. Khan (1998, p. 65) comments that until retailers start to make use of the information they collect there seems to be little justification for collecting it. There is at least one school of thought that suggests data collection is over-emphasised and that the costs of data collection frequently outweigh any advantages gained (O'Malley, 1998, p. 52).

Another principal reason for developing a loyalty scheme, according to Hart *et al.* (1999, pp. 541–62), is to build lasting relationships with customers. Although in some instances there may be a genuine desire on the part of the supplier to enter into a relationship with customers, most loyalty schemes seem to be tactical moves designed to defend short-term positions in highly competitive markets (Uncles, 1994, p. 337) rather than a relationship-building exercise. These schemes are little more than 'classic' sales promotions with short-term incentives to disloyal 'brand-switchers' (Palmer, 1998, p. 114; Uncles, 1994, p. 341).

Profitability is another proposed driver but here again the evidence is conflicting. While loyalty scheme pioneers (e.g. American Airlines' Frequent Flyer programme and Tesco's Clubcard) in a sector may gain additional business in the short term, these incentives rapidly become the 'sector norm' that customers come to expect (Palmer, 1996, p. 22). All too quickly, early benefits can turn into the unavoidable cost of doing business (Uncles, 1994, p. 349) as they become institutionalised and an expected part of the offering (Gruen, 2000, p. 355/6). When loyalty rewards become the expectation in any sector it is doubtful whether anyone is ultimately any better off (Palmer, 1998, p. 117). To exacerbate the situation, once loyalty schemes become the norm and customers come to expect rewards, then there is the costly task of 'continually ratcheting up the loyalty ladder' (Uncles, 1994, p. 348). This is likely, ultimately, to affect the relationship. Over time, customers who receive, in effect, only bribes are likely to become promiscuous and seek the highest bribe available as that is the only satisfaction they receive from the exchange (Tynan, 1997, p. 992).

Box 3.2 Loyalty programmes

It may appear that so-called loyalty schemes are a very recent phenomenon. The technology may be more sophisticated but the principle of 'locking-in' consumers by way of 'promotions' has changed remarkably little. The Co-operative Movement has operated a loyalty scheme for decades, initially as the 'divi' (a dividend based on the amount of purchases made during a period) and later using trading stamps. Pink and green stamps were an important incentive as early as the 1960s. Petrol retailers have been wedded to continuity programmes for many years, with 'low tech' collection devices (cards, stamps, etc.) being replaced later by more technologically sophisticated mediums (e.g. Esso Tiger Cards, Mobil/BP Nectar Cards). Airline frequent flyer programmes (e.g. Virgin Freeway, Air France Frequent Plus) have grown to the extent that very few non-cut-price airlines are without one. Store loyalty cards are but the latest ploy in marketing continuity programmes that have been around for decades.

If there is so much doubt about the validity of these programmes, why do 'loyalty scheme saturated sectors' continue to invest so heavily? It may simply be a case of 'follow the leader'. When Tesco launched its loyalty scheme, Sainsbury were adamant that they would not follow suit, a decision reversed within 12 months.[2] Another reason may be that it is very difficult to measure the effectiveness of a loyalty programme. This stems from the difficulty of comparing the performance of companies that run them with companies that do not (Palmer, 1998, p. 114). In this situation it may be perceived as safer for the supplier to retain a scheme rather than chance losing custom.

It is perhaps ironic that attempts to apply RM in consumer markets have concentrated on 'low-involvement' categories such as **FMCG products**, **white and brown goods**, and services such as supermarkets and petrol retailers (O'Malley and Tynan, 1999, p. 589; see Box 3.2). Many such schemes would seem to have been introduced not for proactive but for defensive reasons (Khan, 1998, p. 65). As a result, customers, according to Mintel (quoted by Khan, 1998), are getting more out of loyalty schemes than retailers (see Box 3.2).

Loyalty in context

Features such as loyalty cards may have a part to play in relationship maintenance but they cannot realistically be taken as a proxy for the relationship marketing philosophy. Loyalty programmes are not a marketing panacea and are often not much more than sophisticated sales promotions where costs may frequently outweigh advantages (O'Malley, 1998, p. 52). At best, loyalty schemes act as reinforcing mechanisms since it appears, on the whole, that they reward the 'already loyal' rather than anyone else (Ward *et al.*, 1998, p. 85). Participation in many of these programmes is strictly an economic decision on the part of the customer and has no influence (not even negative influence) on related behaviours (Bhattacharya and Bolton, 2000, p. 343). David Sainsbury's dismissive description of Tesco loyalty cards as 'electronic

Green Shield stamps' was probably closer to the truth than many gave him credit for at the time. From a customer perspective, many loyalty schemes offer 'me too' benefits, which may be nice to have (because most people like getting something for nothing) but these are no guarantee of continued loyalty and are often marginal to their brand choice decision (Uncles, 1994, p. 341). Given the evidence, it would appear to be becoming increasingly obvious that loyalty schemes have little effect on underlying affective commitment (Palmer, 1998, p. 117) or do little to directly affect the chances of account retention (Bolton *et al.*, 2000, p. 103). As Dowling and Uncles (1997, p. 71) note 'most loyalty schemes do not fundamentally alter market structure. They might help to protect incumbents and might be regarded as a legitimate part of the marketing armoury, but at the cost of increasing market expenditure.'

Unrealistic relational development

It is suggested in Chapter 5 that certain industries are more or less likely to benefit from relational strategy development. On a more individualistic note, it may also be the case that, even where the general indication is that a particular business may benefit from relational strategies, there are reasons why attempting to develop such relationships may be a fruitless pursuit. These 'unrealistic' RM scenarios may be determined by either the customer or the supplier.

Unrealistic customer relationship development

According to Palmer (1996, p. 20), a number of unrealistic customer scenarios exist where:

- there is no reason why, or little likelihood that, a buyer will purchase again from a supplier;
- buyers want to avoid a relationship as it may lead to a dependency on a seller;
- buying processes are formalised in a way that prevents either party developing relationships based on social bonds;
- a buyer's confidence lowers the need for risk reduction (see Chapter 6);
- the costs associated with a relationship put the buyer at a cost disadvantage in a price-sensitive market.

Low likelihood of repurchase

With the growth of travel the percentage of purchases made at diverse, temporary locations (e.g. airports) increases. A buyer who is unlikely ever to repatronise a supplier will see no benefit from relationship formulation and may indeed be annoyed by the tactics associated with it (e.g. data capture).

Dependency avoidance

This situation may exist when any benefits associated with the relationship are outweighed by lost opportunities elsewhere. For example, some companies offer improved terms for exclusive agreements (e.g. estate agencies' commission rates). Customers may decide, however, that a sole-agent relationship would limit them (e.g. restrict the chances of a quick sale through a larger number of estate agents) and choose instead to open up the contract to other suppliers. They are forgoing any benefits of the relationship (e.g. reduced commission) in favour of the benefits of plurality (e.g. wider coverage). The implication is that, although consumers may be naturally inclined towards reducing choice, when forced to forgo all choices, or when they feel excessive pressure to conform to the beliefs of others, customers react against that pressure (Sheth and Parvatiyar, 2000, p. 185).

Formalised contracts

Formalised buying situations (such as those involving government agencies) may be compromised and jeopardised by too close an association between buyer and seller. Indeed, such relationships may be contractually or legally barred. In these situations the establishment of relationships may be neither welcomed by, nor be in the long-term interest of, either party.

Low-risk situations

In many exchange situations risk (as potentially a major driver to 'relationship seeking') is minimal. As a consequence consumers are unlikely to see either the need or the justification for closer relationships (see Chapter 6).

Price-sensitive markets

It may prove more profitable for buyers in certain markets to keep their eyes open for the best deal available rather than narrow the field and commit themselves to one supplier. Indeed, they may well prefer to play suppliers off against each other using an organisation's potential insecurity to gain added value.

In situations such as these, where the consumer will be unlikely to perceive any advantage from a relationship, suppliers should be looking to qualify whether costly relationship-building strategies are a viable proposition. The problem, or indeed paradox, from the perspective of the supplier, is the difficulty of knowing that some of these situations exist (e.g. where the customer is unlikely to repatronise) unless the customer volunteers the information.

Unrealistic supplier relationship development

This 'relationship avoidance' is not necessarily one way and may also be sought by the supplier in certain situations. These scenarios closely mirror Palmer's (1996, p. 20) customer list, and include situations where:

- there is no reason why a seller would ever see a buyer again;
- a seller seeks to avoid a relationship in which it becomes dependent on a buyer;
- buying processes become formalised in a way that prevents either party developing relationships based on social bonds;
- the seller has little opportunity to develop relationships due to the undifferentiated nature of the market;
- the ethos of the industry makes relationship-building inappropriate.

Low likelihood of repurchase

Situations where a customer is unlikely to repatronise a particular supplier (perhaps because the buyer's home base is many miles from that supplier, or where, by the nature of the product or service, a second purchase is unlikely) may suggest that investment in relationship building is unlikely to provide a profitable return.

Dependency avoidance

This may reflect the supplier's desire not to put all of their eggs in one (or a few) basket(s). This may be particularly relevant in business-to-business situations where the number of customers is, generally, lower, although it may also exist in some financial services (or other potentially high-risk associations) where the level of exposure may make the organisation vulnerable to high loss. This scenario may be very difficult to manage from the supplier's perspective if the buyer is, or has the potential of being, a substantial customer and if that customer is pushing for a closer relationship. An example of where 'dependence avoidance' may be considered is where a supplier appears overly dependent on one or a few retailers, leaving it vulnerable to changes in market circumstances (as some UK suppliers of Marks & Spencer discovered to their cost when the company changed its 'buy British' policy in 1999).

Formalised contracts

This situation mirrors the buyer's dilemma. Suppliers may be at risk (particularly in public contracts) from legal action should they even attempt to build a relationship with a public body's representative as this may be construed as bribery or corrupt practice.

Undifferentiated markets

Although RM has been presented as of potential benefit in undifferentiated markets, a different interpretation may be considered. Suppliers of largely undifferentiated products or services where customers are likely at any time to switch should consider whether 'seduction' (e.g. promotional discounts) rather than potentially costly relational strategies are more cost effective. In reality, this is what is happening in the UK supermarket industry where some of the major players (e.g. Tesco, Sainsbury) have chosen what they would call relational strategies based upon loyalty programmes, while others (e.g. Asda, Morrisons) have opted for the promotional route.

Price-sensitive markets

This situation may exist where companies rely on market opportunism. Blois (1998, p. 258) suggests that the US company NECX Inc. is such an organisation. In a case study, Blois noted that the company exists principally to take advantage of uncertainties in both supply and demand in the computer supplies market. Blois argues that this company would feel inhibited about 'exploiting' shortage situations if it were to develop 'relationships' with its customers.

Relationships in context

Relationships are inherently dynamic and are never settled in a way that 'enables us to take a moral audit' (Smith and Higgins, 2000, p. 91). There is no doubt, however, that some companies seem to have the knack of handling relationships. Grönroos (2000, p. 4) quotes Fergal Quinn, founder and president of Superquinn stores in the Irish Republic, as saying that, if the supplier handles relationships well, the customer will come back. Quinn calls this the 'boomerang principle', the beauty of which is that 'you and the customer end up on the same side . . . so that the relationship with your customer is not an adversarial one, it's a partnership'. Tesco too is fêted as an organisation that has handled its relationships with customers well.

On the other side of the coin, the danger comes when the relationship metaphor becomes accepted as truth. Many authors treat consumer–organisational relationships as though they were literally true (O'Malley and Tynan, 1999, p. 594) when realistically they will never be more than weak associations. As Van den Bulte (1994, p. 416) notes, after long and repeated use, a metaphor may become so hackneyed that people forget that it is a metaphor and sublimate its relationship with reality. Perhaps this is happening with RM. Indeed, when some kinds of repeat behaviour (particularly spurious loyalty) are treated as 'relationships', one may suspect that relationship as a metaphor may be rather ill suited (Carlell, 1999, p. 8).

Loyalty, as we have noted, is a very much used and abused term. Although RM and loyalty marketing (or for that matter CRM) have several common components (e.g. the use of information technology, customer knowledge and direct customer communications), it is questionable whether the association is any deeper (Hart *et al.*, 1999, p. 541). Loyalty programmes and other behaviour-based initiatives suggest that this view of relationships formation is more akin to a stimulus–response function (Barnes and Howlett, 1998, p. 15) than anything resembling a relationship. Rarely are loyalty programmes more than sophisticated sales promotions where the loyalty is to the programme and not the brand (O'Malley, 1998, p. 52). Whereas loyalty schemes may play a part in relationship maintenance, they cannot be realistically taken as proxy for the RM philosophy (Pressey and Mathews, 1998, p. 39).

Whatever the level of the relationship, it cannot be expected to last forever. Various terms exist for describing termination of relationships within marketing and these will be covered in more detail in the following chapters. Suffice to say at this stage that long-term relationships can carry with them the seeds of their own destruction (Grayson and Ambler, 1999, p. 138). It is certainly not a foregone conclusion that relationships will mature gracefully. Whether prompted by some experience within the relationship or not, many relationships will suffer and potentially disintegrate from basic boredom or fatigue. Satisfaction is certainly no defence against termination as the customer can *always* be more satisfied somewhere else. Declining customer 'loyalty' (however it is defined) may build up in small steps that may not be discernible until it is too late (Gummesson, 1999, p. 187): Laura Ashley and Marks & Spencer may have been in the past victims of this creeping apathy.

It is important, therefore, that any reference to the term 'relationship' is made in the recognition that not all relationships are close and enduring. Relationships exist at many different levels. What might be said about all relationships, however, is that they determine the type and nature of the customer–supplier interaction. As such, and at whatever level they exist, they are of interest to the marketer.

Summary

This chapter looked at the central concepts associated with 'relationships'. It examined whether customers can have relationships with organisations and whether relationships always have to be interpersonal. It suggested that, although personal relationships may be stronger, relationships with organisations were possible and that they often acted as a prelude to and/or as a mediating factor in the establishment of interpersonal and non-personal business relationships.

The chapter looked at 'learning relationships' based on 'knowing' the customer and (crucially) acting on this knowledge. It examined how 'motivational investment' affects the types of relationships that exist and how 'supplier-maintained' or 'buyer-maintained' relationships may exist in addition to bilateral and discrete exchange relationships. Higher-level relationships were discussed, including affinity, affinity packages and frequency marketing.

Loyalty as a concept close to the heart of RM was elaborated upon and the perceived antecedents to loyalty outlined. Loyalty-type behaviour was discussed and loyalty schemes put under the spotlight.

The potential for situations where relationship development is unrealistic (from either the customer or the supplier perspective) was discussed and the factors leading to such situations noted.

The chapter concluded by attempting to put relationships into perspective within the RM debate. It suggested that many levels of relationship exist, all of which are of interest to the marketer.

Discussion questions

1 In what ways are relationship metaphors used in marketing?
2 How might relationships develop between organisations and their customers?
3 What different levels of relationship can be seen to exist between buyers and suppliers?
4 What part do loyalty schemes play in relationship development?

Case study   Is personal touch worth it?

Long waits accompanied by interminable ambient music, sluggish callback times and the frustration of repeating a problem to numerous call handlers have resulted in call centres rarely getting a good press. But rather than dispense with them, insurance brand More Th>n has taken the ambitious step of placing its contact centres at the heart of its 'More is . . .' brand strategy.

Last week, Royal & SunAlliance announced that it plans to double the size of the business by 2008 and is hoping a bespoke call-centre service will help it realise its goal. Customers who opt into the scheme will be assigned a named personal customer manager (PCM) who they can contact via a direct phone line and email address. Each PCM will be responsible for 3000 customers.

In customer research carried out by the company, a quarter of respondents revealed that they find dealing with people in call centres one of the most infuriating things in their day-to-day lives. 'People told us they get frustrated with call centres when they have to speak to a different person every time,' says More Th>n managing director Mike Holliday-Williams.

Something needed to change. But the fact that an insurance brand should be the first to adopt such a strategy on a large scale is somewhat surprising, given the sector's generally infrequent contact with its customers. The scheme seems a more obvious solution for sectors that experience more regular contact with customers, such as banking. Some banks, such as NatWest, already offer a limited version of this system, although others only do so for high net-worth individuals or customers with multiple bank accounts.

David Payne, managing director of call-centre consultancy Maia Consulting, questions whether insurance customers really mind dealing with a different person when calls are so infrequent. 'Who can tell whether two emails were answered by the same person, and who remembers the voice of the person they speak to on average once a year?' he argues.

According to a More Th>n spokesman, while some existing customers are averse to developing a personal relationship with their insurer, recent trials at the brand's Liverpool contact centre provide anecdotal evidence that the scheme will help build better relationships and, ultimately, customer loyalty. Holliday-Williams claims that when Liverpool FC was beaten 6–3 by Arsenal in the Carling Cup on 9 January, some customers who supported the North London club taunted the company's Liverpudlian call handlers with gleeful emails.

The opportunity for call-centre staff to build personal relationships should make their job more satisfying and therefore improve staff retention, which will be critical to the success of the scheme; with typical call-centre staff churn at between 10 per cent and 15 per cent, the potential of the brand to build relationships will suffer if a customer calls the PCM only to discover the individual has moved on.

Recognising that call-handlers will not always be available, More Th>n has provided a variety of alternative touch points, such as email and voice-mail access. This impresses Ian Bateman, managing director of Inkfish. 'Customers are choosing different methods for contacting a business,' he says. 'If the scheme makes the right channels available, such as voicemail and email, it does not necessarily need more staff.'

Good training is also vital. Jeff Smith, chairman and chief executive of contact centre management firm Teleperformance, says: 'There are challenges to achieving its goal; getting quality people with the right attitude and appropriate training, the correct application of technology and an understanding that the idea behind the contact centre is primarily to improve customer service, rather than to cut costs, will be key to success.'

Logistically, the scheme is ambitious as PCMs will all have holiday to take and may also have time off sick. Bateman believes it will be hard to make it efficient, and adds that the challenge will come when a particular PCM is not available.

In the event of inaccessibility to the PCM, calls or emails to the customer manager are picked up by other call-handlers. But that solution does not satisfy everyone. 'More Th>n is taking a huge risk with customer expectations,' Payne says. 'Once I have received the contact details for my personal manager, I am going to expect them to answer my every call immediately and remember me personally. Excuses such as being in training, on a break or off duty will not wash with me, as I was promised personal service from my own account manager.'

Employing operators to wait around for assigned customers to call would, of course, be an extraordinarily inefficient move, and, as such, managers without calls from assigned customers will field general customer enquiries. Although More Th>n guarantees a response within 24 hours, the new scheme has no immediate impact on waiting times should a consumer specifically wish to speak to their PCM.

More Th>n should be applauded for attempting to improve the customer experience of call centres. While there is little to suggest it will be quicker to speak to the PCM than general call-centre staff, the personal nature of the system does make the call-handler more accountable. Even if customers are infrequent callers to the company, the fact that it can advertise an investment in customer service is likely to have a positive effect on consumer satisfaction.

(*Source*: Ed Kemp, *Marketing*, 24 January 2007)

Case study questions

1 Why are More Th>n introducing such a strategy?
2 How practical is it to implement such a strategy?
3 Is this investment in customer service likely to have a positive effect on consumer satisfaction?

References

Barnard, N. and Ehrenberg, A.S.C. (1997) 'Advertising: strongly persuasive or nudging?', *Journal of Advertising Research*, **1**, January/February, 21–31.

Barnes, J.G. and Howlett, D.M. (1998) 'Predictors of equity in relationships between service providers and retail customers', *International Journal of Bank Marketing*, **16** (1), 5–23.

Berry, L.L. (2000) 'Relationship marketing of services: growing interest, emerging perspectives', in Sheth, J.N. and Parvatiyar, A. (eds) *Handbook of Relationship Marketing*, Thousand Oaks, CA: Sage, pp. 149–70.

Bhattacharya, C.B. and Bolton, R.N. (2000) 'Relationship marketing in mass markets', in Sheth, J.N. and Parvatiyar, A. (eds) *Handbook of Relationship Marketing*, Thousand Oaks CA: Sage, pp. 327–54.

Blois, K.J. (1997) 'When is a relationship a relationship', in Gemünden, H.G., Rittert, T. and Walter, A. (eds) *Relationships and Networks in International Markets*, Oxford: Elsevier, pp. 53–64.

Blois, K.J. (1998) 'Don't all firms have relationships?', *Journal of Business and Industrial Marketing*, **13** (3), 256–70.

Bolton, R.N., Kanna, P.K. and Bramlett, M.D. (2000) 'Implications of loyalty programme membership and service experience for customer retention and value', *Journal of Marketing Science*, **28** (1), 95–108.

Brown, S. (1998) *Postmodern Marketing II*, London: International Thomson Business Press.

Brown, S. and Patterson, A. (2000) 'Knick-knack, paddy-whack, give a pub a theme', *Journal of Marketing Management*, **16** (6), 647–62.

Bund-Jackson, B. (1985) 'Build customer relationships that last', *Harvard Business Review*, November/December, 120–28.

Buttle, F.B. (1996) *Relationship Marketing Theory and Practice*, London: Paul Chapman.

Buttle, F.B. (1997) 'Exploring relationship quality', paper presented at the Academy of Marketing Conference, Manchester, UK.

Carlell, C. (1999) 'Relationship marketing from the consumer perspective', paper presented at the European Academy of Marketing Conference (EMAC), Berlin.

Christopher, M. (1996) 'From brand values to customer values', *Journal of Marketing Practice*, **2** (1), 55–66.

Dick, A. and Basu, K. (1994) 'Customer loyalty: towards an integrated framework', *Journal of the Academy of Marketing Science*, **22**, 99–113.

Dowling, G.R. and Uncles, M.D. (1997) 'Do customer loyalty schemes work?', *Sloan Management Review*, Summer, 71–82.

Dwyer, F.R., Schurr, P.H. and Oh, S. (1987) 'Developing buyer–seller relationships', *Journal of Marketing*, **51**, 11–27.

East, R. (2000) 'Fact and fallacy in retention marketing', Professorial Inaugural Lecture, 1 March, Kingston University Business School.

Fournier, S. (1998) 'Consumers and their brands: developing relationship theory in consumer behaviour', *Journal of Consumer Research*, **24**, 343–73.

Foxall, G.R., Goldsmith, R.E. and Brown, S. (1998) *Consumer Psychology for Marketing*, London: International Thomson Business Press.

Fredericks, J.O. and Salter, J.M. (1998) 'What does your customer really want?', *Quality Progress*, January, 63–8.

Garbarino, E. and Johnson, M.S. (1999) 'The different roles of satisfaction, trust and commitment in customer relationships', *Journal of Marketing*, **63** (2), 70.

Grayson, K. and Ambler, T. (1999) 'The dark side of long-term relationships in marketing', *Journal of Marketing Research*, **36** (1), 132–41.

Grönroos, C. (2000) 'The relationship marketing process: interaction, communication, dialogue, value', in 2nd WWW Conference on Relationship Marketing, 15 November 1999 to 15 February 2000, Paper 2 <www.mcb.co.uk/services/conferen/nov99/rm> (accessed 15 November 2000)

Gruen, T.W. (2000) 'Membership customers and relationship marketing', in Sheth J. N. and Parvatiyar, A. (eds) *Handbook of Relationship Marketing*, Thousand Oaks, CA: Sage, pp. 355–80.

Gummesson, E. (1999) *Total Relationship Marketing: Rethinking Marketing Management from 4Ps to 30Rs*, Oxford: Butterworth Heinemann.

Gummesson, E. (2000) 'Return on relationships (ROR): building the future with intellectual capital', in 2nd WWW Conference on Relationship Marketing, 15 November 1999 to 15 February 2000, Paper 5 <www.mcb.co.uk/services/conferen/nov99/rm> (accessed 15 November 2000)

Håkansson, H. and Johanson, J. (2001) 'Business network learning: basic considerations', in Håkansson, H. and Johanson, J. (eds) *Business Network Learning*, Amsterdam: Elsevier Science.

Hart, S., Smith, A., Sparks, L. and Tzokas, N. (1999) 'Are loyalty schemes a manifestation of relationship marketing?', *Journal of Marketing Management*, **15**, 541–62.

Hassan, M. (1996) *Customer Loyalty in the Age of Convergence*, London: Deloitte & Touche Consulting Group <www.dttus.com> (accessed 23 November 2007).

Hennig-Thurau, T. (2000) 'Relationship quality and customer retention through strategic communication of customer skills', *Journal of Marketing Management*, **16**, 55–79.

Javalgi, R. and Moberg, C. (1997) 'Service loyalty: implications for service providers', *Journal of Services Marketing*, **11** (3), 165–79.

Kandampully, J. and Duddy, R. (1999) 'Relationship marketing: a concept beyond the primary relationship', *Marketing Intelligence & Planning*, **17** (7), 315–23.

Kelly, S. (2000) 'Analytical CRM: the fusion of data and intelligence', *Interactive Marketing*, **1** (3), 262–7.

Kendrick, A. (1998) 'Promotional products vs price promotion in fostering customer loyalty: a report of two controlled field experiments', *Journal of Services Marketing*, **12** (4), 312–26.

Khan, Y. (1998) 'Winning cards', *Marketing Business*, May, 65.

Kinard, B.R. and Capella, M.L (2006) 'Relationship marketing: the influence of consumer involvement on perceived service benefits', *Journal of Service Marketing*, **21** (6), 359–68.

Levitt, T. (1983) 'After the sale is over', *Harvard Business Review*, November/December, 87–93.

McAdam, P. (2005) 'Give the customers what they want and in most cases, it's not a relationship', *Banking Strategies*, BAI Online <www.bai.org/bankstrategies/current/cover> (accessed 12 April 2007).

McDonald, M. (2000) 'On the right track', *Marketing Business*, April, 28–31.

Mitchell, A. (1998) 'Evolution', *Marketing Business*, November, 16.

Mitchell, A. (2001) 'It's a matter of trust', *Marketing Business*, April, 33.

Möller, K. and Halinen, A. (2000) 'Relationship marketing theory: its roots and direction', *Journal of Marketing Management*, **16**, 29–54.

Neal, W.D. (1999) 'Satisfaction is nice, but value drives loyalty', *Marketing Research*, Spring, 20–3.

O'Malley, L. (1998) 'Can loyalty schemes really build loyalty?', *Marketing Intelligence and Planning*, **16** (1), 47–55.

O'Malley, L. and Tynan, C. (1999) 'The utility of the relationship metaphor in consumer markets: a critical evaluation', *Journal of Marketing Management*, **15**, 587–602.

Palmatier, R.W., Dant, R.P., Grewal, D. and Evans, K.R. (2006) 'Factors influencing the effectiveness of relationship marketing: a meta-analysis', *Journal of Marketing*, **70** (October), 136–53.

Palmer, A.J. (1996) 'Relationship marketing: a universal paradigm or management fad?' *The Learning Organisation*, **3** (3), 18–25.

Palmer, A.J. (1998) *Principles of Services Marketing*, London: Kogan Page.

Palmer, A.J. (2000) 'Co-operation and competition: a Darwinian synthesis of relationship marketing', *European Journal of Marketing*, **34** (5/6), 687–704.

Peppers, D. and Rogers, M. (2000) 'Build a one-to-one learning relationship with your customers', *Interactive Marketing*, **1** (3), 243–50.

Pressey, A.D. and Mathews, B.P. (1998) 'Relationship marketing and retailing: comfortable bedfellows?', *Customer Relationship Management*, **1** (1), 39–53.

Rousseau, D.M., Sitkin, S.B., Burt, R.S. and Camerer, C. (1998) 'Not so different after all: a cross discipline view of trust', *Academy of Management Review*, **23** (3), 393–404.

Selnes, F. and Sallis, J. (2003) 'Promoting relationship learning', *Journal of Marketing*, **67** (3), 80–96.

Sheth, J.N. and Parvatiyar, A. (2000) 'Relationship marketing in consumer markets: antecedents and consequences', in Sheth, J. N. and Parvatiyar, A. (eds) *Handbook of Relationship Marketing*, Thousand Oaks, CA: Sage, pp. 171–207.

Singh, J. and Sirdeshmukh, D. (2000) 'Agency and trust mechanisms in consumer satisfaction and loyalty judgements', *Journal of Marketing Science*, **28** (1), 150–67.

Sisodia, R.S. and Wolfe, D.B. (2000) 'Information technology', in Sheth, J.N. and Parvatiyar, A. (eds) *Handbook of Relationship Marketing*, Thousand Oaks, CA: Sage, pp. 525–63.

Smith, W. and Higgins, M. (2000) 'Reconsidering the relationship analogy', *Journal of Marketing Management*, **16**, 81–94.

Storbacka, K., Strandvik, T. and Grönroos, C. (1994) 'Managing customer relations for profit: the dynamics of relationship quality', *International Journal of Service Industry Management*, **5**, 21–38.

Swaminathan, V. and Reddy, S.K. (2000) 'Affinity partnering: conceptualisation and issues', in Sheth, J.N. and Parvatiyar, A. (eds) *Handbook of Relationship Marketing*, Thousand Oaks, CA: Sage, pp. 381–405.

Too, L.H.Y., Souchon, A.L. and Thirkell, P.C. (2001) 'Relationship marketing and customer loyalty in a retail setting: a dynamic exploration', *Journal of Marketing Management*, **17** (3/4), 287–319.

Tynan, C. (1997) 'A review of the marriage analogy in relationship marketing', *Journal of Marketing Management*, **13** (7), 695–704.

Uncles, M. (1994) 'Do you or your customer need a loyalty scheme?', *Journal of Targeting, Measurement and Analysis*, **2** (4), 335–50.

Van den Bulte, C. (1994) 'Metaphor at work', in Laurent, G., Lilien, G.L. and Pras, B. (eds) *Research Traditions in Marketing*, Boston, MA: Kluwer Academic, pp. 405–25.

Ward, P., Gardner, H. and Wright, H. (1998) 'Being smart: a critique of customer loyalty schemes in UK retailing', *Customer Relationship Management*, **1** (1), 79–86.

Notes

1   Bloemer and de Ruyter were describing 'retail store loyalty' in this definition but it is equally applicable to suppliers in general.
2   Sainsbury originally ran their own loyalty programme. In 2003 they joined the 'Nectar' loyalty scheme together with BP, Debenhams and others.

4 Relationship economics

Key issues

- The economic justification for relationship marketing
- Customer acquisition versus customer retention
- Stages of relationship development
- Lifetime value concepts
- Switching costs
- Relationship longevity

Introduction

It has previously been noted that there is limited agreement on a precise definition of relationship marketing, and many of the philosophical, organisational or economic concepts that surround it. There are, however, a number of key ideas or concepts that have developed through relationship marketing research which, proponents claim, underpin relational marketing theory and practice.

As was noted in Chapter 2, profitability ultimately must be a driving force behind any strategy development. In this chapter, therefore, we will look at the arguments for and against what are described in this context as the economics of relationship marketing or 'relationship economics'.

Relationship economics

One axiom of traditional marketing is the belief that self-interest and competition are the drivers of value creation. That axiom is challenged by relationship marketers who believe that it is mutual cooperation that delivers this value (Sheth and Parvatiyar, 1995a, p. 399). A central feature of RM is, therefore, to distinguish the concept from the microeconomic paradigm (Palmer *et al.*, 2005). However, the illusion that RM is unconcerned about profit because of its apparent philanthropic and cooperative image is false. A principal objective behind companies adopting relational strategies must, at least ultimately, be sustainable profitability. Even though in a relational exchange the focus is more concerned with the longer-term economic benefits profits remain important to all parties in the relationship (Morgan, 2000, p. 485). As Gummesson (1994, p. 17) notes the 'language of management is money, [therefore] a good question is how the relationship portfolio pays off'.

RM is, therefore, not altruistic but based on profit-driven arguments (Buttle, 1996, p. 5) with the profitability of relationships as one of the key goals (Storbacka *et al.*, 1994, p. 22). It is, what Sheth and Parvatiyar (1995b, p. 265) call, 'enlightened self-interest'.

Leaky bucket theory

Historically, the focus of traditional marketing has been on creating new customers. This 'offensive marketing' strategy included, in addition to acquiring wholly new customers, attempting to attract dissatisfied customers away from competitors, particularly in periods of heavy competition (Storbacka *et al.*, 1994, pp. 22–3). Many authors take the view that, although the acquisition of customers is important, it is an intermediate step in the process (Berry and Gresham, 1986, p. 43). The first line of defence for any company is its existing customers (Kotler, 1992, p. 50).

Figure 4.1
Leaky bucket theory

RM, therefore, highlights the proposition that, in addition to 'offensive strategies', companies need 'defensive strategies' which minimise customer turnover (Storbacka *et al.*, 1994, pp. 22–3). The logic behind this double-headed approach is probably best illustrated using the metaphor of the leaky bucket (Figure 4.1). This emphasises the importance of keeping customers while recognising that acquiring customers is, of course, the basis for having any customers to keep (Grönroos, 1995, p. 253).

To succeed, a company must *both* have a flow of new customers and restrict customer exit. The aim is to keep or, where company objectives call for it, increase the number of customers available to the company. To achieve profitability the dual strategies of acquisition and retention must work in tandem.

Customer acquisition

There is a continuous need in a business for 'new blood'. Any fall in the overall number of customers has profitability implications, particularly in service industries where fixed costs (especially staffing costs) tend to be highest. *Every organisation loses customers* through relocation or other forms of termination, if not through some level of competitive switching. Any loss of customers has to be replaced merely for the company to stand still.

Companies in the past have tended to concentrate on the customer acquisition process as, in general, market growth provided a steady supply of new prospects. Yet, even in the halcyon days of high population growth, high sector growth and/or minimal competition the possibility always existed of substitutes or new competitors entering the market. In the third millennium, forecasters suggest low and perhaps negative population growth in many mature markets. This will particularly affect the number of potential customers at the freer spending, lower end of the adult age spectrum. Competitive pressures meanwhile are unlikely to ease and may, with the opening up of national borders, get worse. The likelihood is, therefore, that customer acquisition in relative terms will become more difficult.

Customer retention

Although RM has a dual focus on *both* acquisition and retention strategies, it is the latter that is often given more prominence. Indeed, it has become one of the underpinning convictions of RM that it encourages *retention marketing* first and *acquisition marketing* second (Gummesson, 1999, p. 9). This bias exists because customer retention is perceived as offering significant advantages, particularly in saturated markets (Dawes and Swailes, 1999, p. 36). This is generally supported by academics, many of whom further promote the concept by suggesting that customer acquisition is between five and ten times more expensive than customer retention (e.g. Gummesson, 1999, p. 183). It has, therefore, become widely accepted by more and more companies that it makes a great deal of sense to try to keep existing customers happy rather than devote high levels of marketing effort to new customer acquisition (Barnes, 1994, p. 562).

To further strengthen the argument that the principal focus should be on retention, it is proposed that the longevity of relationships also provides additional profit potential. Reichheld (1996, p. 65), for example, suggests that the benefits are cumulative and that the longer the cycle continues the 'greater the company's financial strength'.

The dual benefits of customer retention can be summarised, therefore, as:

- existing customers are less expensive to retain than to recruit;
- securing a customer's loyalty over time produces superior profits.

These, it is proposed, are the two economic arguments that underpin RM (Buttle, 1996, p. 5). Although this is an oversimplification, there is little doubt that a major impetus for the development of RM has been a growing awareness of these *potential* long-term benefits.

Zero defections?

Despite RM's concentration on retention, no company can possibly hold on to all its customers even in monopoly situations. Although some marketing gurus call for policies leading to 'zero defections', this is neither a possible, practical nor indeed profitable objective. Total customer retention is never achievable as there is always some loss. For example, some customers will move; others will pass away. In a highly competitive market, customers may switch (temporarily or permanently) to another product or service on the basis of factors that may not necessarily be within the control of the company. It is also invariably unprofitable to attempt to achieve total (or even near total) retention as the costs (often in the form of inducements to return) involved in delivering this are likely to be prohibitive. Retention strategy should not, therefore, be aimed at keeping customers at any cost (Gummesson, 1999, p. 26). The company must know when to 'cut and run'. A further potential danger exists in concentrating wholly on retention to the exclusion of customer acquisition.

Retention strategies tested

As with any generalised statements, such as those made in support of RM, there is always a danger that they become accepted truths and prescriptive remedies for all varieties of assorted ills. Although the principles may hold good in many instances, there are several inconsistencies with retention economics which should be challenged before companies consider the full application of relational strategies.

Acquisition and retention costs

It is widely suggested that an important component in calculating the benefits of customer retention is that the front-end costs of customer acquisition exceed the cost of retention. Statements such as 'it costs five to ten times as much to get a new customer as it costs to keep an existing customer' are regularly made in a wide range of general and relationship marketing texts (e.g. Christopher *et al.*, 1991, p. 157; Gummesson, 1999, p. 183). This widely accepted marketing maxim is, however, an oversimplification. It would certainly appear that some evidence supporting the proposal exists although it is highly selective. Research to date by consulting firms such as Bain and Co. (see Reichheld, 1996) has produced company-specific examples (Payne and Frow, 1997) in industries that have certain distinct and non-universal characteristics.

Front-end costs

The industries chosen most frequently as examples of the successful application of customer retention strategies appear all to have high front-end acquisition costs inherent in their make-up (e.g. banks, credit card and insurance). Important among these front-end costs are a number that occur frequently. These are:

■ the high costs of personal selling;

■ commission payments;

■ direct and indirect costs of detailed information gathering;

■ supply of equipment;

■ advertising and other communications expenditure.

Personal selling

Although most businesses are involved to some degree in personal selling, it is more significant in some businesses than in others. One particular area where personal selling has always been seen as necessary is where there is a degree of complexity in the product or service. In the service sector this may be significant as intangibility adds to the complex nature of the offering. Mass marketing media does not generally handle complexity well. The salesperson has the ability to highlight and emphasise product or service features and respond to any questions that a customer may have. Personal selling is, therefore, a high-quality, marketing communications tool used in complex or high-value (for the purposes of negotiation) product sales.

The downside of personal selling is cost. Dependent on the industry, complexity, geography and other factors, salespeople who travel to visit customers can rarely meet more than a limited amount of potential new customers in a given period. Even salespeople based at fixed-site showrooms where customers do the travelling (e.g. a retail store) can only be expected to see limited numbers of new clients in an average day. An additional variable factor is that the **client conversion rate** (i.e. the rate at which prospects are converted into customers) may not be high. Such is the nature of personal selling that costs require constant monitoring if they are not to get out of control (see Box 4.1). All of these factors imply that the cost per customer acquisition will be high where personal selling is a major component in the customer's decision-making process.

Box 4.1   Personal selling

A high-tech company I have worked with discovered that it cost them $120,000 to support a salesperson – including salary, commissions, expenses and fringe benefits. At this company, the average salesperson could make 200 calls a year. They had to attend a lot of meetings and training, and therefore could not make a call a day. Based on those numbers, it cost the company roughly $600 to make a call on a prospect. On average, it took about three calls to convert a prospect into a customer. As a result, the company's new customer acquisition cost was $1,800. Actually it was higher than that – that does not include the cost of promoting target market awareness and interest. Suppose the average new customer spends $5,000 a year and remains loyal for three years. If the profit margin is 10 per cent, the lifetime value of the customer is $1,500. In that case the company lost money on the new customer.

(*Source*: Kotler, 1992, p. 50)

Commission

If commissions are payable (either internally or externally) on sales this may reduce the fixed costs of personal selling although the variable costs of acquisition increase. In circumstances where commissions are payable on sales it is likely that the cost of customer acquisition, relative to retention costs, will be high.

Data collection

Where the data collection required is significant and the issue of contracts or other expensive materials is involved, this may again contribute to high initial costs. In these cases (e.g. insurance) the company may not begin to make a profit on the product or service for one or more years into the lifetime of the contract.

Supply of equipment

This refers to long-term equipment hire (e.g. television rental) or supply (e.g. the free or subsidised supply of satellite or digital TV receivers) where the investment is written off over the calculated lifetime of the contract. Any contract that terminates prior to the full write-off period is, therefore, loss making. In contrast, any contract which lasts beyond that point represents additional profit. The benefits of customer retention in such circumstances are obvious.

Advertising and other communication costs

Where advertising (particularly long-term brand-building) is used to promote 'front of mind awareness'[1] (to ensure a brand's prominence in the marketplace) then the cost of maintaining this awareness may, justifiably, be included in the cost of customer acquisition.

High front-end-cost industries

The likelihood is that, in industries where personal selling, commission, high data collection, equipment supply expenditure or high brand awareness investment (i.e. marketing communications) are involved, then new customer acquisition costs will nearly always exceed the costs of retention. Logic suggests, therefore, that industries where the greater part of expenses are up-front would benefit from writing off these costs over an extended period of time (Figure 4.2). In these instances, the longer the relationship the lower the costs relative to income and the higher the profit is likely to be (see the section on lifetime value, p. 84). Grossman (1998, p. 31), for example, reports that it costs the credit card company MBNA approximately $100.00, on average, to attract a new customer. However, a customer who has been with them for five years represents about $100.00 profit per annum and a ten-year customer approximately $300.00 per year.

Figure 4.2
Typical profit pattern in financial services and other high acquisition cost industries

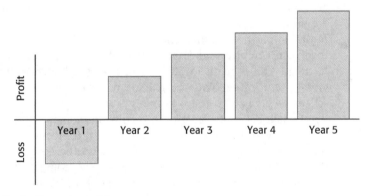

(Not to scale; for illustration only)

Low front-end-cost industries

At the other end of the acquisition costs spectrum, for example in the field of FMCG retailing, the costs of customer acquisition appear marginal as intense personal selling, commissions, detailed information gathering and/or equipment supply are not always necessary to make an individual sale. Indeed, the FMCG consumer would only seem to require one or more of a limited number of drivers, such as location, perceived service quality, price competitiveness, product range and quality and/or promotional offerings, to stimulate a sale. These are the same factors that are seen to influence the customer retention process.

Advertising and other (non-personal selling) marketing communication costs, commonly included in the customer acquisition calculations, again do not fully justify the up-front cost argument. High advertising and sales promotion costs attributed to customer acquisition fail to acknowledge the part played by those same messages in the retention process. Advertising serves to remind buyers of their purchasing preferences (East, 2000, p. 96) and may, therefore, often work defensively to protect the existing customer base rather than aggressively to bring in new buyers (Barnard and Ehrenberg, 1997, p. 38).

If drivers promoting sales to potential new customers are similar or the same as those for existing clients then the cost of acquisition must closely equal the cost of retention. Indeed, if the supplier introduces schemes that reward repeat buying over and above the single purchase (the basis of most retail and airline loyalty schemes) then the cost of retention may exceed the cost of acquisition.

Economics of retention strategies

RM appears to be an expensive alternative to mass marketing and, as such, marketers' commitment to such strategies are only valid when they are deemed to be affordable and practical (Berry, 2000, p. 154). Yet much of the current discussion about RM management ignores how the economic effects of establishing such relationships can be or are measured (Blois, 1999, p. 91). Indeed much of the RM literature depends on the, mostly implicit, suggestion that a causal effect of relationships is always effective performance (Ambler and Styles, 2000, p. 499). The economics of costly relational techniques must, in circumstances where **acquisition/retention cost ratios** are small, be closely scrutinised. This is particularly evident in the case of many costly loyalty schemes which are, perhaps ironically, most prevalent in those sectors where the validity of relational strategies is most highly questionable (e.g. FMCG retailing). Incentives to retention in these schemes are costs that (if profitability is to be maintained) lead ultimately to higher prices. In such markets differentials may occur in costs between the 'loyalty incentivisors' and their lower-priced competition (Palmer and Beggs, 1997). The phenomenon is not new. The history of British supermarket retailing is peppered by swings between price wars and differential advantage strategies. The airline industry too is experiencing this in the competition between established and 'low-cost' airlines.

The evidence that exists suggests that, in industries where recognisable high frontend costs are involved, these are drivers to relational strategies that promote customer retention over customer acquisition. Where acquisition costs are low and/or where the real difference between acquisition and retention costs is marginal, the introduction of costly relational strategies may become a burden.

Claims about the effectiveness of improved retention may also frequently be overblown. According to East (2000, p. 11), authors (e.g. Doyle, 1998, p. 44; Kotler *et al.*, 1999, p. 44) who make claims of 25–85 per cent profit increases based upon increasing retention by as little as 5 per cent rarely consider how difficult (and potentially costly) this is to achieve.

Long-term benefits

Retention economics are also promoted as a time-based form of competitive advantage through the suggestion that investment in long-term relationships brings long-term advantages (Murphy, 1997, p. 1). Relationship investment refers to the time, effort and resources that the supplier invests in building stronger investments (Palmatier *et al.*, 2006, p. 140). Gummesson (1999, p. 183) has coined the phrase **'return on relationships'** (**ROR**) to describe the expectation that there would be a return on this investment. ROR he defines as 'the long-term net financial outcome caused by the establishment and maintenance of an organisation's network of relationships'. The long-term orientation is often emphasised because it is believed that loyalty is cumulative (Reichheld, 1993, p. 65).

Long-term benefits may be considered from two perspectives:

■ relationship stages;

■ the lifetime value of the customer.

Relationship stages

As noted in our earlier definition, relationship marketing is seen as a means of identifying, establishing, maintaining, enhancing and, where necessary, terminating relationships (Grönroos, 1996, p. 7). This definition anticipates that, once a company starts thinking about individual customers (as opposed to mass markets), it should recognise that different customers are at different stages of relational development. Importantly, it also implies that each customer type (e.g. prospect, customer, former customer) should be handled in a different way. This may include different targeted messages (rather than mass communication) and different 'value options' (e.g. rewards) from the exchange.

The recognition of different relational stages in RM also includes the implicit assumption that the higher the stage of development the greater the profitability to the organisation and consequentially the greater the benefits to the organisation. As we will discuss later, this may be an over-simplification in some industries.

Stages models

Various models exist that illustrate this concept (see Figure 4.3) and that may be seen to approximately equate to both consumer and business-to-business relationships. Dwyer *et al.* (1987, p. 15) suggest a five-stage model where each phase represents a major transition in how parties in a relationship regard each other. These are:

■ awareness;

■ exploration;

■ expansion;

■ commitment;

■ dissolution.

Figure 4.3
Relationship
ladders or
stages

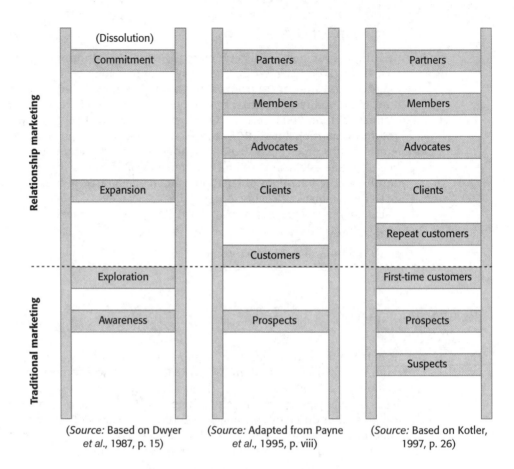

(*Source:* Based on Dwyer *et al.*, 1987, p. 15)

(*Source:* Adapted from Payne *et al.*, 1995, p. viii)

(*Source:* Based on Kotler, 1997, p. 26)

Awareness

Awareness is where one party recognises that the other party is a 'feasible exchange partner'. Interaction has not yet taken place although there may be 'positioning' and 'posturing' by the parties to enhance their attractiveness.

Exploration

Exploration refers to the 'research and trial stage' in the exchange. At this level potential partners consider obligations, benefits and burdens of the exchange. This may well include the psychological and actual costs involved. Dwyer *et al.* suggest that this stage includes sub-phases such as attraction, communication and bargaining, development and exercise of power (see Chapter 9), norm development (e.g. contractual arrangements) and expectation development (e.g. trust and commitment; see Chapter 6).

Expansion

Expansion refers to the period where there is a continual increase in benefits obtained by exchange partners and where they become increasingly interdependent.

Commitment

Commitment relates to the implicit or explicit pledge of relational continuity between the parties.

Dissolution

The inclusion in the model of a dissolution stage reminds us that disengagement always remains a possibility in any relationship.

Dwyer *et al.* (1987, p. 25) make the important point that, although all transactions have relational properties, it makes sense to consider many exchanges as 'practically discrete' (or non-relational). In other words, relationship stages, such as those described, are not automatic and can only exist where both parties recognise the potential benefits of the relationship. Although in organisational (business-to-business) markets these types of close, bilateral relationships can be seen and are explicitly recognised (Blois, 1997, p. 53), doubt must remain whether this level of closeness could possibly exist in consumer goods or even in many consumer services markets where many of the exchange relationships are discrete.

Other models exist which suggest relational stages of customer development. The long-established concept of a 'ladder of loyalty' was adapted by Payne *et al.* (1995, p. viii) to create a 'relationship ladder'. The metaphor of the 'ladder' and 'climbing up' to higher levels of relationship is easy to visualise. Kotler (1997, p. 26) also proposes a stages model which resembles the relationship ladder.

In the three models illustrated in Figure 4.3, although each has a slightly different perspective, they all promote the idea of customers moving upward from one stage to another. They also illustrate the perception that, whereas traditional marketing's interest ends with the sale, RM's interest extends beyond this to the development and enhancement of the customer relationship.

Figure 4.4
Prospect
hierarchy

Increasing
likelihood of
conversion to
active customers

(*Source*: Adapted from Tapp, 1998, p. 150)

In the Kotler model the process starts with the identification of suspects. In mass marketing terms this might be achieved through segmentation and targeting although the 'wastage' (media costs which are judged at a cost per thousand 'hits' invariably include an untargeted audience) would be high. In database marketing terms this may involve the rental of lists of names and addresses of **suspected target groups**. Either way, it is the identification of these potential customers which begins the process.

Prospects are at a higher level than suspects and have, most probably, given some indication that they are likely to purchase the goods or services on offer. Not all prospects are viewed as being of equal potential and, as such, there is a prospect hierarchy (see Figure 4.4). In this hierarchy former customers (known users who have already had experience of the product or service) are considered most likely to revert to being customers. Next best are those customers who have made active enquiries about a product, the assumption being that, having made the effort to contact the company, they are quite probably already motivated to purchase. Referrals are seen as next best in the knowledge that referrals carry considerable weight with most customers and again, in probability, they are likely (having sought information) to be in a frame of mind to purchase. Profiled prospects are those who, based on their profile, give a strong indication that they may purchase, while 'hand raisers' have also indicated in some other way (perhaps in a consumer survey) that they also are potential customers. Finally, suspects might be indicated by demographic or **life-style analysis**. This 'prospect hierarchy' is used, particularly by direct and database marketers, to prioritise customer communication and is an example of how markets may be segmentable against some sort of 'relationship proneness' variable (Buttle, 1996, p. 7).

Kotler (unlike Payne *et al*.) differentiates between first-time and repeat customers. Certainly the decision-making process will be different in each case. With repeat purchases the consumer has actual experience (as opposed to hype or hearsay) to go on. It is at this point that the relational marketer is seen to diverge from the traditional marketer, whose interest is seen to be primarily in the single transaction. The prime task of the relational marketer from this point is to become skilful at moving customers to higher stages of relationship, with each stage representing a strengthening of the company's relationship with the customer (Kotler, 1997, p. 26). This is seen to be in complete contrast with the traditional marketer, who has no ambition to encourage customers to climb the loyalty ladder (Gummesson, 1999, p. 11). Traditional marketing views each transaction independently whereas with RM each further transaction is viewed in terms of its history and its anticipated future (Dwyer *et al*., 1987, p. 12).

The Kotler stages model suggests that the company is looking to transform repeat customers into 'clients', which by definition implies a higher status and some (non-stated) form of psychological contract or 'bond' between the parties. The further jump to the status of 'advocate' implies that the customer moves from being responsive to the company to becoming actively involved in the marketing of the organisation, most commonly through word-of-mouth recommendation. 'Members' implies even greater affinity to the company while 'partnership' suggests a relationship on such a high level that, as predicted in some definitions (e.g. Gordon, 1998, p. 9) of RM (see Chapter 2, page 38), the customer becomes part of the value-creating process.

Marketing reality

As with all relational concepts, it is important with 'stages' or 'ladder of loyalty' theories to separate the reality from the rhetoric. There is, for example, no research to suggest the extent to which those engaged in loyalty marketing actively pursue customers up the ladder of loyalty (Hart *et al.*, 1999, p. 545). Terms such as advocate, member or partner assume a depth of association that few consumers would recognise in relation to companies or organisations they deal with on a daily basis. It is not sufficient simply to imply an affiliation if the customer does not recognise it as such. Even if the supplier regards the process as a long-term commitment on their behalf it will be the customer who will ultimately define the relationship. The real issues are how a company identifies its best customers and how it retains them economically (Moules, 1998, p. 46). Each level also involves higher maintenance costs, so it is important for organisations to determine when (and if) it is worth going to the next level (Kotler, 1992, p. 52).

Some companies have, however, managed to introduce tactics that have successfully created membership-type relationships that assume affiliation of some sort. This does not include so-called 'consumer clubs', which do not normally fulfil the reciprocity conditions required in high-level relationships and are rarely regarded as more than registration or contractual devices by most consumers. Travel organisations are perhaps the furthest advanced and many (particularly airlines) have developed clubs where members are seen to enjoy privileges that ordinary consumers do not enjoy. Some organisations, for example British Airways, have taken this a stage further by openly differentiating between levels of membership dependent on the customer's commitment (determined by expenditure) to the airline. Executive Club members (who can be blue, silver or gold card holders) receive different levels of privileges dependent on their status.

There are also some organisations where explicit relational bonds (or higher-level relationships) are much more evident. These include those where voluntary membership of, for example, political parties or charitable organisations involves, by implication, membership commitment and, perhaps, costs or effort without monetary (but perhaps with psychological) reward. Organisations such as clubs or voluntary organisations may also make explicit that a higher level of relationship can be achieved, usually with increased status potential.[2] Membership of political parties may include the member actively involved in development of the policies of that party – the political equivalent of 'value creation'. Membership of this type can even mean the member becoming involved in the management of the organisation on a part-time or even full-time basis.

A further problem with the 'ladder' or 'stages' theories is the implicit assumption that there is a linear progression from lower to higher status. It should be recognised that a consumer may, regardless of the efforts of the company, demote themselves for a multiplicity of reasons (e.g. better source of supply) or indeed cease altogether to be a customer. Remaining at any British Airways Executive Club level, for example, is determined by the points accumulated in any one membership year. Should customers decide to utilise another (non-affiliated) airline for a number or all of their journeys they are demoted or lose altogether their Executive Club benefits. This differential status has been retained between airlines involved with British Airways in the Oneworld alliance (see Box 4.2). Change of customer status can, therefore, be in either an upward or a downward direction.

Box 4.2 Oneworld frequent flyer programmes (as at 1st August 2007)

Oneworld airline programme	Oneworld emerald status	Oneworld sapphire status	Oneworld ruby status	Entry level to programme
British Airways Executive Club	Gold	Silver	Not applicable	Blue
American Airlines AAdvantage	Executive Platinum	Platinum	Gold	AAdvantage
Cathay Pacific Marco Polo Club	Diamond	Gold	Silver	Asia Miles
Finnair Finnair Plus	Platinum	Gold	Silver	Finnair Plus
Iberia Iberia Plus	Platinum	Gold	Silver	Blue Clasica
Japanese Airlines JAL	JMB Diamond JGC Premier	JMB Sapphire	JMB Crystal	JMB Member
LanChile LanPass	Comodoro	Premium Silver	Premium	LanPass
Malév Duna Club	DC Platinum	DC Gold	DC Silver	DC Blue
Qantas Frequent Flyer	Platinum	Gold	Silver	Frequent Flyer
Royal Jordanian	Platinum	Gold	Silver	Royal Plus

Lifetime value

Recognition of the importance of RM was driven, in part, by the realisation that people trade over lifetimes (Ambler and Styles, 2000, p. 503). The **'lifetime value'** concept suggests that a company should avoid taking a short-term view of the profit (or indeed loss) of any individual but rather should consider the income derived from that company's lifetime association with the customer. As part of a successful customer retention strategy, organisations should project the value of individual customers over time rather than focus on customer numbers (Dawes and Swailes, 1999, p. 36). The idea is not new. Banks, for example, have traditionally offered young people attractive deals to open accounts. Although this may be costly in the short term, these banks are prepared to do this in the knowledge that, traditionally in this sector, customers change infrequently to competitor organisations (although traditional allegiances may be changing, particularly with the introduction of Internet banking).

The lifetime value of a customer is an impetus to implement retention policies. Decisions concerning investment in relational strategies (to promote retention) may be made on the basis of the customer's notional lifetime value, albeit based on historical data. These investments may include those designed to enhance product or service quality in order to maintain or increase competitive advantage, or defensively to discourage defection to the competition. In the latter case the company may effectively be building 'barriers to exit' to promote retention (see switching costs, below). An example of the average lifetime value of an organisation's customers is shown in Box 4.3 below.

Box 4.3 Lifetime value calculation

For an explanation of these calculations please see the appendix to this chapter on page 99.

	Year 1	Year 2	Year 3
Referral rate	5.0%	7.0%	10.0%
Referred customers	–	2,500	2,975
Retention rate	80.0%	82.5%	85.0%
Retained customers	–	40,000	35,063
Total customers	50,000	42,500	38,037
Revenue per customer	£400	£425	£450
Total revenue	£20,000,000	£18,062,500	£17,116,650
Direct costs £225	£11,250,000	£9,562,500	£8,558,325
Acquisition cost £90	£4,500,000	0	0
Marketing costs £25	£1,250,000	£1,062,500	£950,925
Total costs	£17,000,000	£10,625,000	£9,509,250
Profit	£3,000,000	£7,437,500	£7,607,400
Discount rate	1.00	1.12	1.2544
Net present value	£3,000,000	£6,640,625	£6,064,573
Cumulative NPV	£3,000,000	£9,640,625	£15,705,198
Lifetime value	£60	£193	£314

Based on 50,000 acquired and existing customers for Year 1
The formula for the discount rate is: $D = (1 + i)^n$
i = the market rate of interest plus a factor for risk (e.g. 6 per cent and 2 = 0.12)
n = the number of years for which you have to wait (e.g. 0, 1, 2)

The downside of the lifetime value concept is that there is no guarantee that the customer will continue to patronise a supplier at the same level as previously or indeed that he or she will even stay with the company. This is particularly true in businesses with low exit barriers (e.g. retailing) and in rapidly changing, competitive markets (e.g. telecommunications). It may also be the case in industries where substantial sales promotion is used. Indeed, if customers perceive that the only difference between alternative companies is the size of the 'bribe' offered them they are likely to become increasingly promiscuous, actively seeking out the highest bribe available as the only satisfaction to be derived from the exchange (Tynan, 1997, p. 992). The merit of 'lifetime value' in situations such as these must be dubious.

Switching costs

It is difficult to discuss **retention strategies** without referring to the subject of switching costs. Switching costs are effectively **barriers to exit** from the relationship from the perspective of the consumer. Perceived wisdom is that RM strategies work best not only when you have long time horizons but also high switching costs (Kinard and Capella 2006, p. 359). These are costs (monetary and non-monetary) that buyers encounter when switching from one supplier to another. While largely self-evident in complex **business-to-business (B2B)** marketing relationships (sunken costs, search costs, etc.), they can equally be relevant to consumers (Bhattacharya and Bolton, 2000, p. 334). It is important to recognise that the 'real' costs may be greater or less than that customer's perception of them (Stewart, 1998, p. 241).

Switching costs may be created by the supplier, by the consumer or by the relationship itself. This is a controversial area within the RM debate as some costs or barriers are seen as acceptable in that they are the 'natural' barriers created in any good relationship or at the behest of the consumer. Others, however, are seen as coercive and contrary to the principles (if such principles exist) associated with relational strategies. These actual or psychological 'costs', which are not mutually exclusive, may be summarised as:

- search costs;
- learning costs;
- emotional costs;
- inertial costs;
- risk;
- social costs;
- financial costs;
- legal barriers.

Search costs

Search costs are those based on the time and energy spent searching for alternative sources of supply (e.g. searching through catalogues looking for a particular product or service).

Learning costs

Learning costs are based on the time and energy expended learning how to deal effectively and efficiently with a new supplier (e.g. learning the layout of a supermarket you have never used before).

Emotional costs

Relationships over an extended period can create emotional ties with an organisation or the personnel of that organisation. Personal services (e.g. hairdressing) can engender such loyalty as can some iconic brands. In this regard the Internet has seen the development of 'brand community' sites (e.g. Apple, General Motors and Coca-Cola) where members regularly show the depth of their devotion.

Inertial costs

The effort involved in breaking habitual behaviour is frequently underestimated. This tendency is probably best summed up by the phrase 'I can't be bothered to go elsewhere'. This is also associated with the concept of the **zone of tolerance' (ZOT)**. The ZOT is seen as that range of service performance where small increases or decreases in performance quality do not lead to any (positive or negative) action (Yap and Sweeney, 2007, p. 137).

Risk

The move to a new supplier will always involve a degree of risk. Even where the risk is not immediately apparent there is still a general preference to stay with an existing supplier rather than risk a move to another of whom you have no experience. This is best summed up by the inclination of people to remain with the 'devil you know' rather than move to 'the devil you don't'.

Social costs

The existing supplier may, in some way, contribute to the social life of the customer. An exaggerated example might be the existence of 'singles shopping nights' in some supermarkets. A more commonplace example may be the opportunity to socialise with other customers and staff at a company organised event (e.g. preview evenings). This has become more prevalent with the development of Internet-mediated brand communities where companies such as Saab, Jeep and Harley Davidson organise weekend events for avid fans of the product.

Financial costs

The break-up of a relationship may mean financial penalties (e.g. the costs frequently involved in switching mortgage providers) or the loss of rewards or status gained through relationship longevity (e.g. some loyalty schemes, no-claims insurance).

Legal barriers

In some situations, a contractual arrangement ensures that the consumer stays (even against their will) for a period of time in the relationship.

Pressey and Mathews (1998, p. 43) suggest that in developed relationships efforts are made to lock in customers using the types of barrier or cost described above. Relationship marketers, however, suggest that there is more to RM than simply 'locking them in' (Barnes, 1994, p. 556) and that companies that rely on this type of retention are on a 'hiding to nothing'. Thus, when 'enhancement and development of customers' is defined as 'more effective tethering and dissuasion from defection by threat of corrective action' (Worthington and Horne, 1998, p. 39), this is open to criticism. If marketers create excessive barriers or high switching costs, customers are likely to react negatively (Sheth and Parvatiyar, 2000, p. 185).

There does, however, appear to be a distinction between applied costs/barriers (e.g. financial penalties) and those created by the customer (e.g. emotional or social costs) or as a consequence of the relationship (e.g. search, learning or risk-associated costs). Relationships generated by companies which view RM as 'locking in' customers through penalty barriers are seen as inferior relationships to ones where the parties engaged are willing participants. What passes for a relationship in an enforced retention situation is really a 'pseudo-relationship' in that it is one-sided with customers kept, against their will, because the cost of leaving is too high (Barnes, 1994, p. 565). According to Gummesson (1994, p. 17) this type of 'manipulative marketing' can be compared with:

> the use of artificial fertilizer and pesticides which increase short-term harvests but impoverish not only the soil where the crops grow, but the whole of nature for short-term greed. Just like ecology RM sees marketing activities as part of a larger context.

Customer-created barriers, by comparison, are usually the product of mutually recognised satisfaction (or possibly absence of dissatisfaction) created by the supplier to add value to the relationship. An example may be so-called 'strategic bundling' (Payne, 2000, p. 119) where groups of associated products or services are offered with advantages of convenience and/or cost saving. Those barriers that exist as a consequence of the relationship (such as search or learning costs) may not be directly created by the supplier although it may be in that supplier's interest to illustrate the potential costs to the customer. Ultimately long service may act as a switching barrier, but not one that is insurmountable (Stewart, 1998, p. 10).

Relationship longevity

It has been suggested that, when used with skill, customer retention leads to enhanced revenue, reduced costs and improved financial performance. Reichheld (1996, p. 39) echoes this claim by proposing a list of accumulating benefits that contribute to an entire 'life cycle of profits' from the customer. The model (see Figure 4.5) presented assumes:

■ revenue growth over time;

■ cost savings over time;

■ referral income;

■ price premiums.

Figure 4.5
Profit growth
over time

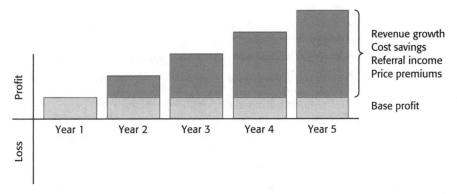

(*Source*: Reprinted by permission of Harvard Business School Press. From *The Loyalty Effect: The Hidden Force Behind Growth, Profits and Lasting Value* by F.F. Reichheld. Boston, MA 1996, p. 43. Copyright © 1996 Harvard Business School Publishing Corporation.)

Revenue growth

Reichheld (ibid., p. 43) suggests that in most businesses customers' spending increases over time. This may indeed be the case in industries with a low turnover of customers (and possibly high exit barriers). It can reasonably be assumed, in these industries, that income will be more likely to increase than decline over time. In general, however, this is a highly optimistic assumption. In businesses with a high turnover of customers and low exit barriers it may be hypothesised that increased revenue from one customer will, most probably, be matched by those customers whose purchases decline or even cease during the same period.

Revenue growth in most businesses cannot be assumed without active intervention on the part of the supplier in expanding the offering (in terms of variety and/or value) relative to the offering of the competition. There are industries (which Reichheld acknowledges) where no customer growth is possible, such as gardening maintenance contracts, which generally involve a 'fixed' level of service. Some other product or service levels may fluctuate over a period due to external factors (such as the amount of gas consumed in cold weather, or the number of telephone calls made) but will generally level out to nil growth over a period of years. Suppliers of this type (e.g. British Gas, BT) have sought to overcome this problem through product and/or service extension (e.g. British Gas Security services, BT Broadband). Alternatively, promotions offering special terms may increase usage in the short term. In general, however, it is difficult (particularly in the current competitive circumstances) to support the notion that longevity (without intervention) automatically leads to greater spending.

Cost savings

As has been noted the ability to amortise costs over a period brings supplier benefits. A certain naivety, on the part of the customer, about other opportunities available in the market may also help in this process. Reichheld (ibid., p. 47) suggests that the operating cost advantages of customer loyalty are particularly strong in retailing as 'a shop selling to a constantly shifting set of customers needs a lot more inventory than a shop serving the same people year after year'. A stable set of customers, he suggests 'can help streamline inventory management, minimise mark-downs and simplify capacity forecasting'.

This type of situation *may* exist where retail inventory is relatively stable (e.g. hardware stores) or where a very close relationship is built up between the customer and a company (e.g. fashion clothes shop). In other areas, particularly the FMCG sector, it is likely to be a different scenario. In an age where customers are less naive, more aware of opportunities and more cynical the costs of facilitating such customers are more likely to rise than to fall. In these markets the customer may, over time, learn to manipulate the supplier to his or her own ends (e.g. the customer who shops for bargains around a number of stores), ultimately leading to increased, not decreased, costs. With the availability of retailers and other suppliers on the Internet the ease of price comparisons may help customers to 'cherry pick' their suppliers and further exacerbate this situation.

Referral income

Again, this may be more likely in some industries than others. Referrals have always been an objective of businesses and are a valuable customer acquisition source. To depend on referrals for revenue growth, however, assumes (all other things being equal) that competitors are inactive and/or that the market is growing at a reasonably substantial rate, neither of which situation currently exists in many industry sectors. In addition, while one company may benefit from a certain number of referrals inward, the competition may themselves be benefiting from referrals away from that company. The best that can be said is that those companies who are 'doing a good job' in the broadest sense of the phrase may marginally benefit from referrals over their competition.

Price premiums

Reichheld (ibid., p. 39) suggests that price premiums may be obtainable from long-term, loyal customers. Such a strategy may again be determined by the naivety of the consumer and the level of exit barriers. In many markets, however, this suggestion totally disregards the fact that widespread use of promotional schemes is helping to create a 'generation of increasingly promotion literate customers' who have become 'adept at leaping from one supplier to another' to take advantage of the best offers (Harlow, 1997). It is highly unlikely, particularly in competitive markets, that the application of price premiums to longer-term customers is realistic. Even where it has been attempted (see Box 4.3) the threat to customer satisfaction makes this a dangerous and potentially costly strategy. The visibility of Internet pricing will make this even less viable in the future.

Box 4.3   Amazon

Between May and September 2000, Amazon.com, the world-famous Internet bookseller, tried out a dynamic pricing strategy that varied the prices of products by determining the profiles of existing customers. Regular customers, it was hypothesised, would be more likely to pay more and, therefore, should be charged more for products! Discussions began on message boards and forums (such as DVDTalk.com) and stories began to spread about price differentials between those who Amazon perceived as new and those they perceived as existing customers. Confusion became outrage as customers found out what was going on. An Amazon spokesperson stated that the experiment 'was done to determine consumer responses to different price levels'. Ultimately the company admitted its mistake and promised its customers it would not happen again.

(*Source*: Based on Mohammed *et al.*, 2002, p. 558)

Knowing your customer

Any discussion of the value of long-term retention must also recognise that not all customers contribute equally to the firm's profit. Indeed, as we have noted, a significant proportion of customers may, over the short or long term, be loss making.

The consequences of losing a profitable customer, therefore, may be very significant whereas the loss of a non-profitable customer may actually be beneficial. A valid assertion has been made that, unless a firm has an RM focus and a subsequent knowledge of individual customer activities, the loss of key customers may go unnoticed (Strandvik and Storbacka, 1996, p. 72). Some UK banks, for example, work on a points system or grids (see Figure 4.6) determined by the services utilised (or indeed not utilised) by the customer. This product-usage and share-of-wallet calculation approximates to that customer's value to the company. Although a crude measure, it allows them to differentiate between potentially profitable and less-profitable customers. In most organisations, the difficulty of calculating 'relationship profitability' stems from the problem in allocating costs to specific customer relationships and promotes the need to identify the cost drivers of those relationships (Storbacka *et al.*, 1994, p. 33). Not only must the individual's gross contribution to the profitability of the relationship (from the firm's perspective) be calculated but also the costs incurred when building and maintaining that relationship (Blois, 1997, p. 63; Palmer, 1998, p. 119).

Figure 4.6
Profit/potential grid. Potential in this model is based on the MOSAIC/Pixel matrix. This evaluates potential for financial services against demographic and lifestyle data.

(*Source*: Adapted from Pompa *et al.*, 2000, p. 37)

Another factor in the long-term relationship calculation is whether any competitive advantage (gained through the introduction of relational strategies) can last long enough to recoup investment. With regard to financial services, the 'product' package is often designed with barriers and costs that discourage customers from defection. The advantage gained through the initial attractiveness of the offering is, therefore, sustained regardless of what products or services are introduced in the interim. Mobile telecommunications suppliers also may incentivise the offering by including a free handset but include a minimum period of rental to cover the cost. Most consumers are intelligent enough to balance the advantages and disadvantages of such arrangements.

At the other end of the spectrum (again, FMCG retailing is a good example) the ability to build barriers to exit is limited. Most retailers depend on some form of customer retention programme offering added value to 'loyal' customers in an attempt to sustain long-term relationships. The problem with loyalty programmes is that the potential always exists for competitors to replicate these relational programmes easily, and doubt must be expressed as to whether they can possibly give companies long-term advantages. It may be hypothesised that where differentiated advantage is perceived to be low or where a programme can be replicated easily the ability of relational strategies to develop lasting competitive advantage is minimal. It may be further hypothesised that the greater the ability to replicate differential advantage, the greater the need to constantly develop and refine RM strategies to keep 'ahead of the field'.

Billions of dollars, euros and pounds are spent each year on customer loyalty technology, before the rewards themselves are taken into account. The expense involved in such cost-escalating strategies may, as has been noted previously, ultimately lead to a divide between relational suppliers and cost-competitive ones and the consequential division of an industry between RM companies and their more 'transactional' competitors. When everyone in an industry is, effectively, offering very much the same incentives (e.g. frequent flyer programmes) the net benefits are marginal. The recent assault on the airline industry (whose introduction of loyalty programmes preceded that of most retailers) by cut-price, 'no frills' airlines such as easyJet and Ryanair, may be an example of this development.

The validity of relationship economics

Interest in RM has grown exponentially, driven primarily by relationship economics (Barnes and Howlett, 1998, p. 15). These economic arguments, however, revolve around one of the smallest words in the English language but the biggest word in business – 'if' (Mitchell, 1997, p. 37). *If* the factors are right and *if* the drivers to relational strategies are in place, the benefits will be forthcoming. The acceptance of relationship marketing as a 'good thing' because it leads to long-term profitability is, however, too simplistic and begs the question of how and with whom these relationships are to be established and what form they should take (Barnes, 1994, p. 562). When it is clear, from past experience, that the average customer will continue to purchase a product or service, then the benefits of relational strategies based on a lifetime value calculation may seem apparent.

The proviso must always be made that all such claims are based on historical data and cannot be guaranteed in the future. Estimates of 'lifetime value', therefore, can be valid from a strategy planning perspective but to rely over much on these forecasts may result in complacency.

Summary

This chapter looked at the economics of relationships. It investigated the arguments surrounding the costs of customer acquisition versus the costs of customer retention and concluded that whereas in many industries it can be stated with some certainty that the cost of acquisition exceeds that of retention, it is by no means a universal truth. The chapter also discussed the benefits of relationship longevity, including stages theories and the concept of lifetime value, and again suggested that although considerable benefits could be achieved under certain industry conditions, this could not be assumed in every case. The switching costs associated with relationship longevity were also discussed and a distinction made between costs positively associated with the relationship and coercive barriers to exit. The chapter concluded by suggesting that the notion that RM leads to long-term profitability is far too simplistic.

Discussion questions

1 What are the different cost drivers associated with (a) customer acquisition and (b) customer retention?
2 What are the potential advantages to be gained from long-term supplier–customer relationships?
3 How would you differentiate between the different stages models discussed in this chapter?
4 What effect do switching costs have on a relationship?

Case study   Return on customer

Marketers around the world are under siege and the primary weapon being used against them is accountability, or lack of it. Financial managers want to know what economic benefits are generated by the resources committed to their companies' marketing, sales and customer service efforts.

With our new metric, **Return on Customer** 5111 (ROC5111), we are proposing a more useful way to communicate the actual benefits of marketing, in financial terms that are more likely to be understood by even the most hardened spreadsheet jockeys.

Our basic argument is that marketing's role is to employ customers to create new shareholder value for the firm. We believe that the single most important gauge of any company's financial success is the efficiency with which its customers actually do create that new value.

Three fundamental principles

1 Customers create all value for a business. All value created by any company's actual business operation must come from its customers at some point. There may be a few exceptions to this, but not many. Asset sales can create value for a business, perhaps, but such gains aren't usually considered part of operating income – and in any case, the asset buyer could often be considered a type of customer. Rents and royalties could also be considered to come from customers, in many cases.

2 Customers create both short-term and long-term value. They generate current-period cash flow by buying things and incurring costs today, and they change their intent or likelihood of buying in the future, which increases or decreases their expected cash flows in the future, eg their lifetime values.

When a customer's likelihood of doing business in the future changes, as the result of the customer's experience, this event actually creates (or destroys) value today, even though the actual cash effects of this event may not be fully realised for weeks, months or even years.

Imagine a CEO announcing publicly that his firm now expects its earnings two years from now to be lower than had been previously forecast. What would happen to his company's stock price? It would go down today, not two years from now, because for investors the firm's value today is a function of its expected cash flows in the future. In the same way, if a customer calls you with a complaint today but gets no satisfaction, his likelihood of buying from you in the future declines, which reduces his lifetime value.

This change in lifetime value represents a value-destroying event that occurs in the current period. It is a loss of value for your firm, and even though the actual cash effect won't be realised until later, that loss of value occurs today, whether or not your firm knows, measures or manages that loss of value.

3 Customers are scarce. In today's business world, customers are even scarcer than capital. If you have a customer for your business, you can almost certainly get the capital you need to serve him. But the market – any market – contains only a finite number of customers, who will each do only so much business in a lifetime, with anybody. Even if there are lots of customers, it's still a finite number. Suppose, for instance, you have two different marketing initiatives available. Initiative A requires investing £4 per customer to create £2 in net new value, generating a **return on investment (ROI)** of 50 per cent. Initiative B requires £12 per customer to create £4 in net new value, for an ROI of 33 per cent. The ROI-maximising company will choose initiative A every time, because every pound invested in this initiative yields 50p in net profit, compared with only 33p in net profit per pound invested in initiative B. But what if you only had one customer? It may not generate the highest ROI, but initiative B would generate twice as much new shareholder value as A does – £4 instead of just £2. The question you should ask now is would you choose differently if you only had a million customers?

Customers create value

Return on Customer (ROC) is designed to account for both the short-term and long-term value that customers create, and it is based on the idea that whatever value a business creates must come from the limited number of customers and prospective customers available to it. Therefore, improving the efficiency with which its customers create value is a worthwhile endeavour. ROC measures the rate at which a business is able to create value from any given customer.

Simply stated, ROC is the sum of the firm's current-period profit from a customer, plus any change in the customer's value, divided by the customer's value at the beginning of the period:

$$\text{ROC} = \frac{\Pi + \text{ALTV}}{\text{LTV}}$$

Where Π = Current-period profit from the customer
ALTV = Current-period change in the customer's lifetime value
LTV = Beginning lifetime value

Profit in this equation is more useful to us if we express it in cash flow terms, and a customer's value should be thought of as the customer's lifetime value (LTV), which is the net present value of future cash flows expected from the customer. It's worth noting that the ROC equation is directly analogous to the ROI equation, except that it is based on the scarcity of customers, rather than the scarcity of capital.

For most companies, analysing customer data to model customer lifetime values is a complex task by itself, although with today's analytics tools many companies are in fact modelling their customers' lifetime values on a regular basis. But the ROC formula also requires analysing the factors that contribute to changes in customer lifetime values – how much does a one-point increase in 'willingness to recommend', for instance, increase the likelihood of repurchase? As an internal decision-making tool, ROC can be highly useful, provided that a number of leading indicators of LTV change have been identified and can be monitored.

Royal Bank of Canada has been focusing on customer relationships in its retail banking business for more than a decade. One of the secrets of the bank's success is that, in evaluating its actions for different customers, the bank optimises overall efficiencies, a term it uses to include both current income and LTV changes in the calculation.

One example of a policy change based on maximising overall efficiencies has to do with courtesy overdraft limits, which used to be offered only to high-net worth customers. Now, anyone who has been a customer for at least 90 days, has a low-risk credit score and has made at least one deposit in the last month will have some level of overdraft protection. This enhances each customer's experience and increases the bank's efficiency during the cheque-clearing process. Between 1997 and 2004 the bank increased the profitability of its average client by 13 per cent, and increased the number of high-value clients by 20 per cent.

New shareholder value

At the enterprise level, we can use publicly reported data for some types of companies to evaluate how efficiently they are using their customers to create new shareholder value. For example, between 2002 and 2004, Verizon Wireless, a joint venture between Verizon and Vodafone, reported $13.7 billion in operating earnings. During this same period, it grew its customer base from 29.4 million handsets in use to 43.8 million, but also halved its monthly customer churn rate, which declined from 2.6 per cent to 1.3 per cent. Altogether, these two actions generated an additional $13.9 billion in customer equity – so the company created more than twice as much value for shareholders as was reflected in its financial statements. Roughly 40 per cent of the increase was attributable to the new customers it acquired, while 60 per cent was attributable to the increase in the value of all its customers due to higher retention rates.

Verizon Wireless generated an average annual ROC of roughly 70 per cent during this three-year period. What this means is that, by focusing on maximising the value created by its customers, the company was able to create shareholder value every year that amounted to about two-thirds of its actual value as a business at the beginning of that year. This was an incredible spurt of value creation, but in this case it was also a one-time event, for the simple reason that monthly churn has already been reduced from 2.6 per cent to 1.3 per cent, and it will be increasingly costly to reduce it further. Many of the company's competitors are running in the opposite direction – spending excessive amounts to acquire customers to replace the ones they are losing, all the while suffering a decline in average lifetime value.

If marketers want a seat on the board, they must be able to communicate the results of their actions in financial terms that can be tied to a company's most basic mission – to create new shareholder value as efficiently as possible. ROC is a metric that help them do this.

(*Source*: Don Peppers and Martha Rogers, *The Marketer*, CRM Supplement, June 2006, Chartered Institute of Marketing)

Case study questions

1 In what ways do customers create both short-term and long-term value?
2 Explain in simple terms the rationale for selecting initiative A over B (point 3).
3 Why is increased shareholder value a better measure than profit and loss?

References

Ambler, T. and Styles, C. (2000) 'Viewpoint: the future of relational research in international marketing: constructs and conduits', *International Marketing Review*, **17** (6), 492–508.

Barnard, N. and Ehrenberg, A.S.C. (1997) 'Advertising: strongly persuasive or nudging?', *Journal of Advertising Research*, January/February, 21–31.

Barnes, J.G. (1994) 'Close to the customer: but is it really a relationship?', *Journal of Marketing Management*, **10**, 561–70.

Barnes, J.G. and Howlett, D.M. (1998) 'Predictors of equity in relationships between service providers and retail customers', *International Journal of Bank Marketing*, **16** (1), 5–23.

Berry, L.L. (2000) 'Relationship marketing of services: growing interest, emerging perspectives', in Sheth, J.N and Parvatiyar, A. (eds) *Handbook of Relationship Marketing*, Thousand Oaks, CA: Sage, 149–70.

Berry, L.L. and Gresham, L.G. (1986) 'Relationship retailing: transforming customers into clients', *Business Horizons*, November/December, 43–7.

Bhattacharya, C.B. and Bolton, R.N. (2000) 'Relationship marketing in mass markets', in Sheth, J.N. and Parvatiyar, A. (eds) *Handbook of Relationship Marketing*, Thousand Oaks, CA: Sage, pp. 327–54.

Blois, K.J. (1997) 'When is a relationship a relationship?', in Gemünden, H.G., Rittert, T. and Walter, A. (eds) *Relationships and Networks in International Markets*, Oxford: Elsevier, 53–64.

Buttle, F.B. (1996) *Relationship Marketing Theory and Practice*, London: Paul Chapman.

Christopher, M., Payne, A. and Ballantyne, D. (1991) *Relationship Marketing*, London: Butterworth Heinemann.

Dawes, J. and Swailes, S. (1999) 'Retention sans frontieres: issues for financial service retailers', *International Journal of Bank Marketing*, **17** (1), 36–43.

Doyle, P. (1998) *Marketing Management and Strategy*, London: Prentice Hall.

Dwyer, F.R., Schurr, P.H. and Oh, S. (1987) 'Developing buyer–seller relationships', *Journal of Marketing*, **51**, 11–27.

East, R. (2000) 'Fact and fallacy in retention marketing', Professorial Inaugural Lecture, 1 March 2000, Kingston University Business School, UK.

Gordon, I.H. (1998) *Relationship Marketing*, Etobicoke, Ontario: John Wiley & Sons.

Grönroos, C. (1995) 'Relationship marketing: the strategy continuum', *Journal of Marketing Science*, **23** (4), 252–4.

Grönroos, C. (1996) 'Relationship marketing: strategic and tactical implications', *Management Decisions*, **34** (3), 5–14.

Grossman, R.P. (1998) 'Developing and managing effective customer relationships', *Journal of Product and Brand Management*, **7**(1), 27–40.

Gummesson, E. (1994) 'Making relationship marketing operational', *International Journal of Service Industry Management*, **5**, 5–20.

Gummesson, E. (1999) *Total Relationship Marketing: Rethinking Marketing Management from 4Ps to 30Rs*, Oxford: Butterworth Heinemann.

Harlow, E. (1997) 'Loyalty is for life – not just for Christmas', paper presented at the Advanced Relationship Marketing Conference, 23 October 1997, Century Communications, London.

Hart, S., Smith, A., Sparks, L. and Tzokas, N. (1999) 'Are loyalty schemes a manifestation of relationship marketing?', *Journal of Marketing Management*, **15**, 541–62.

Kinard, B.R. and Capella, M.L (2006) 'Relationship marketing: the influence of consumer involvement on perceived service benefits', *Journal of Service Marketing*, **21** (6), 359–68.

Kotler, P. (1992) 'Marketing's new paradigm: what's really happening out there?', *Planning Review*, **20** (5), 50–2.

Kotler, P. (1997) 'Method for the millennium', *Marketing Business*, February, 26–7.

Kotler, P., Armstrong, G., Saunders, J. and Wing, V. (1999) *Principles of Marketing*, 2nd European edn, New York: Prentice Hall.

Mitchell, A. (1997) 'Evolution', *Marketing Business*, June, 37.

Mohammed, R.A., Fisher, R.J., Jaworski, B.J. and Cahill, A.M. (2002), *Internet Marketing: Building Advantage in the Networked Economy*, New York: McGraw-Hill.

Morgan, R.M. (2000) 'Relationship marketing and marketing strategy', in Sheth, J.N. and Parvakiyar, A. (eds) *Handbook of Relationship Marketing*, Thousand Oaks, CA: Sage, pp. 481–504.

Moules, J. (1998) 'Stopping the exodus', *Information Strategy*, **3** (5), 46–8.

Murphy, J.A. (1997) 'Customer loyalty and the art of satisfaction', *Financial Times*, FT Mastering Series.

Palmatier, R.W., Dant, R.P., Grewal, D. and Evans, K.R. (2006) 'Factors influencing the effectiveness of relationship marketing: a meta-analysis', *Journal of Marketing*, **70** (October), 136–53.

Palmer, A.J. (1998) *Principles of Services Marketing*, London: Kogan Page.

Palmer, A. and Beggs, R. (1997) 'Loyalty programmes: congruence of market structure and success', paper presented at the Academy of Marketing Conference, Manchester, UK.

Palmer, R., Lindgreen, A. and Vanhamme, J. (2005) 'Relationship marketing: schools of thought and future research directions', *Marketing Intelligence and Planning*, **23** (3), 313–30.

Payne, A. (2000) 'Customer retention', in Cranfield School of Management, *Marketing Management: A Relationship Marketing Perspective*, Basingstoke: Macmillan, pp. 110–24.

Payne, A. and Frow, P. (1997) 'Relationship marketing: key issues for the utilities sector', *Journal of Marketing Management*, **13** (5), 463–77.

Payne, A., Christopher, M. and Peck, H. (eds) (1995) *Relationship Marketing for Competitive Advantage: Winning and Keeping Customers*, Oxford: Butterworth Heinemann.

Pompa, N., Berry, J., Reid, J. and Webber, R. (2000) 'Adopting share of wallet as a basis for communications and customer relationship management', *Interactive Marketing*, **2** (1), 29–40.

Pressey, A.D. and Mathews, B.P. (1998) 'Relationship marketing and retailing: comfortable bedfellows?', *Customer Relationship Management*, **1** (1), 39–53.

Reichheld, F. (1993) 'Loyalty-based management', *Harvard Business Review*, March/April, 56–69.

Reichheld, F.F. (1996) *The Loyalty Effect: The Hidden Force Behind Growth, Profits and Lasting Value*, Boston, MA: Harvard Business School Press.

Sheth, J.N. and Parvatiyar, A. (1995a) 'The evolution of relationship marketing' *International Business Review*, **4** (4), 397–418.

Sheth, J.N. and Parvatiyar, A. (1995b) 'Relationship marketing in consumer markets: antecedents and consequences,' *Journal of the Academy of Marketing Science*, **23** (4), 255–71.

Sheth, J.N. and Parvatiyar, A. (2000) 'Relationship marketing in consumer markets: antecedents and consequences', in Sheth, J.N. and Parvatiyar, A. (eds) *Handbook of Relationship Marketing*, Thousand Oaks CA: Sage, pp. 171–207.

Stewart, K. (1998) 'The customer exit process: a review and research agenda', *Journal of Marketing Management*, **14**, 235–50.

Storbacka, K., Strandvik, T. and Grönroos, C. (1994) 'Managing customer relations for profit: the dynamics of relationship quality', *International Journal of Service Industry Management*, **5**, 21–38.

Strandvik, T. and Storbacka, K. (1996) 'Managing relationship quality', in Edvardsson, B., Brown, S.W., Johnston, R. and Scheuing, E.E. (eds) *Advancing Service Quality: A Global Perspective*, New York: ISQA, pp. 67–76.

Tapp, A. (1998) *Principles of Direct and Database Marketing*, London: Financial Times Management/Pitman Publishing.

Tynan, C. (1997) 'A review of the marriage analogy in relationship marketing', *Journal of Marketing Management*, **13** (7), 695–704.

Worthington, S. and Horne, S. (1998) 'A new relationship marketing model and its application in the affinity credit card market', *International Journal of Bank Marketing*, **16** (1), 39–44.

Yap, K.B. and Sweeney, J.C. (2007) 'Zone of tolerance moderates the service quality-outcome relationship, *Journal of Service Marketing*, **21** (2), 137–48.

Appendix The Lifetime Value (LV) as shown in Box 4.3 is calculated for all or a segment of customers and the supposition is that it can then be attributed back to individual customers. In the example 50,000 customers were recruited at a cost of £90 each totalling £4.5 million. There will always be customers who leave for a variety of reasons and in the example 20 per cent have been lost one year later giving a retention rate of 80 per cent. Of these customers who are carried forward 80 per cent and 82.5 per cent will be retained in years 2 and 3 respectively. Direct and Marketing costs encourage sales and retention. There is also a healthy referral rate of 5 per cent (rising to 10 per cent in year 3) which may be based on 'word-of-mouth' and/or as a result of a 'customer-get-customer' promotion. The profit from these customers is calculated and then discounted (to bring it back to current value) using the formula $D = (1+ i)^n$ where i is the rate of interest plus a factor for risk (6 per cent and 2 in the example). The net present value (NPV) for each year is added cumulatively and divided by the original customers (50,000) to give an individual lifetime value. From this calculation you can determine that the value of the customer in the first year is £60 rising to £314 in year 3. To calculate the value of any individual customer you can attribute the expected behaviour of an individual to the average of the group.

NB: 3 years are shown. Year 1 is not a calendar year but the year of acquisition and may, therefore, include several years worth of customer acquisitions. Year 2 and Year 3 are the first and second years after acquisition.

Notes

1 'Front of mind' awareness is seen as important where infrequent buying decisions are made (e.g. life insurance). The purpose is to ensure that when the consumer is ready to make a decision, the brand is 'front of mind'.

2 In the Chartered Institute of Marketing, for example, you can be a student member, associate member, member or fellow. Each level of membership has different privileges and different costs.

5 Strategy continuum

Key issues

- RM's context within marketing
- The marketing continuum
- Hybrid marketing and portfolios of marketing strategies
- Continuum drivers

Introduction

The discussion concerning the economics of relationship marketing in the previous chapter suggests that, while RM may be beneficial in some instances, it is by no means certain to be beneficial in all. How do we handle a diversity of strategies? How do we decide when particular strategy types are relevant and appropriate?

RM in context

In the 1990s, the debate regarding RM's place within marketing theory could be summed up as a choice between four 'alternative' philosophical viewpoints (Brodie *et al.*, 1997, p. 389; Pels, 1999, p. 19):

- By adding a relationship dimension to the marketing management approach the 'anomalies' identified in traditional marketing could be incorporated into the existing marketing paradigm (see Chapter 2, page 28).
- Exchange relationships (i.e. RM) should be regarded as a new marketing paradigm, suggesting that a paradigmatic shift had taken place in marketing from traditional marketing (TM) towards relationship marketing (see Chapter 2, page 17).

■ Exchange transactions (or TM) and exchange relationships (or RM) are separate paradigms and both paradigms separately coexist.[1]

■ Traditional marketing (TM) and relationship marketing (RM) can coexist as part of the same marketing paradigm.

Put simply, RM may be considered as a concept, as the dominant theory, as one (of two) marketing perspectives or as an integral part of the overall marketing arsenal.

Early texts tended to view RM as a tactical influence on existing concepts, for example the marketing mix (e.g. Christopher *et al.*, 1991). This viewpoint has largely been eclipsed as the strategic value of relational strategies has increased. The argument about whether RM is a new dominant paradigm, however, still rages. As has been noted, many prominent writers (e.g. Sheth and Parvatiyar, 1993; Grönroos, 1994a; Morgan and Hunt, 1994; Gummesson, 1997; Buttle, 1997) believe that a paradigm shift has taken place.

Despite RM's promotion to the highest level of marketing theory, however, there still remain doubts as to whether companies would *always* (or indeed would *ever*) find it suitable and/or profitable to develop relational strategies (e.g. Palmer, 1996, p. 18; Grönroos, 1997, p. 408). Kotler (1997, p. 26), for example, suggests that reports of the demise of traditional mass marketing are 'somewhat premature' and that companies such as Coca-Cola, Gillette and Kodak will continue primarily to practise traditional **mass-marketing** techniques (e.g. mass communication using mass media) into the foreseeable future. Mayer *et al.* (2000, p. 391) too argue that claims that mass markets and mass consumption are dead are not borne out by empirical evidence. A good example of this is the budget airline Ryanair whose strategy is blatantly transactional. In 2006 they were voted the world's most hated airline in an online poll (Ritson 2006) yet in the same year posted record half-year profits of €329 million, a year-on-year increase of 39 per cent (*Business Weekly*, 6 November 2006).

The logical consequence of this viewpoint is that some marketing activities may remain best handled through a transaction marketing approach (Gummesson, 1994, p. 17). As Dwyer *et al.* (1987, p. 14) note, it is possible that the real or anticipated costs (to either party) of relational strategies may outweigh the benefits of relational exchange. As Grönroos (1997, p. 408) suggests, 'the main thing is . . . not whether a relational strategy is possible or not, but whether the firm finds it profitable, and in other respects suitable, to develop a relational strategy or a traditional strategy'. The implication is that, if companies cannot justify, economically, a relational approach, then they would be best advised to retain (or re-adopt) a transactional strategy.

The view that transactional marketing and relational marketing can coexist suggests that the RM should not be considered simply as a replacement for TM strategies but as another perspective in marketing. This implies that RM is not a clearly defined, delimited phenomenon but a 'helpful perspective' in approaching marketing (Gummesson, 1994, p. 8). The argument remains, however, whether RM and TM are exclusive relative to an individual company or industry or as part of the same paradigm (Brodie *et al.*, 1997, p. 389; Coviello *et al.*, 1997, p. 516), perhaps extremes on a 'marketing strategy continuum' (Grönroos, 1995, p. 252).

RM/TM continuum

Research conducted by Brodie *et al.* (1997, pp. 389–402) supports the marketing strategy continuum hypothesis. Their evidence suggests that, at managerial level, a combination of TM and RM approaches are used by firms and that managers maintain a 'portfolio' of strategy types. Although their case and survey results suggested that certain types of marketing (either TM or RM) are more common in some sectors than others, it did not imply exclusivity. The researchers noted that firms at the transactional end of the continuum tended to be larger and longer-established businesses, but this might be an element of sluggishness in adopting new strategies. The researchers' analysis otherwise fails to identify clearly specific characteristics of firms dominated by one or the other practice. This may support the suggestion that 'drivers', other than strictly industry typology, may be involved.

Although, as we might expect with the level of interest in RM so high, general marketing practice does show a considerable shift towards customer orientation, Brodie *et al.*'s conclusion (p. 389) is that both transactional and relational marketing approaches can and do coexist. Möller and Halinen (2000, p. 43) too recognise that purely relational (or indeed purely transactional) types rarely exist and that it is better portrayed as a continuum of varying degrees of relational complexity. Exchanges, therefore, can be considered as falling somewhere along a spectrum ranging from the discrete to the relational (Blois, 1999, p. 4). Pressey and Mathews (1998, p. 48) also seem to suggest a multivarious approach when they note, in a retail context, that a customer's relationship cannot be classed as one that fits the characteristics of RM yet is not as 'discrete' as TM. The relationship is, therefore, between RM and TM and, as such, has parts of both. The strategies used may, therefore, be called a 'portfolio of types'.

In this marketing continuum model RM would be placed at one end. Here the general focus would be on building relationships with customers (and other stakeholders). At the other end of this continuum is TM, where the focus is short term and based on one transaction at a time (Grönroos, 1994b, p. 10). Whereas collaboration is the core property of RM, traditional marketing is prejudiced in favour of competition. The concept of a marketing continuum between the two perspectives allows for elements of both to be represented.

Grönroos (p. 11) suggests that industry type may influence a company's position on the continuum (see Figure 5.1). He predicts that at one extreme is the end-user, packaged consumer-goods market with a marketing mix approach based on discrete, transactional exchange and where customers are more sensitive to price than the development of any longer-term relationship. RM, and the relationship metaphor, it is suggested, are of less value in this mass consumer marketing context than it can be in high-contact, inter-organisational and service marketing contexts (O'Malley and Tynan, 1999, p. 597). At this end of the continuum, traditional measures, such as the technical quality of the output and the monitoring of market share, are used. Customer opinion is determined by ad hoc customer surveys as face-to-face contact is limited. Internal marketing (see Chapter 8) is not seen as a priority.

Figure 5.1 The transactional/ relational continuum and drivers

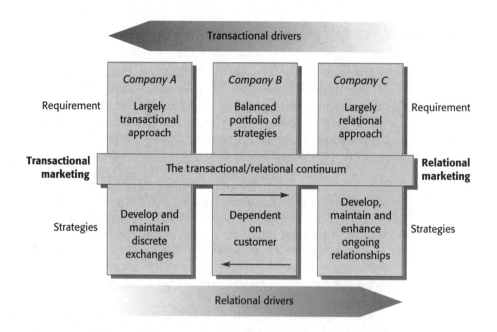

At the other end of the continuum are distribution channels, services and business-to-business marketers, who, it is proposed, would benefit from the application of relationship type strategies. The concentration here is on the long term, with the use of an interactive approach based on the development, maintenance and enhancement of ongoing relationships. Sensitivity to price is much less important at this end of the continuum as customers are seeking other benefits which are delivered via the relationship with the supplier. The dominant measurement criteria here is the quality of interactions with the consumer and the successful management of the customer base. Customer feedback is in 'real time' (i.e. feedback is part of the interaction) and continuous. As the interface with the consumer is so crucial (it is often referred to as 'the moment of truth') the role of internal marketing is of strategic importance.

The strict industry division may be somewhat overstating the case by suggesting that consumer goods companies would never benefit from relational strategies and that distribution channels, services and business-to-business would always benefit from them. For example, research suggests customers perceive greater relational benefits with high contact services rather than the more standardised ones (Kinard and Capella, 2006, p. 365). What the concept of a marketing continuum suggests is that, although RM strategies may well be attractive for many products, services and markets, their application may be inappropriate for others (Palmer, 1996, p. 18). Nor does the adoption of RM strategies guarantee success. As Ambler and Styles (2000, p. 499) note, there are plenty of 'counter examples of poor but profitable relationships and those with good but unprofitable ones'.

Grönroos (1994b, p. 13) notes that the more a firm moves to the right on the marketing strategy continuum, away from the transaction-type situation, the more the market expands beyond the core product (see Figure 5.2) and the more that has to be invested in interactive marketing (Grönroos, 1995, p. 252). Barnes (1994, pp. 566–7) hypothesises that, in moving away from TM at some point on this continuum, it may be said that a transaction approach to marketing ceases to be appropriate and the possibility for the establishment of a genuine relationship begins.

Figure 5.2
RM/TM
continuum

Marketing implications

Grönroos (1995, p. 253) suggests that the marketing implications across the strategy continuum (RM versus TM) are substantially different concerning:

■ the dominant marketing orientation;

■ the dominant quality function;

■ the customer information system;

■ interdependency between business functions;

■ the role of internal marketing.

Dominant marketing orientation

RM suggests that marketing should not be restricted to 'marketing mix' activities nor should it be wholly the responsibility of the marketing department (see Chapter 8). In TM, the marketing role of personnel outside of the marketing department is negligible and elements such as advertising, campaigning and price promotions form the core. In RM, these elements are there but as supporting activities to interaction and internal marketing strategies.

Dominant quality function

In TM it is normally enough if the output is of acceptable quality. In RM, although the technical quality has to be acceptable, it is no longer the only quality dimension. Rather, all the interactions within the firm (contact, information systems, etc.) support the quality perceptions of the customer.

Customer information system

A firm pursuing a TM strategy will normally have little, if any, direct customer contact. TM relies instead on ad hoc customer satisfaction surveys and market-share statistics for information about the behaviour and attitude of customers. A firm that applies RM strategies would monitor customer satisfaction by continuous contact and by directly managing its customer base (see Chapter 11).

Interdependency between business functions

The level of interdependency between functions and departments in an organisation depends on whether the firm has chosen a TM- or an RM-type strategy. In TM the marketing department takes care of the marketing function. In RM the interaction between, in particular, marketing, operations and human resources becomes critical to success (see Chapter 8).

Role of internal marketing

Preparing the non-marketing employees – Gummesson (1999, p. 45) calls these 'part-time marketers' (see Chapter 8) – for their marketing tasks is an important element of RM strategy. Firms operating such strategies have to take a proactive approach towards getting the commitment required to develop marketing behaviour among all employees. The more people in the firm are involved in marketing, the greater the need for active internal marketing. In TM this need is limited.

Four marketing types

Brodie *et al.* (1997, p. 386) take the continuum concept one stage further by suggesting that there may be four main types of marketing practised. These researchers agree on the distinction between the transactional (TM) and relational (RM) forms but suggest that the latter can be further broken down into the following three types:

- **database marketing (DbM)**;
- **interactive marketing**;
- **network marketing**.

The forms of marketing suggested by these various types together with the features associated with each are illustrated in Figure 5.3.

It may be that the three relationship types suggested by Brodie *et al.* may be described in more general terms as direct marketing, relationship marketing (consumer) and relationship marketing (business-to-business). This may be relevant as many of the descriptors seem to fit what is generally accepted to be meant by these more commonly used terms. This supports Möller and Halinen's (2000, p. 48) conjecture that different exchange characteristics and exchange contexts require different types of relationship marketing. This also suggests overlap between the terms (and, as such, the strategies) of the various types:

| | ◄ TM perspective ► | ◄ Relationship marketing perspective ► | | |
Type	**Transaction marketing**	**Database marketing**	**Interaction marketing**	**Network marketing**
Focus	Economic transactions	Information and economic transactions	Interactive relationship buyer and seller	Connected relationship between firms
Parties involved	Firm and buyer in the general market	Firm and buyer in the specific target market	Individual seller and buyer (a dyad)	Sellers, buyers and other firms
Communication pattern	Firm 'to' market	Firm 'to' individual	Individuals 'with' individuals	Firms 'with' firms (involves individuals)
Type of contract	Arm's length, impersonal	Personalised (yet distant)	Face-to-face interpersonal	Impersonal-interpersonal (distant–close)
Duration	Discrete, one-off (but perhaps over time)	Discrete and over time	Continuous* (ongoing and adaptive)	Continuous* (stable yet dynamic)
Formality	Formal	Formal (yet personalised by technology)	Formal and informal (social and business)	Formal and informal (social and business)
Balance of power	Active seller, passive buyer	Active seller, less passive buyer	Buyer and seller mutually active and adaptive	All firms active and adaptive
May describe**	*Transactional marketing*	*Direct/database marketing*	*Relationship marketing (consumer)*	*Relationship marketing (business-to-business)*
Overlap				

* may be long or short term
** author's interpretation

Figure 5.3 Four marketing types   (*Source*: Adapted from Brodie *et al*., 1997, p. 386)

- Transactional marketing and database/direct marketing overlap. Although contact can be personalised (using technology), database marketing is still distant and largely formal, with an active seller and a largely passive buyer.

- Database/direct marketing and consumer RM overlap in that both are marketing 'to the individual' as opposed to utilising mass-marketing techniques.

- Consumer RM and business-to-business RM share a number of similarities in that they both emphasise the long-term value of continuous relationships.

Continuum drivers

A logical progression from these arguments is the proposition that market factors determine (at any particular point in time) the value of (and thus the choice between) relational and transactional strategies. The concept of a continuum may be the basis for determining those departmental, company or industry factors, or 'drivers', that affect (or should affect) strategic decision-making in a given market situation. Drivers that may influence whether the company adopts a relational or transactional strategy are shown in Box 5.1. Some of these drivers have been discussed in previous chapters while others will be referred to in more detail in subsequent chapters.

The term 'drivers' is preferred to 'antecedents' for although much RM literature describes relational factors (e.g. trust) as 'antecedents to positive relational outcomes' the empirical evidence does not always support this type of association (Grayson and Ambler, 1999, p. 132). 'Drivers', on the other hand, suggests factors that are likely to 'promote' RM rather than 'predict' it as an outcome.

Box 5.1 Drivers affecting strategic decision-making

Drivers promoting relational strategies	Drivers against using relational strategies
• High acquisition costs relative to retention costs	• Acquisition/retention cost differential minimal
• High exit barriers	• Low exit barriers
• Competitive advantage sustainable	• Competitive advantage unsustainable
• Buoyant/expanding market	• Saturated market
• High risk/high salience products or services	• Low risk/low salience products or services
• High emotion involved in exchange	• Low emotion involved in exchange
• Requirement for trust and commitment	• Requirement for trust only
• Perceived need for closeness	• No perceived need for closeness
• Satisfaction beneficial to retention	• Repeat behaviour strategy beneficial

The concept of the strategy continuum implies that an 'optimum position' exists (whether determinable or not) and that each company's individually tailored perspective is dependent on the balance between the various transactional or relational drivers. In business as well as in life, relationships are inherently unstable (Blois, 1997, p. 367) and this balance is constantly changing as factors ebb and flow, strengthen or weaken. Research suggests, for example, that customer relationships do not equally influence all exchange outcomes (Palmatier *et al.*, 2006, p. 147). These constantly changing circumstances suggests a permanent 'danger area' either side of the optimum position owing to the difficulty (if not impossibility) of calculating the outcome of particular TM and RM strategies at any given point in time (see Figure 5.4). The two biggest dangers are:

■ at the transactional end of the spectrum, not recognising the desire of customer for an increased level of 'customer service' (see case study Chapter 3);

■ at the relational end of the spectrum, overestimating the level of service expected by the customer, resulting in defection to lower-cost (and lower-service) competitors.

Figure 5.4
RM/TM
continuum

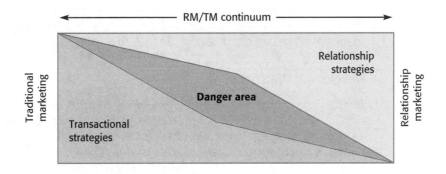

The nearer the middle of the hypothesised continuum, the greater the danger of misapplication of strategies is likely to be. To make matters worse each situation requires individual judgement. The uniqueness of relationships makes the mechanical transfer of successful practices among different companies dubious at best'.

(*Source*: Håkansson and Snehota, 2000, p. 83)

Hybrid managerial approach

As rational and intuitively sensible as the introduction of relational strategies may appear in theory, observation of these policies, over time, will be the only real test. Observation of real-world marketing practice indicates that a hybrid managerial approach (suggested by the continuum concept) may be the most appropriate response to prevailing market circumstances (Chaston, 1998, p. 273). An example of this is the airline industry where the advent of the budget airline has caused many international and national carriers to strip out much of the service content at the promotional end of the market while maintaining relational strategies for higher classes of travel. Möller and Halinen (2000, p. 45), for example, note that companies operating in fast moving consumer goods industries, consumer durables, industrial goods and services often employ two modes. Grönroos (1995, p. 252) suggests that, whether a company is largely transactional or largely relational, there may be situations where both types may benefit from taking another approach. This would suggest the use of multiple marketing strategies (Voss and Voss, 1997, p. 279) that:

■ develop and maintain discrete exchanges (TM);
■ develop, maintain and enhance ongoing relationships (RM).

Within a single operation customers too may prefer (or demand) a differentiated approach. In a survey of US bank customers (quoted in Mohammed *et al.*, 2002, pp. 490/1) researchers noted a distinction between transactional customers, who generally tended to be relatively self-sufficient people who sought out financial information and tended to be price sensitive, and relationship-orientated customers who wanted more face-to-face service and were less price sensitive. The survey estimated a 62 : 38 per cent split between transactional and relational types! A more recent US survey showed similar results with only 31 per cent of customers receptive to the notion of having a relationship with their bank (McAdam, 2005, p. 3).

Developing RM concepts

The continuum/drivers hypothesis may relate to other developing RM concepts. The notion of the three forces of marketing equilibrium (elaborated by Gummesson, 1996, p. 34) suggests that, even if RM puts emphasis on collaboration, it is the combination of competition, collaboration and regulatory institutions in each specific situation that creates the balance or marketing equilibrium (Gummesson, 1997). With competition (TM) and collaboration (RM) represented on the continuum and the regulatory mechanisms as a variable influence on the relevant drivers, the continuum hypothesis would seem in accord with this concept.

The concept of hybrid models may offer greater benefit than that of unswerving allegiance to a single, purist philosophy. Thus, there may exist a number of alternative marketing styles, any of which, depending on the customer–supplier relationship, may be more applicable (Chaston, 1998, p. 277). Rather than suggesting that RM is taking over as the new marketing paradigm, it may be more beneficial to accept it as part of marketing's arsenal. It is not transactional marketing versus relationship marketing or mass marketing versus customer-specific marketing that should be the argument because all of these things are going on (Kotler, 1997, p. 27). It may not, however, be as beneficial to dress up (using relational rhetoric) largely transactional strategies as relational as is frequently the case with CRM. A healthier interpretation is that relationship marketing is not an appropriate strategy for all customers; moreover, multiple relationship marketing strategies may be necessary for different market segments (Berry, 2000, p. 157). As Brown (1998, p. 31) notes, the very idea of a single, all-embracing, general theory of marketing today is 'laughingly absurd'.

Clearly most consumers of mass-produced, mass-distributed, convenience goods are not looking for a relationship with the seller and a transactional, mix-management approach may well satisfy them best (Baker, 2002, p. 146). This contradicts Gruen's (1995, p. 449) view that the objective of RM is to move exchanges away from discrete transactions towards relational exchange with its underlying assumption that relational exchange is always preferable. Rather it suggests that strategies should be appropriate to given situations. As Berry (2000, p. 157) notes, 'importantly some customers may be profitable as transactional customers even if they are not profitable as relational customers'.

Summary

This chapter investigated the arguments for a hypothesised 'strategy continuum'. It recognised that, while RM may be beneficial in some instances, it may not be relevant to all. RM, the text proposed, is perhaps best regarded not as a dominant marketing paradigm but as a 'helpful perspective' in marketing. The suggestion is made, therefore, that a strategy continuum may exist with traditional marketing and relational marketing at either end. Any company, at any point in time, may adopt one or more of a 'hybrid' range of strategies that may be dominated by one or other end of the strategy continuum.

This idea is developed further by the suggestion that the RM end of the continuum may be segmented into database marketing interactive marketing, and network marketing, and proposed that they may be seen as approximately equivalent to direct marketing, consumer RM and business-to-business RM. The proposal that drivers to particular strategies exist was also introduced and will be expanded upon in Chapter 6.

Discussion questions

1 Take four companies with which you are familiar. Where would you place them on the hypothetical RM/TM continuum?

2 What factors led to your decision to place them at this point on the continuum?

3 Suggest, for a company with which you are familiar, a range of marketing strategies that might be termed a 'portfolio of strategy types'.

Case study   Understanding and addressing your client's needs

The most common first question I get asked about loyalty and relationship marketing is 'What should my company do?' My reply is almost always, 'Well, what do you need?' That is, what trend, change, issue or opportunity is prompting the discussion in the first place? Once we can answer that question, we can bring the full spectrum of strategic and tactical options into play.

This column focuses on both parts of this problem – *understanding* the need and *addressing* the need. The two are closely related. The confidence we have in understanding the need helps us decide how specific we can get in addressing the need. While the details of the interaction vary widely based on the nature of the company, the process itself is easily summarised.

Discovery: understanding the need

The companies we work with usually fall somewhere in the spectrum between fact-based and brand-based. Regardless of the company type, our objective is the same – get to the root causes that drive the need for a new or revised loyalty or relationship strategy or programme. If we can get to a point where both sides agree on the situation, it is far, far easier to evaluate and agree on the next steps. The end result of this first phase drives the direction of the second phase, where programmes, campaigns and strategies are developed to improve the business.

Fact-based discovery sounds like it is straightforward. But ask any business intelligence analyst how easy it is to spot changes in the core business and they'll tell you how hard it is to find signals in the noise. Companies that religiously track key performance metrics are the easiest to help. Ninety-day repurchase rate declining? No problem. Average transaction size declining? No problem. Churn rate rising? No . . . well, that's not always so easy. The drawback to such metrics is the search for causality. The metrics often show the effect, but we don't necessarily know the cause. So much of the discovery process is probing to develop hypotheses about root causes for particular performance metrics.

Brand-based discovery is trickier. Companies with a brand-centric mindset will look beyond the short-term numbers and focus on how programmes fit into the overall personality of the brand. The discovery process is focused on clearly defining the brand personality, understanding the brand promise(s) and setting boundaries for what is acceptable and what is not. Brand-centric companies usually have a persona established for their target customer, which helps to define the audience. But using personas occasionally oversimplifies the problem. In these cases, discovery includes teasing out the secondary segments in the customer base and understanding their needs.

It is usually faster and easier to get a good sense of the possibilities when companies have elements of both types of discovery. Since there are limits on the available strategies imposed by both the facts and the brand, we can zero in on a smaller set of options as we develop the strategy and programme designs.

Strategy: addressing the need

The strategy phase needs to address three key subjects: eligibility, objectives and benefits.

Once discovery is performed, understanding and addressing these three areas becomes much more straightforward. Going back to the ubiquitous question of 'What should my company do?' we can lay out a path aligned with the company's current reality. In the vast majority of cases, when a prudent amount of effort is applied to the discovery phase, the strategy phase is shorter, more productive, more focused and the results are easier to communicate and sell internally.

Eligibility is the strategy that defined which customers can (or should) be programme members, or part of clubs, or programme tiers, or promotional programmes, or e-mail programmes, etc. We generally think of customer segmentation and targeting as part of the eligibility question. In this phase we will resolve the entire customer base into smaller segments, and think through the behaviour or information needed to make a customer eligible for various parts of the programme.

One key question that must be answered is whether all customers are eligible for the programme. This is not always ideal due to the cost of programme delivery and communications. Looking at specific examples, a brand-centric company may only want its elite customers invited into a programme, or it may want to include elites based on spending and non-elites based on behaviour that predicts the possibility for high value. A fact-based company may know that it is losing market share among families under 30, and specifically target clubs based on that demographic.

Objectives are an innocuous and dangerous step. Many companies load in every positive objective they can think of, and make it impossible for any programme to succeed. It is crucial to focus on the objectives that will allow your strategy to be crisply defined, whether that is a focus on frequency, average transaction size, cross-category purchasing, churn rate, up sell/cross-sell, ARPU, 90-day repurchase rates or retention. The eligibility and targeting strategy must be tied to one or two of these objectives. Our experience shows the more focused the objective, the higher likelihood of success. One of our clients came to us with a fanatic focus on frequency, and as a result their programme is very successful at driving 60-day repurchasing and overall frequency. Average transaction size is up only slightly, but they were not concerned with that metric, so the programme is not encumbered with extraneous benefits or tactics to drive transaction size.

As you might guess, a company with a clear understanding of underlying root causes, customer segments and eligibility, and segment-based objectives has an easy time putting together a benefit structure. Appropriate alignment of frequency, lock-in, recognition, cross-sell or other strategies with the prior factors becomes a focused and structured discussion. When this process is not followed, and a company jumps directly to benefit strategy, the conversation is far more difficult since there is no way to evaluate the various opinions around the table. A common output is a programme with a wide range of benefits, trying to satisfy the needs of every one of the company's customers.

Connecting the discovery and strategy phases is a critical success factor for relationship and loyalty marketing programme design. This extra work at the beginning of the process pays rich dividends in the long run. You will see an increase in the likelihood of a positive ROI from specific initiatives within the programme. Channelling expenditures to the customers most likely to respond will help ensure the programme's value proposition is more focused and easier to understand.

Michael Greenberg is vice president of marketing for Loyalty Lab, a San Francisco-based developer of customer loyalty programmes for the retail industry, and writes a monthly column for Chief Marketer. *He can be reached at Michael@LoyaltyLab.com.*

(*Source*: Michael Greenberg, <http://chiefmarketer.com/loyalty_needs_08072007> (accessed November 2007)).

Case study questions

1 Why does the author believe that the process he is describing requires a two-stage process?
2 Are the strategies described designed to establish relationships or are other motives apparent?

References

Ambler, T. and Styles, C. (2000) 'Viewpoint: the future of relational research in international marketing: constructs and conduits', *International Marketing Review*, **17** (6), 492–508.

Baker, M.J. (2002) 'Quo vadis? retrospective comment', *The Marketing Review*, **3** (2), 145–6.

Barnes, J.G. (1994) 'Close to the customer: but is it really a relationship?', *Journal of Marketing Management*, **10**, 561–70.

Berry, L.L. (2000) 'Relationship marketing of services: growing interest, emerging perspectives', in Sheth, J.N. and Parvatiyar, A. (eds) *Handbook of Relationship Marketing*, Thousand Oaks, CA: Sage, pp. 149–70.

Blois, K.J. (1997) 'Are business to business relationships inherently unstable?', *Journal of Marketing Management*, **13** (5), 367–82.

Blois, K.J. (1999) 'A framework for assessing relationships', competitive paper, Proceedings of the European Academy of Marketing Conference (EMAC), Berlin, pp. 1–24.

Brodie, R.J., Coviello, N.E., Brookes, R.W. and Little, V. (1997) 'Towards a paradigm shift in marketing: an examination of current marketing practices', *Journal of Marketing Management*, **13** (5), 383–406.

Brown, S. (1998) *Postmodern Marketing II*, London: International Thomson Business Press.

Buttle, F.B. (1997) 'Exploring relationship quality', paper presented at the Academy of Marketing Conference, Manchester, UK.

Chaston, I. (1998) 'Evolving "new marketing" philosophies by merging existing concepts: application of process within small high-technology firms', *Journal of Marketing Management*, **14**, 273–91.

Christopher, M., Payne, A. and Ballantyne, D. (1991) *Relationship Marketing*, London: Butterworth Heinemann.

Coviello, N., Brodie, R.J. and Munro, J. (1997) 'Understanding contemporary marketing: development of a classification scheme', *Journal of Marketing Management*, **13** (6), 501–22.

Dwyer, F.R., Schurr, P.H. and Oh, S. (1987) 'Developing buyer–seller relationships', *Journal of Marketing*, **51**, 11–27.

Grayson, K. and Ambler, T. (1999) 'The dark side of long-term relationships in marketing', *Journal of Marketing Research*, **36** (1), 132–41.

Grönroos, C. (1994a) 'From marketing mix to relationship marketing: towards a paradigm shift in marketing', *Asia–Australia Marketing Journal*, **2** (1), 9–29.

Grönroos, C. (1994b) 'From marketing mix to relationship marketing: towards a paradigm shift in marketing', *Management Decisions*, **32** (2), 4–20.

Grönroos, C. (1995) 'Relationship marketing: the strategy continuum', *Journal of Marketing Science*, **23** (4), 252–54.

Grönroos, C. (1997) 'Value-driven relational marketing: from products to resources and competencies', *Journal of Marketing Management*, **13** (5), 407–19.

Gruen, T.W. (1995) 'The outcome set of relationship marketing in consumer markets', *Integrated Business Review*, **4** (4), 447–69.

Gummesson, E. (1994) 'Making relationship marketing operational', *International Journal of Service Industry Management*, **5**, 5–20.

Gummesson, E. (1996) 'Relationship marketing and imaginary organisations: a synthesis', *European Journal of Marketing*, **30** (2), 31–44.

Gummesson, E. (1997) 'Relationship marketing: the emperor's new clothes or a paradigm shift?', *Marketing and Research Today*, February, 53–60.

Gummesson, E. (1999) *Total Relationship Marketing: Rethinking Marketing Management from 4Ps to 30Rs*, Oxford: Butterworth Heinemann.

Håkansson, H. and Snehota, I.J. (2000) 'The IMP perspective: assets and liabilities of business relationships', in Sheth, J.N. and Parvatiyar, A. (eds) *Handbook of Relationship Marketing*, Thousand Oaks, CA: Sage, pp. 69–93.

Kinard, B.R. and Capella, M.L (2006) 'Relationship marketing: the influence of consumer involvement on perceived service benefits', *Journal of Service Marketing*, **21** (6), 359–68.

Kotler, P. (1997) 'Method for the millennium', *Marketing Business*, February, 26–7.

Lowe, S., Carr, A.N. and Thomas, M. (2004) 'Paradigmapping marketing theory', *European Journal of Marketing*, **38** (9/10), 1057–64.

McAdam, P. (2005) 'Give the customers what they want (and in most cases, it's not a relationship)', *Banking Strategies*, BAI Online <www.bai.org/bankstrategies/current/cover> (accessed 12 April 2007).

Mayer, R., Job, K. and Ellis, N. (2000) 'Ascending separate stairways to marketing heaven (or careful with that axiom, Eugene!)', *Marketing Intelligence & Planning*, **18** (6/7), 388–99.

Mohammed, R.A., Fisher, R.J., Jaworski, B.J. and Cahill, A.M. (2002), *Internet Marketing: Building Advantage in the Networked Economy*, New York: McGraw-Hill.

Möller, K. and Halinen, A. (2000) 'Relationship marketing theory: its roots and directions', *Journal of Marketing Management*, **16**, 29–54.

Morgan, R.M. and Hunt, S.D. (1994) 'The commitment–trust theory of relationship marketing', *Journal of Marketing*, **58** (3), 20–38.

O'Malley, L. and Tynan, C. (1999) 'The utility of the relationship metaphor in consumer markets: a critical evaluation', *Journal of Marketing Management*, **15**, 587–602.

Palmatier, R.W., Dant, R.P., Grewal, D. and Evans, K.R. (2006) 'Factors influencing the effectiveness of relationship marketing: a meta-analysis', *Journal of Marketing*, **70** (October), 136–53.

Palmer, A.J. (1996) 'Relationship marketing: a universal paradigm or management fad?', *The Learning Organisation*, **3** (3), 18–25.

Pels, J. (1999) 'Exchange relationships in consumer markets?', *European Journal of Marketing*, **33** (1/2), 19–37.

Pressey, A.D. and Mathews, B.P. (1998) 'Relationship marketing and retailing: comfortable bedfellows?', *Customer Relationship Management*, **1** (1), 39–53.

Ritson, M. (2006) 'Don't be scared of being despised', *Marketing*, 1 November, 23.

Sheth, J.N. and Parvatiyar, A. (1993) *Relationship Marketing: Theory, Methods and Application*, Atlanta, GA: Atlanta Center for Relationship Marketing.

Voss, G.B. and Voss, Z.G. (1997) 'Implementing a relationship marketing programme: a case study and managerial implications', *Journal of Services Marketing*, **11** (4), 278–98.

Notes

1 For arguments supporting 'paradigm-crossing' and the co-existence of multiple truths see Lowe *et al.*, 2004.

6 Relationship drivers

Key issues

- Risk, salience and emotion
- Trust and commitment
- Closeness
- Customer satisfaction
- Inertia

Introduction

In the previous chapter the concept of 'drivers' towards relational strategies was introduced. Box 6.1 summarises these suggested drivers, a number of which were discussed in Chapter 4, including:

- high customer acquisition costs (see page 75);
- high exit barriers (see page 86);
- sustainable competitive advantage (see page 93);
- buoyant/expanding market (see pages 90).

In this section we will look at those other drivers that appear to have an important bearing on the decision to develop a relationship marketing approach, in particular:

- risk, salience and emotion;
- trust and commitment;
- perceived need for closeness;
- customer satisfaction.

Box 6.1 Drivers promoting/against relational strategies

Drivers promoting relational strategies	Drivers against using relational strategies
■ High acquisition costs relative to retention costs*	■ Acquisition/retention cost differential minimal*
■ High exit barriers*	■ Low exit barriers*
■ Competitive advantage sustainable*	■ Competitive advantage unsustainable*
■ Buoyant/expanding market*	■ Saturated market*
■ High-risk/high-salience products or services	■ Low-risk/low-salience products or services
■ High emotion involved in exchange	■ Low emotion involved in exchange
■ Requirement for trust and commitment	■ Requirement for trust only
■ Perceived need for closeness	■ No perceived need for closeness
■ Satisfaction beneficial to retention	■ Repeat behaviour strategy beneficial

* See Chapter 4

Risk, salience and emotion

Risk, salience and emotion are all psychological aspects involved in some way in every exchange or purchase. Although they are wholly subjective, the levels of risk, degree of salience involved and the emotion generated *will* affect the choice of product or service and supplier involved, as well as the 'level' of relational involvement the customer will seek or, in some circumstances, allow.

An explanation of what is meant by risk, salience and emotion in a marketing context may be appropriate:

■ **Risk** may be defined as 'the perceived probability of loss interpreted by the decision-maker' (Rousseau *et al.*, 1998, p. 395) and presumes an element of consumer vulnerability in the exchange.

■ **Salience** may be regarded as the level of importance or prominence associated with the exchange. Intuitively one knows that some purchases have more personal relevance that others and that this has an impact on behaviour (Uncles, 1994, p. 343).

■ **Emotion** is the complex series of human responses (sometimes negatively described as 'agitation of the mind' or 'cognitive dissonance') generated as a result of the exchange.

Risk, salience and emotion are separately definable concepts, but are not mutually exclusive. There is a close association between the level of risk perceived in, the salience associated with and the emotion generated by any given exchange situation. Thus high risk is often associated with high-salience products or services and with a high-emotional outcome although any measures are *highly subjective* and may differ from individual to individual. It is quite possible to imagine, for example, that a particular exchange relationship will generate a perception of high levels of risk, salience and emotion with one customer yet, if the situation were to be replicated, only generate low levels with another.

High risk, salience and emotion

Much of the relationship marketing literature (e.g. Sheth and Parvatiyar, 1995, p. 288/9, 2000, p. 180; Bhattacharya and Bolton, 2000, p. 334) suggests that the greater the perceived risk, the greater a customer's propensity to engage in relational-type behaviour. Consumer confidence is itself a prime relational benefit influencing relational response behaviour (Kinard and Capella, 2006, p. 365). Case studies of companies that appear to benefit from relational strategies are frequently those involving 'high-risk purchases', either with a large single monetary outlay (e.g. vehicle purchases) or with payments over an extended period (e.g. financial services). These latter extended payments are often associated with high opportunity or actual costs as a possible consequence of incorrect decision-making at the initial sale. One reason why so-called high-risk purchases may benefit from RM strategies is that a relationship, over time, is likely (but not certain) to lower the perceived risk as the consumer 'learns' more about the terms and security of the arrangement and, more generally, gets to know the supplier. RM may also be well suited in cases where the unforeseen future is continuously defined and redefined by those involved in the relationship (Tzokas and Saren, 2000, p. 12/3). Even in a situation where these long-term experiences create some doubt about the supplier, this learning exercise in itself may reduce risk by indicating those areas of the relationship where the supplier can and cannot be trusted. The existence of risk, therefore, creates an opportunity for trust that would not be needed if actions could be taken with certainty and no risk (Rousseau *et al.*, 1998, p. 395).

The case studies quoted in support of relational strategies are also generally highly salient to the consumer, either representing major and current status symbols or as affecting status or quality of life at some point in the future (e.g. pensions, investments). In situations characterised by high risk and high salience, the customer may enter the service encounter with certain specific expectations associated with rather intense emotions (Cumby and Barnes, 1998, p. 55) and may be seeking specific reassurance and reduction of cognitive dissonance. These situations appear to benefit from the closer ties and more frequent communication associated with RM strategies and tactics.

There may be a built-in redundancy in risk-reducing relationships. Over time the perceived risk may reduce with increased self-confidence leading, perhaps, to consumers manifesting increased transactional marketing behaviours (Sheth and Parvatiyar, 2000, p. 180). On the contrary, leading brands are believed to offer psychological reassurances against the risk attached to purchasing and as a consequence create a sense of belonging (Wright and Sparks, 1999, p. 431). There may, therefore, be forces working both for and against the establishment of long-term relationships associated with risk.

Low risk, salience and emotion

At the other end of the spectrum are those products and services that may be defined as low (actual or opportunity) cost, decidedly low risk and low salience. As a result, suppliers at this end of the spectrum, such as FMCG retailers and repetitive services (e.g. library services), are rarely involved in exchange situations that generate the emotional intensity of major purchases. In these industries there is little need for the supplier to devote time and resources to anything more than basic reassurances, guarantees and warranties, and no apparent motive on the part of the customers to seek anything more than a tenuous relationship.

Personalised services

There are, however, some products and services that, seemingly, generate emotions out of proportion to their value. These tend to be highly personalised and usually associated with self-esteem. These categories include products such as clothing and services such as hairdressing or beauty. If the benefits associated with these products and services are important emotionally to a customer, then they are highly salient and the customer is likely to be risk averse. In these situations, relational strategies may help secure that customer's patronage. With most consumers these personal goods or services involve a trade-off. Thus the introduction of 'personal shoppers', personal trainers or expert stylists, at an increased cost to the consumer, may be acceptable to a percentage of the population although the core value of the service is low.

With highly personalised services there is frequently a high level of personal risk potential and salience *perceived by the customer*, and a resultant high degree of emotion generated, despite the relatively low cost in monetary terms (but perhaps a high cost in psychological terms). This situation may also promote or 'drive' RM strategies.

Trust and commitment

The requirement for trust and commitment appears to be an important indicator of when RM strategies may be potentially valuable. Equally, the existence of trust and commitment among parties is seen by some to be central to the success of relationship marketing strategies (Morgan and Hunt, 1994, p. 22; Palmatier *et al.*, 2006, p. 149) and the main means by which the affective strength of a buyer–seller relationship can be judged (Bejou and Palmer, 1998, p. 8). Trust and commitment are frequently discussed together in RM literature, with few authors mentioning one without the other (Pressey and Mathews, 1998, p. 41).

Trust

Trust is defined in various ways in the marketing literature. Both Lewicki *et al.* (1998, p. 438) and Morgan and Hunt (1994, p. 23) define **trust** as confidence in the exchange partner's reliability and integrity. This does not, however, mention the insecurity that trust is seen to overcome. In a risk-taking context partners will necessarily exhibit signs of vunerability as a precondition of trusting behaviour (Mitchell *et al.*, 1998, p. 159). A more comprehensive definition, therefore, might be 'an acceptance of vulnerability to another's possible, but not expected, ill will or lack of good will' (Blois, 1997, p. 58). Trust here is shown to be a psychological state comprising an intention to accept this vulnerability, based upon the positive expectations of the intentions or behaviour of others (Rousseau *et al.*, 1998, p. 394). Young (2006, p. 440) sees two levels of trust. The first is cognitive, calculative and rational, whereas the second is personal trust based on more emotional reasoning.

Trust is not itself a behaviour (as for example is cooperation) nor a choice (as in taking a risk) but an underlying condition that can result from such activities (Rousseau *et al.*, 1998, p. 395). Trust is seen as an important driver to both relationships and relationship enhancement in that it would appear to reduce risk perception more effectively than anything else. It is effectively a fundamental relationship model building block (Wilson, 1995, p. 337). From another perspective, trust may also be seen as a psychological outcome of a trusting relationship (Swaminathan and Reddy, 2000, p. 400) and/or associated with outstanding performance. In this regard, trust may be a consequence rather than an antecedent or, more likely, a cumulative build-up of both (Ambler and Styles, 2000, p. 496).

Scholars have seen trust as an essential ingredient in a healthy personality, as a foundation for interpersonal relationships, as a prerequisite for cooperation and as a basis for stability in social institutions and markets (Lewicki *et al.*, 1998, p. 438). It is seen as the glue that holds relationships together across different encounters (Singh and Sirdeshmukh, 2000, p. 163). As Baier (1986, p. 234) puts it: 'we inhabit a climate of trust as we inhabit an atmosphere and notice it as we notice air, only when it becomes scarce or polluted'.

As well as generating cooperative behaviour, trust may (Rousseau *et al.*, 1998, p. 394):

- reduce harmful conflict;
- decrease transactional costs (e.g. negating the need for constant checks);
- promote adaptive organisational forms (e.g. network relationships);
- facilitate the rapid formation of ad hoc work groups;
- promote effective response to a crisis.

Those suggested advantages involved with organisational groups seem, however, to assume that trust negates ambition. Given human nature and the intense political manoeuvring frequently seen within organisations, this viewpoint may be questionable.

Implicit in the above definitions and descriptions of trust is the general expectation that the word of another can be relied upon. So strong is this expectancy that in certain relationships it is generally seen to supersede normal commercial decision-making. For example, customers are seen to place a high value on trust when dealing with financial services organisations (Alexander and Colgate, 1998, p. 67). Thus, when some UK financial advisers were seen to sell products designed to return their companies or principals a handsome profit (a notion encouraged in many sectors of industry) and themselves very satisfactory commissions, the British government decided it was 'mis-selling' and highly publicised action was taken to refund customers.

The importance of trust has become central to discussions concerning Internet sales. Lack of trust in (often newly created and therefore unknown) suppliers to supply to the quality expected (or indeed at all) has been cited as one of the major suppressors of Internet sales. In response, a number of established organisations (that customers might be expected to 'trust' based on their size and/or reputation) have stepped in to offer 'seals of approval' to legitimise Internet businesses. In the UK these include BT's 'Trustwise', Barclays' 'Endorse', Royal Mail's 'Trust' and the Consumer Association's 'Which Web Trader'.

Trusting situations

Many different words or terms seem to be used to describe trusting situations. These, according to Mitchell *et al.* (1998, p. 160), may be summarised under the following headings:

- probity;
- equity;
- reliability;
- satisfaction.

Probity

Probity focuses on honesty and integrity that may be realised in business terms as professional understanding and reputation (p. 160). Reputation matters, and in particular the historical trustworthiness of parties following previous interactions. Although trust may be managed by individuals, companies can trade on their previous trustworthiness (even if the person who was responsible for generating the trust initially has gone elsewhere) because it can be 'institutionally captured' by the organisation (Shepherd and Sherman, 1998, p. 437) (see also Chapter 3).

Equity

Factors such as fair-mindedness, benevolence, caring, values and sincerity are in evidence here. Helpful advertising and/or cause-related sponsorship or promotions may help communicate this message to the consumer. Equity may also suggest an implied contract with mutual expectations and perceived obligations (Mitchell *et al.*, 1998, p. 160). Trust is not, however, simply cooperation (which may be coercive) but is seen to have more altruistic motivations (Rousseau *et al.*, 1998, p. 394).

Reliability

Reliability relates to the firm having the required expertise to perform its business effectively and reliably. It is emphasised through dependability, quality and consistency, and may be associated with high levels of predictability on the part of consumers as to the product or service they can expect. This may be expressed through the inherent qualities associated with the corporate name or brand or through guarantees and warranties issued by the company (Mitchell *et al.*, 1998, p. 160). It may be important to note that, when customers are not able to evaluate product or service quality, it is brand reputation that often drives the exchange (Selnes, 1998, p. 318).

Satisfaction

This will be covered more fully in the following section but is included here in its capacity as a predictor of trust. There would appear to be considerable overlap between trust and satisfaction as they both represent an overall evaluation, feeling or attitude about the other party in a relationship (ibid., p. 308). Satisfaction may be developed through personal experience or, less directly, through opinion and the experience of peers. It is associated with the perceived standard of delivery and may well be dependent on the duration of the relationship. Anticipated levels of satisfaction may also have an important effect on the duration of trust (Mitchell *et al.*, 1998, p. 160). In addition to being a potential antecedent, satisfaction may also be seen as an outcome of a trusting relationship (Swaminathan and Reddy, 2000, p. 400).

Since trust is built generally through experience, the more positive experiences the consumer has with the company, the more trusting he or she is likely to become (Grossman, 1998, p. 33) Trust is, therefore, a belief in a person's (or organisation's) competence to perform a specific task under specific circumstances (Sitkin and Roth, 1993, p. 373). In other circumstances no such trust (or active distrust) may exist. This is because relationships are multifaceted. It is quite possible for parties to hold, simultaneously, different views of each other as to each party's trustfulness in particular situations. For example, a company may be trusted as regards quality but not to deliver on time. Trust (and for that matter distrust) involves movement towards certainty (Lewicki *et al.*, 1998, p. 438) although complete certainty can never be reached. Trust is almost always regarded as a beneficial force; however, excessive trust (or suppression of distrust) may be at the root of 'group-think' dynamics (p. 453), where logic is suppressed in favour of group integrity, or may lead to claims of naivety.

Commitment

Relationship commitment, it is suggested, is central to relationship marketing and, according to Wilson (1995, p. 337), is the most commonly used dependent variable used in buyer–seller relationship studies. To many it is the 'end-game state' of relationship marketing (Dann and Dann, 2001, p. 352). It is, however, frequently an ill-defined concept. In RM literature it would seem to be regarded as a situation where one or other of the party's intention is to act and their subsequent attitude towards interacting with each other (Storbacka *et al.*, 1994, p. 28). Commitment implies the importance of the relationship to the parties and their desire to continue it (Wilson, 2000, p. 250). It also suggests that both parties will be loyal, reliable and show stability in the relationship with one another (Bejou and Palmer, 1998, p. 10). It is, therefore, a desire to maintain a relationship, often indicated by an ongoing investment into activities which are expected to maintain that relationship (Blois, 1997, p. 58). As it may take time to reach a point where a commitment may be made, it may also imply a certain 'maturity' in a relationship (Bejou and Palmer, 1998, p. 10). High levels of commitment are also associated with perceptions of 'future rewards, relationship identification, limited desire to seek out alternatives, the amount of effort expended in a relationship, the investment made in the relationship and the individuals assumed responsibility' (Grossman, 1998, p. 33).

Commitment is undoubtedly connected with the notion of trust but it is less clear which, if any, assumes precedence. Whether commitment is the outcome of growing trust or whether trust develops from the decision to commit to one or a few suppliers is not immediately clear. In addition, a breakdown in commitment may be the result of a breakdown in trust or vice versa. As with trust, commitment may also be seen as a potential 'psychological outcome' of a strong relationship (Swaminathan and Reddy, 2001, p. 400). It may also be associated (negatively) with greater competition and the availability of alternative relational parties (Bejou and Palmer, 1998, p. 10). Dann and Dann (2001, pp. 352–3) distinguish between two types of commitment: affective commitment, based on a liking, emotional attachment and sense of bonding with the other party, and calculative commitment based on a balance sheet of costs and benefits. They go on to note (p. 353):

> There is an evident bias in the literature towards preferring the affective side of commitment for long-term relationships. In reality, performance of the relationship is every bit as influenced by the profit and loss calculations of calculative commitment as it is by the sensitive 'touchy-feely' approach of affective commitment.

Trust and commitment

Notionally trust and commitment appear inseparable in the RM debate. This may well indicate that, if one or other is missing, the relationship is unlikely to be more than a 'hands off' or transient arrangement. This is because trust and commitment are invariably associated with the prerequisite that the relationship is of significantly high importance to one or both parties that it warrants maximum efforts at maintaining it (Morgan and Hunt, 1994, p. 23). According to Doyle (1995, p. 38), trust and commitment often require new forms of behaviour from marketers. They may have to set aside long-held beliefs and prejudices to accommodate the relationship.

Situations which may benefit from relational strategies are, therefore, likely to be those where the consumer and/or the supplier (but not necessarily both) regard the formation of a relationship as important. Where the supplier alone recognises the importance of a relationship, relational strategies designed to 'lock-in' customers over time seem a logical development (see Chapter 4). Indeed generating relationship benefits and promoting customer dependency may be more effective strategies for increasing customer commitment than for building trust (Palmatier et al., 2006, p. 149).

Where the customer alone recognises the importance of a relationship (e.g. in situations of high risk) the supplier may use this desire to attract customers through the development of strategies perceived by the customer as satisfying this need.

What these descriptions of trust and commitment suggest is that, whatever the industry, it is important to build trust and commitment if the establishment of a relationship is the end goal (Pressey and Mathews, 1998). Conversely, it may be hypothesised that, if trust and commitment are generally prerequisites to a sale, then relationship building is an important step towards achieving this.

There may be a number of precursors to trust and commitment, including (Morgan and Hunt, 1994, pp. 24–5):

- relationship termination costs;
- relationship benefits;
- shared values;
- communication;
- opportunistic behaviour.

Relationship termination costs

Relationship termination costs are *all* of the costs expected from terminating the relationship, including the lack of comparable alternative partners, relationship dissolution expenses as well as other switching costs (see Chapter 4).

Relationship benefits

Relationship benefits directly influence trust and commitment (ibid.). RM theory suggests that partner selection may be a critical element in competitive strategy as partners deliver superior 'value benefits'. Partners that receive superior benefits are likely to be more committed to a relationship.

Shared values

Shared values also directly influence both trust and commitment. The extent to which the partners have beliefs in common about behaviours, goals and policies that are important, appropriate and right for a particular situation is likely to affect commitment to the relationship.

Communication

Communication may directly influence trust and, indirectly, commitment. The sharing of meaningful and timely information is likely to build up both trust and commitment.

Opportunistic behaviour

Opportunistic behaviour (i.e. taking advantage of the relationship partner) on the part of one of the relationship participants is likely to directly influence (negatively) trust and, indirectly, commitment. When a party engages in opportunistic behaviour, such perceptions can lead to decreased trust and, as a consequence, the lessening of commitment.

It is worth noting that although trust and commitment play important roles other factors such as relationship satisfaction, efficiency, equity and reciprocity can also be important (Palmatier *et al.*, 2006, p. 152).

Transactional marketing

O'Malley and Tynan (1999, p. 593) have noted that there is empirical evidence to suggest that there is very little trust, commitment or indeed mutual respect in consumer markets. This may only be partly correct as at the more transactional end of the spectrum trust may be implicit as the consumer relies on the 'promises' of the supplier and/or the brand as regards safety, reliability and value for money for products and services. Often the customer, particularly in the case of services, must buy before 'experiencing the purchase' (Berry and Parsuraman, 1991, p. 107) basing their decision on how much they trust the supplier/brand. This implies that trust is most applicable when the outcome is unclear. The breaking of this trust may be seen to be a potential dissatisfier and a reason for defection.

A high degree of trust can, therefore, exist between parties without much feeling of commitment (Håkansson and Snehota, 2000, p. 77). In the FMCG sector consumers have no reason to commit themselves to one or a few suppliers because of the availability of supply in a largely undifferentiated market. At the other extreme, what at first might appear to be 'commitment' on the part of one party (e.g. the consumer) may hide the fact that they have few other exchange possibilities and are 'trapped' rather than committed to the relational exchange (Bejou and Palmer, 1998, p. 10).

The irony is that it is the FMCG sector, where commitment is low, that is the industry most heavily involved in 'loyalty schemes'. If commitment is a rarity in these businesses then loyalty is also in short supply. Indeed, most loyalty schemes, while rewarding repeat behaviour, are little more than technically advanced promotions that have little to do with retention, and may actively work against the development of long-term commitment. Exit barriers in this industry are low and the psychological costs nearly non-existent. At this end of the industry spectrum seduction is the favoured option (Tynan, 1997, p. 993). The risk is that 'promiscuous customers' will be attracted by the best deal with little regard for who supplies it. Indeed, a breakdown in commitment may well be associated with greater competition and availability of alternative relational partners (Bejou and Palmer, 1998, p. 10).

Commitment implies a state of maturity in a relationship that does not seem to exist at the transactional end of the spectrum (ibid.). There is no need to commit oneself either to a brand or a supplier; rather, consumers seem content to work with a 'portfolio of brands' (including retailer brands) until such time as a better alternative is available (Barnard and Ehrenberg, 1997). If the requirement for the successful application of RM is both trust and commitment, and not just one or the other (Morgan and Hunt, 1994), then many such industries fail to fulfil this criterion.

Perceived need for closeness

Some relationships will always be closer than others. Closeness, therefore, is a construct that is integral to the notion of relationship in that very close and less close relationships exist in virtually all circumstances (Barnes, 1997, p. 229). Closeness can be physical, mental or emotional and can strengthen the feeling of security in a relationship (Gummesson, 1999, p. 17). When the 'distance' between the parties is shorter, deeper relationships are likely to develop (Pels, 1999, p. 27). Conversely, when the distance is greater the relationship (if a relationship can be said to exist) is functional and at 'arm's length'. Close relationships are acknowledged to be more solid and likely to be longer lasting – precisely the characteristics relational marketers are looking for (Barnes, 1997, p. 229).

Different groups may be more or less 'prone' to the development of close relationships (Barnes and Howlett, 1998, p. 16). Not all customers want close relationships and some may only be interested in developing them with some parties and not with others (Pels, 1999, p. 27). A certain percentage may already have a moderately close relationship with a supplier and may wish that it were closer, while others might wish that it were less close. A continuum of closeness may, therefore, be said to exist (Barnes, 1997, p. 229) which may, to an extent, resemble the relational–transactional continuum (see Chapter 5).

According to Barnes (p. 237), degrees of closeness in a relationship may be linked, among other things, to the frequency of two-way communication with employees, and to the trust, empathy and mutuality of perceived relationship goals, and are usually associated with core products and services that involve high risk and involvement. Establishing close customer relationships in settings that are not characterised by frequent personal contact or high levels of involvement or emotion may, therefore, be a challenge. This concept seems to have bypassed some organisations. What is seen as a relationship as defined by many marketing programmes (e.g. customer contact/updates) is not likely to be a relationship in the eyes of the customer in that it is mostly one-sided and lacking in two-way communication (p. 229).

This view of the importance of 'closeness' also has implications for direct marketers whose implicit objective is to develop or otherwise exploit relationships with customers, in particular those using technology as a surrogate for 'close relationships' (see Chapter 11). Targeted mailings, in general, fail to satisfy the criteria as the 'normal' response rate is low, with many customers rejecting the 'communication'. This applies even when the 'return on investment' on the campaign is satisfactory. Companies that rely on frequent mailings to 'keep their customers informed' are merely throwing messages at consumers (in effect a refinement on mass marketing), not communicating with them.

Moves to utilise technology to save staff costs (e.g. cash machines, Internet information services) may also discourage the development of close relationships. By removing the human element in the process the company reverts to relying solely on the easily replicated 'core product and support services' (see Chapter 11) to achieve any 'differentiation' from its competitors.

Customer satisfaction

Relationship marketing theory suggests that profitability is enhanced when customer retention is high. Retention in competitive markets is generally believed to be a product of customer satisfaction (Buttle, 1997, p. 143). In addition, customer satisfaction has been shown to be positively associated with return on investment (ROI) and market value (Sheth and Sisodia, 1999, p. 80), although these are sometimes regarded as poor measures of actual company performance in the long term.

Satisfaction can be perceived from a number of different viewpoints (see Box 6.2). Most researchers agree that satisfaction is a psychological process of evaluating perceived performance outcomes based on predetermined expectations (e.g. Sheth and Sisodia, ibid.). Customers are, therefore, satisfied when their 'expectations of values' are positively disconfirmed (Buttle, 1997, p. 143). In contrast, the greater the (negative) gap between the level of expectation and the matching of such expectations, the greater the level of dissatisfaction experienced by the customer (Hutcheson and Moutinho, 1998, p. 706). Figure 6.1 illustrates these concepts.

Box 6.2   Satisfaction is ...

'an evaluation of emotion'

(Hunt, 1977, p. 460)

'favourability of the individual's subjective evaluation'

(Westbrook, 1980, p. 49)

'summary psychological state resulting when the emotions surrounding disconfirmed expectations is coupled with the consumers prior feelings about the consumption experience'

(Oliver, 1981, p. 27)

'a positive outcome from the outlay of scarce resources'

(Bearden and Teel, 1983, p. 21)

'the consumer's fulfilment response. It is the judgement that a product or service itself, provided (or is providing) a pleasurable level of consumption-related fulfilment, including levels of under- or over-fulfilment'

(Oliver, 1997, p. 13)

'related to a subjective evaluation of emotions. The emotion occurs as a function of disconfirmation and relative output to input. The end result is a positive or negative feeling of fulfilment'

(Andreasson, 2000, p. 161)

Figure 6.1
Expectation and
realisation of
service

Satisfaction drivers

What drives customer satisfaction? Fournier and Mick (1999, p. 2) note that the customer-satisfaction paradigm suggests that:

■ confirmed standards lead to moderate satisfaction;

■ positively disconfirmed (i.e. better than expected) standards lead to high satisfaction;

■ negatively disconfirmed (i.e. worse than expected) leads to dissatisfaction.

This may, however, be an over-simplification of a complex series of reactions. Cumby and Barnes (1998, pp. 58–60) suggest that drivers exist on five levels and that these generally involve progressively more personal contact with the service supplier:

■ core product or service;

■ support services and systems;

■ technical performance;

■ elements of customer interaction;

■ affective dimension of services.

Core product or service

This is the basic product or service provided by the company and, probably, provides the supplier with the least opportunity to differentiate or add value. However, in the competitive marketplace the company must get the core product or service right otherwise the whole relationship is at risk. With services in particular, the inability to patent the service and the ease of copying largely precludes the use of service features for competitive advantage (Devlin and Ennew, 1997, p. 73).

Support services and systems

These include the peripheral and support services that enhance the provision of the core product or services (e.g. staffing levels, delivery, technical support). The customer may well receive an excellent core product or service from the supplier but be dissatisfied with the supplier because of inferior support services and systems.

Technical performance

This level of the 'customer satisfaction model' deals with whether the service provider gets the core product or service *and* the support services and systems right. The emphasis is on keeping the promises made to the consumer (e.g. on-time delivery, correct billing). There may be nothing wrong with the core product or service and the supplier may have the services and systems in place but they do not (perhaps because of management failings) get them right on every occasion. Customer dissatisfaction may result from this failure to deliver to the customer's expectations.

Elements of customer interaction

This level relates to the way the service provider interacts with the customer either face-to-face or through technology-based contact (e.g. telephone etc.). How do we treat customers? Are they treated with courtesy? Do we make it easy for them to do business with us? Understanding of the importance of applying this level of consideration implies that the company has thought beyond the simple provision of core products and services and support.

Affective dimensions of service

Beyond the basic interactions of the company are the messages, sometimes subtle and often unintentional, that companies send to their customers that leave them with either positive or negative feelings towards them. Cumby and Barnes (1998, p. 58) note that research evidence exists showing that a considerable amount of customer dissatisfaction has nothing to do with core products and services or with how that 'core' is delivered or provided to the customer. Indeed, the customer may be satisfied with most aspects of the interaction. The problem is with the 'little things' that may not even be noticed by staff (see Box 6.3).

Box 6.3   Frustrations

- I used to be able to telephone my bank if I had a problem and my problem would normally be sorted out then and there. Now my bank uses a 'customer care centre'. I now have to call this centre (which is frequently engaged), try to remember the first, third and fourth letter of my password (which I frequently forget) and explain (usually from the very beginning as the call centre operator does not know me) my problem. They cannot usually answer my question because they need first to speak to my bank, which they promise to contact. I may then receive a telephone call at home during office hours (usually taken by my answerphone so I have no opportunity to question what I am told) a few days later either part-answering or not answering my query. I then have to call the customer care centre back and the cycle begins again. Not only was my query not answered immediately but it would seem to me that the duplication of effort on the part of the bank hardly suggests efficiency.

- A large cable telephone operator has written to me on two separate occasions urging me to join them. As I am less than happy with my current telephone provider I called the company on both occasions to find out more. Both times the company told me that cables have yet to be laid in my street. Discussing this with some students, I find that the same thing has happened to many of them. I am beginning to think that it is not a mistake, as I had been told, but that the company is 'mass mailing' to judge whether it would be worth laying cables in the first place. Is this ethical or sharp practice?
- A well-known insurance company wrote to me a while ago suggesting that they could 'almost certainly' cut the cost of my home insurance. I called them only to be quoted a premium almost £200 more than my current insurer. The operator said it was because of the area in which I lived. As these rates are based almost always on post codes why did this company bother writing to me in the first place?
- Every time I go to the doctor I receive an appointment. Regardless of what time of day the appointment is it is *always* late. The reason is, I am told, that the doctor allows a certain time for each appointment and that this time allowance is always exceeded. It would seem too obvious that the surgery should review the time schedule on the basis of the average time the doctor spends with patients.
- I was involved for many years with a UK ceramics company for which I was (on behalf of a large North American department store) that company's largest customer. Towards the end of each year I would contact the company to check on the January/February shipments. Each time, without fail, I would be told there was a delay. When I asked why, I would be told (each and every time) that the problem was that the factory was closing for Christmas. The fact that Christmas happened every year did not seem to influence the company's planning programmes in any way.

Cumby and Barnes (ibid.) make the point that it is quite possible for the supplier to get things right on the first four levels and to dissatisfy the customer because of something that happens on the fifth level. This emphasises the importance of 'critical episodes' in the exchange process, as discussed in the following section.

Episode value

Service researchers have long argued that the consumer's experience and subsequent satisfaction are primarily an outcome of the interaction between personnel and the consumer (Möller and Halinen, 2000, p. 33; Palmatier *et al.*, 2006, p. 141; Kinard and Capella, 2006, p. 365) and that these may be described in the form of 'episodes'. Indeed, one definition of relationships in RM is as 'the sum of meaning-filled episodes which relational partners co-produce' (Buttle, 1997, p. 148). Bitner *et al.* (1990, p. 73) define them as 'specific interactions between customers and . . . employees that are especially satisfying or unsatisfying' [sic]. Not all of these episodes have the same importance or carry the same weight (Storbacka *et al.*, 1994, p. 30). Some are routine and others critical. Customer satisfaction can be increased, it is suggested, if episode value is improved by increasing the benefit and/or reducing the sacrifice for the buyer (Selnes, 1998, p. 305).

According to Storbacka *et al.* (1994, p. 30), the definition of a **'critical episode'** is an episode that is of 'great importance to a relationship and upon which the continuation of a relationship is dependent'. Not keeping up the standard expected by the customer in an exchange may be seen to have a negative effect that may trigger a critical episode. Critical episodes are customer specific, and even a 'routine episode' can become critical if the *perceived* level of service is not met. Thus episodes indicative of high quality in one relationship may be deemed indicative of poor quality in another (Buttle, 1997, p. 153). These 'critical episodes' within the relationship are seen to have a considerable effect on customer satisfaction. The importance of episode value will be returned to in Chapter 7.

The customer satisfaction process

While the literature differs on the definition of satisfaction (see Box 6.2) most descriptions share common elements, including (Giese and Cote, 2000, p. 1):

■ customer satisfaction is a response (emotional or cognitive);
■ the response relates to a specific focus (e.g. expectation, experience);
■ response occurs at a particular time (before, during or after consumption).

Although this may be the case in certain instances, this does not take account of satisfaction (or dissatisfaction) that develops over time and is based upon episodes in the relationship (see Chapter 7).

Jones and Sasser (1995, p. 93) suggest that the ability to 'listen to the customer' is at the heart of any successful strategy to 'manage' customer satisfaction. They suggest five categories of approach to this process:

■ customer satisfaction indices;
■ feedback;
■ market research;
■ front-line personnel;
■ strategic activities.

Customer satisfaction indices

Customer satisfaction indices are among the most popular methods of tracking or measuring customer satisfaction. Indeed, businesses of all sorts now divert considerable energies into tracking customer satisfaction in this way (Mittal and Lassar, 1998, p. 178). These studies are, however, 'static and cognitively orientated' (Strandvik and Storbacka, 1996, p. 73) and are frequently criticised for reporting overly positive results (Nowak and Washburn, 1998, p. 443). There is also a problem with how questions are asked. Different results can be achieved with the same satisfaction survey dependent on how it was operationalised (Giese and Cote, 2000, p. 1). There is an added difficulty of equivalence across countries and/or cultures where knowledge and meaning may make comparisons difficult (see Reynolds and Simintiras (2000)). Jones and Sasser (1995, p. 91) point out that, as important as they believe 'satisfaction surveys' to be, it would be fatal for a business to rely solely on them.

Mittal and Lassar (1998, p. 178) note that many companies measure satisfaction in the hope that, if the scores are high, the customer will stay with them. They warn, however, that even a satisfied customer will leave for the lure of a competitor's offer. Their research (p. 183) suggests that, even at a satisfaction rating of five (on a five-point scale) nearly 20 per cent of healthcare customers and over 30 per cent of car repair customers were 'willing to switch' to another supplier. At a score of four (a level most companies would be quite happy with) the potential desertion figures reached 32.4 per cent and 78.6 per cent respectively. Reichheld (1993, p. 71) also recognises that customer satisfaction is not a surrogate for retention. According to his research, between 65 per cent and 85 per cent of customers who defected claimed they were satisfied or very satisfied before leaving. Whatever else satisfaction indices tell us, they do not predict loyalty.

Feedback

Feedback in this context includes comments, complaints and questions. It may be among the most effective means of establishing what the customer regards as a satisfactory level of performance and what 'dissatisfiers' exist within the operation as it is based on actual performance rather than contrived situations (e.g. market research).

Market research

In addition to research among customers and non-customers into potential 'satisfiers', 'dissatisfiers' and 'customer expectations', market research can be used when they become customers (to establish those drivers which brought the customer to the company) and when they end the relationship (to establish those factors which caused the customer to go elsewhere). Again, more valuable information may be achieved in the latter rather than the former as it is based on actual behaviour rather than perception.

Front-line personnel

Direct contact with staff can provide a good means of listening to the customer. Many customers, rather than formally complain to a company, will simply break the relationship, and front-line staff provide the only opportunity for a less formal sounding board for complaints which might otherwise not be heard. The crucial factor here is how this information is fed back into the decision-making process.

Strategic activities

Actively involving the customer in company decision-making may be a means of pre-empting potential 'dissatisfiers' and establishing potential 'satisfiers'. Jones and Sasser (1995) use the example of Southwestern Airlines, which invited frequent flyers to the first round of interviews with prospective flight attendants.

Benefits of customer satisfaction

Much of the marketing literature takes as a 'given' the notion that customer satisfaction is a proxy for repatronising behaviour (Hutcheson and Moutinho, 1998, p. 706). As a result, many companies adopt strategies to improve customer satisfaction with the perceived objectives of strengthening bonds and achieving customer loyalty (Ravald and Grönroos, 1996, p. 19).

Great claims are made regarding higher customer satisfaction levels. It is suggested that customer satisfaction increases customer loyalty, reduces price elasticity, insulates market share from competitors, lowers transaction costs, reduces failure rates and the costs of attracting new customers, and improves the firm's reputation in the marketplace (Sheth and Sisodia, 1999, p. 80). Jones and Sasser (1995, p. 89) suggest that, except in a few rare instances, customer satisfaction is the key to securing customer loyalty and to generating superior long-term financial performance.

In simple terms, therefore, the generally accepted model suggested is as shown in Figure 6.2.

Figure 6.2
Simple 'return on relationship' model

Potential flaws

As with many highly subjective concepts, these 'claims' should be treated as generalisations and even then with an element of scepticism. The simple model that justifies these arguments may be inherently flawed, particularly in industries where relationships are of more marginal importance. Although it may have an implicit logic, it is based on an oversimplification that often creates practical problems (Storbacka *et al.*, 1994, p. 23).

As Mittal and Lassar (1998, p. 178), Buttle (1997, p. 145), O'Malley (1998, p. 48) and others have noted, satisfaction does not always imply loyalty. The first-mentioned authors suggest two compelling reasons why not:

- A dissatisfied customer may continue his or her patronage.
- A satisfied customer may be willing (indeed eager) to patronise alternative suppliers in the hope of a 'more satisfying' result.

Dick and Basu (1994, p. 101) indicate graphically the first anomaly by cross-classifying the concepts of 'relative attitude' (strong or weak) to an organisation and 'repeat patronage' (high or low) as shown in Figure 6.3.

Figure 6.3
Relative
attitude–
behaviour
relationship

(*Source*: Adapted from Dick and Basu, 1994)

Customers who have a strong relative attitude and who are seen to frequently repatronise the supplier may be seen as loyal (at least for the time being). Those with a weak
attitude (patently dissatisfied), however, may be 'spuriously loyal' as their reasons for
staying with the supplier may be linked to having no other option but to continue the
relationship. Dick and Basu also point out that 'latent' loyalists exist who hold a positive attitude but who may be prevented from patronising the supplier for reasons other
than potential satisfaction (e.g. location). Customer satisfaction has been used as a
proxy measure of loyalty because it has been assumed that satisfaction affects buying
intentions in a positive way. Research suggests, again, that this is far too simplistic.

As regards loyal customers seeking other suppliers, this may be explained by the
fact that customers always have the potential, whatever the current situation, to be
more satisfied elsewhere. This may be particularly evident in those situations where
the 'switching barriers' are low and where the benefits of developing a close relationship with a supplier are not perceived as important by the customer.

The view that customer satisfaction is the key to securing customer loyalty is,
therefore, far from a fully robust concept. It is not sufficient to have customers who
are merely satisfied. In addition, satisfying customers that have the freedom to make
choices is not enough to keep them loyal (Jones and Sasser, 1995, p. 91; Stewart,
1997, p. 112). Satisfaction does not always result in retention and it is equally apparent that dissatisfaction does not necessarily result in defection (Buttle, 1997, p. 145;
O'Malley, 1998, p. 48). Indeed, the gap that appears to exist between satisfaction and
loyalty calls into question the assertions managers often make about the direct association between them (Mittal and Lassar, 1998, p. 178) (see Chapter 3).

Traditional customer satisfaction theory assumes that the customer has expectations and comparison standards (Strandvik and Storbacka, 1996, p. 73) to compare
with product or service performance in deriving satisfaction judgements (Fournier
and Mick, 1999, p. 11). It also presumes objectivity. This assumption of rationality is
perceived to be a problem, not just in this particular scenario but generally in marketing theory, which emphasises positive decision-making as being at the centre of
consumer behaviour (East, 1997a, p. 41) when real-life observation suggests cus-

tomers can be fickle. Research calls into question the continued dominance of the customer-satisfaction paradigm (Fournier and Mick, 1999, p. 18) and suggests 'value-expectation' is a flawed measure because of its multi-facetedness, complexity (Ravald and Grönroos, 1996, p. 19) and subjectivity.

Inherent satisfaction may be the basis of one form of loyalty, particularly where the customer has exerted some effort in establishing the 'best deal' available in the marketplace. Other situational drivers (such as time and opportunity costs) may, however, result in 'default loyalty' where satisfaction plays little or no part. Research by East (1997b, p. 7), for example, notes that convenience of location may be a stronger motivator in FMCG retailing than supermarket loyalty schemes. Mintel's (1996) research came to similar conclusions.

In FMCG retailing in particular, strategies designed to encourage simple repeat behaviour or to minimise disruption of consumer inertia (see the following section) may be considerably more beneficial than costly, interactive, relational strategies. In industries with lower or more complex comparability a different need exists. Continual reassurance and frequent comparison may be required to ensure that customers remain relatively satisfied.

Inertia

One further element in the 'customer satisfaction' debate that is frequently underrated is the part played by '**inertia**'. Customer satisfaction is regarded, generally, as a positive, proactive force that drives behaviour patterns. Satisfaction is not, however, always the result of positive input but may be simply the result of things not going wrong (Johnson and Mathews, 1997, p. 536). In other situations the level of 'satisfaction' may be due to a lack of motivation and/or the ability of a customer to evaluate the level of service (Bloemer and de Ruyter, 1998, p. 501).[1] In the former case this may be described not as satisfaction but as inertia. Rather than 'driving' a customer to repatronise a supplier, this non-response to other external attractions suggests habitual behaviour. This may be similar to what Fournier and Mick (1999, p. 10) refer to as 'satisfaction-as-resignation', which involves 'passive submission and unresisting acceptance of that which is imposed'.

Inertia-type behaviour might be defined as behaviour that would occur anyway, assuming no external stimuli. This variety of satisfaction is passive and simply reflects the willingness of customers to stay with a supplier until they perceive (if ever) that something better is available in the market or other factors (e.g. customer moves away) cause a change. Stability in markets occur because habits may rarely change (East, 1997a, p. 40). It may be hypothesised, therefore, that in many situations it is not positive 'customer satisfaction' driving consumers to act but lack of stimulation to act otherwise. The distinction between positive and neutral satisfaction (or inertia) is important as, in certain industries, it again challenges the idea that customer satisfaction leads to long-lasting relationships (Storbacka et al., 1994, p. 28). Marketers should not equate inertia with loyalty (Cumby and Barnes, 1998, p. 56).

It is quite probable (although not a universal truth) that consumer inertia or unwillingness to change from the present behaviour may be the norm in many industries. The 'comfort zone'[2] described is the difference between an adequate and a desired level of service (Storbacka *et al.*, 1994, p. 26), which becomes a 'zone of inertia' where customers do not act or react to increased levels of service quality. Effectively customers are indifferent to small increases or decreases within the zone (Yap and Sweeney, 2007, p. 137). In this situation, any small increase in service level or quality (all other things being equal) merely helps maintain inertia or habitual behaviour rather than actually driving the competitive process (see Figure 6.4). This inertial form of routine human behaviour may help explain why aggregate responses to surveys are very weak measures (East, 1997a, p. 41). In relationship terms, an analogy to marriage suggests that, whatever bond holds couples together, it is largely responsive rather than proactive, particularly after time has elapsed. The natural tendency of relationships is towards erosion of sensitivity and attentiveness over time. Familiarity may not always breed contempt but it may well create inertia! In commercial situations, it has been observed that individuals who remain 'loyal' in the long-term indeed show signs of this inertia (Bejou and Palmer, 1998, p. 16).

Figure 6.4 The inertia effect on expectation and realisation of service

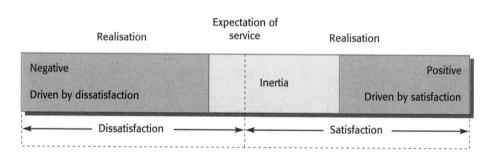

The concept of inertia in many ways runs counter to one of the main planks of the customer satisfaction paradigm, that excellent services necessarily improve profitability (e.g. Buttle, 1996, p. 9). Rather it suggests that, in certain industries, no benefit is achieved from the extra effort expended. Once resources have been allocated to the achievement of latent customer satisfaction (or, more descriptively, customer inertia), up to a threshold level (and not beyond) any additional investment will not yield any return in the form of increased customer retention (Hassan, 1996, p. 9) or, ultimately, increased profitability. Indeed, if keeping up with customers' needs in a highly competitive market involves ever greater investment, the potential is for ever falling, not rising, profits as expectations on quality is believed to have diminishing returns (Strandvik and Storbacka, 1996, p. 74). An increased level of satisfaction *may*, in itself, be counter-productive as it may well increase expectations and, therefore, increase dissatisfaction rates (Hutcheson and Moutinho, 1998, p. 718). This is directly contrary to another fundamental principle of RM in that its concern is to meet, or preferably exceed, customers' expectations (Buttle, 1996, p. 8).

By direct contrast, any decrease from whatever level of service the customer now expects, possibly regardless of what the market generally has to offer, may ferment switching behaviour. The marketing emphasis here, far from being upon increasing satisfaction, may be directed at retaining the status quo. This may be achieved not by increasing customer satisfaction but by minimising dissatisfaction as the switching costs of dissatisfaction may well outweigh the benefits of satisfaction (Hutcheson and Moutinho, 1998, p. 706). The danger is that the competition may move the goalposts and what was previously acceptable is no longer the standard to be achieved.

The reason that 'inertial behaviour' seems to contradict some widely held concepts of RM may be because its application appears to coincide with more repetitive transactional exchanges at the TM end of the transactional–relational continuum (see Chapter 5). In situations where RM is seen to be beneficial the development of customer satisfaction through differential, relational strategies may be advantageous. In repetitive, more transactional relationships, strategies that promote repetitive behaviour may be more profitable.

Satisfaction – the reality

The simple model (customer satisfaction→customer retention→profitability) is too simplistic and possibly misleading for many businesses. While intuitively a useful goal, an increased level of satisfaction could prove counterproductive in certain industries as it may well increase expectation and, by definition, lead to increased dissatisfaction rates (Hutcheson and Moutinho, 1998, p. 718). This may simply reflect the obverse of the Buddhist principle that when you decrease your desire you increase your chances of happiness. Evidence from the US market suggests that, despite the increased focus on satisfaction and service quality among many American companies, customer satisfaction rates in that market are at an all-time low and other expressions of dissatisfaction at an all-time high (Fournier *et al.*, 1998, p. 42). Jan Lapidoth Sr, in an interview about his time at SAS (quoted by Gummesson, 1999, p. 185), describes a concept known as the 'service paradox' (Box 6.4). This suggests that less profitable customers are frequently the most satisfied while the more profitable are frequently less satisfied. A further, and supporting, paradox has emerged in research by Gwynne *et al.* (2000, p. 559). This is that customers who are generally happy about what they have received thus far and are generally positively disposed toward the supplier are likely to be more demanding in terms of their future expectations. Conversely customers who are disgruntled appear to temper their expectations.

Box 6.4 The service paradox

Gummesson (1999, p. 185) introduces the notion of a 'service paradox', which suggests that the most loyal customers do not always mean the most satisfied or the most profitable. Gummesson quotes a definition of the service paradox as described to him by Jan Lapidoth Sr on his experiences at SAS. He states that 'the less profitable customers are, the more satisfied they are, while the more profitable customers are less satisfied'. Lapidoth illustrates this with the example of flights between New York and Europe. The price of fares on this route differ dramatically. Full Business Class is $3,000.00. The business traveller is highly profitable but highly demanding. Value for the business traveller is high quality, punctuality, comfort, etc. The Economy Class customer contributes marginally to profits but is grateful for the low price and not so demanding. Value for the economy traveller is in low prices. The likelihood is that the business traveller is less satisfied than the economy traveller despite the business traveller getting better service.

(*Source*: Based on Gummesson, 1999, p. 185)

Summary

A model was introduced at the end of Chapter 3 that suggested that there were a number of per-ceived 'drivers' to relational and transactional strategies. In this chapter drivers were introduced that had not been previously discussed.

The existence of high risk, high salience and, consequently, high emotion in an exchange transac-tion appears to suggest that RM strategies would be beneficial as the customer may perceive that a close relationship is necessary in such situations. At the other end of the spectrum, low risk, low salience and low emotion suggest that the customer does not perceive the benefits of staying with one or a few suppliers and is, consequently, more opportunistic.

The perceived need for trust and commitment in deep relationships provided another indicator of those situations where relational strategies may be seen as beneficial. At the transactional end of the continuum, although there are indications that a certain level of trust is a necessary ingredient, the existence of commitment is not usually observed.

The concept of closeness was also discussed. When the 'distance' between the parties is shorter, deeper relationships are likely to develop. Conversely, when the distance is greater, the relationship is functional and at arm's length. Again, observation of these characteristics in a relationship may be an indicator of whether RM strategies are likely to be beneficial.

The complexities surrounding the concept of customer satisfaction were examined and it was con-cluded that the widely accepted model (customer satisfaction *leads to* customer retention which *leads to* profitability) is too simplistic and may cause difficulties in certain industries. The perceived need for positive customer satisfaction in a relationship may, however, prove a reasonable indicator (or driver) of the benefits of relational strategies. At the other end of the continuum, strategies which promote habitual behaviour may be more indicative of transactional marketing.

The importance of these themes is such that they will be referred to again in later chapters.

Discussion questions

1 Explain the association between risk, salience and emotion.
2 Explain the association between trust and commitment.
3 Why will close relationships be stronger than arm's length relationships?
4 Describe a situation where inertia may determine the duration of a relationship.

Case study   Why should we trust you?

Only 57 per cent of consumers are inclined to trust companies. As if this all-time low is not bad enough news, resistance to marketing is also now at a peak, with just 6 per cent of consumers admitting to trusting any form of advertising.

Though marketers are acutely aware of the importance of gaining trust, many fail to earn it, not least those in the tobacco, petrochemical, fast food, utilities, construction, telecoms, financial services, alcohol and travel sectors, which all fund themselves at the wrong end of consumer trust rankings complied by Corporate Culture in exclusive research for *Marketing*.

'It is no surprise that fast food ranks close to the bottom,' says McDonald's senior vice-president and chief marketing officer for Europe Jill McDonald, who adds that her company size and status as market leader means that it generally bears the brunt of negative perceptions of the sector.

The firm's own research backs up the findings and McDonald is well aware of the many reasons for mistrust of the sector, including concern over obesity, the negative portrayal of the industry in the media, as well as fears among consumers that her brand, in particular, represents globalisations and Americanisation.

Fast-food brands are attempting to rectify the problem and McDonald's in particular has taken significant steps over the past year toward greater transparency. The chain has created a website called makeupyourownmind.co.uk, which invites consumers to become quality scouts for the brand and record their experiences online. The effect of its efforts has yet to be seen, but at least it is taking steps in the right direction.

Utilities firms also come under fire from consumers, who say the sector has a reputation for unreliable service. Brands singled out for specific criticism include Powergen, which is trusted by 31 per cent of consumers, and British Gas (35 per cent).

A spokesman for Powergen acknowledges the negative impact of price rises and customer service issues, but emphasises efforts to improve perceptions; the firm pulled its call centres out of India last summer and hopes to have recruited 3500 additional customer services staff by the end of this year. He adds that the brand had seen an 80 per cent reduction in complaints over the past year.

However, John Drummond, chief executive of Corporate Culture, warns that charting customer satisfaction through the number of complaints received will never produce an accurate picture, as only 25 per cent of consumers would write to complain if they lost trust in a company.

Telecoms has come under scrutiny thanks to hidden costs and outsourcing to foreign call centres. NTL/Telewest is trusted by just 31 per cent of consumers and reports that of the total number of complaints it received last year, 15 per cent related to firms that failed to be transparent in marketing or selling telephone services.

It comes as little surprise that financial services firms are trusted by only a third of consumers; the sector has been dogged by reports of hefty pay cheques for its directors, branch closures and fears among consumers about the mis-selling of endowments.

So, what does it take to win over consumers? Some brands such as John Lewis, British Airways, Sony and Virgin seem to have the answer, and top the trust rankings, particularly among young people.

Boots is the overall victor, with 85 per cent of consumers saying they trust it. This is partly due to its longevity and familiarity, according to Drummond, who adds that the firm is at an advantage because it sells products that can make a positive difference to consumers' health.

High-ranking sectors include food firms, supermarkets, technology and car manufacturers. Premium grocers Marks & Spencer and Waitrose are both consistently cited as trusted brands, indicating that the efforts of supermarket and food brands in labelling their products with nutrition guidelines, as well as a greater emphasis on organic product and attempts to boost green credential, have paid off.

Drummond says that Marks & Spencer has also effected a huge turnaround by keeping a finger on the pulse of what is important for its customers.

The technology sector is a high achiever and brands such as Microsoft and Apple gained trust scores of 69 per cent and 61 per cent respectively. Consumers believe that technology improves their lives and are willing to put aside concerns over data protection and privacy according to the research. Google comes second behind Boots in the overall ranking, with 84 per cent of consumers deeming trustworthy.

Sadly for companies that did not fare so well, Drummond warns that must be aware of the limitations of their communications in influencing trust. 'The experience the consumer has of a company and the experiences of their acquaintances are extremely important,' he says. The research shows that, if a company earns consumer trust, 54 per cent will recommend the product to others, while consumers tell about 50 per cent more people about a bad experience than a good one.

Marketers must also tread especially carefully with middle-aged men, since they are the most likely to mistrust firms until companies actively earn their trust: 71 per cent of females trust companies until there is a problem, compared with 61 per cent of men. If those men are from London, marketers are in even more trouble, as 43 per cent say they are likely not to trust a company at all, or to trust it very little – the highest of all the UK regions.

'It is important to remember that consumer trust is never static,' concludes Drummond. Even those flying high, then, must be careful to ensure they do not lose that hard-gained trust; once gone, it is becoming all the harder to get back.

(*Source*: Melanie Godsell, *Marketing*, 10 January 2007)

Case study questions

1 What reasons are given for the high degree of mistrust amongst consumers?
2 Why do certain suppliers/brands appear to be more trusted than others?

References

Alexander, N. and Colgate, M. (1998) 'Building relationships in retailing through financial services: insights and implications', *Customer Relationship Management*, **1** (1), 64–78.

Ambler, T. and Styles, C. (2000) 'Viewpoint: the future of relational research in international marketing: constructs and conduits', *International Marketing Review*, **17** (6), 492–508.

Andreassen, T.W. (2000) 'Antecedents to satisfaction with service recovery', *European Journal of Marketing*, **34** (1/2), 156–75.

Baier, A. (1986) 'Trust and antitrust', *Ethics*, **96** (2), 231–60.

Barnard, N. and Ehrenberg, A.S.C. (1997) 'Advertising: strongly persuasive or nudging?', *Journal of Advertising Research*, January/February, 21–31.

Barnes, J.G. (1997) 'Exploring the importance of closeness in customer relationships', American Marketing Association Conference, Dublin, June, pp. 227–38.

Bearden, W.O. and Teel, J.E. (1983) 'An investigation of personal influences on consumer complaining', *Journal of Marketing Research*, 20 February, 21–8.

Bejou, D. and Palmer, A. (1998) 'Service failure and loyalty: an exploratory empirical study of airline customers', *Journal of Services Marketing*, **12** (1), 7–22.

Berry, L.L. and Parsuraman, A. (1991) *Marketing Services*, New York: The Free Press.

Bhattacharya, C.B. and Bolton, R.N. (2000) 'Relationship marketing in mass markets,' in Sheth, J.N. and Parvatiyar, A. (eds) *Handbook of Relationship Marketing*, Thousand Oaks, CA: Sage, pp. 171–207.

Bitner, M.J., Booms, B.H. and Tetreault, M.S. (1990) 'The service encounter: diagnosing favorable and unfavorable incidents', *Journal of Marketing*, **54**, 71–84.

Bloemer, J. and de Ruyter, K. (1998) 'On the relationship between store image, store satisfaction and store loyalty', *European Journal of Marketing*, **32** (5/6), 499–513.

Blois, K.J. (1997) 'When is a relationship a relationship?', in Gemünden, H.G., Rittert, T. and Walter, A. (eds) *Relationships and Networks in International Markets*, Oxford: Elsevier, pp. 53–64.

Buttle, F.B. (1996) *Relationship Marketing Theory and Practice*, London: Paul Chapman.

Buttle, F.B. (1997) 'Exploring relationship quality', paper presented at the Academy of Marketing Conference, Manchester, UK.

Cumby, J.A. and Barnes, J. (1998) 'How customers are made to feel: the role of affective reactions in driving customer satisfaction', *Customer Relationship Management*, **1** (1), 54–63.

Dann, S.J. and Dann, S.M. (2001) *Strategic Internet Marketing*, Milton, Qld: John Wiley & Sons.

Devlin, J.F. and Ennew, C.T. (1997) 'Understanding competitive advantage: the case of financial services', *International Journal of Bank Marketing*, **15** (3), 73–82.

Dick, A. and Basu, K. (1994) 'Customer loyalty: towards an integrated framework', *Journal of the Academy of Marketing Science*, **22**, 99–113.

Doyle, P. (1995) 'Marketing in the new millennium', *European Journal of Marketing*, **29** (12), 23–41.

East, R. (1997a) 'Inertia rules', *Marketing Business*, November.

East, R. (1997b) 'The anatomy of conquest: Tesco versus Sainsbury', working paper, Kingston Business School, UK.

Fournier, S.B. and Mick, D.G. (1999) 'Rediscovering satisfaction', *Journal of Marketing*, October, **63** (4) 2–5.

Fournier, S.B., Dobscha, S. and Mick, D.G. (1998) 'Preventing the premature death of relationship marketing', *Harvard Business Review*, **76** (1), 42–9.

Giese, J.L. and Cote, J.A. (2000) 'Defining consumer satisfaction', *Academy of Marketing Science Review* 1 <www.amsreview.org/articles/giese01-2000.pdf> (accessed 23 November 2000).

Grossman, R.P. (1998) 'Developing and managing effective customer relationships', *Journal of Product and Brand Management*, **7** (1), 27–40.

Gummesson, E. (1999) *Total Relationship Marketing: Rethinking Marketing Management from 4Ps to 30Rs*, Oxford: Butterworth Heinemann.

Gwynne, A.L., Devlin, J.F. and Ennew, C.T. (2000) 'The zone of tolerance: insights and influences', *Journal of Marketing Management*, **16** (6), 545–64.

Hassan, M. (1996) *Customer Loyalty in the Age of Convergence*, London: Deloitte & Touche Consulting Group <www.dttus.com> (accessed 23 November 2000).

Hunt, H.K. (1977) 'CS/D: overview and future research direction', in Hunt, H.K. (ed.) *Conceptualisation and Measurement of Customer Satisfaction and Dissatisfaction*, Cambridge, MA: Marketing Science Institute.

Hutcheson, G.D. and Moutinho, L. (1998) 'Measuring preferred store satisfaction using consumer choice criteria as a mediating factor', *Journal of Marketing Management*, **14**, 705–20.

Johnson, C. and Mathews, B.P. (1997) 'An evaluation of consumers' interpretation of satisfaction', paper presented at the Academy of Marketing Conference, Manchester, UK, pp. 527–38.

Jones, T.O. and Sasser, W.E. (1995) 'Why satisfied customers defect', *Harvard Business Review*, November/December, 88–99.

Kinard, B.R. and Capella, M.L (2006) 'Relationship marketing: the influence of consumer involvement on perceived service benefits', *Journal of Service Marketing*, 21 (6), 359–68.

Lewicki, R.J., McAllister, D.J. and Bies, R.J. (1998) 'Trust and distrust: new relationships and realities', *Academy of Management Review*, 23 (3), 438–58.

Mintel (1996) *Customer Loyalty in Retailing*, London: Mintel.

Mitchell, P., Reast, J. and Lynch, J. (1998) 'Exploring the foundations of trust', *Journal of Marketing Management*, 14, 159–72.

Mittal, B. and Lassar, W.M. (1998) 'Why do customers switch? The dynamics of satisfaction versus loyalty', *Journal of Services Marketing*, 12 (3), 177–94.

Möller, K. and Halinen, A. (2000) 'Relationship marketing theory: its roots and direction', *Journal of Marketing Management*, 16, 29–54.

Morgan, R.M. and Hunt, S.D. (1994) 'The commitment–trust theory of relationship marketing', *Journal of Marketing*, *58* (3), 20–38.

Nowak, L.I. and Washburn, J.H. (1998) 'Antecedents to client satisfaction in business services', *Journal of Services Marketing*, 12 (6), 441–52.

Oliver, R.L. (1981) 'Measurement and evaluation of satisfaction process in retail selling', *Journal of Retailing*, 57, 25–48.

Oliver, R.L. (1997) *Satisfaction: A Behavioural Perspective on the Consumer*, New York: McGraw Hill.

O'Malley, L. (1998) 'Can loyalty schemes really build loyalty?', *Marketing Intelligence and Planning*, 16 (1), 47–55.

O'Malley, L. and Tynan, C. (1999) 'The utility of the relationship metaphor in consumer markets: a critical evaluation', *Journal of Marketing Management*, 15, 587–602.

Palmatier, R.W., Dant, R.P., Grewal, D. and Evans, K.R. (2006) 'Factors influencing the effectiveness of relationship marketing: a meta-analysis', *Journal of Marketing*, 70 (October), 136–53.

Pels, J. (1999) 'Exchange relationships in consumer markets?', *European Journal of Marketing*, 33 (1/2), 19–37.

Pressey, A.D. and Mathews, B.P. (1998) 'Relationship marketing and retailing: comfortable bedfellows?', *Customer Relationship Management*, 1 (1), 39–53.

Ravald, A. and Grönroos, C. (1996) 'The value concept and relationship marketing', *European Journal of Marketing*, 30 (2), 19–30.

Reichheld, F.F. (1993) 'Loyalty based management', *Harvard Business Review*, March/April, 64–73.

Reynolds, N.L. and Simintiras, A. (2000) 'Establishing cross-national equivalence of the customer satisfaction dissatisfaction construct', *European Business Management School*, Working Paper EBMS/2000/7.

Rousseau, D.M., Sitkin, S.B., Burt, R.S. and Camerer, C. (1998) 'Not so different after all: a cross-discipline view of trust', *Academy of Management Review*, 23 (3), 393–404.

Selnes, F. (1998) 'Antecedents and consequences of trust and satisfaction in buyer–seller relationships', *European Journal of Marketing*, 32 (3/4), 305–22.

Shepherd, B.H. and Sherman, D.M. (1998) 'The grammars of trust: a model and general implications', *Academy of Management Review*, 23 (3), 422–37.

Sheth, J.N. and Parvatiyar, A. (1995) 'Relationship marketing in consumer markets: antecedents and consequences', *Journal of the Academy of Marketing Science*, 23 (4), 255–71.

Sheth, J.N. and Parvatiyar, A. (2000) 'Relationship marketing in consumer markets: antecedents and consequences', in Sheth, J.N. and Parvatiyar, A. (eds) *Handbook of Relationship Marketing*, Thousand Oaks, CA: Sage, pp. 171–207.

Sheth, J.N. and Sisodia, R.S. (1999) 'Revisiting marketing's lawlike generalizations', *Journal of the Academy of Marketing Sciences*, 17 (1), 71–87.

Singh, J. and Sirdeshmukh, D. (2000) 'Agency and trust mechanisms in consumer satisfaction and loyalty judgments', *Journal of Marketing Science*, **28** (1), 150–67.

Sitkin, S.B. and Roth, N.L. (1993) 'Explaining the limited effect of legalistic remedies for trust/distrust', *Organisational Science*, **4**, 367–92.

Stewart, T.A. (1997) 'A satisfied customer is not enough', *Fortune Magazine*, **136** (July), 112–13.

Storbacka, K., Strandvik, T. and Grönroos, C. (1994) 'Managing customer relations for profit: the dynamics of relationship quality', *International Journal of Service Industry Management*, **5**, 21–38.

Strandvik, T. and Storbacka, K. (1996) 'Managing relationship quality', in Edvardsson, B., Brown, S.W., Johnston, R. and Scheuing, E.E. (eds) *Advancing Service Quality: A Global Perspective*, New York: ISQA, pp. 67–76.

Swaminathan, V. and Reddy, S.K. (2000) 'Affinity partnering: conceptualisation and issues', in Sheth, J.N. and Parvatiyar, A. (eds) *Handbook of Relationship Marketing*, Thousand Oaks, CA: Sage, pp. 381–405.

Tynan, C. (1997) 'A review of the marriage analogy in relationship marketing', *Journal of Marketing Management*, **13** (7), 695–704.

Tzokas, N. and Saren, M. (2000) 'Knowledge and relationship marketing: where, what and how?', *2nd WWW Conference on Relationship Marketing*, <www.mcb.co.uk/services/conferen/nov99/rm> (accessed 15 November 1999 to 15 February 2000 Paper 4)

Uncles, M. (1994) 'Do you or your customer need a loyalty scheme?', *Journal of Targeting, Measurement and Analysis*, **2** (4), 335–50.

Westbrook, R.A. (1980) 'Intrapersonal affective influence upon consumer satisfaction with products', *Journal of Consumer Research*, **7** (June) 49–54.

Wilson, D.T. (1995) 'An integrated model of buyer–seller relationships', *Journal of the Academy of Marketing Science* **23** (4), 335–45.

Wilson, D.T. (2000) 'An integrated model of buyer–seller relationships', in Sheth, J.N. and Parvatiyar, A. (eds) *Handbook of Relationship Marketing*, Thousand Oaks, CA: Sage, pp. 245–70.

Wright, C. and Sparks, L. (1999) 'Loyalty saturation in retailing: exploring the end of retail loyalty cards?', *International Journal of Retailing and Distribution Management*, **27** (10), 429–39.

Yap, K.B. and Sweeney, J.C. (2007) 'Zone of tolerance moderates the service quality–outcome relationship, *Journal of Service Marketing*, **21** (2), 137–48.

Young, L. (2006) 'Trust: looking forward and back', *Journal of Business and Industrial Marketing*, **21** (7), 92–3.

Notes

1 Bloemer and de Ruyter (1998) call it 'latent satisfaction'.
2 Yap and Sweeney (2007) call this the 'Zone of Tolerance'.

Part II

The core firm and its relationships

As has been previously noted, a feature of 'older' definitions of relationship marketing was a concentration on the 'traditional' supplier–customer relationship. Later contributions to the RM debate were seen to widen the scope to incorporate other relationships. The rationale behind this was that in order to serve your customer properly you had to attend to all the firm's core relationships.

Although there are numerous models, and no single definition, there was a growing consensus that, in addition to a customer focus, a company should be considering a range of partnerships with suppliers, internal customers, institutions and intermediaries (Clarkson *et al.*, 1997, p. 173). In this respect RM is similar to the much older 'stakeholder theory' (Tzokas and Saren, 2000, p. 6). These 'network' or extended relationship theories, ideas and concepts have been advanced by a number of eminent marketing writers, including Christopher *et al.* (1991; 1994), Kotler (1992), Millman (1993), Hunt and Morgan (1994), Doyle (1995), Peck (1996), Buttle (1996) and Gummesson (1996). These writers adopted a view of marketing that continued to acknowledge the importance of managing customer relationships, but recognised that this is only one part of the relationship marketing equation. Although this view has, more recently, been challenged (see Chapter 13) it still best represents what distinguishes RM from other relational concepts and strategies. The common theme is that firms should compete through the development of relatively long-term relationships with all their stakeholders (Hunt, 1997, p. 431; Reichheld, 1996, p. 3). Whether the relational model is represented as 'six markets' (Christopher *et al.*, 1991, p. 13; 1994, p. 21), 'ten players' (Kotler, 1992), 'four partnerships' (Buttle, 1996, p. 3), 'four partnerships and ten relationships' (Hunt and Morgan, 1994, p. 21), or '30Rs' (Gummesson, 1996; 1999, pp. 20–22), the common ground between these theories appears to be the concept of 'the core firm and its partnerships' (Doyle, 1995, p. 34).

The move to RM is seen, therefore, as a move from a dyadic relationship to a multi-faceted series of interrelationships not necessarily dominated exclusively by the supplier–customer interaction. This view of marketing represents a change of emphasis over and above traditional marketing. No longer is marketing simply about exchange (i.e. the transfer of goods and money in the marketplace). It also entails the creation and maintenance of dialogue between suppliers, sellers, customers, clients and others such that all parties are satisfied with the purchasing process (Uncles, 1994, p. 335). Different authors give varying prominence to each stakeholder group, and Gummesson (1999, pp. 20–22) in particular goes into considerable detail regarding the possible relationships a company and its stakeholders can be involved within. For relative simplicity, however, these various relationships may be broken down into four principal groupings. These are customer partnerships, internal partnerships, supplier partnerships and external partnerships. In Part II we will look at each of the four principal groupings in turn. Box II.1 and Figure II.1 show how the relationships types suggested by the different authors are related to each other.

Box II.1 Core relationships

	Customer partnerships	Supplier partnerships	Internal partnerships	External partnerships
Doyle (1995) The core firm and its partnerships	**Customer partnerships**	**Supplier partnerships**	**Internal partnerships** Employees Functional departments Other SBUs	**External partnerships** Competitors Governments External partners
Hunt and Morgan (1994) Four partnerships and ten relationships	**Buyer partnerships** Intermediate Final consumer	**Supplier partnerships** Goods suppliers Service suppliers	**Internal partnerships** Business units Employees Functional department	**Lateral partnerships** Competitors Non-profit organisations Government
Christopher et al. (1991; 1994) Six markets	**Customer markets**	**Supplier markets**	**Internal market** **Employee market**	**Referral market** **Influence market**
Gummesson (1996; 1999) 30Rs	**Classic market relationships** Classic dyad (customer/supplier) Classic triad (above+competitor) Classic network (distribution channels) **Special market relationships** Full-time/part-time marketers The service encounter Many-headed customer/supplier Customer's customer relationship Close versus distant relationship The monopoly relationship The customer as a member The electronic relationship Parasocial relationship (symbol etc.) The non-commercial relationship The green relationship The law-based relationship The criminal network		**Meta relationships** Profit centres Internal customer Quality (e.g. design manufacturing) Employee Matrix relationships Marketing services Owner/financiers	**Mega relationships** Personal/social Mega (e.g. government) Alliances Knowledge relationship Mega alliances (e.g. EU, NAFTA) Mass media

Figure II.1 The core firm and its relationships

● Core firm and its relationships   Doyle (1995)
❷ Four partnerships and ten relationships   Hunt and Morgan (1994)
❸ Six markets   Christopher *et al.* (1991)
❹ 30Rs   Gummesson (1996; 1999)

References

Buttle, F.B. (1996) *Relationship Marketing Theory and Practice*, London: Paul Chapman.

Christopher, M., Payne, A. and Ballantyne, D. (1991) *Relationship Marketing*, London: Butterworth Heinemann.

Christopher, M., Payne, A. and Ballantyne, D. (1994) *Relationship Marketing*, Oxford: Butterworth Heinemann.

Clarkson, R.M., Clarke-Hill, C. and Robinson, T. (1997) 'Towards a general framework for relationship marketing: a literature review', paper presented at the Academy of Marketing Conference, Manchester, UK.

Doyle, P. (1995) 'Marketing in the new millennium', *European Journal of Marketing*, **29** (12), 23–41.

Gummesson, E. (1996) *Relationship Marketing: From 4Ps to 30Rs*, Malmö: Liber-Hermods.

Gummesson, E. (1999) *Total Relationship Marketing: Rethinking Marketing Management from 4Ps to 30Rs*, Oxford: Butterworth Heinemann.

Hunt, H.K. (1997) 'CS/D: overview and future research direction', in Hunt, H.K. (ed.) *Conceptualisation and Measurement of Customer Satisfaction and Dissatisfaction*, Cambridge, MA: Marketing Science Institute.

Hunt, S.D. and Morgan, R.M. (1994) 'Relationship marketing in the era of network competition', *Journal of Marketing Management*, **5** (5), 18–28.

Kotler, P. (1992) 'Total marketing', *Business Week*, Advance Executive Brief No. 2.

Millman, A.F. (1993) 'The emerging concept of relationship marketing', in Proceedings of the 9th Annual IMP Conference, Bath, 23–25 September.

Peck, H. (1996) 'Towards a framework for relationship marketing: the six markets model revisited and revised', *Marketing Education Group (MEG) Conference*, University of Strathclyde, UK.

Reichheld, F.F. (1996) *The Loyalty Effect: The Hidden Force Behind Growth, Profits and Lasting Value*, Boston, MA: Harvard Business School Press.

Tzokas, N. and Saren, M. (2000) 'Knowledge and relationship marketing: where, what and how?' *2nd WWW Conference on Relationship Marketing* <www.mcb.co.uk/services/conferen/nov99/rm> (accessed 15 November 1996 to February 2000, Paper 4)

Uncles, M. (1994) 'Do you or your customer need a loyalty scheme?', *Journal of Targeting, Measurement and Analysis*, **2** (4), 335–50.

7 Customer partnerships

Key issues

- Customer focus
- Service industries
- Customer service
- Episodes and service chains
- Dissolution, exit and withdrawal
- Profit chains

Introduction

As was discussed in the opening chapter, one of the most significant perceived differences between relationship marketing and traditional marketing is that RM is seen to extend marketing's focus beyond the single dyadic relationship of buyer and seller (Gummesson, 1999, p. 1) and to embrace other organisational relationships. Despite this overall change in emphasis, the customer–supplier relationship is still a core issue in RM and indeed across the whole marketing discipline (Möller and Halinen, 2000, p. 31). Christopher *et al.* (1991, p. 21), while acknowledging the benefits of a 'broadened view of marketing', are in no doubt that 'customer markets' should remain the primary focus and, as such, they place them firmly at the centre of their six-markets model of relationship marketing (Figure 7.1).

Figure 7.1
The six-markets
model

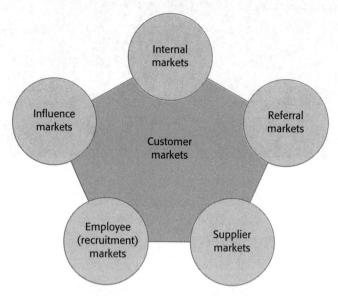

(*Source*: Adapted from Christopher *et al.*, 1991, p. 21)

Customer focus

Another supposed difference between traditional marketing and RM is in the way customers are perceived and valued. Traditional marketing stands accused of treating customers as pawns in a competitive game. By its very nature, this 'market focused' approach is seen to concentrate on increasing market share and emphasising short-term profitability. The priorities of traditional marketers are seen as the 'capture' of anonymous customers, either before competitors or away from them, and manipulating these captives for short-term gain. Target segments were as personal as it got in this marketplace battlefield.

RM, in contrast, focuses not on what you can do *to* your customer but on what you can do *for* your customer (Worthington and Horne, 1998, p. 39) and what you can do *with* your customer, to ensure customer satisfaction. The aim is to treat your customers as valued partners, to establish their needs and develop their loyalty through quality service. As the company statement quoted in Box 7.1 elegantly puts it, 'obsession with the customer should be the most vital factor in business success'.

Box 7.1 Customer focus

The following is a statement from the Burnley Building Society:[1]

> Obsession with the customer should be the most vital factor in business success. The main priority of any business must be to win and keep customers, as failure to do so results in no profits, no growth, no jobs, therefore, no business.

This very 'modern' statement of the importance of the customer was issued by the Burnley Building Society in 1850 yet it appears as relevant today as it did a century and a half ago.

Customer focus motivation

This change of emphasis is not, as has been discussed, wholly altruistic. Company prosperity is still the long-term aim. What is different is that this is perceived, in particular circumstances, to be better achieved by focusing on the individual needs of the customer rather than the agglomerated marketplace. Neither is this change in attitude wholly associated with better and/or more advanced strategy development per se. The development of relational strategies may be seen, in part, as a recognition that the balance of power has shifted from producer to consumer and that many of the strategies of the past are no longer appropriate. The less naive and more worldly-wise buyers of today are more than ever aware that it pays to play the field (Mitchell, 1997, p. 37). In such a marketplace the supplier can no longer count on unquestioning brand loyalty and must offer something more in return for patronage than promotional bribery if sustainable advantage is to be achieved and maintained.

In today's competitive markets there are more and more undifferentiated or little differentiated products and services. Storbacka *et al.* (1994, p. 29) conclude that the degree of differentiation in provider strategies seem to be inversely dependent on the degree of market concentration. In oligopolistic markets there are seldom major differences between the providers. If the core product or service offering leaves little scope for competitive advantage then competitive advantage must be found elsewhere. To this end the development of a 'relationship' with your customer *may* be the most effective way of building something unique and sustainable that your competitor will find difficult to replicate (Buttle, 1996, p. 1).

The realisation that marketing's focus on traditional models was insufficient in the modern marketplace was highlighted (if not driven) by the dramatic changes in national economies. The marketing priority was shifting away from products to services with the growing domination of service economies in major western markets, what Vargo and Lusch (2004, p. 2) call the 'service-centred view' or 'new dominant logic'. The realisation of the importance of the customer-focused approach in service marketing, over and above the market focus, was a major factor in further promoting the relationship marketing concept.

The importance of the reconceptualisation of both products and services in the development of RM cannot be overstated. For this reason a discussion of the nature of services and the importance of customer interaction may, at this stage, be appropriate.

Services

The word 'service' is a frequent feature in the modern marketing vocabulary and never more so than when discussing relationship marketing in general and the supplier–customer partnership in particular. The extensive use of the word and its rapid evolution and development demonstrate the importance of this sometimes elusive concept. Service, in a marketing context, is regarded principally in two ways. The term is used firstly to describe those businesses where the greater part of the company's central offering is intangible. These '**service industries**' are generally seen to have a number of characteristics that appear to differentiate them from physical goods industries.[2] In addition to **intangibility**, these are **inseparability**, **variability**, **perishability** and non-ownership. These characteristics are outlined in Box 7.2.

Box 7.2   Special characteristics of services

Intangibility: A 'pure' service cannot be assessed in the physical sense. It is an abstraction that cannot be directly examined before purchase. The intangible process characteristics that define services include such factors as reliability, personal care, attentiveness, friendliness and these can only be verified once a service has been purchased and 'consumed'. Few services are wholly intangible, however, and many include a tangible element (e.g. a concert programme). Intangibility has a number of implications for the consumer, including increased uncertainty and potential risk.

Inseparability: Products may be produced in one location and sold in another. The production and consumption are, therefore, said to be separable. This is not the case for services, which are produced and consumed at one time and place. This inseparability occurs whether the producer is human (e.g. a doctor) or machine (e.g. an ATM machine). With services, marketing becomes a means of facilitating complex producer–consumer interactions, rather than being merely an exchange medium.

Variability: There are two dimensions to variability. These are the amount the production varies from the norm and the extent it needs to be varied to suit the individual customer. As the customer is usually involved in the production process of a service at the same time as they consume it, it can be difficult to carry out monitoring and control of the production to ensure consistent standards. This is exaggerated in situations where personnel are providing services on a one-to-one basis (e.g. hairdressers) where they must adapt the 'service production' to fulfil an individual customer's needs.

Perishability: Services cannot be stored. For example, if a hotel fails to fill all of its rooms on a particular night, these cannot be 'carried over' to subsequent nights.

Non-ownership: The inability to 'own' a service relates to the characteristics of intangibility and perishability. Where a service is performed no ownership is transferred from the buyer to the seller. The buyer is merely buying the right to a service process (e.g. a solicitor's time).

(*Source*: Adapted from Palmer, 1998, p. 11)

The second most frequent use of the word 'service' is in connection with the phrase 'customer service'. The definition of customer service is difficult to qualify accurately but the term is generally used to describe those features of the offering or exchange that extend beyond the 'core' product or service. The phrase is further seen to imply added value (or, over time, relational benefits[3]) derived as a result of contact between buyers and sellers. Although the two concepts of 'service industries' and 'customer service' are related they are best approached, from an analytical perspective, separately.

Service industries

The intangible nature of service industries has always posed a problem for traditional marketers. Marketing research and teaching has for decades been dominated (and to an extent still is) by 'corporate product marketing'. The realisation that traditional marketing models were proving imprecise when applied to services drove some marketers to consider new approaches and concepts. Indeed, service marketers (together with their industrial marketing colleagues) can be said to have driven marketing research into new areas and been largely responsible for the development of the 'modern' RM approach. As Grönroos (1995, p. 252) notes:

> It is quite natural that the seeds of modern relationship marketing first started to grow in service marketing research. In fact, service marketing started to develop as a discipline because the marketing mix management paradigm and some of its key models fitted service firms' customer relations badly.

Service firms have in theory always been 'relationship orientated' as the very nature of service businesses is relationship based (Grönroos, 1995, p. 252). The reasons behind this are manifold. In service industries a process or performance takes place where the customer is seen to be heavily involved in the creation and delivery (see Box 7.2, inseparability). Service delivery is, therefore, simultaneous with consumption (Johns, 1999, p. 963) and indeed is both defined and co-created with the consumer (Vargo and Lusch, 2004, p. 4). As most service providers compete with companies very similar to themselves (resulting in so-called 'parity offerings') they frequently counter the effect of direct competition by building relationships with their customers. The services literature is clear on the difficulty that consumers have about judging the quality of the service as the 'intangibility' aspect makes it difficult to examine or sample the service (Czepiel, 1990, p. 15–16). The difficulty in evaluating services may suggest it is less likely that consumers will switch after they have developed a relationship with a service supplier (Javalgi and Moberg, 1997, p. 166). In services marketing there is always some form of direct contact (although not necessarily physical) between the customer and the service firm. The repeated encounters provide the occasions where the parties are able to develop a more complex relationship (Czepiel, 1990, p. 16). This '**service encounter**' is such an important part of service delivery that it is frequently called the 'moment of truth'[4] (Johns, 1999, p. 965). This phrase underlines the crucial role each service encounter plays in customer evaluation of a service (Odekerken-Schröder et al., 2000, p. 107).

This customer involvement in service industries can vary considerably. It may sometimes be for a long time, sometimes for a short time, sometimes on a regular basis and sometimes as a one-off encounter (Grönroos, 1995, p. 252). Services can also be defined on the basis of the closeness of the contact. Relationships play an important part in high-contact services (e.g. hairdressers, financial advisers). In low-contact or 'production-line' services (e.g. fast food, FMCG retailing), however, suppliers provide a more standardised service and the best investment here will be in hiring and training staff rather than developing relational programmes (Kinard and Capella, 2006, p. 365).

There is also a significant social aspect to any service relationship. Czepiel (1990, p. 13) sums up the importance of the social nature of services when he comments:

> Service encounters are interesting phenomena with short-run and long-run effects. In the short-run they are the social occasion of economic exchange in which society allows strangers to interact . . . In the long-run encounters provide the social occasions in which buyer and seller can negotiate and nurture the transformation of their accumulated encounters into an exchange relationship. The concept of a marketplace-relationship, the mutual recognition of some special status between the exchange partners, is especially interesting in services marketing.

Modern service marketers, therefore, view marketing as an interactive process within a social context where relationship building and management are the vital cornerstones (Grönroos, 1994, p. 5). Indeed, service encounters can be regarded, first and foremost, as social encounters (McCallum and Harrison, 1985, p. 35), the variety of which goes a long way to explaining the problem of variability (see Box 7.2). It is this social contact that makes it feasible to envisage creating a relationship with the customer, if both parties (or perhaps either; see Chapter 3) are interested in such an association (Grönroos, 1995, p. 252).

Goods versus services

Although RM was (and is) principally seen as a development of, and of particular benefit to, services marketing, its application in the field of consumer goods appears to be growing (see Chapter 13). Although criticism of this broad application exists it reflects a recognition that the boundaries between goods and services (i.e. the distinctions between the tangible and the intangible dimensions of the offer) are becoming blurred (Pels, 1999, p. 2). Although services are frequently described as 'intangible' and their central offering as an 'activity' rather than a tangible object, much 'service output' has a tangible component (Johns, 1999, p. 959). Examples of the importance of this tangible component in service industries can be seen when it is recognised that a restaurant's reputation is, in part, built on the provision of food and drink and a retailer's classification based on the type of physical goods supplied.

Products, meanwhile, are more than ever recognised as having intangible attributes. Indeed, many manufactured products are marketed on the basis of these attributes rather than the hard components or features of the offering (e.g. an automobile's prestige status or a beer's macho image). It is indeed a paradox of marketing that these product manufacturers look to promote the intangible element of their offering while service providers frequently look to create tangible features such as physical evidence (e.g. a bank's impressive façade) to establish their credibility (see Shostack, 1977). Vargo and Lusch (2004, p. 8) describe the association between goods and services in terms of a 'flow of information' and that 'service is the provision of the information to (or use of information for) a consumer who desires it, with or without an accompanying appliance'.

The traditional view of marketing saw services as the occasion where the producer's production process and the consumer's consuming process intersected (Strandvik and Storbacka, 1996, p. 68). In other words, services augmented the product but the product remained the core of the exchange. The RM perspective goes beyond product specifications. Goods and services become part of a holistic, continuously developing service offering (Grönroos, 1999). It implies that the goal of marketing is to customise offerings, to recognise the consumer is always the co-producer and that the more that the customer can be involved in the process the better the fit with their needs (Vargo and Lusch, 2004, p. 11).

Thus the line between products and services and the dominance of the core product appears to be fast fading.[5] Whereas marketers used to talk about the consumption of goods and services they now talk about product experiences (Slater, 1997, pp. 193–4). What once appeared to be a rigid polarity has now become a hybrid (McKenna, 1991, p. 15). Successful marketing is now seen to depend on the capability of firms to add value through different types of service, to the core solution offered to customers (Storbacka *et al.*, 1994, p. 22).

Such is the overlap being witnessed that Strandvik and Storbacka (1996, p. 68) suggest that the goods/services distinction should be removed altogether and that all companies should regard themselves as service companies. In their 'service management' conception, physical products (goods) are seen as 'frozen services' where the real quality or benefit of the purchase is not revealed until it is actually used (consumed) by the buyer. Grönroos (1996, p. 11) too notes that successfully executed RM demands that the firm defines its business as a service business and understands how to create and manage a total service offering.

Firms are having to alter their structures to accommodate this sea-change. Some are even reinventing their businesses. Supermarkets are becoming financiers and major manufacturers are finding other ways to operate other than remaining dependent on sales (e.g. leasing, financing). Movement away from core product towards a total service offering is apparent.

Customer service

Customer service is regarded, in the RM literature, as a separate though related concept to service marketing. Whereas service marketing is seen as embracing all aspects relating to services industries, customer service is seen as wider in application (in that it relates to both product and service suppliers) but narrower in focus, being directly and intimately connected to the customer satisfaction process.

Although definitions of customer service vary, what they all have in common is that they are concerned with relationships at the buyer–seller interface (Clark, 2000, p. 213). Customer service is associated with the building of bonds to ensure long-term relationships of mutual advantage to both parties (Christopher *et al.*, 1991, p. 5). The provision of high levels of customer service involves understanding what (and how) a customer buys and determining how additional value can be added to differentiate it from competing offers (Clark, 2000, p. 212). According to Buttle (1996, p. 9), relationship marketers must believe that excellent customer service produces improved profitability. The quality of this service leads (it is suggested) to customer satisfaction that leads in turn to relationship strength and longevity and (ultimately) results in relationship profitability (Storbacka *et al.*, 1994, p. 23). As we have previously discussed (see Chapter 6), this is rather a simplistic model that is unlikely to stand up to close scrutiny across a wide range of industries. It may, however, be used as a starting point in establishing why customer service is regarded, by relationship marketers, as a crucial element in the marketing process and why so much time and money is being spent by practitioners on measuring customer service levels (see Chapter 6).

Customer service and RM

From the earliest days of relationship marketing research, customer service (created at the supplier–customer interface) has been regarded as a core component in the RM process. As Möller and Halinen (2000, p. 33) note, by the late 1970s RM researchers were arguing that a consumer's quality experiences and subsequent satisfaction with the service were primarily an outcome of an interactive relationship between the personnel and the consumer. Christopher *et al.* (1991, p. 4), more broadly, saw relationship marketing as the unifying concept that brought the individual concepts of customer service, quality and marketing together. It was their judgement that one of the biggest challenges to an organisation was to bring these three critical areas into closer alignment (see Figure 7.2).

Figure 7.2
Relationship marketing orientation

Customer service levels should be determined by research-based measurement of customers nee ds and competitors' performance and must recognise the needs of different market segments

Quality must be determined from the perspective of the customer based on regular research and monitoring

The total quality concept should influence the *process* elements (e.g. managing the 'moments of truth' in the customer encounter)

(*Source*: Adapted from Christopher *et al.*, 1991, p. 4)

Christopher *et al.* (1991, p. 4) suggest that customer service, quality and marketing work in harmony with:

- customer service levels being determined by research-based measurement of customer needs and competitor performance, and in recognition of the needs of different market segments;
- quality being determined from the perspective of the customer based on regular research and monitoring;
- the total quality concept influencing the *process* elements (e.g. managing the 'moments of truth' in the customer encounter) associated with the marketing (or more strictly the relationship marketing) concept.

Traditional marketing, they suggest (p. vii), conceived these three elements as independent 'rather like spotlights shining on a stage and beaming light, often of different intensity at different points on a stage'. The task facing the organisation, they suggest, is to bring about an alignment of the three 'beams' so that the impact upon the customer is more effective. Their conviction was that the point of overlap best describes what RM is all about.

Customer service, therefore, can be seen as playing an important role in the realisation of RM strategies. Its influence at the macro level is complemented by its importance at the micro level of individual relationships and interactions. At this end of the scale customer service may be seen as being concerned with the building of relationships (Clark, 2000, p. 213) through the management of an ongoing sequence of episodes. These episodes, it is suggested, require analysis on an episode by episode basis as well as at the long-term relationship level (Storbacka *et al.*, 1994, p. 22) to establish the success or otherwise of customer service strategies. The influence of customer service at the macro and micro levels emphasises that, although RM takes a holistic view of relationships, it should not ignore the importance of the constituent parts.

Episodes

The concept of a relationship made up of a series of episodes (some of which are 'critical episodes') was introduced briefly in Chapter 6. In terms of customer service it is perhaps the transition from a routine episode to a critical episode that may be seen as determining the adequacy (or otherwise) of customer service performance. As Storbacka *et al.* (ibid., p. 30) note:

> Every episode does not carry the same importance or weight in the customer's evaluation of the relationship. Some [are] routine . . . others [are] 'critical episodes'. A 'critical episode' can be defined as an episode that is of great importance for the relationship. The continuation of the relationship is dependent (both in a negative and positive way) on 'critical episodes' . . . The definition of 'critical episode' is customer specific . . . A routine episode can become critical if, according to the customer, the adequate level of performance is not met.

Critical episodes[6] are, therefore, those specific interactions between customers and the firm's employees that are especially satisfying or especially dissatisfying (Bitner *et al.*, 1990, p. 73). According to Strandvik and Storbacka (1996, p. 73), long-term relationships can be defined as being made up of a 'string of episodes'. They emphasise that when analysing relationship benefits and when attempting to calculate relationship costs the configuration of these episodes has to be understood.

Configuration of episodes

Every relationship will have a number of different types of episodes that differ in content, frequency, duration, etc. and so will be configured differently. During an episode, the customer experiences one or several 'interactions' during which the actual service is produced. As former SAS president Jan Carlzon points out, 'SAS is created 50 million times a year, fifteen seconds at a time' (quoted in Grossman, 1998, p. 32). These interactions may be said to constitute a 'service chain' that can be analysed from both the customer's and the provider's perspective. The customer's perspective of the service chain may be called the 'customer's service path'. Problems frequently come about because managers rarely have responsibility for, or focus upon, the whole service episode. The customer, meanwhile, sees no such distinction, viewing it all as part of the complete service (Strandvik and Storbacka, 1996, p. 72). The association between interactions, episodes and the service chain/customer service path are illustrated in Figure 7.3.

Figure 7.3
Interactions and episodes

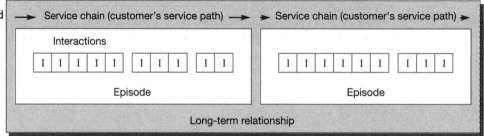

(*Source*: Based on Strandvik and Storbacka, 1996, pp. 71–4)

A company that is service orientated has learnt the importance of service elements of the overall transaction and customer service in the development of added value. A service orientation carries with it the need for a shift in managerial thinking from emphasising the value of transactions to developing the value in relationships (Ballantyne, 2000, pp. 3–6).

Building customer relationships

Relationships rarely develop overnight. Relationships evolve, sometimes over a great amount of time. During this period customers may be seen to move through stages of development. Dwyer *et al.* (1987, p. 15) identified five general phases through which relationships evolve with each phase representing a major transition in how parties regard one another (see Figure 7.4). This model may apply to both business-to-consumer and business-to-business relationships and there is likely to be considerable variation in the length of each stage dependent on the type and purpose of the relationship. The phases are:

■ awareness;
■ exploration;
■ expansion;
■ commitment;
■ dissolution.

Figure 7.4
Evolution of
relationships

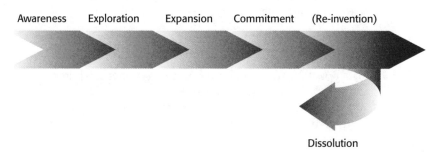

(*Source*: Based on Dwyer *et al.*, 1987, pp. 15–20)

Awareness

Awareness refers to one party's recognition that the other party is 'a feasible exchange party'. Interaction has yet to take place but there may be considerable 'positioning' and 'posturing' to enhance each other's attractiveness.

Exploration

This refers to the 'search and trial period' in the relational exchange. It is in this phase that potential relational partners consider the 'obligations, benefits and burdens' of the relationship. Trial purchases may be made but 'the exploratory relationship is very fragile in the sense that minimal investment and interdependence make for simple termination' (Dwyer *et al.*, 1987, p. 16). The exploration phase is conceptualised in five self-explanatory subprocesses:

- attraction (i.e. why is this likely to be a worthwhile relationship?);
- communication and bargaining;
- development and exercise of power;
- norm development (i.e. normalisation of the relationship);
- expectation development (i.e. what do we want from the relationship?).

Expansion

Expansion refers to the continual increase in benefits obtained by the exchange partners and their increasing interdependence. The critical distinction between this and the previous phase is that 'the rudiments of trust and joint satisfaction established in the exploration stage now lead to increased risk-taking' (ibid., p. 18).

Commitment

Commitment refers to the implicit or explicit pledge, made by the partners, to continue the relationship. At this stage the benefits include the 'certainty' developed from mutually anticipated roles and goals, the 'efficiency' established as a result of bargaining and the 'effectiveness' that comes from trust.

Dissolution

The possibility of withdrawal or disengagement, while not being relationship development as such, is integral to the model. Dissolution is always an option and will, ultimately, always take place (see the section on customer/supplier dissolution or exit, p. 162). Reinventing relationships that have passed their sell-by date may prevent dissolution.

As discussed in previous chapters, not all relationships are as complex or as highly motivated as those suggested by the relationship formulation process outlined above. All relationships, however, have some elements that are recognisable in this model.

Customer service failure

Customer service failures test the commitment of an organisation's customers (Bejou and Palmer, 1998, p. 11). When such a situation exists, however, it may not be the problem per se that causes a critical episode to develop but the company's response to that problem (Stewart, 1998a, p. 9). Every customer will react differently. Each has a propensity to 'stick to' or 'switch' from the status quo and the magnitude of this propensity will depend on the profile of that individual (Hassan, 1996, p. 4) at any point in time. It is also likely that amounts of tolerance will vary from industry to industry or situation to situation. Tolerating a problem does not mean that a 'negative critical incident' is forgotten. Incidents within a relationship are not wholly discrete and further negative incidents may trigger 'memories' of past incidents (Stewart, 1998a, p. 11). Customers are, therefore, seen to engage in a historical evaluation process over time. This evaluation process includes not only the problem itself but also a review of previous problems and how these were handled (p. 10).

Problems may not necessarily lead to long-term dissatisfaction or desertion. Satisfactory response by the supplier *may* lead to renewed levels of satisfaction or, as is sometimes claimed (e.g. Bejou and Palmer, 1998, p. 11), greater satisfaction than existed prior to the incident. Described as the 'recovery paradox' it suggests that if the recovery is highly effective this offers the possibility of achieving higher satisfaction levels than if the failure never happened (Magnini *et al.*, 2007, p. 213). Research by Andreassen (2000, p. 160) suggests that the complainer is usually focused on restoring justice or equity and that a customer's judgement is driven by perceived fairness of the outcome. As Andreassen (p. 167) points out, fairness does not imply that the customer is right. Even when the customer has received an unsatisfactory response from the supplier this may not immediately lead to 'exit' from, or dissolution of, the relationship (for a definition of 'exit', see p. 162). The negative impact may be compensated by the fact that the overall service quality is perceived to be high enough to sustain the relationship (Odekerken-Schröder *et al.*, 2000, p. 110). There may also be substantial switching costs that are powerful barriers to relationship discontinuation with a particular supplier (Stewart, 1998a, p. 10).

Relationship duration

Relationship duration, as one would intuitively suppose, is a mediating influence on the dissolution and a barrier to 'exit'. The effect of relationship duration may, however, not be as straightforward as it would seem. There would appear to be evidence (Bejou and Palmer, 1998, pp. 15–16) that in the early stages of a relationship there is a 'honeymoon period' when some teething problems or even critical episodes may be tolerated. There is no clear evidence why this aberration should exist. Perhaps it is as simple as a reluctance to admit the failings of a new supplier in whom research resources (time and effort) have been expended. Bejou and Palmer's research suggests that this level of 'toleration' drops to a low point after a short period before building up slowly again over time (see Figure 7.5).

Figure 7.5
Tolerance of critical negative incidents

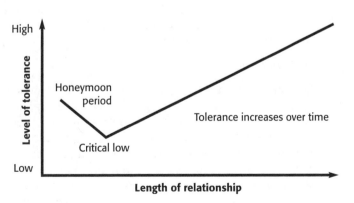

(*Source*: Based on Bejou and Palmer, 1998, pp. 15–16)

Relationship duration may have other effects. Exiting the relationship may be seen as less complicated at an earlier stage than later when heavy investment in the relationship may result in high switching costs (Boote and Pressey, 1999, p. 8). Alternatively, it has been claimed that an individual with a history of positive experiences may be more forgiving of a failure than a first-time customer (Magnini *et al.*, 2007, p. 215).

Customer/supplier dissolution or exit

Whereas many RM models imply continual customer development (e.g. 'the ladder of loyalty', Chapter 4) these fail to acknowledge that some relationships (ultimately *all* relationships) will be terminated.[7] In the real world there is *always* the possibility of dissolution of, or 'exit' from, a relationship.

If the concept of relationship breakdown is examined more closely it may be seen to include three distinct types:

- **dissolution**
- **customer exit**
- **supplier withdrawal**

Dissolution

Dissolution suggests some form of agreed separation. This can be either where both parties agree that it would be in their best interests to go their separate ways or that one party (usually the more powerful of the two) forms this view and the other acquiesces. This form of agreed separation is most likely, but not exclusively, to manifest itself in business-to-business markets, where higher levels of relationship are observed to develop, rather than in consumer markets, where relationships are less likely to be formally acknowledged or contractually arranged. An example of an exception to this generalisation is, for example, a solicitor–client relationship. In the case of most day-to-day commercial relationships there would appear to be little driving or compelling either party to formally acknowledge dissolution.

Customer exit

Customer 'exit' has been defined as a 'term used to denote the economic phenomenon of a customer ceasing patronage of a particular supplier' (Stewart, 1998b, p. 235). In more everyday language, it is where the customer decides to end the relationship. Unlike dissolution, the supplier has little input into the final decision although they may use argument or incentives in an attempt to prevent it. Exit may be most prevalent where competition is high and many alternative sources of supply exist. What is most important, however, is that the customer is aware of these alternatives. Customers who do not have (or know about) alternatives, even when generally dissatisfied, are likely to remain 'spuriously loyal' (Dick and Basu, 1994, p. 101; see Figure 6.3, p. 134). In these situations customers may use their 'voice' (i.e. complain) but effectively stay 'loyal'.

Exit is normally seen to be considered when the consumer recognises a (relative or actual) decline in performance although, as we have argued previously, customer dissatisfaction does not necessarily result in exit. This perceived decline does not necessarily mean that quality standards have fallen but may mean that better quality is seen or perceived to be available elsewhere. Stewart (1998b, p. 235) summarises those situations when exit can be expected as:

> where competition prevails and alternatives are available to the customer, who is aware of them and alert to any absolute or relative deterioration in performance.

'Exit' and 'voice' have their positive sides (see Box 7.3). They are traditionally seen as the means by which 'wayward businesses and organisations respectively, are made aware of their lapses and can begin to right their affairs' (p. 236). Customer 'voice' has long been seen as a means of recovering a critical situation (so-called '**problem recovery**'). Some writers would even suggest that recovery can lead to even greater levels of satisfaction (e.g. Bitner, 1990, p. 76; Bejou and Palmer, 1998, p. 11) although research by Levesque and McDougall (1996, p. 14) supports the contention that satisfactory problem recovery, at best, leads to a return to former satisfaction levels. Problem recovery remains a controversial concept as any satisfaction exhibited may be as a result of satisfaction with the 'bribe' (if a bribe such as a refund, discount, etc. is used as settlement to a problem) rather than satisfaction with the company per se.

A major problem associated with customer exit is how it can be recognised by the supplier as happening or even as having happened. According to Clark (2000, p. 212), 98 per cent of dissatisfied customers never complain about poor service but as a result 90 per cent will not return to the supplier. Except where customers choose to voice their decision to leave or where the relationship is particularly close and of high enough volume that desertion is quickly noticed, exit may go unrecognised. Customers may also choose to use negative 'word-of-mouth' as part of that complaining behaviour (Boote and Pressey, 1999, p. 3). This may cause significant, yet largely unseen, damage to the supplier. Since the advent of the Internet this behaviour has been taken to a new dimension (see Box 7.4 and case study). To complicate matters further exit may only be temporary, particularly in areas such as FMCG. Customers may choose, in the short term, to sample from another supplier or they may be temporarily attracted away by the incentives of competitors only to return at a later date.

Box 7.3 Complaining on the Internet

In the past decade the Internet has become a popular medium for individuals or groups who wish to complain about public and private organisations. There is even a website <www.howtocomplain.com> that advises newcomers on the best way to go about it. Some websites, known as 'gripe sites' are specifically aimed at particular companies such as United Airways <www.untied.com> and McDonald's <www.mcspotlight.com>. Some organisations pay considerable attention to the views of its customers while others do their best to shut the sites down (see case study).

Supplier withdrawal

As the phrase implies, supplier withdrawal is where the separation is at the instigation of the supplier. In our earlier definition of relationship marketing it was suggested that terminating relationships was part of the RM marketing process (see Chapter 2). Without doubt, some (many, perhaps, in certain industries or companies) customers are definite 'burdens' (Håkansson and Snohota, 1995, p. 522). It is indeed quite possible that a small number of highly profitable customers may subsidise a larger number of customers on which the company actually loses money (Sheth and Sisodia, 1999, p. 83). It may even be the case that increasing customer retention in some firms may actually *decrease* profitability and *destroy* value (Reichheld, 1996, p. 34). For these reasons supplier withdrawal must always remain an option.

Supplier withdrawal or termination, as we noted previously, may be managed in two ways. The first is 'customer de-selection' or 'adverse selection' (Smith, 1998, p. 4), effectively 'dumping' the customer. This may be easier said than done (particularly if the customer believes they are on to a good thing). Withdrawal of certain services and/or discriminatory pricing may be ways that this could be achieved, but the danger is that dissatisfaction may spread from the immediate customer to a wider audience. The general outcry in the UK over the closure of Post Office branches in 2007 was an example of this. The second option is by managing the database (see Chapter 11) in such a way as to either exclude unprofitable customers or, at the very least, minimise losses. Neither is an easy option but may be necessary to protect future prosperity.

Box 7.4   The value of complaints

The story of the customer who held a service engineer hostage for three hours until she could force Currys to replace her new, but defective, washing machine would be amusing if it was not so indicative of something a bit more profound when it comes to company–customer relationships.

Yes, it was illegal, but this woman's actions are an example of how customers are increasingly demanding that companies not only listen to them, but learn. The more fervently companies preach customer care, the more they will be held to account when they fail to deliver.

It's surprising that at a time when just about everything can be copied and improved upon by rivals, so many companies are failing to put into place not only a process, but a culture that encourages listening and learning. This is such a missed opportunity – what better way to collect customer intelligence that is proprietary to each and every company than its complaints?

Most companies have a system to deal with complaints. But too often they are formulaic systems, which deal with complaints efficiently but do little to contribute to learning and thus improvement.

The problem is that there are complaints, and then there are complaints. Some are doubtless just big whinges, some are because the customer has made a silly mistake – it's a myth that the customer is always right – but others, if intelligently fed back into strategic thinking, could actually make a competitive difference. This moves well beyond customer satisfaction surveys as a way to gauge customer feeling and hence potential loyalty. Surveys have inherent problems. First, they are too one-directional. They ask customers how they think the company is doing based on its set of criteria. Second, the answers are so aggregated that the level of 'satisfaction' becomes little more than a number on a grid. Meaningless, in other words. And, finally, they talk about satisfaction at a single point in time, which is already in the past. Complaints, on the other hand, are living, breathing focus groups showing what customers don't like, and what they expect, today *and* tomorrow. They could also be about to become big business.

A number of websites are springing up in the US such as eComplaints.com and PlanetFeedback, the latter set up by a Procter & Gamble veteran. The sites provide platforms for consumers to vent their spleen about bad company experiences. Everyone can read the complaints, which are listed anonymously, while they also get redirected to the relevant companies. While eComplaints.com gives the companies a chance to respond, it twists the knife with a constant ranking of the worst offenders. And here's the really clever part: these web ventures also plan to make money through selling back to those companies what could be some very valuable market research.

So it could be that companies will have to listen whether they like it or not. Some won't, if the tale of Dixons and the non-delivery of a dishwasher is true. When the frustrated customer tried to ring the retailer's customer services director, he was told that the customer services director has a policy of not speaking to customers. Dixons vigorously denies this. Maybe it should take advantage of another website, set up for frustrated businesses. It's called customerssuck.com. Really!

(*Source*: Laura Mazur, 'Why firms must listen and learn from complaints', *Marketing*, July 2000)

Profit chains

Many RM authors have visualised the benefits of RM customer–supplier partnerships through the medium of 'customer relationship life cycles' or 'profit chains' (Gummesson, 1999, p. 184). Probably the simplest model was discussed in Chapter 6 and is shown again in Figure 7.6.

Figure 7.6
Simple 'return on relationship' model

As has been noted, this model may be inherently flawed as it is based on an oversimplification that, in many industries, creates problems (Storbacka *et al.*, 1994, p. 23). Customer satisfaction does not always lead to retention, nor does retention always lead to profitability (see relationship economics, Chapter 4).

Gummesson (1999, p. 184) describes a broader model (Figure 7.7) which suggests that building good internal quality operations leads to happy and contented employees producing quality products, which in turn results in customer satisfaction, retention and profitability. This model stems from what Gummesson calls the 'indisputable logic' that when everybody is happy the company will do well. Simple logic should, however, always be treated with a degree of scepticism. As Gummesson himself admits, the general validity of such an argument can be questioned as 'market logic' sometimes follows other patterns.

Figure 7.7
'Return on relationship' model

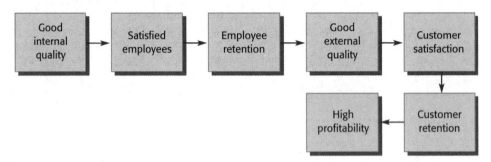

(*Source*: Gummesson, 1999, p. 184)

Storbacka *et al.* (1994, p. 23) also challenge the basic assumption that improving quality leads directly to customer satisfaction and that this necessarily drives profitability. Instead they put forward their own model (Figure 7.8) that reflects some of the many complexities associated with relational strategy development. This model implies that, although a linkage of sorts can be made between the basic components (highlighted in the model), there are so many intermediary stages that any direct association is tenuous. As the old saying goes, 'there's many a slip 'twixt cup and lip'.

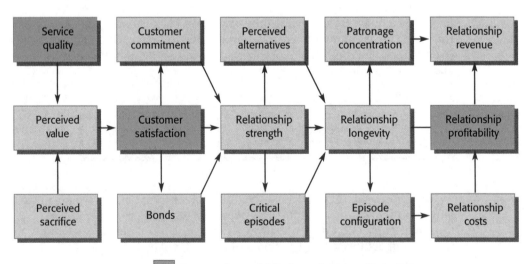

Figure 7.8 Complex 'return on relationship' model   (*Source*: Adapted from Storbacka *et al.*, 1994, p. 23)

The Storbacka *et al.* model shows a much more complex route to profitability fraught with dangers for the relationship marketer. More in-depth descriptions of the arguments associated with these concepts are shown in Box 7.5.

The lesson that appears to be emerging is that paths to sustained profitability through customer–supplier partnerships are fraught with complexity beyond the scope or control of most companies. This is one reason why the argument for greater accountability in marketing (often called 'marketing metrics') is so fraught with danger. Many things that matter most in marketing are immeasurable! On the other hand while firms continue to strive to outperform their competitors, offering 'legendary service' can be risky (Kotler, 1992, p. 51) as again there is no guarantee that this will translate into retention.

Box 7.5 Description of factors in complex return on relationship model (Figure 7.8)

Perceived service quality: Customer's cognitive evaluation of the service across episodes compared with some explicit or implicit comparison standard.

Perceived sacrifice: Perceived sacrifices (e.g. price, physical effort) across all service episodes in the relationship compared with some explicit or implicit comparison standard.

Perceived value: Service quality compared with perceived sacrifice.

Customer satisfaction: Customer's cognitive and affective evaluation based on the personal experiences across all service episodes within the relationship.

Commitment: The parties' intentions to act and their attitude towards interacting with each other; high relationship value will affect commitment positively (see Chapter 6).

Relationship strength: Measured both as purchase behaviour and as communication behaviour (word of mouth, complaints). Loyalty (repetitive purchase behaviour), which is based also on positive commitment by the customer, indicates a stronger relationship (see Chapter 3). The bonds between the customer and the service supplier also affect the behaviour.

Bonds: Exit barriers that tie the customer to the service provider and maintain the relationship. These are legal, economic, technological, geographical, time, knowledge, social, cultural, ideological and psychological bonds (see Chapter 4).

Critical episodes: Episodes that are of critical importance for the continuation of the relationship. Episodes can be critical based on the size of the values exchanged during the episode compared with the parties' resources and based on the experiences during the episode (see Chapter 6).

Patronage concentration: The share of a customer's cash-flow in a certain industry in which the customer chooses to concentrate on one provider.

Relationship longevity: The length of the relationship.

Episode configuration: The episode types and number of each type that occur over time in the relationship between a provider and a customer.

Relationship revenue: The total revenue generated from a customer relationship during a fiscal year.

Relationship costs: The total cost incurred from serving a customer relationship – including direct and indirect costs – during a fiscal year.

Relationship profitability: Relationship revenue minus relationship costs.

(*Source*: Based on Storbacka *et al.*, 1994, p. 25)

Summary

This chapter looked at the central relationship between a customer and supplier. It discussed the focus of RM as being what you can do *for* or *with* as opposed to what you do *to* your customer. Service industries were reviewed initially from the perspective of their influence on RM and what effect this has on the customer–supplier strategy. Customer service was discussed extensively, both as a component central to RM and from the perspective of breaking down customer service into episodes and interactions. Relationship formulation was analysed, as was the nature of relationship dissolution and customer satisfaction. Customer service failures and the concepts surrounding dissolution and exit were examined. Finally the ideas surrounding profit chains and the 'return on relationships' were analysed and debated.

Discussion questions

1 How might organisations operationalise their 'obsession with the customer'?
2 Why are the boundaries between products and services becoming blurred?
3 Imagine a frequent flyer's relationship with an airline. What situations have the potential to become critical episodes if service failure occurs?
4 What, according to your judgement, are the most important factors in the 'profit chain' illustrated in Figure 7.8?

Case study Complaints are there to be heard

Ryanair's attempts to close down a website run by a disgruntled customer provide a cautionary tale for marketers thinking of getting heavy-handed with the growing breed of digitally-savvy consumers.

No longer do hard-done-by customers have to rely on writing to their local MP or appearing on the BBC's *Watchdog* to get justice. Now, with a little technical nous, consumers can establish virtual shrines to their grievances by launching a 'gripe' or 'suck' site with the ability to tear a brand's reputation to shreds.

At the end of last year, a panel on behalf of the World Intellectual Property Organisation concluded that one such gripe site, www.ryanaircampaign.org, set up by Michael Coulston, could remain under his ownership.

The budget airline had failed in its bid to convince the panel that the site fulfilled the three criteria necessary for the domain to be transferred to it. First, that it had made use of the Ryanair trademark in bad faith; second, that it had no rights or legitimate interests in the business; and third, that it could be mistaken for the carrier's official site.

It is hard to see what Ryanair gained from pursuing the action. As well as resulting in the airline coming across as a corporate bully and suppressor of free speech, its action brought Coulston's site to the media's attention, which in turn has led to it attracting visitors in their droves.

Since the case came to light a few weeks ago, Coulston, who set up the site after Ryanair lost his luggage, says the total number of visitors has surged from 12,000 to more than 31,000. He adds that he has been inundated with Ryanair horror stories to the extent that there is now a backlog to be posted on the site.

Nick Johnson, partner at media law firm Osborne Clarke, describes Ryanair's approach as heavy-handed. 'There are times when this kind of action is justified if something misleading about your brand is being said, but the downside is that it gives that gripe more publicity and makes it seem more credible than it might be,' he says. 'It probably left [the decision to pursue the case] to its lawyers, rather than its consumer brand people,' adds Marc Giusti, creative director at digital agency Good Technology.

Website-hosted stories of bad customer-service experiences are now one of the most influential factors governing consumer behaviour. According to Hotwire's Blog Impact Barometer 2006, produced in conjunction with Ipsos/MORI, reviews written by customers or individuals on a blog are believed by 15 per cent of consumers; conversely, only 4 per cent would trust an email from a company.

Managing this flood of information is a priority for marketers, and there are ways of doing so without resorting to litigation. Speed of response is one of the most important factors when dealing with negative online comment, says Graham Lee, account director at online PR company *Immediate Future*. He suggests marketers should be ready to stand up to criticism, though he concedes that this 'requires a degree of transparency that is difficult for some companies'.

A more brutal way of trying to suppress criticism is to anticipate the likely names of irksome websites and register them before the gripers do. Johnson points to the example of Procter & Gamble, which has registered ihateproctelandgamble.com and, interestingly febrezekillspets.com. However, he adds that this approach has limited effectiveness, as Wal-Mart found when it registered ihatewalmart.com, only to find that someone else then registered irealyhatewalmart.com.

Nevertheless, brand-protection companies such as netnames.com are doing a successful trade in snapping up potentially damaging web addresses on behalf of companies; more than 30% of firms in the FTSE 100 subscribe to its service, which aims to prevent these websites reaching the light of day.

Gripe sites and bloggers are also proving a lucrative source of income for digital consultancies, which are being called upon to provide marketers with more sophisticated ways to track what is being said about them.

Companies can receive alerts every time a site is updated, while free tools such as technorati.com trawl the blogosphere. Agencies such as Good Technology and Market Sentinel also use bespoke software that enables brands to 'listen' to what is being said about them, identify opinion-formers and receivers and offer advice on how to respond.

Simon Rogers, director of Market Sentinel, believes good customer service must sit at the heart of any response. 'The most obvious thing to do is talk to the customer and try to deal with the problem, instead of putting your finger in your ears,' he says, citing Dell's decision to ignore blogger Jeff Jarvis's complaints, allowing him to achieve a high profile and dominate its image online.

Although they make uncomfortable reading, consumer moans can provide insight to marketers on what customers really think of their brands. If a site's content is robust but fair, companies have a choice between engaging with the disgruntled customer and making improvements or ignoring the criticism. With the influence of the net rising all the time and the advent of the web 2.0 age, choosing to do the latter is extremely dangerous.

Data file 'Gripe' sites

Land Rover Discovery

<www.haveyoursay.com>

Site dedicated to exposing 'the truth about the new Discovery'. Angry customer Adrian Melrose claims Land Rover has no culture of customer care and is run by 'old-fashioned, arrogant bigwigs'. It has attracted postings from around the world, not all of which are negative.

easyJet

<www.easyjetcomplaints.blogspot.com>

Describes the difficulties experienced by customer Dave Griffiths. The site is the first listed by Google when searching for 'easyJet' and 'complaints'. Its days may be numbered though, as easyGroup is quick to crack down on sites using the words 'easy' and 'easi'.

Carphone Warehouse

<talktalkhell.wordpress.com>

The problems related to Carphone Warehouse's TalkTalk service are well-documented, and now a blog has sprung up to have a moan about it. It is run by an anonymous 'young lady' who writes that she was 'very fed up' with the service she received.

(*Source*: Gemma Charles, *Marketing*, 10 January 2007, p. 15)

Case study questions

1 Did Ryanair do the right thing by pursuing the legal action?
2 What might be the best response for companies such as Ryanair, Land Rover, easyJet and Carphone Warehouse?

References

Andreassen, T.W. (2000) 'Antecedents to satisfaction with service recovery', *European Journal of Marketing*, **34** (1/2), 156–75.

Ballantyne, D. (2000) 'Interaction, dialogue and knowledge generation: three key concepts in relationship marketing', in 2nd WWW Conference on Relationship Marketing, 15 November 1999 to 15 February 2000, Paper 7 <www.mcb.co.uk/services/conferen/nov99/rm> (accessed 15 November 2007)

Bejou, D. and Palmer, A. (1998) 'Service failure and loyalty: an exploratory empirical study of airline customers', *Journal of Services Marketing*, **12** (1), 7–22.

Bitner, M.J. (1990) 'Evaluating service encounters: the effects of physical surroundings and employee responses', *Journal of Marketing*, **54**, 69–82.

Bitner, M.J., Booms, B.H. and Tetreault, M.S. (1990) 'The service encounter: diagnosing favorable and unfavorable incidents', *Journal of Marketing*, **54**, 71–84.

Boote, J.D. and Pressey, A.D. (1999) 'Integrating relationship marketing and complaining behaviour: a model of conflict and complaining behaviour within buyer–seller relationships', European Academy of Marketing Conference (EMAC), competitive paper, Berlin.

Buttle, F.B. (1996) *Relationship Marketing Theory and Practice*, London: Paul Chapman.

Christopher, M., Payne, A. and Ballantyne, D. (1991) *Relationship Marketing*, London: Butterworth Heinemann.

Clark, M. (2000) 'Customer service, people and processes', in Cranfield School of Management, *Marketing Management: A Relationship Marketing Perspective*, Basingstoke: Macmillan, pp. 110–24.

Czepiel, J. (1990) 'Managing relationships with customers: a differentiating philosophy of marketing', in Bowen, D., Chase, R. and Cummings, T. (eds) *Service Management Effectiveness: Balancing Strategy, Organisation and Human Resources*, San Francisco, CA: Jossey-Bass, pp. 299–323.

De Chernatony, L. and Segal-Horn, S. (2001) 'Building on service characteristics to develop successful service brands', *Journal of Marketing Management*, 17 (7/8), 645–69.

Dick, A. and Basu, K. (1994) 'Customer loyalty: towards an integrated framework', *Journal of the Academy of Marketing Science*, 22, 99–113.

Dwyer, F.R., Schurr, P.H. and Oh, S. (1987) 'Developing buyer–seller relationships', *Journal of Marketing*, 51, 11–27.

Grönroos, C. (1994) 'From marketing mix to relationship marketing: towards a paradigm shift in marketing', *Management Decisions*, 32 (2), 4–20.

Grönroos, C. (1995) 'Relationship marketing: the strategy continuum', *Journal of Marketing Science*, 23 (4), 252–4.

Grönroos, C. (1996) 'Relationship marketing: strategic and tactical implications', *Management Decisions*, 34 (3), 5–14.

Grönroos, C. (1999) 'The relationship marketing process: interaction, communication, dialogue, value', in 2nd WWW Conference on Relationship Marketing, 15 November 1999 to 15 February 2000, Paper 2 <www.mcb.co.uk/services/conferen/nov99/rm> (accessed 15 November 2000)

Grossman, R.P. (1998) 'Developing and managing effective customer relationships', *Journal of Product and Brand Management*, 7 (1), 27–40.

Gummesson, E. (1999) *Total Relationship Marketing: Rethinking Marketing Management from 4Ps to 30Rs*, Oxford: Butterworth Heinemann.

Gwinner, K.P., Gremler, D.D. and Bitner, M.J. (1998) 'Relational benefits in services industries: the customer's perspective', *Journal of the Academy of Marketing Science*, 6 (2), 101–4.

Håkansson, H. and Snohota, I. (1995) 'The burden of relationships or who next?', in proceedings of the 11th IMP International Conference, Manchester, UK, pp. 522–36.

Hassan, M. (1996) *Customer Loyalty in the Age of Convergence*, London: Deloitte & Touche Consulting Group <www.dttus.com> (accessed 23 November 2007).

Javalgi, R. and Moberg, C. (1997) 'Service loyalty: implications for service providers', *Journal of Services Marketing*, 11 (3), 165–79.

Johns, N. (1999) 'What is this thing called service?', *European Journal of Marketing*, 33 (9/10), 958–73.

Kinard, B.R. and Capella, M.L (2006) 'Relationship marketing: The influence of consumer involvement on perceived service benefits', *Journal of Service Marketing*, 21 (6), 359–68.

Kotler, P. (1992) 'Marketing's new paradigm: what's really happening out there?', *Planning Review*, 20 (5), 50–2.

Levesque, T. and McDougall, G.H.G. (1996) 'Determinants of cost satisfaction in retail banking', *International Journal of Bank Marketing*, 14 (7), 12–20.

McCallum, J. and Harrison, W. (1985) 'Interdependence in the service encounter', in Czepiel, J.A., Solomon, M.R. and Surprenant, C.F. (eds) *The Service Encounter: Managing Employee/Customer Interaction in Service Businesses*, Lexington, MA: Lexington Books, pp. 25–48.

McKenna, R. (1991) *Relationship Marketing*, London: Addison Wesley.

Magnini, V.P., Ford, J.B., Markowski, E.P. and Honeycutt, E.D. (2007) 'The service recovery paradox: justifiable theory or smoldering myth?', *Journal of Service Marketing*, 21 (3), 213–25.

Mitchell, A. (1997) 'Evolution', *Marketing Business*, June, 37.

Möller, K. and Halinen, A. (2000) 'Relationship marketing theory: its roots and direction', *Journal of Marketing Management*, **16**, 29–54.

Odekerken-Schröder, G., Van Birgelen, M., Lemmink, J., De Ruyter, K and Wetzels, M. (2000) 'Moments of sorrow and joy', *European Journal of Marketing*, **34** (1/2), 107–25.

Palmer, A.J. (1998) *Principles of Services Marketing*, London: McGraw-Hill.

Palmer, A.J. (2005) *Principles of Services Marketing*, 4th edn, London: McGraw-Hill.

Pels, J. (1999) 'Exchange relationships in consumer markets?', *European Journal of Marketing*, **33** (1/2), 19–37.

Reichheld, F.F. (1996) *The Loyalty Effect: The Hidden Force behind Growth, Profits and Lasting Value*, Boston, MA: Harvard Business School Press.

Sheth, J.N. and Sisodia, R.S. (1999) 'Revisiting marketing's lawlike generalizations', *Journal of the Academy of Marketing Sciences*, **17** (1), 71–87.

Shostack, G.L. (1977) 'Breaking free from product marketing', *Journal of Marketing*, **41**, April.

Slater, D. (1997) *Consumer Culture and Modernity*, Cambridge: Polity Press.

Smith, P.R. (1998) *Marketing Communications: An Integrated Approach*, 2nd edn, London: Kogan Page.

Stewart, K. (1998a) 'An exploration of customer exit in retail banking', *International Journal of Bank Marketing*, **16** (1), 6–14.

Stewart, K. (1998b) 'The customer exit process: a review and research agenda', *Journal of Marketing Management*, **14**, 235–50.

Storbacka, K., Strandvik, T. and Grönroos, C. (1994) 'Managing customer relations for profit: the dynamics of relationship quality', *International Journal of Service Industry Management*, **5**, 21–38.

Strandvik, T. and Storbacka, K. (1996) 'Managing relationship quality,' in Edvardsson, B., Brown, S.W., Johnston, R. and Scheuing, E.E. (eds) *Advancing Service Quality: A Global Perspective*, New York: ISQA, pp. 67–76.

Vargo, S. and Lusch, R. (2004) 'Evolving to a new dominant logic for marketing', *Journal of Marketing*, **67** (1), 1–17.

Worthington, S. and Horne, S. (1998) 'A new relationship marketing model and its application in the affinity credit card market', *International Journal of Bank Marketing*, **16** (1), 39–44.

Notes

1 I am indebted to Rebecca Burrell for drawing this statement to my attention.

2 See Palmer, 2005 for a full discussion of the distinguishing features of service.

3 Gwinner *et al.* (1998, p. 102) define 'relational benefits' as 'those benefits (that a) customer receives from long-term relationships above and beyond the core service performance'.

4 The phrase 'moment of truth' is often ascribed to Jan Carlzon of SAS.

5 Not all researchers agree with this viewpoint. For example, see De Chernatony and Segal-Horn (2001, p. 655).

6 Bitner *et al.* (1990) call these 'critical incidents'.

7 Dwyer *et al.*'s (1987, p. 15) five-stage model discussed previously (see Chapter 4) is an example of one that includes the possibility of separation although most models appear (sometimes conveniently) to ignore it.

8 Internal partnerships

Introduction

Relationship marketing has, as the concept developed, wholeheartedly embraced the idea of a 'broadened view of marketing' (Christopher *et al.*, 1991, p. 21). To this end, aspects of RM theory development have mirrored, and to a certain extent borrowed from, events taking place in other areas of business research, including trends in organisational structure (Gummesson, 1999, p. 7). Whereas traditional marketing focused wholly on the external customer, RM stressed the additional significance of the internal customer (Gummesson, 1991, p. 69). The RM concept calls, therefore, not only for an external marketing orientation but also for an 'internal marketing' (IM) focus on employees (Javalgi and Moberg, 1997, p. 173). A variety of terms, including **internal partnerships**, **internal relationships** and **internal marketing**, have been used to describe the concepts discussed in this chapter. Although authors in some cases imply certain nuances and priorities, the terms are used here (perhaps controversially in some people's eyes) interchangeably to avoid confusion. If a distinction is required *internal marketing* can be seen as the process towards the development of *internal partnerships*.

Customer–employee interface

Recognition of the importance of the employee–customer interface has, in large part, promoted interest in internal marketing. Research suggests that the quality of relationships a company has with its customers is largely determined by how employees at the front line make customers feel (Barnes and Howlett, 1998, p. 21). It is also suggested that where the customer–supplier interface is more immediate, the internal climate has a strong impact upon employee satisfaction and customer retention (Payne, 2000a, p. 118), although a direct causal linearity between the two cannot be assumed (Ballantyne, 1997, p. 355). As service offerings are largely through human interaction of some kind, the suggestion is that in service organisations a 'relationship' between employees and customers is almost inevitable (Kandampully and Duddy, 1999, p. 320). Furthermore, relational strategies are more effective when they are built with individual front line staff rather than the firm itself (Palmatier *et al.*, 2006, p. 136).

Internal marketing strategies in service companies in particular are recognised as being of the utmost importance. Whereas a service firm's contact with its customers is normally through its own employees, manufacturing firms in contrast rely on intermediaries or (increasingly) technology (e.g. call centres) to develop some type of relationship. Another factor particularly promoting IM in service companies is that these organisations are invariably labour intensive. As such, internal marketing can help these organisations attract, keep and motivate quality personnel, which in turn helps them improve their capability to offer quality services (Berry, 1983, p. 27).

The stimulus for this internal marketing concern was, therefore, the growth in the importance of services marketing. Despite this, there is no insurmountable reason why internal marketing strategies should be limited to this area (Gummesson, 1991, p. 69). Although the importance of the internal dimension is seen to be particularly relevant to service industries, any organisation's final output, be it a good or service, is almost always the product of a series of operations and processes performed by employees (Buttle, 1996, p. 3). If we accept Vargo and Lusch's (2004, p. 9) hypothesis that value is defined and co-created with the consumer rather than being imbedded in outputs the distinction may be superfluous.

Theory development

The ideas associated with internal marketing and internal partnerships have had a chequered career. The early views of internal marketing were more akin to the 'persuasion of staff to a management-determined situation' (Varey and Lewis, 1999, p. 929), whereas the concept of the internal customer evolved originally through the idea of 'selling jobs' and making them more attractive for employees (Reynoso, 1996, p. 77). In more recent times internal marketing and internal partnerships have become associated with a wide number of (sometimes overlapping) concepts, among them:

■ The concept of employees as (internal) suppliers and customers (Gummesson, 1991, p. 69; Christopher *et al.*, 1991, p. 79). This assumes chains of internal customers (administrative and manufacturing/processing) within an organisation. An employee who, in the normal course of a job, would not deal directly with an external customer would be expected to treat internal customers as if they were external to the organisation.

■ The breaking down of functional barriers within the organisation (Doyle, 1995, p. 29).

■ Efforts to 'sell' the message of an organisation to its internal audience, using similar techniques to those used in the organisation's relationship with its external audiences (Palmer, 1998, p. 201).

■ Marketing that takes place between profit centres inside a decentralised company (Gummesson, 1991, p. 69).

■ The orchestration of staff working together and attuned to the company's mission, strategy, goals (Christopher *et al.*, 1991, p. 29) and the wider operations of the company with its environment (Hogg *et al.*, 1998, p. 893).

■ Any activity within an organisation that focuses staff attention on the internal activities that need to be changed in order to enhance the external marketplace performance (Ballantyne, 1997, p. 346).

■ Activities that improve internal communication and customer consciousness among employees (Hogg *et al.*, 1998, p. 880).

■ Meeting the needs of employees so that they can meet the needs of their customers (Shershic, 1990, p. 45).

■ The development of a company marketing orientation (Gummesson, 1991, p. 69; Varey and Lewis, 1999, p. 926; Hogg *et al.*, 1998, p. 879).

■ How to get and retain customer-conscious employees (Grönroos, 1990, p. 88).

Varey and Lewis (1999, p. 931) while acknowledging the diversity of meanings and usage for the internal marketing concept, see it from a different viewpoint. They conceive that internal marketing can be seen as:

■ a metaphor;

■ a philosophy;

■ a set of techniques;

■ an approach.

Internal marketing as a metaphor suggests that organisational jobs and employment conditions are 'products' to be marketed with the employee as both buyer and consumer. As a philosophy, internal marketing suggests that human resource management (HRM) requires 'marketing-like' activities to 'sell' the requirement of management. The concept also implies that HRM should adopt marketing techniques such as research, segmentation, promotional communications and advertising internally to inform *and* persuade. Finally, internal marketing may be regarded as a style of management with key (and perhaps contradictory) objectives of flexibility and commitment.

These ideas converge to suggest the prime constituents of IM. It was this broader concept that Christopher *et al.* (1991, p. 30) were describing when they noted that internal marketing was:

> recognised as an important activity in developing a customer-focused organisation. In practice, internal marketing is concerned with communications, with developing responsiveness, responsibility and unity of purpose. Fundamental aims of internal marketing are to develop internal and external customer awareness and remove functional barriers to organisational effectiveness.

Internal marketing is perceived as a holistic approach to the business in general but to HRM and marketing in particular (Hogg *et al.*, 1998, p. 880). As internal interactions inevitably occur between departments in organisations, organisational dynamics are of particular relevance to both the service products and service delivery (Reynoso, 1996, p. 77; Reynoso and Moores, 1996, p. 55). Indeed, it is perceived as so important to the success of an operation that Gummesson (1991, p. 74) proposes that marketing in the future should be presented and taught from this holistic perspective and be truly integrated with other functions of the firm. In practical terms this would encompass HRM policies designed to attract, select, train, motivate, direct, evaluate and reward personnel (Palmer, 1998, p. 201) and indeed extend this influence to other parts of the organisation by breaking down the traditional functional barriers that exist in many companies. Gummesson (1991, p. 72) sees this as a change from 'marketing management' to 'marketing-orientated company management'.

The internal market[1]

Internal marketing, in the general sense, is seen to describe 'any form of marketing within the organisation which focuses attention on the internal activities that need to be changed in order that marketing plans can be implemented' (Christopher *et al.*, 1991, p. 26) and that enhances external marketplace performance (Ballantyne, 1997, p. 346). Internal marketing is essentially a way of enabling an organisation to recruit, motivate and retain customer-conscious employees in order to boost employee retention and customer satisfaction levels (Clark, 2000, p. 217). It can be broadly interpreted as those activities that improve internal communications and customer consciousness among employees, and the link between those activities and external marketplace performance (Hogg *et al.*, 1998, p. 880). In addition to this general meaning, the term can be applied to the concept that every person in an organisation is both a customer and a supplier (Buttle, 1996, pp. 3–4). The essence of internal marketing is not, according to Varey and Lewis (1999, p. 926), a phenomenon of the post-industrial era since there is some evidence of associated attitudes and methods in literature produced early in the twentieth century. What is new is the active market-orientated approach.

Internal marketing benefits

Internal marketing focuses on the three core value-adding activities, innovation, effective processes and customer support, and builds networks which design in quality (Doyle, 1995, pp. 26–7). It involves retaining customer-conscious employees (Grönroos, 1990, p. 88) and the development of employee empowerment to better satisfy the needs of the customer. Internal partnerships reflect the belief that if management wants its employees to deliver an outstanding level of service to customers, then it must be prepared to do a great deal for its employees (Reynoso, 1996, p. 77).

Internal marketing, therefore, is seen as a requirement for the successful implementation of the internal partnership concept and, ultimately, of RM. According to Buttle (1996, p. 12) the goal is to promote the development of the new culture, to persuade employees that it is sensible to buy into the new vision, and to motivate them to develop and implement RM strategies. In this way internal marketing partnerships become a core business philosophy (Palmer, 1998, p. 201) rather than solely the preserve of the marketing department.

The functional interface

The CIM definition of marketing as 'management process' implies a functional marketing department responsible for a fixed number of responsibilities closely associated with the traditional marketing mix. Indeed, in recent years, the claim has been made that marketing was more and more restricted to the promotional aspects of that mix. RM strategies imply breaking down functional barriers in an organisation. The oft-repeated maxim (at least in marketing circles) that 'whereas not everything is marketing, marketing is everything' (see McKenna, 1991, p. 18 and Ballantyne, 1997, p. 345 for variations on this theme) suggests that a **marketing orientation** means more than can possibly be handled by the marketing department alone. Rather, marketing orientation means 'the organisation-wide generation of market intelligence, dissemination of that intelligence across departments and organisation-wide responsiveness to it' (Kohli and Jaworski, 1990, p. 4). This organisational-wide stance is supported by evidence[2] from experienced marketers who see little distinction between a business plan and a marketing plan. Marketing in this context should be leading the effort of designing and building cross-functional business processes and should, therefore, be at the heart of the organisation's strategic planning.

A clear implication of research by Bitner (1990, p. 76) also suggests the need for coordination among functional areas particularly in service organisations. She notes that 'typically decisions about employees and the design of physical evidence are made, not by marketers, but by human resource managers, operations managers and design professionals'. This observation emphasises the need to create the organisation of marketing around cross-functional processes as opposed to organisational functions (Payne, 2000b, p. 47). According to Doyle (1995, p. 23):

Marketers have generally made the mistake of seeing the subject [Marketing] as a fundamental discipline rather than an integrated business process. Marketing Directors have sought to make Marketing decisions rather than share responsibility for satisfying customers with cross-functional teams. Unfortunately the only decisions where Marketing has sole responsibility tended to be tactical; promotions, line extension and superficial positioning policies.

Human resources

Over the past few decades, firms have begun to recognise that, more often than not, the limiting factor to their success is far more predicated on the availability of satisfactory skilled people than the availability of other resources such as capital or raw materials (Christopher *et al.*, 1991, p. 26). Recent studies on the major concerns of managers back up the importance of internal resources. The studies show employee communication and involvement, the redesign of business processes and the importance of the perceived relationship between employees and customer satisfaction as being top of managers' hit-lists (Varey and Lewis, 1999, p. 926).

Nowhere is the importance of human assets more evident than in service operations, many of which can no longer be valued on the basis of their physical assets but on the basis of 'intellectual capital'. This intellectual capital, according to Gummesson (1999, p. 190) comes in two types:

- individual capital;
- structural capital.

Individual capital

Individual capital covers the employees and their qualities, including knowledge, skills and motivation, plus the individual's network of relationships inside and outside the company.

Structural capital

Structural capital, as we have noted previously (see Chapter 3), is the embedded knowledge inseparable from its environment and which does not evaporate when an employee leaves. This includes established relationships, the climate and culture, systems, contracts, image and branding. Core competencies, based on specific knowledge, reside in the organisation's staff and the systems that it has developed (Doyle, 1995, p. 28). As the success of 'individual capital' development has the potential to enhance 'structural capital', maintaining the former is crucial. The firm has a responsibility, therefore, to develop company-specific skills and to motivate its staff to harness these skills energetically to deliver superior value to the customer (p. 28).[3]

Teamwork

Research by Reynoso and Moores (1996, p. 58) suggests that one of the key factors contributing to any discrepancy between service quality specifications and the actual service delivered is poor teamwork. It is the existence of **'functional silos'** that are seen to act independently and with little coordination that is frequently the major cause both of disagreement and 'non-goal congruence' (a frequent criticism coincidentally of CRM). For a firm pursuing RM strategies, the internal interface between marketing, operations, personnel and other functions is of strategic importance (Grönroos, 1994, p. 12). This viewpoint acknowledges that all activities in a company are interrelated – what Gummesson (1991, p. 65) calls 'inter-functional dependency'. The interesting issue is whether a holistic marketing orientation calls for more marketing department direct authority over the operating activities of the firm (Ballantyne, 1997, p. 345) or whether the marketing function per se has reached its sell-by date and that cross-functional teams are the answer to the functionality problem. In many ways this conundrum is at the heart of the current RM/CRM debate (see Chapter 13). It is unlikely that any solution is right in every case. Each company will need to find an organisational form that is both effective and complements its climate and culture.

Part-time marketers

Many companies have centralised marketing and sales staff, who might be called 'full-time marketers'. These employees do not, however, represent all the marketers and salespeople the firm has at its disposal (Grönroos, 1996, p. 8). Gummesson (1990) has coined the phrase **'part-time marketers' (PTM)**, in his book of the same name, to describe these non-marketing specialists who, regardless of their position in the company, are crucial to the company's marketing effort. These PTMs include all of those employees who, in any way, influence customer relations, customer satisfaction and the customer's perceived quality (Gummesson, 1991, p. 60). As Grönroos (1996, p. 8) notes, in many situations their impact on customer satisfaction and quality perception is more important to long-term success in the marketplace than that of the full-time marketer.

Christopher *et al.* (1991, p. 17) too recognised the part that both marketers and part-time marketers play in the marketing process. They further subdivide these categories based on the frequency of contact with the company to produce four types, as shown in Figure 8.1:

- *Contractors*: Contractors have frequent or periodic customer contact and are heavily involved with 'conventional' marketing activities, including sales and customer service roles. They should be well versed in the company's marketing strategy, well trained and motivated to serve the customer on a day-to-day basis. They should be recruited based on their potential to respond to customer needs and evaluated and rewarded on this basis.
- *Modifiers*: Modifiers, while not directly involved with conventional marketing activities, have frequent customer contact. This group includes receptionists,

Figure 8.1
Employee
influence on
customers

	Involvement with marketing	Not directly involved with marketing
Frequent or periodic customer contact	**Contractors**	**Modifiers**
Infrequent or no customer contact	**Influencers**	**Isolateds**

(*Source*: Adapted from Christopher *et al.*, 1991, p. 17)

accounting staff, delivery personnel, etc. Modifiers should have a clear view of the organisation's marketing strategy and the part they play in it. They should be trained in the development of customer relationship skills and monitored and evaluated on this basis.

■ *Influencers*: Influencers are involved with elements of conventional marketing, but they have infrequent personal contact. They are, however, very much part of the implementation of the organisation's marketing strategy. Roles include research and development, market research, etc. A major skill to be nurtured here is 'customer responsiveness'. Influencers should be evaluated and rewarded according to customer-orientated performance standards. Opportunities to meet customers in a programmed way may be also be valuable.

■ *Isolateds*: Although these employees have neither regular contact with customers nor regular input into conventional marketing activities, their performance could affect successful fulfilment of the company's marketing strategy. Included in this category, for example, are staff members from personnel and data processing departments. The appropriate attention should be given to maximising the impact of their activities on marketing strategy and they should be rewarded accordingly.

Climate and culture

The management of individual encounters is, according to Bitner (1990, p. 69):

nested within broader management issues of organisational structure, philosophy and culture that also can influence the service delivery and, ultimately, customer perception of service quality.

Organisations are not, after all, tangible objects but rather social constructs made up of people, activities, thoughts, emotions and other intangibles (Gummesson, 1994, p. 10). As Payne *et al.* (1995, p. 95) note, **organisational climate** and **organisational culture** have become recognised as the foundation of long-term marketing effectiveness. They define these linked concepts as:

■ *climate*: the policies and practices that characterise the organisation (and, in turn, reflect its cultural beliefs).

■ *culture*: the deep-seated, unwritten system of shared values and norms within the organisation (which in turn dictates its climate).

The climate and culture of an organisation are dependent on how the employees view that organisation and its goals (Hogg *et al.*, 1998, p. 881). In particular, they affect both how the individual perceives his or her role within the organisation and how those roles relate to the wider operation of the organisation with its environment (p. 893). Internal marketing and the development of internal partnerships suggest the creation of an organisational climate where cross-functional quality improvements can be sponsored and worked upon by the people whose job processes are involved (Christopher *et al.*, 1991, p. 79).

Change within organisations frequently causes concern among employees even if that change will ultimately benefit them in some way. With the dramatic change inherent in today's strategy development, a supportive organisational culture is required to successfully implement changes. Dangers are also inherent in change. Climatic problems can quickly develop if issues are not dealt with before extensive change takes place.

Employee retention and loyalty

It is unarguable that the longer an employee stays with a company, the more familiar he or she will become with the business. It may also be generally true that longevity of employment increases learning. According to Reichheld (1993, p. 68) this learning increases the value of the employee to the company based upon how long the worker is expected to stay and grow with the business. This may be somewhat overstating the point in that 'longevity' in itself cannot guarantee 'value', and 'long service' can sometimes be associated with fixed ideas and inflexibility. The general point being made, however, is that experience is frequently sacrificed in favour of expediency, particularly in cost-cutting exercises, a situation highlighted recently (April 2000) in a British government report. Although the expression 'our employees are our greatest assets' is often heard, it is frequently no more than a platitude (Christopher *et al.*, 1991, p. 16).

Empowerment

Empowerment was a buzzword of the 1990s. An important driver towards empowerment strategies came from the difficulty of non-homogeneity of delivery in service
markets and the need for speedy decision-making at the customer interface.
According to Bowen and Lawler (1992, p. 37) the more enduring the relationship,
and the more important it is in the service package, the stronger the case for empowerment. The firm must be able to create an intra-organisational environment in
which employees are flexible and prepared to take decisions without referring back to
management (Chaston *et al.*, 2000, p. 637). Empowerment, however, appears to have
been the second-choice solution. In the 1970s, in a bid to overcome the non-homogeneity difficulty, companies (e.g., McDonald's) took a 'production-line' approach to
services (Bowen and Lawler, 1992, p. 31). Through duplication of activities, simplification of tasks and clear divisions of labour, companies were able to keep
organisational control and produce efficient, low-cost, high-volume service operations with satisfied customers. This system would appear to work well in highly
repetitive and relatively simple operations (e.g. fast food outlets or FMCG retailers).

It is, however, one of the oft-repeated social criticisms of the move from manufacturing economies to service-led economies that skilled jobs are being replaced by low-paid
and little-skilled service operations. To an extent (and particularly where there is a production-led approach) this is true. In general, however, it is the rules and lines of
authority which most restrict the innate personal skills of employees being fully (and
satisfactorily) realised. Empowerment, therefore, according to Tom Peters, is necessary
to 'dehumiliate' work by eliminating those policies and procedures of the organisation
that demean and belittle human dignity (quoted in Zemke and Schaaf, 1989, p. 68).

In other areas of service (and indeed some product) provision there is a need for
more complex interactions than suggested by the production-line approach. In some
cases these interactions may involve instant decision-making on the part of the
employee (e.g. information desk, complaints office). In these cases, organisational
control cannot be maintained at the point of interaction (although guidance may be
involved beforehand and, potentially, censure afterwards). Effectively, the manager
must trust the employee to make a decision that will be best from the company's perspective. It is this trust that underlies empowerment.

Empowerment looks to the performer of the tasks for solutions to problems, and
to these employees to suggest new services and products and to solve problems creatively and effectively. Jan Carlzon, former CEO of SAS (quoted in Bowen and Lawler,
1992, p. 32), sees it as freeing employees from 'rigorous control by instructors, policies and orders, and to give freedom to take responsibility for ideas, decisions and
actions'. This, he predicts, will 'release hidden values that would otherwise remain
inaccessible to both the individual and the organisation'.

Operationalising empowerment

Bowen and Lawler (ibid.) define 'empowerment' as the sharing, with front-line employees, of four organisational ingredients that in production-led service and many product industries would be in the hands of senior managers. These are:

■ information about organisational performance;

■ rewards based on organisational performance;

■ knowledge that enables employees to understand and contribute to organisational performance;

■ power to make decisions that influence organisational direction and performance.

Research by Lindgreen and Crawford (1999, p. 235) suggests that, for employee empowerment to work, there has to be investment in proper customer-focused staff training to enhance such different skills as industry knowledge, customer service, communications, presentation and teamwork. When managers in organisations establish policies, procedures and behaviour that show concern for the organisation's customers they are, according to Schneider (1980, p. 53) 'service enthusiasts'. This contrasts strongly with managers interested simply in systems maintenance and routine adherence to uniform operating guidelines and procedures ('**service bureaucrats**').

As well as recognising the value of interpersonal relationships and the importance of showing concern for the customer, the difference between the 'service enthusiast' and the 'service bureaucrat' is the former's emphasis on the flexible application of rules, procedures and systems maintenance. This assumes that all employees' workplace objectives are congruent with those of the organisation and that some form of consent must exist between employers and employees (Palmer, 1998, p. 200).

Empowerment benefits and cautions

Empowerment has a number of perceived benefits. According to Bowen and Lawler (1992, pp. 32–3), it results in:

■ quicker online response to customers' needs during service delivery;

■ quicker online response to dissatisfied customers during service recovery;

■ employees feeling better about their jobs and themselves;

■ employees interacting with customers with more warmth and enthusiasm;

■ empowered employees being a great source of service ideas;

■ great 'word of mouth' advertising and customer retention.

As with most management concepts, empowerment benefits should be considered against the potential downside (see Box 8.1). To begin with, although the benefits are clear, the implementation is fraught with difficulty. Most commonly, problems involve managers who wish to retain authority or employees who have no wish to have such a responsibility. It is also clear that some customers may prefer to be served by non-empowered employees, for example in self-service situations (p. 37). Empowerment may not, therefore, always be the preferred option. Despite Peter's warnings about the belittling nature of some service jobs, Bowen and Lawler (p. 37) note that the production-line approach makes sense if a company's core mission is to offer high-volume service at the lowest cost because 'industrialising' services can take advantage of economies of scale by leveraging volume throughput. The added value of this may be seen to be cheap, quick and reliable service versus high-level customer interaction or alternatively performing a straightforward 'transaction' versus 'managing a relationship'.

Box 8.1   The downside of empowerment

In January 2002 customer service agents at Carphone Warehouse were empowered to raise credit notes to the value of £10 per customer if a customer complained about the quality of service. This not only led to an increase in credit notes but, perversely, to an increase in complaints. A hundred accounts were analysed over a period of three months. The resulting analysis showed that 35 per cent of customers who had received a credit in the first month complained subsequently and requested a credit note.

(*Source*: Chouglay, 2002)

There are also (and inevitably) costs associated with empowerment. These are summarised by Bowen and Lawler (pp. 33–4) as:

- higher investment in selection and training;
- higher labour costs;
- slower/inconsistent service delivery as individual treatment slows down the operation;
- poor reaction of customers who see employees negotiating 'special deals' or terms with other customers;
- too many 'give-aways' and bad and costly decisions.

Empowerment, therefore, may produce benefits, particularly, but not exclusively, in service industry settings. It must be recognised, however, that it is not a panacea for every internal management problem.

Internal marketing implementation

Obtaining and understanding the employee perspective is a critical tool in managing customer satisfaction as it enables managers to exercise internal marketing – in effect meeting the needs of employees so that they can meet the needs of customers

(Shershic, 1990, p. 45). Internal marketing, it is claimed, is a relationship development process in which staff autonomy and know-how combine to create and circulate new organisational knowledge. This process will highlight those existing internal activities that require change to enable enhanced quality in marketplace relationships (Ballantyne, 1997, p. 354). It is built on the premise that employees want to give good service just as customers want to receive it, and managers who make it easier to achieve this will find that both customers and employees are likely to respond positively (Schneider, 1980, p. 54).

At a tactical level internal marketing may include ongoing training and encouragement of formal and informal communications (such as newsletters), whereas at a strategic level internal marketing extends to the adoption of supportive management styles and personnel policies, customer service training and planning procedures (Hogg *et al.*, 1998, p. 880). Doyle (1995, p. 29) suggests that the development of internal strategies requires a three-stage approach:

- The organisation has to demonstrate a commitment to the security and development of its employees that ranks at least equal to that of its shareholders.
- The organisation has to create a structure where functional barriers are torn down. It will have 'flatter' organisational levels, empowerment for front-line staff and will focus efforts on the three core value-adding processes of operations, customer support and innovation.
- Top management must then provide leadership by reinforcing these values and offering a vision of what the organisation will become.

Reynoso and Moores (1996, p. 57) suggest that implementing an internal customer approach involves a number of processes. These include the creation of internal awareness, the identification of internal customers and suppliers, the identification of the expectations of the former, the communication of those expectations to internal suppliers, and the development of a measure of internal customer satisfaction and feedback mechanisms. The danger inherent in all of these proposals is that internal marketing may be limited in what it contributes to the wider issues of organisational culture as it all too often defaults to an internal communications exercise (Meldrum, 2000, p. 13).

Staff development

It appears that the satisfaction of staff with their work is positively related to customer satisfaction only when that work is customer orientated. In a detailed analysis of over 16,000 bank staff, over 25 per cent of employees revealed that they were dissatisfied, in particular, with the key support mechanisms provided by management intended to facilitate deeper relationships with customers (McAdam, 2005, p. 5). There is no evidence, however, that a broader causality between staff satisfaction and customer satisfaction exists (Ballantyne, 1997, p. 356). Grönroos (1996, p. 10) advocates what he terms a '**process management perspective**' (PMP). PMP, he suggests, is very different from the traditional functionalistic management approach based on 'scientific management' principles. A PMP approach would see department boundaries broken down and the work-flow (including sales and marketing activities, productive, administrative and distributive activities and a host of 'part-time' marketing activities) organised and managed as a value-creating process.

Knowledge may be the key driver to staff effectiveness (and indeed satisfaction). As Gummesson (1987, p. 23) notes, all 'contact personnel' must be well attuned to the mission, goals, strategies and systems of the company otherwise they would be unable to handle those crucial 'moments of truth' that occur during the interaction with customers. This is particularly evident in service firms where the interface with the customer is broad and intense, but may also be generally true of all companies.

Reward systems too may play a crucial role in internal partnership development. At present, sales and marketing management are widely rewarded with a mix of basic salary and performance-related bonus or commission. As Buttle (1996, p. 13) notes, the common performance criteria include sales volume and customer acquisition data that only reflects the short term. Under an RM strategy employees are more likely to be rewarded by customer profitability, account penetration and customer retention (see Box 8.2).

According to Kandampully and Duddy (1999, pp. 321–2) an RM programme should:

> be considered the firm's life-blood – percolating through all ranks, departments, functions and assets of the firm – with the ultimate aim of simultaneously offering and gaining value at all levels. The firm's marketing, management, operations, finance and human resources should constitute nurturing organs assisting the firm to develop, create and nurture the continuous flow of value between the respective stakeholders inside and/or outside the organisation.

Box 8.2 Partnership in action

John Lewis Partnership is a retail organisation that has always treated its staff as integral to the business. Staff members are not only called 'partners' in practice but are so in reality. They share in all 'partnership benefits', including dividends, and, through their representative, have a say in the strategic and tactical development of the store group. In an age of intense retail competition, will John Lewis be forced to restructure more in line with other UK retailers? It would seem not if communiqués from head office are to be believed. There may have to be some rebalancing of priorities, however. According to John Lewis Partnership's administration director, writing in the organisation's internal magazine, the *Gazette*, 22 May 1999, 'the Partnership is a commercial enterprise, and if it is to survive in an increasingly competitive world it must balance the interests of "partners" with the expectations of customers'.

Conclusion

RM's environment is not only the market and society in general but also includes the organisation and it is, therefore, dependent on changes in organisational design (Gummesson, 1994, p. 10). Internal marketing is widely seen as a prerequisite for the successful implementation of RM, although responsibility for its implementation may not be solely the domain of marketers (Clark, 2000, p. 220). According to Grönroos (1994, p. 13), if internal marketing is neglected then external marketing suffers or fails. Research by Barnes and Howlett (1998, p. 21) suggests that the quality of relationships a company has with its customers is very much determined by how employees make customers feel. Schneider (1980, p. 63) reports research which concludes that if employees perceive a strong service orientation customers report they receive superior service. It works both ways. The success of RM is itself dependent, to a large extent, on the attitudes, commitment and performance of employees. If they are not all committed to their role as marketers (full-time and part-time) and are not motivated to perform in a customer-orientated fashion, RM strategy will fail (Grönroos, 1996, p. 12).

The adoption of RM concepts internally suggest a recognition of the need for a new type of organisation with a new type of management (Gummesson, 1994, p. 10). There is a broad recognition of the failure of conventional 'chimney stack' management with its functional bunkers (including marketing) 'embodying an abstract notion of marketing orientation . . . but a practical unwillingness to get out in the field and deliver on customer service and satisfaction' (O'Driscoll and Murray, 1998, p. 395). Doyle (1995, p. 35), for example, predicts that the changes will lead to smaller marketing departments staffed by a few generalists with big responsibilities for achieving results through teams of internal and external partners and (p. 38) goes on to suggest that:

> Marketing Managers will have to work more effectively as team players; proactively putting teams together and co-operating with other functions to enhance the core processes of innovation, order fulfillment and customer service. Functional boundaries in the 'professional core' will be seen as irrelevant and general management skills will be much more prized.

Marketing researchers in general strongly endorse these sentiments. Chaston (1998, p. 280) sees internal marketing as requiring priority over any other organisational process when seeking to achieve the goal of customer satisfaction. Grönroos (1996, p. 12) sees RM success as highly dependent on a well-organised and continuous internal marketing process. Buttle (1996, p. 193) cites evidence from the service sector (including the Post Office, banking, hospitality and not-for-profit organisations) that also suggests that organisations are 'likely to be less effective externally if the expectations of internal relational partners are not met'.

Increasing numbers of companies have recognised the need for internal marketing programmes, and the implementation of such programmes has gained momentum in recent years (Clark, 2000, p. 220). On a cautionary note, Varey and Lewis (1999, p. 927), while acknowledging that internal marketing is an evolving subject, note that there is not yet any firm theory or a strong base of empirical evidence to show how and why it is of value to managers. Adoption of internal marketing strategies is, therefore, no guarantee of success. In 1995, Doyle (1995, p. 26) cited three companies, Marks & Spencer, Virgin Airways and The Body Shop, as examples of companies which had eliminated functional boundaries and which had no marketing directors or conventional marketing departments. Over the past few years these three companies have had mixed fortunes. Marks & Spencer, in particular, has faced considerable problems in the past decade. British Airways, cited as the 'most famous' of internal marketing advocates (Clark, 2000, p. 220), has also had continuing difficulties despite the introduction of its 'hearts and minds' employee programme. The argument for internal marketing is strong in theory although, perhaps, more difficult to implement and sustain.

Summary

This chapter looked at internal partnerships (also referred to as internal marketing). It highlighted the importance of the employee–customer interface and the development of an internal marketing approach to the overall success of relational strategies. It reviewed the significance of human resource management in the development of internal marketing and the broader need to remove all functional barriers from the organisational environment. The importance of full-time and part-time marketers was acknowledged and the advantages of teamwork considered. The benefits of employee retention and loyalty were noted and the effect of climate and culture on that employee loyalty discussed. Empowerment was seen as a recognisable feature of internal marketing, but it was noted that costs as well as benefits accompany such a policy. Finally, the means of implementing internal marketing was discussed.

Discussion questions
1 What are the basic concepts that underlie internal marketing strategies?
2 Suggest ways in which functional barriers (e.g. between marketing and human resource management) could be broken down.
3 What are the principal advantages and disadvantages of empowerment?
4 What type of organisational climate and culture might best suit the implementation of relationship marketing?

Case study   Who are your most ardent fans?

It's been more than 40 years since the Rolling Stones officially began their career in the music industry. Certainly by almost any standard they are the world's most successful rock and roll band, and one of Britain's most memorable exports.

As one of the group's longstanding fans I can vouch for their ability to get and keep customers. Though I adore their music, I attribute their success more to their development of a strong brand and their phenomenally effective marketing. They know the value of creating a loyal audience. And what I like best is that they always deliver a high-spirited performance even when they're playing songs for the thousandth time.

Who are your most ardent fans? Let us take a lesson from the Stones about creating loyalty, but, instead of focusing on external audiences, let's turn inward to our employees. It's true, your employees are your most important audience. You stand little chance of success if they are not completely sold on your product or service. If they're not sold, it shows. Then why not consider undertaking a marketing initiative to turn your employees into your most loyal and vocal fans? That may sound utterly unnecessary, because, after all, you hired your employees to be avid supporters, correct? Correct. But are they as motivated as they could be? Probably not. Studies show that only about 30 per cent of employees are truly engaged in their jobs. Which means that fully 70 per cent are either not engaged or are actively disengaged and negatively affecting your business. Think about what would happen if you turned a larger percentage of your employees into actively engaged fans.

Why market to employees?

There are four good reasons for marketing to your employees. Knowledge is power. The better your employees understand the company, the more competent they will feel and the better they'll be able to deliver what your brand promises customers. First, engaged employees are motivated employees. They will do the best job they can to support your projects and programmes and to ensure your company's success. Second, loyal employees are enthusiastic sales people. Their belief in your product and service will be contagious, which means you attract and keep more customers. Third, employees who believe in their company will go above and beyond to make sure that customers are happy. Great service leads to customer loyalty, which leads to greater bottom line results. Fourth, employees who feel they successfully contribute to the organisation are more likely to be long-term employees. Reduced turnover contributes positively to productivity and to your bottom line.

What are the steps to internal marketing?

Internal marketing comprises the same steps as external marketing and relies heavily on effective communication. Ultimately, you want to educate, engage and empower your employees. When we work with clients, this is the process we follow to create a motivated, loyal workforce:

1 **Set a course**. Conduct a SWOT analysis (Strengths, Weaknesses, Opportunities, Threats) to evaluate your current position.
2 **Know your audiences**. Define each group in your company according to their needs. For example, managers are an audience separate from front-line supervisors, and customer-facing employees are different from back of house. Identify all the various audiences and clearly understand the types of information they need to be better informed and engaged.
3 **Assess the climate**. Surveys and interviews are two methods of assessing current levels of support among all audiences. How receptive are people to change? How motivated are they to support a particular effort? Your plan will be quite different for employees who are hostile than for those who are positive.
4 **Define your key messages**. Determine the most important information people need to know, but remember that too much information can be just as confusing as not enough.
5 **Match vehicles to the message**. The most effective communication plan incorporates a variety of vehicles that address the different ways people receive information: print, one-on-one meetings, group meetings, email, video, and so on.

6 **Choose your champions**. Influential people at all levels of your company can deliver your message. Select thought leaders among all groups to be champions or special messengers who help create buzz and generate acceptance among their peers.

7 **Execute the plan**. Think through a timetable for each vehicle. Reinforce your message with consistent and frequent communication.

8 **Measure and adapt**. You should establish measurement standards that will enable you to know how well the plan is working. At points all along the way you can take the organisation's pulse and do a course correction wherever you feel the plan is not fulfilling your goals. Every plan should be dynamic, allowing for enhancements wherever necessary.

Training as a marketing tool

Poor performance is quite often attributable to poor training. How many times have you hired an employee but failed to fully introduce that person to his or her new environment? Yes, we often have the best intentions, but too often we lack the time or the proper processes for helping new employees learn the company's core values, its brand attributes and benefits, and even their own jobs.

Internal marketing begins as soon as a new employee is hired. What a perfect time to reinforce a new person's enthusiasm. From the time you offer employment, or bring someone to orientation, you should be communicating the values of your organisation.

Recently a friend of mine went to work for a global enterprise and his experience exemplifies the benefits of internal marketing via training. For months he shadowed people in a host of jobs, learning what it was like to manufacture the products, drive a route or stock a convenience store. The company set him up to succeed by acclimatising him to the total process of producing, packaging and selling the products. As a result, he can do a better job. And because he recognises the investment the company has made in him, he wants to invest his efforts in the company.

Attracting the best employees

Companies that market consumer goods would never dream of doing business without sophisticated marketing, religiously using marketing tools like advertising and promotional offers to create awareness and loyalty among their customers. Why do they do it? It works.

Think of companies such as Coca-Cola and McDonald's, entities that have built their brands to enormous levels of success among consumers the world over. They spend millions to inform and inspire a variety of audiences to buy their products, targeting the types of consumers they want to attract.

Now imagine that, when you build a culture where employees are 100 per cent fans, word spreads. You begin to attract not only customers, but also employees. The right kind of employees. Employees who want to be motivated, engaged and inspired to do an outstanding job. And once you've hired them, use internal marketing to continue to light their fire, ignite employee performance and wow your customers.

(*Source*: Susan Drake, *The Marketer*, November 2006)

Case study questions

1 In what ways does the case study match what has been written in the RM literature and discussed in this chapter?

2 What is your understanding of the term 'thought leaders'?

References

Ballantyne, D. (1997) 'Internal networks for internal marketing', *Journal of Marketing Management*, **13** (5), 343–66.

Barnes, J.G. and Howlett, D.M. (1998) 'Predictors of equity in relationships between service providers and retail customers', *International Journal of Bank Marketing*, **16** (1), 5–23.

Berry, L.L. (1983) 'Relationship marketing' in Berry, L.L., Shostack, G.L. and Upsay, G.D. (eds) *Emerging Perspectives on Service Marketing*, Chicago, IL: American Marketing Association, pp. 25–8.

Bitner, M.J. (1990) 'Evaluating service encounters: the effects of physical surroundings and employee responses', *Journal of Marketing*, **54**, 69–82.

Bowen, D.E. and Lawler, E.E. (1992) 'The empowerment of service workers: what, why, how and when', *Sloan Management Review*, **33** (Spring), 31–9.

Buttle, F.B. (1996) *Relationship Marketing: Theory and Practice*, London: Paul Chapman.

Chaston, I. (1998) 'Evolving "new marketing" philosophies by merging existing concepts: application of process within small high-technology firms', *Journal of Marketing Management*, **14**, 273–91.

Chaston, I., Badger, B. and Sadler-Smith, E. (2000) 'Organisational learning style and competencies', *European Journal of Marketing*, **34** (5/6), 625–46.

Chouglay, N. (2002) 'Customer perceptions of payment in a service perspective', Middlesex University Business School, unpublished.

Christopher, M., Payne, A. and Ballantyne, D. (1991) *Relationship Marketing*, London: Butterworth Heinemann.

Clark, M. (2000) 'Customer service, people and processes', in Cranfield School of Management, *Marketing Management: A Relationship Marketing Perspective*, Basingstoke: Macmillan, pp. 110–24.

Doyle, P. (1995) 'Marketing in the new millennium', *European Journal of Marketing*, **29** (12), 23–41.

Egan, J. (2007) 'Sidelined? the future of marketing in the contemporary organisation', *Irish Journal of Management*, **27** (2), 99–118.

Grönroos, C. (1990) 'Relationship approach to the marketing function in service contexts: the marketing and organization behaviour interface', *Journal of Business Research*, **20**, 3–11.

Grönroos, C. (1994) 'From marketing mix to relationship marketing: towards a paradigm shift in marketing', *Management Decisions*, **32** (2), 4–20.

Grönroos, C. (1996) 'Relationship marketing: strategic and tactical implications', *Management Decisions*, **34** (3), 5–14.

Gummesson, E. (1987) 'Using internal marketing to develop a new culture: the case of Ericsson quality', *Journal of Business and Industrial Marketing*, **2** (3), 23–8.

Gummesson, E. (1990) *The Part-time Marketer*, Karlstad: Centre for Service Research.

Gummesson, E. (1991) 'Marketing orientation revisited: the crucial role of the part-time marketers', *European Journal of Marketing*, **25** (2), 60–7.

Gummesson, E. (1994) 'Making relationship marketing operational', *International Journal of Service Industry Management*, **5**, 5–20.

Gummesson, E. (1999) *Total Relationship Marketing: Rethinking Marketing Management from 4Ps to 30Rs*, Oxford: Butterworth Heinemann.

Hogg, G., Carter, S. and Dunne, A. (1998) 'Investing in people: internal marketing and corporate culture', *Journal of Marketing Management*, **14**, 879–95.

Javalgi, R. and Moberg, C. (1997) 'Service loyalty: implications for service providers', *Journal of Services Marketing*, **11** (3), 165–79.

Kandampully, J. and Duddy, R. (1999) 'Relationship marketing: a concept beyond the primary relationship', *Marketing Intelligence and Planning*, **17** (7), 315–23.

Kohli, A.K. and Jaworski, B.J. (1990) 'Market orientation: the construct, research propositions and managerial implications', *Journal of Marketing*, **54**, 1–18.

Lindgreen, A. and Crawford, I. (1999) 'Implementing, monitoring and measuring a programme of relationship marketing', *Marketing Intelligence and Planning*, **17** (5), 231–9.

McAdam, P. (2005) 'Give the customers what they want (and in most Cases, it's not a Relationship)', *Banking Strategies*, BAI Online <www.bai.org/bankstrategies/current/cover> (accessed 12 April 2007).

McKenna, R. (1991) *Relationship Marketing*, London: Addison-Wesley.

Meldrum, M. (2000) 'A market orientation', in Cranfield School of Management, *Marketing Management: A Relationship Marketing Perspective*, Basingstoke: Macmillan, pp. 3–15.

O'Driscoll, A. and Murray, J.A. (1998) 'The changing nature of theory and practice in marketing: on the value of synchrony', *Journal of Marketing Management*, **14** (5), 391–416.

Palmatier, R.W., Dant, R.P., Grewal, D. and Evans, K.R. (2006) 'Factors influencing the effectiveness of relationship marketing: a meta-analysis', *Journal of Marketing*, **70** (October), 136–53.

Palmer, A.J. (1998) *Principles of Services Marketing*, London: Kogan Page.

Payne, A. (2000a) 'Customer retention', in Cranfield School of Management, *Marketing Management: A Relationship Marketing Perspective*, Basingstoke: Macmillan, pp. 110–24.

Payne, A. (2000b) 'Relationship marketing: the UK perspective', in Sheth, J.N. and Parvatiyar, A. (eds) *Handbook of Relationship Marketing*, Thousand Oaks, CA: Sage, pp. 39–67.

Payne, A., Christopher, M. and Peck, H. (eds) (1995) *Relationship Marketing for Competitive Advantage: Winning and Keeping Customers*, Oxford: Butterworth Heinemann.

Reichheld, F.F. (1993) 'Loyalty based management', *Harvard Business Review*, March/April, 1993, 64–73.

Reynoso, J. (1996) 'Internal service operations: how well are they serving each other?', in Edvardsson, B., Brown, S.W., Johnston, R. and Scheuing, E.E. (eds) *Advancing Service Quality: A Global Perspective*, New York: ISQA, pp. 77–86.

Reynoso, J.F. and Moores, B. (1996) 'Internal relationships', in Buttle, F.B. (ed.) *Relationship Marketing: Theory and Practice*, London: Paul Chapman, pp. 55–73.

Schneider, B. (1980) 'The service organization: climate is crucial', *Organizational Dynamics*, Autumn, 52–65.

Shershic, S.F. (1990) 'The flip side of customer satisfaction research', *Marketing Research*, December, 45–50.

Varey, R.J. and Lewis, B.R. (1999) 'A broadened conception of internal marketing', *European Journal of Marketing*, **33** (9/10), 926–44.

Vargo, S. and Lusch, R. (2004) 'Evolving to a new dominant logic for marketing', *Journal of Marketing*, **67** (1) 1–17.

Zemke, R. and Schaaf, D. (1989) *The Service Edge: 101 Companies That Profit From Company Care*, New York: New American Library.

Notes

1 This should not be confused with the term 'internal market', associated with systems used in some public service and other organisations.

2 See Egan (2007).

3 This view is consistent with resource advantage theory, core competence theory and the services centred dominant logic (Vargo and Lusch, 2004).

9 Supplier partnerships

Key issues

- Vertical versus horizontal relationships
- Partnering
- Partnership costs
- Partnership benefits

Introduction

As the boundaries between organisations have become less clear and organisations have started to recognise the benefits of collaboration, researchers have become interested in understanding the dynamics of these relationships (Shaw, 2003, p. 147). Relationship marketing theory suggests that interdependence reduces transaction costs and generates better quality while keeping management costs lower (Sheth and Parvatiyar, 2000, p. 123). Relationships become resources because they contribute to the organisation's ability to efficiently and effectively produce market offerings that have value (Hunt *et al.,* 2006, p. 77).

An organisation's external relationships can be seen to have a vertical and horizontal dimension (Palmer, 2000, p. 689). These can be described as:

- vertical relationships representing those that integrate all or part of the supply chain through component suppliers, manufacturers and intermediaries;
- horizontal relationships represented by organisations that are at the same point in the channel of distribution (including competitors) who seek to cooperate and collaborate for mutual benefit.

These horizontal and vertical relationships are not mutually exclusive (see Figure 9.1) and it is quite possible for an organisation to have a number of bilateral and multilateral relationships of both sorts. When it comes to relationships of this type, not only is polygamy allowed – it is highly recommended (Gummesson, 1999, p. 129)!

Figure 9.1
Horizontal and
vertical
relationships

Whereas joint ventures have clear legal boundaries, other forms of relationships and channel partnerships seldom have legal structures that define them (Wilson, 2000, p. 260). They may instead involve an understanding between the parties to cooperate in the expectation that both parties will benefit.

Although many aspects of these relationship types have similar features, it may be valuable to investigate them separately. This chapter will, therefore, concentrate on **vertical relationships** (described as supplier partnerships or partnering), whereas Chapter 10 will look more closely at **horizontal relationships**. To differentiate the latter, horizontal relationships are termed 'collaborations'.

Supplier partnerships

Partnerships between customers and suppliers come in many forms and under many different guises: for example, Christopher *et al.* (1991, p. 24) note that Phillips called them in the past 'vendor partnerships' and AT&T labelled them 'co-makerships'. Although 'supplier partnerships' is the term used here for these vertical relationships, it refers, more broadly, to any two-way relationship within the vertical chain and is sometimes more simply known as 'partnering'. Supplier partnerships are, evidently, the other side of the 'customer partnerships' coin, so aspects relating to general relationships between 'partners' discussed previously apply. There is, therefore, no need to repeat again those aspects of the supplier–customer relationship outlined in Chapter 7. However, whereas the earlier chapter largely (but not exclusively) looked at the relationships from the consumer goods and services perspective (popularly referred to as **business-to-consumer**, or **B2C)** this chapter will concentrate on relationships further back in the supply chain. The most common way of describing these is as '**business-to-business**' **(B2B)** relationships, this term having largely replaced the term 'industrial goods and services marketing'.

We referred earlier to the concepts of organisational as well as personal relationships. As Håkansson and Snehota (1989, p. 187) note, when it comes to B2B, 'no business is an island', thus, by the very nature of the interdependency of most B2B markets, business relationships of one sort or another are inevitable. Whereas infinite supply would mean there would be little need for organisational interaction, under conditions of scarcity inter-organisational exchanges are essential (Levine and White, 1961, p. 587). Interdependence might be defined as where the interests of one party cannot be achieved without reference upon another (Rousseau *et al.*, 1998, p. 395). Because each partner's individual success is linked to the success of the other, the organisations may actively pursue common goals (Hunt *et al.,* 2006, p. 72).

The problem with discussing B2B relationships is that such is the wide variety of relationship types that the all-encompassing term 'relationship' may be too general to provide wholly constructive insight (Blois, 1999, p. 1). This chapter will attempt as far as possible to overcome this difficulty.

Business-to-business relationship research

It was the pioneering research work of the Industrial Marketing and Purchasing Group (IMP) into the complexities of the B2B markets and the relationships within them (Naudé and Holland, 1996, p. 40) that, in part, led to the development and application of relationship theory in this sector. Indeed, even the earliest development of theory by the group implicitly assumed that relationships enhanced performance (O'Toole and Donaldson, 2000, p. 328) and provided a grounding for what has developed since in relational marketing research. The recognition of the importance of 'relationships' came from real-life evidence that was slowly building up of a movement away from the traditional adversarial relationships between suppliers and their customers towards a new form of relationship based on cooperation (Christopher *et al.*, 1991, p. 24). As Brennan (1997, pp. 759–60) notes:

> In the field of business-to-business marketing researchers associated with the International Marketing and Purchasing (IMP) Group . . . published evidence to support the assertions that inter-firm buying and selling must be seen as related activities, and that the marketing function must be at least as concerned with inter-firm relationship development and management as with conventional marketing mix management.

IMP researchers also suggested that a two-level approach was evident, the first 'including short-term episodes . . . exchange of goods and services, information, financial and social aspects' and the second, and longer-term, 'processes leading to adaptation and institutionalisation of roles and responsibilities' (Grönroos, 2000, p. 7). Webster (1992, p. 10) also saw a 'clear evolution away from arm's length transactions and traditional hierarchical, bureaucratic forms of organisation towards more flexible types of partnerships, alliances and networks' within the B2B sector. Håkansson and Snehota (2000, p. 75), meanwhile, saw the four cornerstones of the IMP research into B2B markets as:

- relationships that exist between buyers and sellers;
- business relationships that are connected (by networks);
- a relationship being a combination that includes elements of both market and hierarchy;
- relationships that are confrontational (and therefore innovative).

Business relationships

Although the importance of IMP research cannot be over-emphasised in the study of industrial relationships, the existence of 'trading partnerships' is not new. In the B2B field marketing concepts associated with long-term relationships have a long history of acceptance and effective practice (Barnes, 1994, p. 562). For example, personal relationships between the employees and owners/directors of companies have for some time been explicitly recognised by both buyer and seller organisations and individuals within those organisations (Blois, 1997, p. 53). Relational 'bonding' between B2B traders is not even a twentieth-century phenomenon. In the pre-Industrial Revolution world such associations were quite prevalent between traders, partly because of the need, in turbulent, minimally legislated and sometimes dangerous markets, to do business with others you could trust (Sheth and Parvatiyar, 1995, p. 403). Indeed, it was only with the growth and formalisation of mass-market distribution that traditional relationships between traders in the distribution chain became so strained and only with the advent of mass production and mass consumption that marketers began to accept a more transactional approach (Sheth and Parvatiyar, 2000, p. 130).

This observable tension in the distribution chain was most evident in relationships between brand suppliers and their retail intermediaries. Both parties had their minds focused on the final consumer but, while their individual objectives overlapped, they frequently differed considerably in strategy implementation. During the so-called 'golden age of marketing' from the mid-1950s to the mid-1970s, it was the brand supplier who financed the development of individual brands and dominated and manipulated the means of distribution. Only rarely did brand owners and retailers work together to achieve a result that would satisfy both parties. Most often suppliers used 'pull strategies' with the objective of attracting customers 'over the heads' of the retailer. When 'push strategies' (effectively using trade incentives and promotions to 'push' product through the distribution chain) were used they tended to be one-off tactics rather than strategic cooperative activity. The retailers, on their part, felt no responsibility to any one supplier, being concerned more with overall profit margins than with specific brands.

The third quarter of the twentieth-century saw a change in the balance of power between suppliers and retailers, particularly in the FMCG sector, although initially little movement towards cooperation. As the power of larger supermarket retailers grew, suppliers were often played off against each other. Information regarding production capacity on one side and sales on the other was regarded as commercially sensitive and distrust of one's supplier or customer was the norm.

Only when vertical integration took place through 'acquisition' (forward or backward in the supply chain) was information seen to flow up and down the chain and, even then, somewhat hesitantly. The commonest justification for acquisition of this sort was protection of either the sources of supply (backward integration), or product markets (forward integration) with the improvement of information flow as a secondary benefit. The problems with these forms of integration were often that capital requirements and lack of flexibility typically led to inter-business subsidisation and transfer pricing as a way of shielding the internal business units from market forces (Sheth and Sisodia, 1999, p. 82). Despite these weaknesses, the acquisition route to effective and efficient distribution synergy dominated corporate strategy in the 1970s and 1980s. As the twentieth century came to a close, however, there was a growing recognition that the theoretical benefits sought through coordinating elements of the distribution chain might be better achieved in other ways. Rather than attempting to encompass all or a significant part of the distribution chain, companies were encouraged to concentrate their organisational efforts on their 'core competencies'. This thinking led to consideration of alternative strategies such as outsourcing and partnering.

Outsourcing was another approach that was not new. As Gummesson (1999, p. 128) notes, the 'make or buy' choice has always been an issue in manufacturing although the outsourcing of services is a more recent (but rapidly growing) phenomenon. Nor was partnering without precedent. Despite the general distrust in the typical distribution chain, there were partnerships which proved to be the exceptions to the rule. Partnering-type relationships existed between companies such as Whirlpool and Sears, and McDonald's and Coca-Cola, the latter of which has lasted for over 50 years (Sheth and Parvatiyar, 1995, p. 408). Similarly, Mitsubishi Electric and Westinghouse Electric have been engaged in an alliance for more than 60 years, as have Phillips and Matsushita (Sheth and Parvatiyar, 2000, p. 132). What had before been limited to a few companies was, however, now developing as mainstream strategy.

Partnering

Partnering can take many forms, so a rather generalised definition must suffice:

> Partnering is a relationship between customer and supplier organisations, recognised as such by the parties involved, whose principal objective is a shared increase in the effectiveness and efficiency of joint responsibilities within the remit of their relationship.

The *raison d'être* of a partnership approach is, therefore, to improve the efficiency and effectiveness with which a value-adding system functions (Brennan, 1997, p. 770; Hunt *et al.*, 2006, p. 77). Sheth and Sisodia (1999, p. 82) suggest that, through partnering, buyers and sellers can gain many of the advantages of vertical integration without the drawbacks associated with acquisition. These advantages include:

■ lower transaction costs;

■ assurance of supply;

■ improved coordination;

■ higher entry barriers.

This type of cooperation between buyers and sellers may manifest itself in a number of ways. They may engage in cooperative behaviour and coordinated activities in areas such as marketing, production, finance, purchasing or research and development (Hunt *et al.*, 2006, p. 72). They may include the establishment of long-term contractual commitments, the divulging of personal information, and the adaptation of the production, delivery and buying processes to meet the requirements and needs of both the buyer and the seller (Palmer, 2000, p. 693). This adaptation of processes has become particularly prevalent in the motor vehicle manufacturing and FMCG distribution sectors where strategies for fast-flow replenishment (e.g. 'just-in-time' strategies) are seen as necessary for competitive advantage. In the retail field, such replenishment strategies are often referred to as supplier/retailer collaboration (SRC). The GEA Consulting Group (1994), in a study for Coca-Cola, defined SRC as where:

> both retailers and suppliers share proprietary internal and external data and/or share policies and processes used in decision-making with the clear objective of sharing the benefits.

Technology has driven this information exchange even further than was envisaged in the past and systems now exist that allow selected suppliers to monitor sales of any of their products. The development of customer–supplier partnering agreements has grown considerably in the past decade. Margins in the B2B sector are continually tightening, further promoting the requirement for greater efficiency and effectiveness. Rapid technological development has increased the cost of research and development (R&D) and the 'window of opportunity' for getting products and services to market has shortened, forcing companies to work together in joint research projects and joint product development programmes (Sheth and Parvatiyar, 1995, p. 410). Ideas associated with total quality management and efficient and effective management of the channels of distribution have also created a need for the flow of information between customers and suppliers.

As a result of changing markets and available technology, suppliers and retailers appear to be changing the habits of a lifetime. Whereas before they regarded each other with suspicion many now see each other as allies in the distributive chain.

Culture gap

Critical to partnering is a good understanding between partner firms. In particular, a knowledge and acceptance of each other's organisational cultures would appear crucial to successful business relationships (Phan *et al.*, 1999, p. 8; Arnett *et al.*, 2007, p. 87). Kanter (1994, pp. 99–100) talks about the need for 'chemistry' and 'compatibility' when selecting partners and that success will have more to do with people-centred factors than financial or strategic. Not only should there be an acceptance of cultures between organisations but also the adaptation of cultural styles and organisational mind-sets to allow partnerships to flourish. Brennan (1997, p. 766) notes the scale of the cultural divide to be bridged when he compares the 'old' with the 'desired' inter-organisational cultures that promote relationship development (see Box 9.1).

Box 9.1   Company organisational cultures

Old inter-organisational culture

We are involved in a zero sum game; if we gain then they must lose.

Information is power; the more we know about them the better. The less they know about us the better.

Trust is for mugs; I respect my counterpart as a tough negotiator; I trust him as far as I could throw him.

They are out to screw us and we're out to screw them.

Personal success is about winning; if I can consistently negotiate concessions from my counterpart then my career will go from strength to strength.

Desired organisational culture

We are involved in a positive sum game; together we must aim to increase our business success.
Information sharing is the key; unless we share information on a large scale, we will be unable to maximise our joint efficiency and effectiveness.
Trust will emerge naturally; gradually we will learn that each other is trustworthy, and this will improve relationship effectiveness since we will no longer have to keep checking up.
This is a valuable relationship; it is very unlikely that my counterpart will risk damaging it to obtain short-term advantage.
Personal success is about mutual success; if I can demonstrate that the strength of this relationship has contributed to my company's success my career will go from strength to strength.

(*Source*: Brennan, 1997, p. 767)

Customer and supplier organisations are represented in these partnering arrangements by their employees leading to relationship development on a personal as well as organisational level. These personal bonds can be powerful and enduring although empirical evidence would suggest that they can lessen or break down once one of the participants leaves their respective organisation. Social bonds have been observed to reduce a buyer's perceived levels of risk and simplify the reordering process (Palmer, 1996, p. 22). They help build up trust between parties in the relationship by creating other situations, outside of formal meetings, by which to observe a partner. As partners interact more frequently, they tend to gain more information about their partner which reduces uncertainty (Palmatier *et al.*, 2006, p. 149).

Partnership costs and benefits

According to Brennan (1997, p. 770), the purpose of a partnership approach must be to improve the efficiency with which a value-adding system functions. He candidly notes:

> If there is no improvement in overall systematic efficiency, then the only way one party can gain is at the expense of another, in which case the firms are playing a 'zero-sum game' and are back to old-style adversarial relations. Partnering can only flourish in a 'positive-sum game' where there are real economic advantages associated with this approach to doing business.

From his research in the automobile industry, Brennan notes that the primary benefits for the supplier and the customer of the partnership approach are that:

- The supplier gains an in-depth understanding of the customer's requirements and can be proactive in suggesting product improvements.
- The supplier's personnel become familiar with the customer's 'way of doing things', potentially reducing misunderstandings and improving the speed of response.
- Greater supplier involvement (as a 'member of the team') at an early stage in new projects and new product development can increase the 'speed to market'.
- There is a reduction or elimination of the 'cost of sales' (or marketing costs) for the customer.
- The supplier is not exposed to the hazards of the marketplace, implying greater certainty about future revenues.
- The 'partner–supplier' usually gains privileged access to information about long-term customer plans, enabling a proactive stance to be taken and subsequent reinforcement of its 'preferred supplier' position.
- There is an increased information flow and greater information trustworthiness.
- The ability of both partners to focus on those aspects of the value-added chain that are their 'core competencies' is increased, enabling them to leave other aspects to their trusted partner.

Although these advantages are substantial, there is always a downside to any strategy. Partnership costs are, therefore, inevitable. Brennan (1997, p. 771) describes the potential costs to the customer and/or supplier of the partnership approach as:

■ The reduction (or dulling) of 'market incentivisation' normally created by vigorous competition (i.e. the risk that the supplier or customer becomes complacent).

■ The likelihood that external suppliers will be unwilling to bid against favoured suppliers.

■ The risk of becoming heavily committed to the wrong partners (effectively 'backing the wrong horse').

■ The sunken (i.e. committed) costs (related to customer-specific or supplier-specific investment in physical or human assets) that are more or less worthless outside of the partnership.

As with any strategy development, the costs and benefits need to be carefully considered before progressing to any partnership agreement.

Power

Power imbalance is directly related to the degree of one partner's dependence on another and this has been a focal issue in traditional and relational research (Wilson, 2000, p. 253). In organisational relationships, the 'balance of power' is rarely symmetrical (Gummesson, 1999, p. 16) with one party usually the stronger of the two. As Gummesson (1994, p. 9) notes, this is acceptable to a degree in an imperfect market but from a welfare perspective it may prove unacceptable over the long term. The balance of power will often affect how partners behave. If, for example, during a dispute the aggrieved party has the upper hand, they may adopt a more aggressive complaint resolution strategy than the aggrieved party with less authority over the situation (Boote and Pressey, 1999, p. 9).

Power and dependency in a relationship are very much a function of the relative importance to both parties (Storbacka et al., 1994, p. 29). Imbalance of power, where one partner is seen as dominant and the other dependent,[1] creates opportunities for individual parties to pursue short-term advantage, whereas 'balanced or symmetrical dependence represents a mutual safeguard and a collective incentive to maintain a relationship' (Palmer, 1996, pp. 20–1). According to Weitz and Jap (2000, p. 235), partners in a relationship are more likely to engage in constructive conflict resolution when they are power-equals. If the power is imbalanced, then the more powerful party has little incentive to engage in joint problem-solving. It will come as no surprise to many small and medium-sized enterprises (SMEs), therefore, that relationship power imbalances are most evident when larger companies are involved. As a consequence there is a strong suggestion that the quality of buyer–seller relationships is higher among small-scale businesses operating in 'closed communities', as typified by many less developed economies (Palmer, 2000, p. 700).

An imbalance of power is potentially disruptive to any relationship. Successful partnerships appear to design agreements so that, as far as possible, power/dependence issues are avoided. However, at any particular time one partner may be a net-gainer in the partnership. The disincentive to 'cut and run' is based on the view that future gains can only be made through continuance of the relationship (Dodgson, 1993, p. 92).

The downside of B2B partnerships

As may be expected, other pitfalls (in addition to those related to costs or imbalances of power) exist for potential partners. In all relationships disagreements are probable, indeed inevitable. Complaining behaviour within a buyer–seller context can be seen as different from complaining within a consumer behaviour setting as organisational buying may involve more complexity (Boote and Pressey, 1999, p. 3). In one respect a positive 'spin' can be put on this if parties perceive these disagreements as an effective way of bringing problems out into the open, as opposed to bristling with anger and looking for new partners (Hunt and Morgan, 1994, p. 25). Even in the most serious of disagreement situations, the opportunity to threaten the ultimate sanction of leaving the relationship may be heavily restricted by barriers to exit, in particular those sunken costs of relationship development. Structural bonds develop over time as the level of investment, adaptation and shared technology grows until a point is reached when it may be difficult to terminate a relationship (Wilson, 1995, p. 339). The limited room to manoeuvre within a relationship may be a major negative. Partners trapped in such a situation are reminiscent of the 'spurious loyalists' discussed in Chapter 6.

Another potential downside relates to the length of the relationship. Despite the generally held view that the longer the association the more profitable it can be, there is also a darker side to relationships in the longer term. Inherent drawbacks exist in relationships that last any duration (Grayson and Ambler, 1999, p. 132). There is, for example, an intellectually coherent point of view that suggests that there are considerable disadvantages associated with getting 'too cosy' over time with your supplier (or customer) and that in practice these disadvantages outweigh the advantages of partnering (Brennan, 1997, p. 766). Moorman *et al.* (1992, p. 323) observes that long relationships between service providers show evidence of becoming stale or that the partners become too similar in thinking and, therefore, have less value to add. Palmer (2000, p. 696) suggests that a 'dynamic tension' in the buyer–seller relationship may be essential to achieve continuous improvements in value delivery. Long-term relationships settle into predictable patterns and lack the tension of newly formed associations. A lack of such tension, Palmer suggests, is characterised by 'gullible buyers with a low propensity to complain' and 'results in less collective benefit available to the partners'.

There appears, therefore, to be an in-built redundancy factor in relationships that do not reinvent themselves from time to time. Indeed, research suggests (Grayson and Ambler, 1999, p. 132) that many partners reach a stage where they begin to believe it is time for a change. It is interesting to note that it is in those industries where creative, fresh ideas are an important currency (e.g. advertising) that the turnover of relationships (e.g. client and agency) is perceived as greatest.

One complaint made against B2B partnering relationships is that, rather than representing a new style of business development, they are often 'old style' transaction marketing under a new guise. It may be perceived in certain industries, for example, that, whereas individual companies no longer compete against each other, 'supply chain' now competes against 'supply chain' (Christopher, 1996, p. 62) and 'network' competes against 'network' (Doyle, 1995, p. 24). There is a further serious charge that partnering relationships can have anti-competitive implications where partnering is used as a process by which a seller seeks to restrict the choice set of buyers (Palmer, 1996, p. 22). An additional danger exists when social bonds associated with close inter-organisational relationships become so pervasive that they lead to economic inefficiencies and, at the extreme, corrupt networks of buyers and sellers (p. 21). Palmer (p. 22) notes that it is ironic that, while western companies seek closer relationships, many of those same companies have been applying pressure, through their governments, to have such practices curtailed in Japan.

Finally, although academics as well as the popular and business press highlight the trends towards increased buyer–seller cooperation, the trend is not universal and there is some evidence of the benefit of a spectrum of strategies. Cannon and Perreault Jnr (1999, p. 6) note, for example, that while GM (General Motors) use adversarial tactics to drive down costs, Chrysler actively cooperate with suppliers to achieve similar goals! Whether or not to partner is another example of selecting the most appropriate strategy.

Summary

This chapter has distinguished between vertical supplier–customer relationships (partnerships) and horizontal (collaborative) relationships within the business-to-business (B2B) sector. It has looked at the types of vertical relationship associated with supplier–customer partnerships (or partnering) and established that the generic objectives of these relationships is to improve the efficiency and effectiveness within the value-adding system. The importance of understanding organisational cultures was noted and the likelihood that failure is possible without changes to these cultures proposed. The reasons for the development of partnering were discussed as well as the perceived benefits and costs. The 'darker side' of longer-term relationships was also debated.

Discussion questions
1 Distinguish between vertical and horizontal relationships.
2 What part does the balance of power between the parties play in a relationship?
3 Why are closer ties likely to develop in business-to-business rather than business-to-consumer relationships?
4 Why might partnering relationships lead to 'the reduction (or dulling) of market incentivisation'?

Case study Building bridges

Managing a team can be tricky enough. But when that team is not in the office with you every day it can be even harder. Marketers can find themselves having to worry about a number of extended teams – people from other businesses, other departments or other offices who are crucial to getting the job done. So how should they best manage their extended team?

One of the key relationships a marketer has to manage is the company's group of agencies. These, after all, are the businesses that deliver the marketing programmes. Yet there is arguably great scope for getting more out of the agencies. 'Very few marketers manage agency relationships to optimum effect,' says Nick Turner, a consultant at Deloitte. Trust is certainly an issue here. 'One issue is the provision of response data to agencies', says Turner. 'Clients are not giving enough information on whether campaigns are effective. It really does limit the effectiveness of the agency.'

It takes time to share information, and many marketers still prefer to keep the agency at arm's length. Marketers are not helped by the fact that the data they have access to within their organisation might be limited in the first place.

Once they have appointed agencies, marketers use different strategies to organise them. Frequently they appoint a lead agency to develop the main strategy and hire a roster of other agencies to implement the work in different disciplines. Traditionally, the lead shop has been the advertising agency, though as direct and digital communications grow more important this is changing.

Not every company works this way. AOL, for example, operates with a dozen different agencies, which director for brand marketing, Tim Ryan, describes as 'an extension of my team'. Rather than appoint a lead agency, Ryan leads the strategy, with input from key people from across his agencies. Every week AOL holds breakfast meetings to talk through the development of communications.

AOL is one of a number of businesses that are looking for ways to deepen ties with agencies and improve the flow of information. Shell is another. Like AOL, it believes in regular meetings with its agencies to ensure face-to-face communication is maintained, and it holds quarterly get-togethers to update all its agencies on the company's objectives and activities.

BSkyB has also taken steps to improve communication with agencies. Over the past couple of years, it has reduced its roster of research agencies and now holds regular away-days with people from its six main agencies to showcase new products and educate them about where the company is heading.

'There was some concern among the agencies about sitting down with their rivals,' says marketing strategy director Danny Russell. 'But they found it very valuable to find out what other people had been researching for us, and we are now happy to share internal information with them that we wouldn't have done before.'

One issue when dealing with agencies is setting boundaries. Many agencies operate across different disciplines, and will seek to build their business by extending their work for a client into different areas (e.g. from sales promotion into experiential marketing). While this may be a natural development of the relationship, at other times it can be unwelcome – and it is up to the marketer to say so.

Perhaps the most extreme system for setting boundaries is operated by the Central Office of Information (COI), which has a series of rosters for different areas of its communications, including advertising, direct marketing, digital marketing and so on.

When a government department wants to run a campaign, it conducts pitches within the rosters for each particular aspect of that campaign. The direct agency is only hired for the direct work, while the digital agency can only do the digital side. The COI is undoubtedly effective in letting agencies know exactly what they can and can't do, though its inflexibility can be frustrating for agencies. For marketers in the private sector, a more informal judgment call is often required. . . .

Companies are investing in systems to allow marketers to work with remote teams more easily. Deloitte has worked with two brewing companies to build asset management systems so that, if an idea works in one geographical market, it can be transferred to another quickly without having to start from scratch. Shell has also introduced a digital system that allows agencies around the world to track the progress of campaigns. Meanwhile, firms such as Huddle have been set up to facilitate greater collaboration online.

Such developments are aiding the rise of sole practitioners. For example, Mike Moran, a former marketing director at Toyota, now runs two consultancies, The Orchard Consultancy and The Automotive Partnership. The rationale is that companies can hire him with a specific marketing problem in mind, then he can coordinate with marketing services providers to address it. Moran cites one client for whom The Orchard Consultancy turned round a new corporate website and internal communications programme in 13 days. It worked with a PR company and web firm, but the different businesses only met twice during the whole process.

This sort of process takes the idea of the extended team to a new level, and Moran believes it will become increasingly popular as companies look to replace large fixed marketing teams with more flexible resourcing solutions. 'The underlying message is that marketers need to invest more time in what is happening in technology and what it means for the way they work,' he says. 'Technology forces you to innovate, and takes you out of the cosy corporate world where waste is endemic.'

A note of caution is sounded by Colin Ashurst, senior teaching fellow at Durham Business School. He warns that the rise in remote working must be matched by instruction in how to use the new tools effectively, or you risk creating more work for yourself than you had before. The challenge is to recreate the balance of formal and informal working that comes naturally when you are dealing with people face to face.

'There are horror stories about the lack of effectiveness of people working in mobile teams,' he says. 'If you aren't careful, you can find the time needed to manage such teams exploding, as you can no longer do things informally. There is no consensus on how to manage people in these circumstances – when do you use email, the phone or web conferencing, for example?'

Despite all the possibilities raised by technology, the issue remains one of time. Marketers must be more than people managers – they have to develop strategies, sell them internally and build the profile of marketing within their organisations. But they need to have built good internal and external relationships to do this effectively. So the challenge is finding the time needed, while ensuring they leave enough time to do the rest of the job.

(*Source*: Chris Ellery, *The Marketer*, June 2007 (abridged))

Case study questions

1 What problems does the article foresee in the client–agency relationships?
2 What problems could exist when a company has multiple suppliers with whom it has relationships?

References

Arnett, D.B, Laverie, D.A. and McLane, C. (2002) 'Using job satisfaction and pride as internal marketing tools', *Hotel and Restaurant Administration Quarterly*, **43** (2), 87–96.

Barnes, J.G. (1994) 'Close to the customer: but is it really a relationship?', *Journal of Marketing Management*, **10**, 561–70.

Blois, K.J. (1997) 'When is a relationship a relationship?', in Gemünden, H.G., Rittert, T. and Walter, A. (eds) *Relationships and Networks in International Markets*, Oxford: Elsevier, pp. 53–64.

Blois, K.J. (1999) 'A framework for assessing relationships', competitive paper, European Academy of Marketing Conference (EMAC), Berlin, pp. 1–24.

Boote, J.D. and Pressey, A.D. (1999) 'Integrating relationship marketing and complaining behaviour: a model of conflict and complaining behaviour within buyer–seller relationships', competitive paper, European Academy of Marketing Conference (EMAC), Berlin.

Brennan, R. (1997) 'Buyer/supplier partnering in British industry: the automotive and telecommunications sectors', *Journal of Marketing Management*, **13** (8), 758–76.

Cannon, J.P. and Perreault Jr, W.D. (1999) 'Buyer–seller relationships in business markets', *Journal of Marketing Research*, **36** (4), 439.

Christopher, M. (1996) 'From brand values to customer values', *Journal of Marketing Practice*, **2** (1), 55–66.

Christopher, M., Payne, A. and Ballantyne, D. (1991) *Relationship Marketing*, London: Butterworth Heinemann.

Dodgson, M. (1993) 'Learning trust and technological collaboration', *Human Relations*, **46** (1), 77–95.

Doyle, P. (1995) 'Marketing in the new millennium', *European Journal of Marketing*, **29** (12), 23–41.

GEA Consulting Group (1994) 'Grocery distribution in the 90s: strategies for the fast flow replenishment', GEA/Coca-Cola consultancy report.

Grayson, K. and Ambler, T. (1999) 'The dark side of long-term relationships in marketing', *Journal of Marketing Research*, **36** (1), 132–41.

Grönroos, C. (2000) 'The relationship marketing process: interaction, communication, dialogue, value', in 2nd WWW Conference on Relationship Marketing, 15 November 1999 to 15 February 2000, Paper 2 <www.mcb.co.uk/services/conferen/nov99/rm> (accessed 15 November 2000)

Gummesson, E. (1994) 'Making relationship marketing operational', *International Journal of Service Industry Management*, **5**, 5–20.

Gummesson, E. (1999) *Total Relationship Marketing: Rethinking Marketing Management from 4Ps to 30Rs*, Oxford: Butterworth Heinemann.

Håkansson, H. and Snehota, I. (1989) 'No business is an island: the network concept of business strategy', *Scandinavian Journal of Management*, **4** (3), 187–200.

Håkansson, H. and Snehota, I.J. (2000) 'The IMP perspective, assets and liabilities of business relationships', in Sheth, J.N. and Parvatiyar, A. (eds) *Handbook of Relationship Marketing*, Thousand Oaks, CA: Sage, pp. 69–93.

Hunt, S.D. and Morgan, R.M. (1994) 'Relationship marketing in the era of network competition', *Journal of Marketing Management*, **5** (5), 18–28.

Hunt, S.D., Arnett, D.B. and Madhavaram, S. (2006) 'For dynamic relationship marketing theory: a reply to Rese', *Journal of Business and Industrial Marketing*, **21** (2), 92–3.

Kanter, R.M. (1994) 'Collaborative advantage', *Harvard Business Review*, July/August, 96–108.

Levine, S. and White, P.E. (1961) 'Exchange as a conceptual framework for the study of inter-organisational relationships', *Administrative Science Quarterly*, **5**, 583–601.

Moorman, C., Zaltman, G. and Deshpande, R. (1992) 'Relations between providers and users of market research: the dynamics of trust within and between organisations', *Journal of Marketing Research*, **29**, 314–28.

Naudé, P. and Holland, C. (1996) 'Business-to-business marketing', in Buttle, F. (ed.) *Relationship Marketing Theory and Practice*, London: Paul Chapman.

O'Toole, T. and Donaldson, W. (2000) 'Relationship governance structures and performance', *Journal of Marketing Management*, **16**, 327–41.

Palmatier, R.W., Dant, R.P., Grewal, D. and Evans, K.R. (2006) 'Factors influencing the effectiveness of relationship marketing: a meta-analysis', *Journal of Marketing*, **70** (October), 136–53.

Palmer, A.J. (1996) 'Relationship marketing: a universal paradigm or management fad?', *The Learning Organisation*, **3** (3), 18–25.

Palmer, A.J. (2000) 'Co-operation and competition: a Darwinian synthesis of relationship marketing', *European Journal of Marketing*, **34** (5/6), 687–704.

Phan, M.C.T, Styles, C.W. and Patterson, P.G. (1999) 'An empirical examination of the trust development process linking firm and personal characteristics in an international setting', European Academy of Marketing Conference (EMAC), Berlin.

Rousseau, D.M., Sitkin, S.B., Burt, R.S. and Camerer, C. (1998) 'Not so different after all: a cross discipline view of trust', *Academy of Management Review*, **23** (3), 393–404.

Shaw, E. (2003) 'Marketing through alliances and networks', in Hart, S. (ed.) *Marketing Changes*, London: Thomson, pp. 147–70.

Sheth, J.N. and Parvatiyar, A. (1995) 'The evolution of relationship marketing', *International Business Review*, **4** (4), 397–418.

Sheth, J.N. and Parvatiyar, A. (2000) 'The evolution of relationship marketing', in Sheth, J.N. and Parvatiyar, A. (eds) *Handbook of Relationship Marketing*, Thousand Oaks, CA: Sage, pp. 119–45.

Sheth, J.N. and Sisodia, R.S. (1999) 'Revisiting marketing's lawlike generalizations', *Journal of the Academy of Marketing Sciences*, **17** (1), 71–87.

Storbacka, K., Strandvik, T. and Grönroos, C. (1994) 'Managing customer relations for profit: the dynamics of relationship quality', *International Journal of Service Industry Management*, **5**, 21–38.

Webster Jr, F.E. (1992) 'The changing role of marketing in the corporation', *Journal of Marketing*, **56** (October), 1–17.

Weitz, B.A. and Jap, S.D. (1995) 'Relationship marketing and distribution channels', *Journal of the Academy of Marketing Science*, **23** (4), 305–20.

Weitz, B.A. and Jap, S.D. (2000) 'Relationship marketing and distribution channels', in Seth, J.N. and Parvatiyar, A. (eds) *Handbook of Relationship Marketing*, Thousand Oaks, CA: Sage, pp. 209–44.

Wilson, D.T. (1995) 'An integrated model of buyer–seller relationships', *Journal of the Academy of Marketing Science*, **23** (4), 335–45.

Wilson, D.T. (2000) 'An integrated model of buyer–seller relationships', in Sheth, J.N. and Parvatiyar, A. (eds) *Handbook of Relationship Marketing*, Thousand Oaks, CA: Sage, pp. 245–70.

Notes

1 Palmer (1996, p. 20) alternatively calls this 'absence of symmetrical dependence'.

10 External partnerships

Key issues

- Horizontal partnerships
- Networks
- Industry collaboration
- External collaboration
- Relationship life cycles
- Legislative, agency and pressure group relationships

Introduction

In the previous chapter, a distinction was made between vertical relationships (partnering) and horizontal relationships (collaboration). This chapter will concentrate on those horizontal relationships that were earlier described as being represented by organisations at the same point in the channel of distribution[1] (including competitors) who seek to cooperate and collaborate for mutual benefit. In addition, this chapter will look at other relationships (e.g. with governments) that are, strictly speaking, non-commercial, but which have the potential to affect the commercial viability of an organisation.

Horizontal partnerships

Over the past two decades there has been considerable growth in the number of horizontal partnerships between competitors or other complementary players. These types of collaboration are significantly changing the competition landscape (Thomas, 2000, p. 530) as well as greatly extending the complexity of inter-firm relationships. The rise of strategic network competition, where firms compete within networks with other networks (Hunt *et al.*, 2006, p. 72), has further changed the competitive nature of whole industries including aviation and automobile manufacturing. **Resource dependence theory** (Varadarajan and Cunningham, 2000, p. 282) suggests that few organisations are self-sufficient in critical resources, but this is more than casual relationships. Internationalisation, rapid advances in technology, a changing industrial base and increasingly active customers are among the reasons why organisations are entering these alliances, partnerships, joint ventures, licensing agreements and networks (Shaw, 2003, p. 149).

As with the previous chapter, the concentration here is almost wholly on the business-to-business (B2B) sector. Although the beginnings of a growth in consumer networks (particularly via the Internet; see Box 10.1) are apparent, these appear at an early stage of development, but may prove to be very significant in the future (see Chapter 11). It is in the B2B sector that collaborations and networks of associations and relationships are currently more obviously developing. It is also more evident that many of the 'higher forms' of relationship discussed in previous chapters are more likely to develop in the B2B sector than in most consumer markets.

Box 10.1 Consumer network developments

Although consumer networks (effectively consumers collaborating to achieve a particular objective) are rare in today's economy, they do exist and there is some evidence to suggest that they are likely to increase in the future. In the past families and friends have got together to buy in bulk (e.g. a whole carcass from the butcher) at a much reduced price. Indeed the origins of the Co-operative Movement had the collective spending power of the consumer as its driving force. In more recent years 'share portfolio' clubs have developed where pooled resources cut costs and shared decision-making potentially increases efficiency and effectiveness.

The limitation with these types of collaboration is usually geographical as extended distribution arrangements add to costs. It is also generally true that the more widespread the membership, the less collaborators have an opportunity to meet. The Internet has the potential to remove this geographical dependence. Already there is the example of the American consumer who, unhappy about the price quoted for her new car, used the Internet to trawl for other potential buyers. As a result she was able to return to the dealership with multiple orders for which she was now quoted a significantly lower price.

That consumer networks have potential is evident. Whether they will become widespread is less certain. To succeed they invariably rely on a 'leading partner' who effectively fulfils the function of an intermediary, or 'middleman'. The distinction between the leading partner as the customer or the supplier becomes, therefore, very blurred. Chaffey *et al.* (2000, p. 196) see an alternative in the form of market intermediaries working on behalf of clients. They suggest that 'as customers become aware of the value of information and as technology on the Internet enables them to protect private information relating to site visits and transactions so the opportunity for intermediaries to act as "customer agentsî grows". The sole source of revenue for these new 'infomediaries' will derive from the value they generate for their clients.

Relationship research

According to Blois (1998, p. 256), an observer watching two organisations' behaviour is able to make an assessment of the current state of the relationship between them when:

- the observer has knowledge of the contractual terms under which the exchange is being conducted;
- the observer can observe the exchange process over an extended period of time;
- the participants give explanations of the reasons why the observed actions were undertaken.

Subject to some measure of access, research of this type may be seen as relatively straightforward in the B2B sector. Indeed, many researchers (especially from the IMP Group) have taken advantage of the relative visibility in the sector to examine, sometimes in great detail, the interactions between partner companies and their employees. This contrasts with the consumer goods sector (B2C), where most relationships are non-contractual and where consumers' motivations (despite the valiant attempt of researchers) are largely hidden, making assessment of relationships considerably more difficult. Add to this the probability that many consumers have little motivation to explain their actions (if indeed they actually know why these actions took place) and the difficulties of RM researchers in the B2C area are evident.

As a result of the greater openness in B2B marketing a considerable volume of research literature has been produced. While not always consistent (particularly in the language used to describe these relationships), this has provided a wealth of evidence about why networking and collaboration are becoming so widespread.

Networks and collaboration

There is considerable confusion in the usage and meaning of terms such as **networks**, **collaborations** and other associations (e.g. **alliances**). These terms change meaning with different authorship and are frequently used interchangeably depending on the circumstances described. In respect to this chapter the following descriptions are offered:

■ *Networks*: Networks are seen as relationships between individuals (as opposed to organisations). 'Networkers' utilise their 'contacts' in a sometimes systematic, but more often ad hoc, way. These 'personal contact networks', according to Chaston (1998, p. 276), are 'constituted of formal and informal co-operative relationships whereby individual owners/managers seek to build links with each other in their market with the aim of obtaining the necessary information and knowledge to optimise organisational performance'.

■ *Collaborations*: Collaborative relationships are perceived as more formal relationships between organisations in the sense that they are recognised on a company-wide basis. These may be contractual, but as Gummesson (1999, p. 130) notes, 'trust cannot be assured through contracts and those that believe that lawyers can prevent the risks and hurdles of collaboration are bound to be disillusioned'. By the very nature of business, however, they are likely to include more formal meetings and involve the establishment of agreements and procedures on the form and nature of the collaboration.

Networks

Networking was a buzzword of the 1990s which continues to have resonance in the new millennium. As networking is more individual than organisational it may be valid to suggest that 'networking' is more effective on a smaller rather than a larger scale. It has been suggested, for example, that personal networks offer opportunities for small firms, in particular, to compete more effectively with larger companies (Chaston, 1998, pp. 275–6).

A network consists of a collection of individuals (see Figure 10.1), albeit individuals who are likely to have organisational affiliations and can use the benefits derived from networking for the good of their individual companies. According to Keegan (1999, p. 175), executives from global organisations obtain as much as two-thirds of the information they receive through personal sources. Certain businesses thrive on networking while others actually depend on the network of contacts developed by their employees (e.g. financial services). In general most companies recognise the value in knowledge terms of their staff developing a network of contacts with associate and competitive companies, other industries and other influential players (e.g. government) and explicitly encourage it.

Informal and ad hoc contact is of considerable importance. Formal relationships between these network players are unlikely and may even be barred by government legislation (e.g. if there is any attempt by networkers to manipulate a market). Despite this informality, such networks can be both strong and enduring. Social relationships are not discouraged and can indeed be the 'glue' that holds these networks together.

Figure 10.1
Business-to-business networks

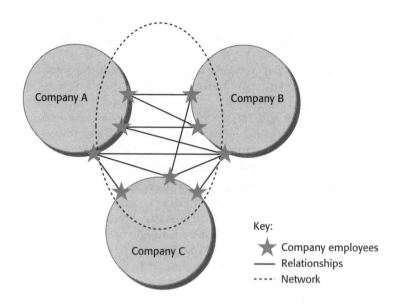

Networks are not a new phenomenon nor is the blur between acceptable and unacceptable commercial relationships behaviour a new debate. Where, for example, should the line be drawn on corporate entertainment? Is it an unfair advantage that a decision maker and potential supplier see each other socially? Is the membership of organisations that promote kinship ethical? Social membership of organisations such as the Freemasons, Rotary Clubs and even working men's clubs has always had a self-help element to it that is clear to members, if sometimes less acceptable to those outside. What is evident is that the growing complexity of network organisations and the interdependency of members renders much subsequent analysis simplistic (Palmer, 2000, p. 690).

Collaboration

The paradox of business in the future is that, according to Doyle (1995, pp. 33–4), to be a successful international competitor, the firm also has to be a committed and trusted cooperator. The firms he is describing engage in cooperative behaviour and the coordination of activities in all areas of the business including marketing, manufacturing, finance, purchasing and research and development (Hunt *et al.*, 2006, p. 72). Over the past decade authors have battled to describe systematically the types of cooperation that were apparent in the marketplace. The number and range of such relationships typically defy neat pigeonholing. Brandenburger and Nalebuff (1996), for example, coined the phrase '**cooptition**' to describe what at first sight appears to be the anomaly of simultaneous competition and collaboration. Even before the term 'cooptition' was used, terms such as alliances, partnerships, joint ventures, joint R&D, minority investments, cross-licensing, sourcing relationships, co-branding, co-marketing and other cooperative descriptions were being used to describe what were being recognised as a 'key requirement' for successfully competing in the global market-place (Sheth and Sisodia, 1999, p. 81).

So pervasive is collaboration seen to be that decades-old marketing concepts are being rewritten in the language of cooperative behaviour. Gummesson (1999, p. 127), for example, updates the 1980s' 'forces of competition' model (involving present and potential competitors, customers and suppliers; Porter, 1985, p. 5) which he inter-prets, 'in the spirit of RM', as 'relationships forces giving birth to alliances'. Governments too have noted the spectacular increase in 'collaborative agreements' and are having to reinterpret anti-competitive legislation to take this into account (e.g. some partners in the 'Star Alliance' have protection from US government anti-trust legislation).

Collaboration should not, however, be mistaken for altruism or an end to competi-tion. Indeed, in some industries competition is more intense than ever as one 'alliance' battles with another in a bid for greater market share (e.g. the airline industry). It is also widely recognised that collaborative relationships can, if restrictions are not observed, have anti-competitive implications (Palmer, 1996, p. 22). They can give birth to 'power networks' which create partly locked markets (Gummesson, 1999, p. 131). So potentially powerful are these collaborations that legislators around the world keep a very close eye on such agreements and have developed powers, where necessary, to prohibit them (see Box 10.2, p. 214).

Collaboration types

Collaboration can be crudely divided into two types:

- *Industry collaboration*: with competitors in the same market sector and where objectives may include effectiveness and efficiency of distribution channels, ser-vicing or other support facilities and market sector growth or market sector dominance. Distinguishing features of intra-industry strategic collaborations are that the partners tend to be rivals competing for market share in the same prod-uct/service market, in the same market segments, in different segments or in different geographic markets (Varadarajan and Cunningham, 2000, p. 216).

- *External collaboration*: where collaborators (usually from different industries) bring different skills, competencies and assets to the relationship. The objective of exter-nal collaboration is often to take advantage of a new sector or to promote existing sector differentiation (e.g. Mercedes and Swatch – see Box 10.4, p. 216).

Industry collaboration

Industry collaboration is becoming a key marketing strategy as firms recognise the possibilities of a 'positive-sum game' where a degree of cooperation results in greater value creation and enlargement of the market for all participants (Sheth and Sisodia, 1999, p. 81). Industry collaboration is not new. Trade associations have existed for centuries and were set up with the aim of setting of agreed standards. They often used generic advertising to encourage market growth (e.g. British Meat Board, International Wool Secretariat).

According to Sheth and Sisodia (p. 82), market share will continue to be an important concept but it is fundamentally a 'zero-sum' or 'win–lose' proposition compared with industry collaboration. Most authors agree that collaboration (like partnering) should aim to be a 'win–win' relationship if it is to succeed. Equity is also seen as vital. In this type of relationship, parties must treat each other as equals and partners, otherwise there is the likelihood that one party will act covertly to out-manoeuvre the other (Gummesson, 1999, p. 130).

Market-share thinking, therefore, has to be counterbalanced with a 'market-growth orientation' as an industry growing the total market collaboratively is often less costly to its individual firms (Sheth and Sisodia, 1999, p. 82). There is also what Gummesson calls 'tacit alliances', which emerge through such industry consensus and which result in all members acting in the same way. The plus side of these 'tacit alliances' is that they can instil ethical behaviour into an industry. On the negative side they may uphold past bad practices at the expense of the future of the industry.

Alliances

The current growth area in industry collaboration is in so-called alliances. This is where a group or groups of competitors (as opposed to the whole industry) collaborate to achieve cost and efficiency objectives. At one extreme a strategic alliance can encompass all the functional areas; at the other extreme it may be limited in scope to a single functional area (e.g. marketing) or value activity (Varadarajan and Cunningham, 2000, p. 274). It is in the airline industry that the development of alliances is most prevalent (see Box 10.2). An airline may, for example, belong to one group for sales purposes but to another for engine maintenance – even if that means servicing its sales competitor's aircraft (Palmer, 2000, p. 689). For the airlines involved the objectives of such alliances are improved competitiveness, increased sales, increased revenue and lower cost through coordination of destinations, timetables, reservation systems, ticketing and staffing (Gummesson, 1999, p. 129).

Box 10.2   British Airways 'Oneworld alliance'

The complexity of collaboration in the airline industry is illustrated in this extract by Nigel Piercy, which describes British Airways' (BA) 'alliance' negotiations from 1997 to 1999 (for the current list of Oneworld members, see Chapter 4):

> From the base of the proposed BA/AA (American Airlines) alliance, BA is committed to a larger network operating under the new 'Oneworld' umbrella brand. Progress towards this goal has continued while the alliance with AA has been blocked [by the US and European regulators]. Key stages in this building process, leading to the announcement of the 'Oneworld' brand in 1998 have been:

- August 1997 – Richard Branson of Virgin [a long-term objector regarding BA's competitive strategies] makes a surprise press announcement that BA has a 'secret global deal' involving BA/AA with Japan Airlines and KLM, which should be stopped.

- September 1997 – plans to include Iberia of Spain in the alliance fall through, but by January 1998 a looser code-sharing agreement with BA and AA holding equity in Iberia is being discussed with BA and AA each taking a 10 per cent stake.

- October 1997 – BA and Finnair announce a marketing and network alliance in Scandinavia to challenge the Scandinavian Airlines Systems' (part of the Star Alliance) dominance.

- January 1998 – BA and Lot Polish Airlines announce a partnership to counter Lufthansa's strength in Poland.

- May 1998 – news breaks of an imminent end to the dispute between BA and USAir, as a prelude to USAir joining the BA/AA alliance (AA and USAir already have a marketing agreement).

- September 1998 – BA/AA widen their alliance to include Cathay Pacific in Hong Kong, Australia's Quantas and Canadian Airlines.

- September 1998 – the Oneworld alliance branding is announced by BA.

- September 1998 – although designed specifically to avoid regulatory issues, the European Commissioner announces that he is scrutinising the plans and may take action.

- December 1998 – Finnair, the state-controlled Finnish carrier, joins Oneworld.

- January 1999 – Japan Airlines plans to introduce code-sharing flights with BA and Cathay Pacific, seen as a move by Asia's largest carrier towards alliance.

(*Source*: Adapted from Piercy, 1999, pp. 45–6)

Industry-driven alliances have a history that stretches back across the twentieth century. A good example is the Associated Merchandising Corporation (AMC). AMC was formed at the beginning of the twentieth century to source merchandise for a number of North American department stores, including Bloomingdales of New York, Filenes of Boston, Bullocks of Los Angeles and other, originally independent, stores, each of which held a 'share' of AMC's equity. Although the ownership of these stores is now concentrated in fewer hands, it still operates on the basis of delivering collaborative gains in merchandise cost and distribution efficiency and effectiveness to its 'member' stores. In Japan conglomerate-type industrial groups, known as *Keiretsus*, have existed since after the Second World War (and their precursors, *Zaibatus,* since the nineteenth century). These *Keiretsus* are made up of a complex web of interacting independent companies, often with interlinked ownership, which cooperate with each other as 'systems' through which to share skills and resources to achieve competitive advantage (Chaston, 1998, p. 275; Varadarajan and Cunningham, 2000, p. 289).

Alliances come in all shapes and sizes. They can vary considerably in intensity and duration, may be 'one-shot projects', limited but continuous cooperation or take parties so close that the next step is to consider merger (Gummesson, 1999, p. 127).

External collaboration

Collaboration frequently (and with growing regularity) means arrangements between organisations from different market sectors, each of which bring different skills, competencies and assets to a relationship. Inter-industry collaborations[2] are often propelled by 'the convergence of industries and the complexity and muliplicity of technologies underlying the product [or service] of these emergent industries' (Varadarajan and Cunningham, 2000, p. 288). These relationships may be for the purposes of improving the total package offering (e.g. the collaboration between British Airways and Hertz) or to create a distinctive advantage in an existing market sector (e.g. Sky Television and Granada Television with a variety of Premier League football teams). Alternatively, they may be developed to take advantage of a new market sector (see Boxes 10.3 and 10.4). It is in the area of 'new sector development', particularly those associated with recent technological advances, that collaborations are expected to have the greatest growth potential.

Box 10.3 Handbag.com

Handbag.com is, in Internet parlance, a 'vertical portal' (or 'vortal') aimed at women. Vertical portals are Internet sites which include links to other (often retail) sites and where revenue is largely derived from advertising and sponsorship.[3] Handbag.com was launched in October 1999 as a 50/50 joint venture between the pharmaceutical and beauty product retailer Boots and Hollinger Telegraph New Media. Boots brought to the venture extensive experience of retailing to the site's target female market. Hollinger Telegraph New Media (the media management and investment division of Hollinger International) brought extensive experience of Internet publishing, including the *Electric Telegraph*, one of the UK's best online news websites. Having established itself as a highly successful portal Handbag.com became part of the Hearst Digital Network, the digital division of the National Magazine Company Limited in October 2006.

Box 10.4 The Smart Car

The concept of the Smart Car was initially championed by Swiss Watch manufacturer Swatch. As Swatch had no experience of automobiles they sought to collaborate with established car manufacturers. Initially they approached Volkswagen before teaming up with the Mercedes division of Daimler-Benz. Designed as a fun, sporty vehicle for young people it was originally nicknamed the Swatchmobile. The eventual name, 'Smart', was nothing to do with its perceived advantages of an electronic car designed for the city but an anagram for Swatch Mercedes Art. In 1994, a joint venture was established. The first concept car was premiered at the Atlanta and Paris Car Shows in 1996 and the first production line model, the Smart Fortwo, came out in 1998. Although Swatch were to pull out of the venture because of initial heavy losses, the project would probably never have got off the ground without them and the vision of the Swatch CEO Nicholas Hayek.

Developing collaborative relationships

Successful collaborations of any sort are not created overnight but develop over time, dependent upon the desired level of closeness and/or the complexity of the relationship. Collaborative relationships mature with interaction, frequency, duration and the diversity of challenge that relationship partners encounter and face together (Lewicki *et al.*, 1998, p. 443), ultimately becoming part of the structural capital of the organisation (Gummesson, 1999, p. 5). Tzokas and Saren (2000, p. 8) suggest that this development can be represented by a 'relationship life cycle' that develops through different stages. Each of these stages, they suggest, present unique requirements and opportunities for those involved. These life cycle stages are shown in Figure 10.2.

Tzokas and Saren suggest that specific knowledge requirements are a necessity at each stage of the cycle. At the introduction stage partners seek a mutual understanding of each other's capabilities and concerns and their potential for strategic, behavioural, cultural and purpose 'fit'. Trust at this stage is based on rational evaluation. At the experimental stage the first joint tasks are undertaken, testing the effectiveness and efficiency of the relationship and helping develop appreciation by the collaborators of each other's capabilities. Trust is at this stage seen to be based on a working knowledge of the partnership. At the identification stage closer and more ambitious collaboration may be undertaken and the boundaries between the organisations may begin to dissolve. Organisational and relational skills are required at this point to maintain the strategic purpose and direction of the collaboration. Identification-based trust, characterised by a mutual sharing of values, becomes more evident. In the final (continuous renewal or dissolution) stage two options are put forward. If the relationship has run its course (e.g. if it has become stale or less productive), then dissolution may be the end result. Alternatively, renewal may take

Figure 10.2
Relationship stages

(*Source*: Adapted from Tzokas and Saren, 2000, p. 8)

place if partners identify new tasks to be performed and have the ability to reinvent the relationship. Trust at this stage is integral to the operation.

Tzokas and Saren's model illustrates the potential for collaborative relationships. The existence of such relationships implies a degree of mutual dependency that blunts the ability of either partner to part from the other without some degree of inconvenience (Brennan, 1997, p. 770). The 'usual warnings' must, however, be made concerning models of this type. The movement is not necessarily unidirectional as relationships can be scaled down as well as up, depending on perceived needs at a particular point in time. In addition, many relationships will never reach the stage where organisational boundaries are seen to dissolve if partners are content to operate at a lower relationship intensity.

Downsides

A variety of environmental factors influence the stability (and indeed the acceptability) of cooperative relationships, including the general values of the society in which the exchanges occur and the specific history of actions and reactions by individuals within that society (Palmer, 2000, p. 690). There is a very fine line between cooperation and collusion (Sheth and Sisodia, 1999, p. 81) and different societies are prone to draw the line according to established national practice. Thus, what is acceptable cooperation in Japan may be regarded as anti-competitive in the USA and the European Union. Even within national boundaries regulators are prone to 'move the goalposts' in support of their own companies' self-interest. For example, whereas in the UK it is acceptable for former public utilities to come under foreign ownership, UK companies cannot do the same in much of Europe.

Operational defects may also prove damaging. According to Palmer (2000, p. 687), cooperation that is too pervasive may have the effect of reducing efficiency and effectiveness in a market. For example, the extensive networks of cooperative relationships among Japanese distributors can add three levels to the distributive system with a consequent increase in costs. A further common occurrence in systems where social relationships become intermingled with business relationships is that 'altruism' may be extended by one partner (e.g. accepting goods which fail to meet their expectations of value) to preserve the standing of the other partner (Palmer, 2000, p. 700). Another problem associated with making relationships work is 'culture clash' (see Chapter 9). The potential battle between two corporate cultures can be hazardous. Confrontation between value systems and cultural shock are, according to Gummesson (1999, p. 130), the rule rather than the exception.

The value of replacing one competitive system with another (albeit collaborative) system must also be questioned. As Palmer (2000, p. 700) notes:

> The development of co-operative marketing alliances, which result in competition between networks of organisations, rather than between individual organisations may transfer this selfish instinct to the network rather than the individual firm.

The danger also exists that marketers are misreading the partnership and collaboration runes and that relationships of this type are a phase rather than a wholly new direction. Certainly, while the number of collaborative agreements continues to rise, there are still examples of mega-mergers continuing apace. There is also evidence of a growing number of equity investments between collaborators that may drive further mergers in the future. Alternatively, this may simply reflect the diversity of the marketplace and the need for a spectrum of strategies.

Collaborations need to be constantly worked upon if they are to succeed. Gummesson (1999, p. 131) recognises the problems associated with maintaining relationships when he proposes:

> The advice provided by a marriage councillor is surprisingly well suited for the advice needed for a company entering an alliance – choose your partner carefully, invest in a win–win relationship, stay attractive to your partner, develop a sound economy, and search for a division of labour that works for all parties. Good vibrations are needed, even if it is not passionate love. Still we know that decisions on cohabitation are taken under uncertainty with no guarantee whatsoever of the outcome.

Other relationships

Other important external liaisons exist in addition to those so far discussed in this and the previous chapter. These include relationships with:

■ local, national and supranational legislators;

■ national and international agencies;

■ pressure groups.

Legislators

Companies have long recognised the importance of maintaining good relationships with legislators. After all, legislators have it within their power to considerably benefit or jeopardise the health of commercial organisations. There is, however, a significant difference between the types of relationship permitted with legislators and those between commercial firms. Whereas commercial companies (within the scope of anti-competitive legislation) are free to establish whatever depth of relationship the parties see fit, relationships with legislators at anything less than arm's length are perceived as potentially corrupt practice in most developed economies. To suggest it never happens would be naive. Both parties are, however, aware that there are boundaries (albeit unclear) that they should avoid crossing.

'Lobbying'[4] is the all-embracing term most often used to describe the methodologies applied to influence government. Although the term implies influence through argument, the general meaning is 'to influence or solicit' (politicians) and a wider range of techniques are used in addition to straightforward argument. Thus, lobbying may take the form of information transmission (ensuring legislators have the information to make a decision), influence (ensuring that the company's or industry's position is clear), general 'public relations' activities (e.g. social events, trips) and political party funding.

Having the ear of government (or the potential future government) is seen as so important that substantial sums are spent (and sometimes mis-spent) on funding such activities. It is often said that only companies with monetary resources can indulge themselves in political lobbying. On the other hand democracy works best when governments can discuss proposals with appropriate interest groups (Baines *et al.*, 2004, p. 372). Companies also see it as useful to bring political appointees into their businesses for advice and lobbying purposes. In the UK, for example, the most common type of interest declared in the House of Common's Register of Members' Interests is payments from organisations that employ them generally as advisers (Filkin, 2000, p. 34). The line between acceptable and unacceptable influence is very blurred.

In addition, it should not be forgotten that governments (local, national and supranational) are large existing and potential customers and that, from the supplier perspective, relationship maintenance will be directed to this end (Zineldin, 2000, p. 20). Given the level of public accountability for this expenditure, however, the development of personal relationships is (technically) severely restricted.

Agencies

As with legislators, local, national and international agencies (or Quangos) can be influential in many industries (e.g. road building and construction) in that they often have the ear of governments and, in many cases, have substantial buying power. There has been a considerable growth in 'agencies' in many countries (e.g. UK, New Zealand), with a growing number of previously directly controlled departmental operations being privatised. As with legislators, the level of relationship will be determined by acceptable practice. The greater freedom of previously government-run businesses (e.g. the UK Post Office) has meant some easing of the 'rules' (written and unwritten) covering formal and informal relationships between these organisations and those in the private sector. The high public profile of such organisations, however, normally ensures that such relationships rarely reach the levels established between other commercial companies.

Pressure groups

There are a growing number of pressure groups whose actions can influence and affect the commercial viability and long-term success of a business. Direct conflict with such pressure groups can appear inequitable at times with apparently small, ill-financed groups taking on large, multinational corporations. They can, however, have an influence with consumers and legislators considerably out of proportion to their size, as companies such as Shell and McDonald's can testify. Frequently (but by no means always) commercial organisations find themselves in opposition to such groups. Whereas complete agreement may not always be possible, maintaining a dialogue with such groups may be in an organisation's best interest.

Conclusion

There is little doubt that horizontal relationships are of current and growing importance in many industries. Gummesson (1999, p. 127) suggests that, for companies such as Corning, collaboration is so central to their business strategy that the corporation calls itself a 'network of organisations'. He goes on to note (p. 129) that five US corporations were represented in 400 formal alliances and countless informal ones. These include IBM (136), AT&T (77), Hewlett-Packard (65), Digital Equipment (63) and Sun Microsystems (45). In those industries driven by new technologies, the value of such strategies is particularly apparent with partners and collaborators bringing diverse skills and knowledge to the relationship.

There is, however, no guarantee that such collaborations will always produce results. In a study by McKinsey (quoted in Gummesson, 1999, p. 130), of 49 collaborations studied, one-third failed. Whereas collaboration in general is seen as beneficial and can contribute to the effectiveness and efficiency of an operation, such outcomes are far from a foregone conclusion. Important decisions need to be made concerning the validity of all such collaborations, the level of closeness and the probable duration. In addition, companies should not just have 'collaboration'-forming strategies but plans in place to be implemented when such relationships have run their course.

Summary

This chapter looked at horizontal partnerships and other potential partnerships external to the organisation. It noted the considerable increase of such arrangements between competitors and other complementary players, which may or may not come from a single industry. The chapter differentiated between 'networking' and 'collaborations', subdividing the latter into 'industry collaboration', usually with competitors, and 'external collaboration' with other companies that could offer different skills, competencies and assets to a partnership. The chapter noted that successful collaborations are not created overnight and presented a 'relationship life cycle', describing the factors observed at each stage in the relationship. The importance of other relationships with, for example, governments, agencies and pressure groups was also highlighted.

Discussion questions

1 Distinguish between network and collaborative strategies.
2 Where would you draw the line between collaboration and collusion?
3 Suggest examples of (a) industry collaboration and (b) external collaboration.
4 Why might organisations wish to maintain relationships with consumer or other pressure groups?

Case study   Bouncing ideas around

If it's a basic fact of business life that change doesn't stop, innovation is concerned with harnessing useful ideas for change to create business value. Look at the wider picture. The world is transforming. As we enter a new era characterised by 'information on demand', every business must grapple with the challenges of new technologies, emerging business models and the much greater but still uncertain role of nations such as China and India.

The *IBM Global CE5 Study 2006* – based on interviews with more than 750 of the world's top CEOs and leaders – reveals interesting insights on innovation. The findings show that it is no longer just about new products and services; business leaders are now renewing their business models and operations, too. Business model innovators gain ground on their competition by achieving greater focus and specialisation. They regularly review their market and decide which business components to retain and which to source externally.

Despite the myth that innovation is too critical and proprietary to involve outsiders, the study shows that collaboration is often indispensable. More than three-quarters of respondents ranked 'business partner' and 'customer collaboration' as top sources for new ideas. Said one CEO: 'If you think you have all of the answers internally, you are wrong.'

The survey suggests that collaboration makes businesses more successful; companies with higher revenue growth reported using external sources significantly more than slower growers. Outperformers used external sources 30 per cent more than underperformers.

Collaboration and business model reinvention often require major cultural change. The results suggest that this change can only be driven from the top. Commented one respondent from the *IBM Global CEO Study 2006:* 'Leading, setting direction, laying the cultural groundwork that stimulates innovation it's essential work for a CEO.'

But where to start? Setting an agenda for innovation involves a set of strategic choices that are often made without sufficient deliberation or with no challenge of assumptions. For example, how to choose between business model, operational and product innovation?

Creating a working environment where inspiration thrives and creativity flourishes remains one of the crucial leadership and management challenges facing companies today. How else will you secure a continuous flow of new ideas that can be turned into value? This means adopting a collaborative, collegiate and team-oriented approach that still leaves room for rewarding individual contributions to innovation.

Despite the value placed on collaboration and partnerships, the study reveals that many CEOs are still only at the planning stage. While 76 per cent of them agree collaboration is critical, only half say their organisations collaborate extensively. Citing a lack of the skills and expertise needed to partner externally, many of them refer to partnering as 'theoretically easy' but 'practically hard to do'. Plugging this capability gap is a matter of urgency: the results show that the higher the level of collaboration, the stronger the financial results.

Many of the CEOs in our study see business and technology integration as fundamental for the newer forms of innovation. Indeed, organisations with high revenue and margin growth are supreme business and technology integrators, benefitting from more effective and efficient business models and 'daring ideas'.

It's tempting to think that innovation is someone else's job, perhaps a task belonging to the R&D team or the marketing department. In IBM, we believe that, although innovation needs orchestration from the top, everyone should be encouraged to think broadly, act personally and contribute to the innovation mix. What will your contribution be?

(*Source*: Trevor Davis and Ian Bradbury, *Management Today*, September 2006)

Case study questions

1 Why is collaboration seen as indispensable?
2 Why is collaboration seen as 'theoretically easy' but 'practically hard to do'?

References

Baines, P., Egan, J. and Jefkins, F. (2004) *Public Relations: Contemporary Issues and Techniques*, Oxford: Elsevier.

Blois, K.J. (1998) 'Don't all firms have relationships?', *Journal of Business and Industrial Marketing*, **13** (3), 256–70.

Brandenburger, A.M. and Nalebuff, B.J. (1996) *Cooptition*, New York: Doubleday.

Brennan, R. (1997) 'Buyer/supplier partnering in British industry: the automotive and telecommunications sectors', *Journal of Marketing Management*, **13** (8), 758–76.

Chaffey, D., Mayer, R., Johnston, K. and Ellis-Chadwick, F. (2000) *Internet Marketing*, Harlow: Pearson Education.

Chaston, I. (1998) 'Evolving "new marketing" philosophies by merging existing concepts: application of process within small high-technology firms', *Journal of Marketing Management*, **14**, 273–91.

Doyle, P. (1995) 'Marketing in the new millennium', *European Journal of Marketing*, **29** (12), 23–41.

Filkin, E. (2000) 'House rules', *RSA Journal*, March, 34–5.

Gummesson, E. (1999) *Total Relationship Marketing: Rethinking Marketing Management from 4Ps to 30Rs*, Oxford: Butterworth Heinemann.

Hunt, S.D., Arnett, D.B. and Madhavaram, S. (2006) 'For dynamic relationship marketing theory: a reply to Rese', *Journal of Business and Industrial Marketing*, **21** (2) 92–3.

Keegan, W. (1999) *Global Marketing Management*, 6th edn. Englewood Cliffs, NJ: Prentice Hall.

Lewicki, R.J., McAllister, D.J. and Bies, R.J. (1998) 'Trust and distrust: new relationships and realities', *Academy of Management Review*, **23** (3), 438–58.

Palmer, A.J. (1996) 'Relationship marketing: a universal paradigm or management fad?', *The Learning Organisation*, **3** (3), 18–25.

Palmer, A.J. (2000) 'Co-operation and competition: a Darwinian synthesis of relationship marketing', *European Journal of Marketing*, **34** (5/6), 687–704.

Piercy, N. (1999) *Tales From the Marketplace: Stories of Revolution, Reinvention, and Renewal*, Oxford: Butterworth-Heinemann.

Porter, M.E. (1985) *Competitive Advantage*, New York: Free Press.

Shaw, E. (2003) 'Marketing through alliances and networks', in Hart, S. (ed.) *Marketing Changes*, London: International Thomson Business Press, pp. 147–70.

Sheth, J.N. and Sisodia, R.S. (1999) 'Revisiting marketing's lawlike generalizations', *Journal of the Academy of Marketing Sciences*, **17** (1), 71–87.

Thomas, M.J. (2000) 'Commentary: princely thoughts on Machiavelli, marketing and management', *European Journal of Marketing*, **34** (5/6), 524–37.

Tzokas, N. and Saren, M. (2000) 'Knowledge and relationship marketing: where, what and how?', in 2nd WWW Conference on Relationship Marketing, 15 November 1999 to 15 February 2000, Paper 4 <www.mcb.co.uk/services/conferen/nov99/rm>.

Varadarajan, P.R. and Cunningham, M.H. (2000) 'Strategic alliances: a synthesis of conceptual foundations', in Sheth, J.N. and Parvatiyar, A. (eds) *Handbook of Relationship Marketing*, Thousand Oaks, CA: Sage, pp. 271–302.

Zineldin, M. (2000) 'Beyond relationship marketing: technologicalship marketing', *Marketing Intelligence and Planning*, **18** (1), 9–23.

Notes

1 Strictly speaking, organisations that collaborate *at* the same point in the distribution but not necessarily *from* the same point in the chain. This is particularly relevant when 'complementary relationships' are discussed.

2 Varadarajan and Cunningham use the word 'alliances' but the meaning in the context of this chapter does not change.

3 This is very much a simplification as Handbag.com has a number of ways of generating revenue including through sales commission. The complexity of 'vortals' is, however, beyond the scope of this book.

4 The word 'lobbying' derives either from the practice of UK Members of Parliament meeting visitors in the lobby of the House of Commons or from the habit of US politicians meeting their petitioners in the lobby of the Willard Hotel in Washington, DC.

Part III

Managing and controlling the relationship

In this third and final part, important aspects of the management and control of relationships are discussed. It should be noted, however, that this is not a prescriptive approach; rather, an attempt to illustrate the various routes taken and the opportunities available dependent on a company's individual requirements.

Chapter 11 looks at the enormous impact that new technologies have had, are having and no doubt will continue to have in the future on the management and control of relationships. According to economist Brad de Long (quoted in Woodall, 2000), 'IT and the Internet amplify brainpower in the same way that the technologies of the industrial revolution amplified muscle power.' As is noted in the text, some relationship marketers would go so far as to suggest that without these developments RM (under whatever guise) would not have become so prominent.

In Chapter 12 concepts surrounding the planning and control of RM are analysed. The text deliberately avoids the promotion of a prescriptive 'checklist' of solutions, although some models are generally accepted as valuable from a planning perspective. Instead, it recommends the need to 'design-in' relational strategies, initially within the current planning process. The chapter also confronts head-on the criticism of RM, in part as a warning against 'prescriptive complacency' and in part to rebalance (if this is needed) any over-enthusiastic claims made on its behalf.

Chapter 13 looks at the direction RM research is heading and what forms it is taking. It takes on board some of the comments made about the first and second edition without (it is hoped) contradicting what has gone before. It is bound to attract criticism from some quarters as it challenges the view that CRM is the way forward in relationship marketing research.

References

Woodall, P. (2000) 'Untangling e-conomics: a survey of the new economy (Part 1)', e-business forum.com, *The Economist*, 27 September.

11 Relationship technology

Key issues

- The language of e-commerce
- Mass customisation
- Loyalty schemes and data gathering
- One-to-one marketing
- Marketing types (RM, DM, DbM and CRM)
- The Internet and the changing marketplace

Introduction

Developments in information technology (IT) and manufacturing technology have had an enormous impact on the theory and practice of marketing in general and relationship marketing in particular. Recent developments have provided exciting new opportunities for developing communications between companies and their customers. Such is the influence of this new technology that it has been claimed that without these advances RM could never hope to be an effective strategy (Zineldin, 2000, p. 9; Sheth and Parvatiyar, 2000, p. 196). Certainly, without these developments few companies would be able to handle the growing complexity of their customer and other core relationships. O'Malley and Tynan (2000, p. 799) suggest that having been initially ignored by strategists, who considered it more appropriate in services and business-to-business (B2B) industries, RM was apparently not 'discovered' by consumer goods marketers until the advent of the technology that made effective data storage and communications processes possible.

The pace of technological change is frantic. Developments are unfolding 'so fast, in so unsettling and complex a manner, that it is very easy to see only thousands of different trees and get thoroughly lost in the wood' (Mitchell, 2000, p. 355). It is easy to get carried away by the prospects of IT and it can be very difficult to tell the genuine from the hype (Gummesson, 1999, p. 89), which may account for the oft-quoted 70–80 per cent failure rate on CRM projects. The speed of this change makes discussion of new technology difficult as even new technology can become outdated quickly. To avoid potential embarrassment, this chapter will concentrate on the actual or potential strategic effects of current technology and its likely successors rather than on the tools themselves.

Buzzwords

A growing problem when discussing the effects of new technology on marketing theory and practice is the myriad of ways these developments are described by different authors. Buzzwords and phrases are created (and subsequently dumped) at a rate that reflects the technocrat's needs to move on to the next best thing. The evident danger is that this form of technological development will lead rather than facilitate the marketing imperative.

The language of electronic commerce is used to convey the strategic priorities of many companies. At the simplest level the prefix 'e-' is seen to imply updated techniques utilising the tools of the technological age (e.g. e-business, e-commerce, e-tail). As Duncan (2000, p. 58) notes, by placing 'e-' in front of it, everyday activities becomes modern, daring and accessible all at one time. The ubiquitous suffix '.com' (or 'dot com'), over and above other suffixes (e.g. co.uk), is seen to convey the message that businesses wish it to be known that they are competing in this technologically developed marketplace. More recently, it has become associated with the dot.com boom and the subsequent collapse in share prices of high-tech companies. On an educational level the number of different concepts with the suffix '-marketing' directly associated with IT and technological developments in manufacturing are growing fast (e.g. one-to-one, permission, virtual). To add to the chaos, it is frequently the case that:

- many conceptual terms have definitions that appear to overlap;
- different authors use the same terms to describe different concepts or different terms to describe the same concept;
- some terms 'evolve' into differently named yet apparently similar concepts;
- terms are denigrated and ditched as the next 'new' idea (if indeed it is new) comes along (see Box 11.3, p. 237).

Perhaps the best example of a number of the above-mentioned scenarios is the term 'relationship marketing' itself. At the end of 1999, RM was used by many practitioners (and some academics) to describe what some called direct or database marketing and others now frequently term 'customer relationship management' (CRM). Indeed CRM has been described as 'technology-enabled RM' (Little and Marandi, 2003, p. 197) and as a 'philosophically related offspring of RM' (Zablah et al., 2003, p. 116). The justification for these interpretations would appear to be more cosmetic than substantial although some academics and practitioners (and many consultants) would, no doubt, disagree. They argue that CRM means so much more (or is it less?).

This multiplicity of terms would suggest that many marketers no longer wish to be confined by strict definitions and that flexibility of description and title takes precedence over clarity.

Ground rules

The 'rule' followed in this chapter has been to describe the impact of IT developments on marketing relationships using those terms that appear to offer maximum clarity and/or best represent the industry consensus. It is also seen fit to discuss manufacturing as well as IT developments as the former is both driving and being driven by the latter.

Manufacturing technology

Mass manufacturing and mass marketing may have dominated commercial activity in much of the nineteenth century and nearly all of the twentieth, but this has not always been the case. In earlier times most people traded for basic needs within a confined geographical area. Suppliers knew their customers well and frequently made or supplied to order. It was only with the coming of the Industrial Revolution that the cost advantages of mass production were fully recognised and the consequent need to market on a mass scale developed. Mass production and mass marketing together drove the enormous increase in consumer spending during the twentieth century and were arguably both responsible for the growing wealth (and so-called consumerism) of developed economies.

Mass customisation

The final decade of the twentieth century saw the beginnings of a reaction against 'mass production' and 'mass marketing' both prompted by and promoting technological developments of every sort. In many ways, the mass-customisation concept can be seen to have developed from service markets where customisation is necessary because of the simultaneity (see Chapter 7) of production and consumption (Bhattacharya and Bolton, 2000, p. 327). Although this should not be over-emphasised (most consumers are still happy to benefit from the cost savings of mass-manufactured products or mass-supplied services), the growing wealth (relative to the cost of living) meant more and more consumers were looking for more individual, personally tailored offerings. As Brookes and Little (1997, p. 98) note, 'in today's fragmented, turbulent marketplace, with its ever shifting demand for innovation and tailor made products and services, the concept of a standard product, a standard service or a standard message no longer makes sense'. Bhattacharya and Bolton (2000, p. 327), too, propose that in mass markets relationship marketing is only possible with some degree of customisation.

While it is perhaps true that these statements are a little overblown (mass-producers such as Coca-Cola or McDonald's certainly have some life left in them) and that the vision sometimes differs from the reality (see Box 11.1), there is evidence that 'mass customisation', as it has become generally known, is a recognisable, although occasionally faltering, trend.

Box 11.1   The vision and reality of mass customisation

Visionary definition
Mass customisation is the ability to provide your customers with anything they want profitably, at any time they want it, anywhere they want it, and in any way they want it.

Realistic definition
The use of flexible processes and organisational structures to produce varied and often individually customised products and services at the low cost of a standardised, mass production system.

(*Source*: Hart, 1995, p. 36)

The term '**mass customisation**' has come to refer to 'the notion that, by leveraging certain technologies, companies can provide customers with customised products while retaining the economic advantages of mass production' (Sheth and Sisodia, 1999, p. 80). In manufacturing industries, mass customisation 'entails the use of flexible processes, structures and management to produce varied and even individualised products' at the same low cost of standardised products (Bhattacharya and Bolton, 2000, p. 327). Mass customisation differs from individually crafted products or services (for which there also appears to be a growing trend) in that it maintains the economies of scale advantages of mass production. In many industrial sectors, the capability is becoming available to produce more and more varieties and choices for the customer although, as Box 11.1 points out, there is still a gap between the vision and the reality.

The individual tailoring of products suggested by 'mass customisation' has been described by Ira Matahia (quoted by Chaffey *et al.*, 2000, p. 292), CEO of Brand Futures Group, as 'complicated simplicity'. Matahia goes on to suggest that as consumers crave individually tailored products there will be a strong demand for unique items. For businesses, this will mean the end of a mass audience orientated approach and the beginning of an 'audience-of-one' (or 'segment of one') approach to marketing. In any discussion on customer sensitivity and mass customisation, however, it is important, according to Hart (1995, p. 41) to stress that consumers do not want to be overwhelmed by choice options, a problem typified by some vehicle manufacturers.

Time to market

In technological industries (i.e. those companies producing, as opposed to simply using, this new technology) time to market is a key factor. Windows of opportunity for any new technically innovative product are smaller than before and product life cycles (PLCs) appear to be getting shorter. The pressure to get a new product to market means that, in general, there is less time than before to spend on research. As Gordon (1998, p. 6) notes, 'marketers used to use market research to help identify issues and assess customer response' but under the more pressurised conditions that now exist this research can 'take more time than the marketer has got'. Market conditions are, Gordon notes, changing so fast that a company addressing current research may quickly find itself dealing with yesterday's issues. In many instances, instead of pre-launch research, companies are using the marketplace as their testing ground. The 'beta testing of prototypes' is a common technique employed online by software development companies and is becoming common in technology-orientated firms (Dann and Dann, 2001, p. 211). These firms are using the flexibility of technologically advanced development methods to 'roll out' (and at the same time adapt) early versions of products while simultaneously testing their response. This testing (as opposed to research) has the advantage of producing results based on actual as opposed to forecast sales while at the same time generating revenue.

Dangers exist in this strategy, particularly in respect of innovation. Technologically orientated companies are prone to deceive themselves into thinking that the extreme novelty of their new invention automatically means there is an untapped market.[1] Palmer (2000, p. 126) calls this self-deception the 'myth of the big market' and it is an example of the potential problems associated with companies reverting to product-driven, as opposed to market-driven, strategies.

Information technology

It is generally acknowledged that IT has potential for relationship building, if used effectively. Developments in IT allow a relationship-orientated management to store and manipulate information about their customers and, ultimately, to provide those customers with a better service. It is, however, very easy to get carried away by the prospects of IT and as a result it is sometimes difficult to tell the genuine from the hype (Gummesson, 1999, p. 89).

In RM terms, perhaps the biggest danger is to assume that technology can always effectively replace or enhance personal contact. Research suggests that consumers have stronger affiliation with individuals rather than companies. The issue of individual versus organisational relationships has significant implications when organisations attempt to increase their service efficiencies (i.e. cut costs) through the use of technology (Palmatier *et al.*, 2006, p. 141). Technology-supported developments aimed at increasing the efficiency of the organisation (e.g. call centres, telephone menus) do not necessarily always increase value or convenience for the customer (see Box 11.2) and are usually justified in cost reduction rather that value-creating terms. To regard technology as an adequate 'agency of surrogacy enlisted to help marketers to recreate the operating styles of yesterday's merchants' (Sisodia and Wolfe, 2000, p. 526) may be naive. Indeed, some organisations, blinded by the possibilities technological manipulation may bring, have lost sight of the personal aspect of relationships. According to Peppers and Rogers (2000, p. 243) in today's 'interactive age' customers:

> are accustomed to having their needs met immediately, conveniently and inexpensively. That's why, for many people, contacting customer service representatives can be an excruciating experience. Between navigating lengthy menus of push-button options, waiting on hold for what seems an eternity, never getting a reply to an e-mail, and not having you or your problems remembered the next time you call back, it's no wonder many customers think customer 'service' is a cruel joke.

Loyalty programmes

The most prominent use of IT in many consumer sectors has been in the management of loyalty (or more strictly usage) programmes, although some would suggest that this has more to do with sales promotion than relationship development. According to Bejou and Palmer (1998, p. 7), for example, many such loyalty programmes are nothing more than crude attempts to increase short-term sales without adding to the long-term relationship with the customer. Others would argue that 'loyalty technology' has augmented the traditional usage programme (based on 'low-tech' stamps or tokens). Uncles (1994, p. 339), for example, suggests three reasons why this might be the case:

- The range of organisations involved in promotions and programmes is much wider, extending beyond high street retailers and petrol stations to encompass international travel, financial services and all levels in the distribution chain.
- National borders are no longer a constraint (e.g. Dunnes Stores' loyalty scheme operates in Northern Ireland and the Republic of Ireland).
- Recognition of some usage schemes is widespread, leading to fairly complex offers to retain customers (e.g. British Airways and Air Miles, Nectar and Sainsbury, BP, Debenhams).

Box 11.2   Technology is no substitute for thought when it comes to customer care

Why do some companies persist in thinking that technology is the answer to tackling customer care issues? After IKEA became the subject of innumerable consumer watchdog-type television and radio programmes about 'voice-mail-jail' you might think it would have dawned on marketing directors everywhere that technology only improves customer service if it helps to solve customers' problems.

In reality, it is a vain hope that companies will learn from the mistakes of others. If marketing departments take any notice at all, they will at best relate the incident to specific areas of direct functional responsibility. They appear unable to think through the strategic issues and relate lessons learnt to all areas of customer contact.

There is a universal failure to respond to the voice-mail-jail issue. If its inability to manage something as simple as voice mail technology could lead to humiliation for the mighty IKEA, what are the implications for the reputation and brand image of all those companies developing call centres without understanding the role technology plays in customer care?

Alfa Romeo (GB) is a case in point. The company is said to have spent over £1 million building and staffing a call centre. But if my experience is anything to go by, all it has got for its money is a mechanism by which to antagonise even the mildest customer who needs anything more than a brochure.

David Reed, writing in the April issue of *Marketing Business*, outlined how Mercedes-Benz UK has put in place a small customer assistance team whose every member is tasked with resolving any issue brought to them by telephone. Alfa Romeo, by contrast, uses a reference number system.

For anything other than the simplest request they log the enquiry/complaint, give the caller a number and say someone will investigate and respond. Responses come in writing and take the 'don't call us, we'll call you' format. Should the caller phone again they find there is just enough information on file to show that they made an enquiry, but not enough to enable the operator to tell them what has been done about it.

Given, as Mercedes-Benz recognises, the low incidence of one-call complaints resolution, this attitude is disappointing. But from here things go from bad to worse.

Alfa Romeo has fallen into the trap of assuming that investment in technology is a substitute for developing processes that lead to good customer care experiences. It seems to find it easier to spend money than commit the time to think about how to deal effectively with the genuine concerns of its customers.

Senior management is responsible for the way customer care is managed. Alfa Romeo (GB) has a customer service director and a customer relations director. It is hard to imagine two more inappropriate job titles.

It's all right for Jeremy Clarkson to enthuse about the latest Alfa: he can give it back at the end of his test drive.

(*Source*: John Edmund, *Marketing Business*, May 1999)

As previously noted, customer 'data' is considered to have value and the potential to augment a relationship. (Storing data for later retrieval is known as 'data warehousing'; manipulation of 'warehoused' data is known as 'data mining'.) Much of the captured and stored data, however, would appear to be surplus to current requirements, although it holds out the possibility of being utilised at a later date.

One-to-one marketing

One-to-one marketing has become, according to Mitchell (2000, p. 354), 'an almost ubiquitous buzz phrase, almost a cliché, used to cover everything from good old-fashioned junk-mail to the most sophisticated forms of mass customised communications and products'. Data collection does offer potential for one-to-one communication where it improves the information flow and the systems are in place such that knowledge will be derived from it. Linking suppliers, distributors and customers through electronic data interchange (EDI) in a network of closer relationships potentially provides enormous cost advantages (Zineldin, 2000, p. 20). Used appropriately, technology can help a company learn from every customer interaction and deepen a relationship by advancing ideas and solutions likely to appeal to that customer (Gordon, 1998, p. 168). These days, as Marty Abrams (2000, p. 7) vice president of Experian notes:

> manufacturing expertise is a given. If you do not make a great product that you deliver at a great price, you do not have a ticket to play. What will differentiate the winners [from] the losers is their ability to reap the efficiencies that come from understanding the nature of individual demands. Not only will the market make goods better, cheaper and quicker, but it will produce the right goods based on an information driven understanding of individual consumer demand applied at an aggregate level.

However utopian this vision may appear, technology can theoretically make this possible. The Internet already enables users to customise what consumers see and hear, how they choose to buy and what specification the product or service should be. This individual attention to individual customer needs has been described as 'one-to-one marketing'. One-to-one marketing implies the development of long-term relationships with each customer in order to better understand that customer's needs and better deliver the 'service' that meets that individual's requirements (Chaffey *et al.*, 2000, p. 290). RM theory provides the conceptual underpinning to one-to-one marketing as it emphasises customer service through knowledge of the customer and deals with the markets segmented at the level of the individual.

For one-to-one marketing to become more than an electric catalogue of product service combinations, there is a need to develop knowledge-based systems that learn more about individual customers so that firms can really create the value the customer wants and be ready to serve that customer when they are ready (or can be tempted) to buy (Gordon, 1998, p. 6). At the current time this level of offering is still some way off. Indeed, many companies cannot handle the information they already receive.

Marketing types

As noted in Chapter 2, certain types of relational marketing have built a following of their own. It may be valuable to examine these in a little more detail.

Database and direct marketing

The 'database' has been described as the engine that enables RM (ibid., p. 194) and as being at the heart of direct marketing. Tapp (1998, p. 6) distinguishes between direct and database marketing by suggesting that:

- **Database marketing (DbM)** is using a database to hold and analyse customer information, thereby helping create strategies for marketing. Tapp suggests a big overlap with direct marketing.

- **Direct marketing (DM)** focuses on using a database to communicate (and sometimes distribute) directly to customers so as to attract a direct response. Tapp emphasises again the overlap with database marketing.

Möller and Halinen (2000, p. 33) suggest that rapidly developing information technology has created a 'primarily practice based and consultant-driven literature on managing customer relationships through databases'. These programmes (under the auspices of RM) are often criticised for not being 'customer-focused'. Rather, it is suggested, they are designed more to raise switching costs and/or rely on database-driven information to 'market at' customers who may or may not want a relationship (Barnes and Howlett, 1998, p. 15). Indeed it could be claimed that the use of the database in DbM is more consistent with a transaction-orientated marketing strategy as the marketer focuses all of his or her efforts on marketing the sales (O'Malley *et al.*, 1999, p. 281).

Caught up, as we are, in the enthusiasm for technology's information-gathering capabilities, it is possible that companies are forgetting that relationships take (at least) two (Fournier *et al.*, 1998, p. 42). Often DbM is little more than enhanced manipulation of customer data to create an illusion of a customised response. In some instances, RM is used, more or less, as a synonym for direct marketing or database marketing (Tapp, 1998, p. 11) and described in such a way as to imply it is just another instrument in the 'marketing mix toolbox' (Bejou and Palmer, 1998, p. 7). Others suggest that RM, DM and DbM are converging to create a powerful new marketing paradigm (Chaffey *et al.*, 2000, p. 290) where RM provides the conceptual underpinning, DM provides the tactics and DbM is the technical enabler. The counter-argument is that those marketers who consider RM to be little more than the development and maintenance of customer databases are ignoring the deeper issues related to the nature of relationships (Barnes, 1994, p. 566) for which technology has, as yet, no substitute. The paradox is that as technology develops and more information becomes available through different media, the importance of human contact may actually be increasing.

This is the basis for the argument that differentiates RM from DbM and DM, which (arguably) are primarily associated with data manipulation over and above personal relationships and short-term tactics rather than long-term strategies. It is unlikely that the majority of direct-marketers could be described as relational (O'Malley *et al.*, 1999, p. 280) and most database marketing is essentially automated transaction marketing (Sisodia and Wolfe, 2000, p. 544). Indeed it is difficult to regard the use of DM and DbM as relational when they have stimulated ethical qualms within and beyond marketing (Smith and Higgins, 2000, p. 83). According to Möller and Halinen (2000, p. 38):

> The database marketing and direct marketing tradition is perhaps best characterised as a practice, since it has no clear disciplinary background, no clearly defined methodologies

nor a premised theory of markets. It has a strong managerial emphasis aiming at enhancing the efficiency of marketing activities, especially communications – its channels and messages . . . The focus is on interactive communication, where the seller is the active partner who plans offers and communication on the basis of customer status (profile) and feedback. Relationships are seen as long-term in nature, but conceptual or other efforts to tackle the dynamism of customer relationships have been limited. The main focus is on how to keep the customer loyal and profitable in an efficient way.

Customer relationship management (CRM)

The latest relational concept to receive 'top billing' is customer relationship management (CRM). As McDonald (2000, p. 31) notes, 'it's the latest place to be – it's fun, colourful and full of promise'. Although it is frequently associated with RM, the term itself emerged from the IT vendor community in the mid-1990s (Payne and Frow, 2005, p. 167). It was used to describe data collection and those activities surrounding the management of the customer–supplier interface (Boulding et al., 2005, p. 156). Although the original discussion of CRM was in the database, data-mining and decision-support literature (Wetsch, 2003, p. 4), the debate spread quickly to marketing. In the period 1992–2002, 191 CRM articles were published in leading marketing journals (Ngai, 2006, p. 586).

Another irony was that despite the fact that relational strategies have always been considered less beneficial in consumer goods markets it is in these markets that the possibilities for relational strategies have become the new orthodoxy (O'Malley, 2003, p. 135). This 'new orthodoxy' goes by the name of CRM. Figures from the Henson Group (Stone et al., 2001, p. 30) show that, in 2000, there was 100 per cent growth (to $7.6 billion) of the global marketplace for CRM software applications and services. Wetsch (2003, p. 2), from a variety of sources, estimates that $12 billion was spent in 2004 on CRM projects and that 26 per cent of US businesses will spend more than $500,000 on CRM technology, with some implementations costing between $60 million and $130 million. CRM is big business!

The distinction between this and direct or database marketing, however, remains elusive. DbM-, DM- and CRM-orientated managers may actually agree with the interpretation of Möller and Halinen, arguing that the problem with RM is that it is too much 'theory based' and not concerned enough with practical and measurable relationship management. This is undoubtedly a valid criticism in many respects. The answer proposed is 'analytical CRM', the explanation of which usually involves the loading of data on individual customers into 'data warehouses' and using business intelligence tools to analyse it (Bray, 2000, p. 1). Even here, however, there appears to be no agreement. Definitions of CRM, according to McDonald (2000, p. 28) include:

- 'a continuous performance initiative to increase a company's knowledge of its customers';
- 'consistent high quality customer support access across all communications channels and business functions and business partners';
- (tongue in cheek) 'ERP[2] is from Mars, CRM is from Venus'.

Box 11.3 Customer relationship management

Customer relationship management (CRM) has been heralded as one of the greatest advances known to man. Ten years ago it was 'total quality management', two years ago it was the 'millennium bug' – the *fin de siècle* mood, not the virus – and most recently 'knowledge management' have kept us humming along to the latest buzz phrase.

Many of these have been bang on the money – with the obvious exception of the millennium bug, which must rank as one of the greatest stings the world has ever seen. However, the problem with buzz phrases is that they begin to take on different meanings to those for which they were originally intended. CRM has for the past three or four years been shortened and transmuted into 'Relationship Marketing', the net result of which is that, to many, such activity has become the sole preserve for those campaigns involving the use of databases or lists. This is nonsense.

So why has it happened? Over the past ten years, the power of computing has soared while costs have plummeted, which means that customer databases, if set up and managed well, are the most potent tool a business can have. Companies can truly become 'knowledge-rich' and exploit that knowledge profitably. It is the tool by which current customer relationships can be managed and the learning tool for acquiring yet more of the valuable customer types.

However, just because these databases are powerful tools for managing relationships doesn't mean database marketing – usually meaning personalised communications – is relationship marketing.

Tony O'Reilly once said 'I'll take the brands, you take the factories. We'll get back together in five years and see who's doing best.' He was, of course, proposing the brand–consumer relationship as a company's most valuable asset and their factories as their most dangerous liability. He wasn't talking about databases, he was talking about bonding. Brands have been successfully building relationships with consumers long before anyone knew how to spell the word database, let alone build one.

Aren't we all, therefore, relationship marketers? Client side, agency side, design, sales promotion, new business development, research, ads – you name it, we're all playing the dating game. If whatever you're doing isn't aimed at developing or maintaining brand relationships, I suggest you are in the wrong business. But, of course, this wasn't what CRM was originally meant to be about.

Ultimately it was such a lack of understanding that led to the petering out of integrated marketing – another buzzwagon of bygone days. At its heart was a great idea, that the brand-consumer relationship was sacrosanct. Unfortunately it too became misunderstood as a term meaning 'coordinated' campaigns; if you wanted to 'do relationship marketing', best get a DM agency in.

So next time you see a buzz phrase coming along, take care that it's in its original form and not in the agency-modified version.

Anyone want to buy some Totally Knowledgeable Quality Customer Management for de-Bugged Millennium Relationships?

(*Source*: Julian Dodds, 'Look out for the bastardisation of buzz phrases', *Marketing*, 29 June 2000).

CRM is usually associated with the use of IT in managing commercial relationships (Ryals, 2000, p. 259), where the database is regarded as 'an agent of surrogacy . . . enlisted to help marketers to recreate the operating styles of yesterday's merchants' (Sisodia and Wolfe, 2000, p. 526). Depending on your source of reference, a number of different aspects are associated with CRM. These include data warehousing, customer service systems, smart cards, call centres, e-commerce, point-of-sale terminals and web marketing together with operational and sales systems including analytical and predictive planning (McDonald, 2000, pp. 28–9; Little and Marandi 2003, p. 199). CRM seems also to fit Zineldin's (2000, p. 14) definition of what he describes as 'Technologicalship Marketing' (TechM). TechM is described as marketing based on technological tools and used by firms to acquire and manage their relationships.

According to Kelly (2000, pp. 264–5), key analytical CRM applications include:

- *Sales analysis*: offering the organisation an integrated perspective on sales and enabling the sales function to understand the underlying trends and patterns in the sales data.
- *Customer profile analysis*: allowing the organisation to distinguish, from the mass of customer data, the individuals as well as the micro-segments.
- *Campaign analysis*: providing the ability to measure the effectiveness of individual campaigns and different media.
- *Loyalty analysis*: measuring customer loyalty with reference to the duration of the customer relationship.
- *Customer contact analysis*: analysis of the customer contact history of any individual.
- *Profitability analysis*: measuring and analysing the many different dimensions of profitability.

Few so far have differentiated the objectives of CRM from those of RM (or indeed DM and DbM) other than the confidence of its promoters to deliver the results (see Box 11.4). Gummesson (2002, p. 327) suggests CRM is in need of 'general theoretical assistance'. Duncan (2000, p. 58) perhaps hits the nail on the head when he suggests that 'today's CRM fever is rather odd'. He goes on to comment that:

> Unless I missed something, the only genuinely new concept added to the 'old' database marketing mix is a new communications channel (in the absence of a suitable acronym, this is called the Internet) and a desire to apply differentiation to all customer contacts.

Box 11.4   Fact, fiction or fad?

Step along there, don't push – there is room for all. The all-new, glitzy, razzmatazz bandwagon is waiting to explode on your senses. Be the first to experience the latest special effects (corporate self-mutilation in full colour) and gloat over your friends and competitors. For the very latest, state-of-the-art, must-have management fad is coming your way, and customer relationship management (CRM) is too good to miss. But what about the previous, now forgotten fads? Remember 'in search of excellence'? Of 43 excellent companies, only six were considered excellent only eight years later! Remember 'TMQ [*sic*]' **[total quality management]**? For most it turned out to be an exercise in getting a certificate to prove that they could make 'rubbish' perfectly every time ('rubbish' being goods and services that customers don't buy). Remember **'BPR' [business process reengineering]**? For most it brought merely cosmetic savings. Remember 'relationship marketing'? The domain quickly became occupied by happy-clappy, touchy-feely, weepy-creepy, born-again zealots without any underpinning process. Apart from which, 'delighting' or 'exciting' all customers is the quickest way to bankruptcy! There are others, of course. The reality is that most fads were merely the clever packaging of long-standing, sound concepts that have always worked – providing certain fundamental conditions are fulfilled.

(*Source*: M. McDonald, 'On the right track', *Marketing Business*, April 2000, p. 28)

The suspicion remains that the largely unspoken assumption among senior managers that CRM is desirable may be misplaced as it is not the panacea (see Box 11.5) it is often claimed to be (Stone *et al.*, 2001, p. 31). The problem is that the 'quick fix' offered by technology often fails to take account of customer care issues (O'Malley, 2003, p. 144). According to KPMG consultants (Sussex and Cox, 2002, p. 1), CRM is falling into disrepute because technology-led approaches fail to deliver real benefits. The forecast of some is that it 'will pass on and be remembered as the late 1990s' . . . fad and . . . as something exploited by the IT industry' (Seddon, 2000, p. 27).

Box 11.5   CRM myths

According to Little and Marandi (2003, pp. 205–6) there are a number of myths surrounding CRM that require correction, including:

- CRM means management of customers. *For management read manipulated. In reality it is often the customer who controls the relationship.*
- CRM software will solve all our problems. *Bringing information together in one place is useful but only if you know what to do with it. There is also the thorny problem of who 'owns' the system and who should have access to it. In reality this is where most fall down.*
- CRM applications will always pay for themselves. *The cost benefit is rarely convincing. Adding this to the number of total expensive failures makes a nonsense of this claim.*
- All customers love new technologies. *No they don't. Even those who are technically literate do not like being manipulated by systems.*
- Our organisation speaks to its customers with one voice. *Anyone with, for example, a credit card or a loan or a mortgage with a company will note how many times they are offered another one by the same company.*

As O'Malley (2003, p. 141) notes, companies are using 'technology that they don't understand very well in order to help implement a process they are unfamiliar with'.

The changing marketplace

Although database technology is important, perhaps the greatest change now and in the future will be in the market itself. Nowhere is this change more evident than in the area of Internet marketing. The Internet is affecting every facet of business life. In the UK in 2002 the number of regular home web users rose to 16.5 million (a 50 per cent annual increase) and the total number of people with Internet connections has risen by a third to around 30 million – almost half the population (Gibson, 2002). By 2007 the dramatic growth was in faster and more flexible broadband technology which had overtaken dial-up services and a UK household penetration of 55 per cent.

Although the Internet has become indispensable in many people's lives, the argument rages as to the effect of online marketing on the customer retention and/or relationship building process. To some (e.g. Zineldin, 2000, p. 14) the Internet is the very encapsulation of 'one-to-one marketing' and, as such, gives companies the ability to establish enduring relationships with individual customers. On the other hand, a study of retailing services carried out by the Canadian-based Bristol Group, reported in *Marketing Business*, April 2000, p. 4, dramatically contradicts this by suggesting that encouraging customers to go online could lead to desertion in the long term. Irvin (2000, p. 9), commenting on the results of this research, outlines the problems:

> 'Everything online' may be the most recent marketing mantra, but it seems that Net is not always best. Encouraging customers to go online can, in some instances, lead to a decline in customer loyalty, referrals to friends and, over the long term, a decline in profits. This, of course, is when the need for whizzy technology overtakes the customer's needs. Price, access to inventory, speed of shipping and other distribution factors are important, but customers also need to feel that the retailer will provide a human touch where necessary.

That the Internet will encourage disloyalty is evident when comparability with the competition's offering is often 'just a click away'. As Scott Reid of Miller Brothers notes (quoted in Chaffey *et al.*, 2000, p. 278), 'the concept of customer loyalty runs against the trend of shopping on the Internet'. On the positive side, it is those websites that manage to make themselves indispensable to the consumer that will be the ones that suffer least from this phenomenon. In addition, the Internet, as a marketing vehicle, does take the concept of targeting to new levels as the user's every movement becomes a piece of marketing information (Prabhaker, 2000, p. 158). Companies can gather information on users in various ways, including (p. 162):

■ registration;

■ electronic address capture;

■ cookies (data written to the user's hard disk, allowing web preferences to be tracked and stored on a file that can be accessed by the cookie owner).

This information can be used to good effect. Rather than rely on demographic information (although this too can be captured), Internet data capture (particularly cookies and related technology) gives the marketer the opportunity to establish actual as opposed to predicted behaviour as the customer moves from site to site (this has data protection implications that will be covered in Chapter 12). Woodall (2000, p. 5) suggests:

> The Internet (in theory) allows customers to seek the lowest price, and firms to get quotes from more suppliers; it reduces transaction costs and barriers to entry. In other words it moves the economy closer to the textbook model of perfect competition, which assumes abundant information, many buyers and sellers, zero transaction costs and no barriers to entry. It makes these assumptions a bit less far-fetched.

'Virtual exchange' is bringing buyers and sellers together electronically rather than having to go to a physical marketplace (Mitchell, 2000, p. 359), offering the promise of substantial cost savings and considerable upheaval in the traditional distribution chain. Adaptations of established associations (e.g. customer/supplier/internal/external) are appearing as Internet technology holds out the potential of new types of relationships. Mitchell (pp. 356–9) predicts substantial changes in the marketplace, as illustrated in Figure 11.1.

Mitchell considers that these new and adapted relationships include:

- marketer–customer;
- agent–customer;
- marketer–marketer;
- customer–customer.

Figure 11.1
Virtual exchange: potential new types of relationships

(*Source*: Adapted from Mitchell, 2000, pp. 356–9)

Marketer–customer

The traditional market relationship will see changes with the rise of 'bottom-up infor-mation flows' and 'dialogues' between the marketer and his or her customer. As Mitchell notes (p. 356):

> the faster the cost of information falls the more it is democratised. Whereas information processing was once the exclusive preserve of giant institutions with gargantuan budgets, more and more ordinary people can afford to do information processing of their own.

In the early vacuum created by relatively low levels of activity by traditional interme-diaries (i.e. retailers), new entrants appeared to flourish strongly (Reynolds, 2000, p. 419) although, for many, long-term survival proved difficult.

Agent–customer

The 'death of the intermediary' suggested by some sources is almost certainly prema-ture. Indeed, the rise in the number of 'cybermediaries', such as Amazon and Lastminute.com, continue (although not at the level of the mid-1990s) and tradi-tional retailers too, albeit after a slow start, have begun to master the Internet. Indeed it is by no means clear whether disintermediation is possible in any but the most spe-cialist of marketplaces (ibid.). The success of price comparison sites such as Moneysupermarket.com and LastMinute.com is an indication that consumers wel-come mediation. One area that will undoubtedly develop is that of 'reverse marketing'. This includes 'infomediaries' such as search agents, buying clubs and 'reverse auctions'. The principal difference will be that 'infomediaries' will (theoreti-cally) be working on behalf of the consumer rather than as an agent for the supplier.

Marketer–marketer

The growth of 'alliances' was discussed in Chapter 10 and it is likely that the Internet will further promote this trend. The Internet relies heavily on customers actively approaching the company. The importance of 'visibility' is, therefore, of considerable importance. Collaboration between companies, whether through links, vertical portals (e.g. hand bag.com) or online communities (e.g. Barclay Square), will undoubtedly increase.

Customer–customer

As noted in Chapter 10 (see Box 10.1) the rise of consumer groups (or communities of interest) is likely to be a feature of the new marketplace. These will comprise groups of individuals who share an interest in a similar subject or purpose. It stands to reason that marketers will find these communities very valuable for targeting purposes and it may be in the interest of marketers to sponsor or otherwise support such ventures.

Summary

This chapter discussed the effects of developments in manufacturing and information technologies. It noted the confusion of terms, particularly when describing relational strategies and tactics. It noted that there is some evidence to suggest that consumers are reacting against mass production and mass marketing, both promoted by and promoting technological development. As a result of this trend and the creation of technologies to support it, 'mass customisation' (the customisation of products while retaining economies of scale) may be an important future development. There still appears, however, to be a gap between the vision and the reality of this concept. In technology-driven industries, time to market is now a major priority. This is affecting companies' ability to undertake market research as it can take more time than marketers have available.

Information technology development has enormous potential for building one-to-one relationships although developments in this area may not always meet with customers' wholehearted approval. Loyalty programmes were highlighted as a prominent utilisation of technology although, in general, they are perceived to be more akin to short-term promotions than longer-term relationship building.

The concepts of direct marketing, database marketing and customer relationship management were discussed and the danger of substituting technology for 'relationship proximity' highlighted. Although RM has been accused of being too much 'theory based' and not concerned enough with practical and measurable relationship management, it serves to underpin the principles associated with these tactics albeit that the reality may be different. The suggestion is that the objectives of all of these 'relational concepts' appear indistinguishable.

The changing marketplace, particularly as a result of developments in Internet technology, was highlighted. The requirement for the customer to be proactive and the 'democratising' of information processing is adapting current, and developing new, relationships.

Discussion questions

1 Why is marketing research expenditure perceived to be difficult to justify?
2 What do you understand by the term 'one-to-one marketing'?
3 Distinguish between the terms 'relationship marketing', 'direct marketing', 'database marketing' and 'customer relationship management'.
4 How is the Internet changing the marketplace?

Case study Reclaiming the customer high ground

Technology is transforming marketing practice. At its best it allows companies to reach vast numbers of customers in novel and cost-effective ways, it provides unprecedented information about customers' buying habits, it helps to standardise the experience a customer has of a business and it enables customers to buy direct from the organisation.

Not surprisingly, the influence of the IT function has grown accordingly over the past decade. Far more surprisingly, and very worryingly, marketers have largely stood back and let IT take over vast swathes of their traditional role, not least those aspects that are directly to do with the customer experience. IT folk, as is their wont, get carried away with what technology can do, rather than what the organisation needs it to do. Unchecked by others, this can take them down avenues that are both extremely costly and threaten to undermine patiently accumulated brand equity.

Call centres and customer relationship management systems are two cases in point. What self-respecting marketer would subject his organisation's valuable customers to lengthy phone queues as they wait to talk to someone about their phone bill or bank account and then, when they finally get through, be unable to properly hear the person on the other end of the line? Likewise does any marketer really believe that a customer will be 'delighted' to be called at dinner time or when they are putting their children to bed to try to cross-sell them another product?

Independent marketing consultant Mike Sommers asks: 'How could any company with a customer mission statement ever decide to move its customer service voice telephony to India? No amount of saving can compensate for the obvious and immediate loss in mutual comprehension, and the signal that the organization cares more about its costs than it does about its customers.'

HSBC has recently attracted negative comment for its alleged decision to score customers and divert the less valuable ones to foreign call centres while dealing with the more profitable ones in the UK. This sort of negative PR can severely damage a brand that it is the marketer's role to protect.

In a piece of research from Forrester last year, called 'Reinventing the marketing organisation', author Peter Kim, a senior research analyst in marketing, claimed that almost 80 per cent of marketers don't influence customer service. This is not the only critical business function that they have lost control of, he argued, claiming that 'the current marketing organisation is broken'. In particular, he said, marketing 'has lost touch with key organisational counterparts and it lacks the ability to effectively influence the cross-channel customer experience'.

He continued: 'As consumers shift media consumption to emerging channels, marketers need new technologies and skill sets to deliver campaigns and provide analytic support. But two departments with the most unproductive relationships with marketing today are Information Technology and Human Resources.'

Marketers don't need to be technologists, but they do need to understand enough about technology to know what technologies really would benefit marketing and, specifically, the organisation's relationship with its customers. They also need to know enough to be able to tell when they are having the wool pulled over their eyes.

'You have to be involved in technology if you are in marketing,' says Simon James, planning director at WWAV Rapp Collins Planning. 'In today's environment the two are inextricably linked.' By extension, you also have to be involved with the IT director. But close collaborative relationships between the two sides that result in technology solutions that enhance the customer experience, build loyalty and generate bottom-line growth are far less common than they should be.

Part of the reason is historic. Some believe that the root of the problem lies in an unholy alliance of IT directors, software consultants and software vendors that developed in the 1990s – an alliance of which Sommers has first-hand experience. In the late 1990s he was hired by Price Waterhouse to run its marketing and customer management division in the UK. It quickly became clear that part of the role was to sell front-office automation technologies from software companies such as Siebel and others.

He explains: 'I was interested in customers and marketing strategy, but I wasn't interested in selling software packages. They were dressed up as CRM systems, but they were effectively automated selling systems that took no account of what customers actually wanted. There were hundreds of people floating around after the systems integration work for Y2K-related enterprise-wide software had come to an end, and this was a brilliant way to use up consultancy time. But as a marketing man, I couldn't see a single benefit to the customer.'

Typically it was the IT director or finance director in the client organisation who had the relationship with the consultants, with marketers left out in the cold. James explains: 'A consultant would come in, do some tax consultancy and save the client considerable amounts of money. The FD would ask "what else can you do for me?" and the consultant would offer a front-office automation solution. The problem is, it's easy to cut costs and streamline operations and processes, but that doesn't make marketing more effective. But marketers are losing the battle because so many of the big decisions have been taken out of their hands.'

Part of the problem is that marketers have grown increasingly busy over the past 20 years, having to deal with a proliferation of external agencies and new channels, often with reduced headcount. Hugh Davidson, visiting professor of marketing at Cranfield University School of Management, says: 'They haven't had enough time to do their existing job, never mind get involved in new areas such as technology.' But they need to seize back the initiative, says Davidson: 'They don't need to get involved in the day-to-day operations, but they should be heavily involved in the strategy behind and specification of a new technology investment.'

It's not easy, however, for marketers to regain control of a situation where not only do the consultants have the ear of other people in the organisation, but new technologies are being implemented with the overriding aim of driving efficiencies and cost savings rather than enhancing the customer experience. But it is in the interests of the organisation as a whole, not just their own, that they seek to do so.

Successful businesses are built around the customer, and customer focus comes from the top and filters down. For example, despite rumours to the contrary, Tesco's success is built on its obsession with the customer, not on its Clubcard data. Sommers points to Tesco chief executive Terry Leahy and Marks & Spencer chief executive Stuart Rose as exemplars of the customer-focused chief executive, and points out that a good chief executive will empower the marketer. 'I used to be marketing director at TSB and the then chief executive Peter Ellwood was brilliant at giving me enough rope to either hang myself with or positively transform the product offering,' he says.

But if you aren't fortunate enough to have a Leahy, a Rose or an Ellwood as your chief executive, you need to work hard to forge stronger relationships at the top of the organisation to ensure you get your voice heard and are taken more seriously. Davidson says: 'Marketers spend too much time building outside contacts with their agencies rather than building strong relationships with the finance director and chief executive.'

The reality of most IT investments is that they are designed to save costs. But a strong marketing director who is respected throughout the organisation can, at worst, ensure that the customer is not adversely affected by a new IT investment, and, at best, ensure that the investment delivers tangible customer benefits.

Mercedes Benz recently worked with marketing consultancy Rocket Science to centralise its European call centres into one operation. But while the justification was an operational cost saving, the customer care director and marketing team were involved at the very beginning of the project to ensure that customers gained some value from the change.

Alan Timothy, 'chief scientist' at Rocket Science, explains: 'We looked at the exercise as a way of working out what information we could gather from callers and how we should treat them in order to enhance the customer relationship. It wasn't just about efficiency.' As he points out: 'It costs no more to do it right than to do it wrong.'

But he adds that marketers are often neither technical enough nor precise enough to be able to identify the kind of information that would benefit the customer. They tend to think and talk broad brush, he argues, and often can't respond adequately to the IT team's query as to what particular piece of information that could be garnered from a customer on the phone would make a real difference in marketing terms.

In one sense, then, marketers need to get better at speaking the language of IT. This means being clear and specific about their requirements and developing a greater understanding of how technology can translate into improved customer knowledge and ultimately an improved customer experience. But they should also encourage IT to speak the language of the business, rather than hide behind its own often impenetrable jargon which, a cynic might say, is designed to deliberately confuse.

Colin Ashurst, senior teaching fellow in information systems at Durham University Business School, says: 'IT people do use scary language, and marketers step back from it. But if marketers constantly brought conversations back to the benefits for the customer, that would help build a common language around the customer and put the technology back in its place.' And back in its place is where the technology needs to be. Even marketers seem to have been seduced into believing that technology is an end in itself rather than an enabler. In 'Reinventing the marketing organisation', Forrester's Kim argues that the way to fix what he calls 'broken' marketing functions is to migrate towards 'customer-centric marketing organisations' (CCMOs). He defines a CCMO as 'A marketing structure in which customer alignment is the primary organising structure, with other groups, such as IT, channel groups and product heads, supporting the cause.' In this structure, technology is 'the backbone', and Kim advocates that the chief marketing officer and chief information officer should jointly assess the status of the existing infrastructure to see if it is capable of serving as a proper technology backbone.

Any such assessment, he writes, should include the evaluation of systems, skills and processes needed to support customer groups and functional specialists. 'The CMO should build costs into the business case where there are gaps, while IT develops a plan to move with marketing. For example, IT staff may be experts with enterprise back-office systems, but running an e-commerce infrastructure may require new thinking.'

This collaborative relationship may sound like a sort of marketing nirvana, but it is one that some organisations are well on the way towards. At Guardian Newspapers, for example, head of CRM, Charles Ping, says: 'We have never had a situation where IT goes off and tries to impose something on our department. We're in a rare and luxurious situation where our view of what we need is exactly shared by the IT department. They are as sceptical as we are about software being the solution to a problem that no one had identified existed.' Collaboration from the outset is clearly central to a successful relationship between marketing and IT. Any proposed technology investment should be critically appraised by all parties to ensure that there is a clear and genuine business benefit. If the cash stacks up and the necessary budget is released, then the process of implementation and final delivery should be successful and harmonious.

Ian Robinson, director of insight at marketing agency Tullo Marshall Warren, says that the most successful IT implementations depend on agreement and recognition at the highest level that the new initiative is a priority, and ensuring that sufficient budget is allocated to the marketing aspects. He cites a CRM strategy the agency worked on for Visit Britain as an example. 'The project was properly budgeted and there was a clear business requirement specification, resulting from interviews with the various stakeholders. Visit Britain has a very switched-on IT function, which recognised where the existing legacy system was falling down, and the whole project went through very smoothly.'

Elsewhere, IT departments are over-stretched and struggle to keep the stakeholders of a particular project, including marketing, happy within the confines of a fixed budget. 'Everyone gets very tense and uptight and it can be a very painful process,' says Robinson. But with the best will in the world, it seems the historic tension between marketing and IT will persist for some time. The two views are neatly summed up by John Simpson, senior director, CRM sales consulting at Oracle EMEA, and by Sommers. Says Simpson: 'The smart companies understand that there is no "divide" these days and have more of a hybrid mentality. Entire departments are dedicated to technology-enabled marketing transformation, bridging the "right-brain left-brain" gap.' And Sommers counters: 'The only IT training marketing people need is how to spot a snake-oil salesman and how to be less gullible in the face of magic-bullet solutions to complex marketing issues.'

(*Source*: Holly Wright, *The Marketer*, July/August 2007)

Case study questions

1 What are the potential advantages and disadvantages of the introduction of new technology?
2 The author suggests that marketers have lost control of the situation. How might they regain it?

References

Abrams, M. (2000) 'Contribution to debate paper', *Interactive Marketing*, **2** (1), 6–11.

Barnes, J.G. (1994) 'Close to the customer: but is it really a relationship?', *Journal of Marketing Management*, **10**, 561–70.

Barnes, J.G. and Howlett, D.M. (1998) 'Predictors of equity in relationships between service providers and retail customers', *International Journal of Bank Marketing*, **16** (1), 5–23.

Bejou, D. and Palmer, A. (1998) 'Service failure and loyalty: an exploratory empirical study of airline customers', *Journal of Services Marketing*, **12** (1), 7–22.

Bhattacharya, C.B. and Bolton, R.N. (2000) 'Relationship marketing in mass markets', in Sheth, J.N. and Parvatiyar, A. (eds) *Handbook of Relationship Marketing*, Thousand Oaks, CA: Sage, pp. 327–54.

Boulding, W., Staelin, R., Ehret, M. and Johnson, W.J. (2005) 'A customer relationship management roadmap: what is known, potential pitfalls, and where to go', *Journal of Marketing*, **69** (October), 155–66.

Bray, P. (2000) 'Analytical customer relationship management', *Microsoft Business Technology*, June, <http://microsoft.com/uk/business_technology/dw/798.htm).

Brookes, R. and Little, V. (1997) 'The new marketing: what does "customer focus" mean?', *Marketing and Research Today*, May, 96–105.

Chaffey, D., Mayer, R., Johnston, K. and Ellis-Chadwick, F. (2000) *Internet Marketing*, Harlow: Pearson Education.

Dann, S.J. and Dann, S.M. (2001) *Strategic Internet Marketing*, Milton, Qld: John Wiley & Sons.

Duncan, C. (2000) 'Customer evolution', *Marketing Business*, May, 58.

Edner, M., Hu, A., Levitt, D. and McCrory, J. (2002) 'How to rescue CRM', *The McKinley Quarterly*, No. 4.

Fournier, S., Dobscha, S. and Mick, D.G. (1998) 'Preventing the premature death of relationship marketing', *Harvard Business Review*, January/February.

Gibson, G. (2002) 'Internet usage soars', *Media Guardian*, 11 June.

Gordon, I.H. (1998) *Relationship Marketing*, Etobicoke, Ontario: John Wiley & Sons.

Gummesson, E. (1999) *Total Relationship Marketing: Rethinking Marketing Management from 4Ps to 30Rs*, Oxford: Butterworth Heinemann.

Gummesson, E. (2002) 'Practical value of adequate marketing', *Management Theory*, **36** (3), 325–49.

Hart, C.W.L. (1995) 'Mass customisation: conceptual underpinning opportunities and limits', *International Journal of Service Industry Management*, **8** (3), 193–205.

Irvin, C. (2000) 'Testing time for technology', *Marketing Business*, April, 9.

Kelly, S. (2000) 'Analytical CRM: the fusion of data and intelligence', *Interactive Marketing*, **1** (3), 262–7.

Little, E. and Marandi, E. (2003) *Relationship Marketing Management*, London: International Thomson Business Press.

McDonald, M. (2000) 'On the right track', *Marketing Business*, April, 28–31.

Mitchell, A. (2000) 'In one-to-one marketing, which one comes first?', *Interactive Marketing*, **1** (4), 354–67.

Möller, K. and Halinen, A. (2000) 'Relationship marketing theory: its roots and direction', *Journal of Marketing Management*, **16**, 29–54.

Ngai, F.W.T. (2006) 'Customer relationship management research (1992–2002): an academic literature review and classification', *Marketing Intelligence and Planning*, **23** (6), 582–605.

O'Malley, L. (2003) 'Relationship marketing', in Hart, S. (ed.) *Marketing Changes*, London: International Thomson Business Press, 125–45.

O'Malley, L. and Tynan, C. (2000) 'Relationship marketing in consumer markets: rhetoric or reality?', *European Journal of Marketing*, **34** (7), 797–815.

O'Malley, L., Patterson, M. and Evans, M. (1999) *Exploring Direct Marketing*, London: International Thomson Business Press.

Palmatier, R.W., Dant, R.P., Grewal, D. and Evans, K.R. (2006) 'Factors influencing the effectiveness of relationship marketing: a meta-analysis', *Journal of Marketing*, **70** (October), 136–53.

Palmer, A.J. (2000) 'Co-operation and competition: a Darwinian synthesis of relationship marketing', *European Journal of Marketing*, **34** (5/6), 687–704.

Payne, A. and Frow, P. (2005) 'A strategic framework for customer relationship management', *Journal of Marketing*, **69** (October), 167–76.

Peppers, D. and Rogers, M. (2000) 'Build a one-to-one learning relationship with your customers', *Interactive Marketing*, **1** (3), 243–50.

Prabhaker, P.R. (2000) 'Who owns the on-line consumer?', *Journal of Consumer Marketing*, **17** (2), 158–71.

Reynolds, J. (2000) 'eCommerce: a critical perspective', *International Journal of Retail and Distribution Management*, **28** (10), 417–44.

Ryals, L. (2000) 'Organising for relationship marketing', in Cranfield School of Management, *Marketing Management: A Relationship Marketing Perspective*, Basingstoke: Macmillan, pp. 249–64.

Seddon, J. (2000) 'From push to pull: changing the paradigm for customer relationship management', *Interactive Marketing*, **2** (1), 19–28.

Sheth, J.N. and Parvatiyar, A. (2000) 'Relationship marketing in consumer markets: antecedents and consequences', in Sheth, J.N. and Parvatiyar, A. (eds) *Handbook of Relationship Marketing*, Thousand Oaks, CA: Sage, pp. 171–207.

Sheth, J.N. and Sisodia, R.S. (1999) 'Revisiting marketing's lawlike generalizations', *Journal of the Academy of Marketing Sciences*, **17** (1), 71–87.

Sisodia, R.S. and Wolfe, D.B. (2000) 'Information technology', in Sheth, J.N. and Parvatiyar, A. (eds) *Handbook of Relationship Marketing*, Thousand Oaks, CA: Sage, pp. 525–63.

Smith, W. and Higgins, M. (2000) 'Reconsidering the relationship analogy', *Journal of Marketing Management*, **16**, 81–94.

Stone, M., Woodcock, N. and Starkey, M. (2001) 'Assessing the quality of CRM', *Marketing Business*, July/August, 31–3.

Sussex, P. and Cox, C. (2002) 'Next generation customer relationship management: strategic CRM', KPMG, Chartered Institute of Marketing Seminar, March.

Tapp, A. (1998) *Principles of Direct and Database Marketing*, London: Financial Times/Pitman.

Uncles, M. (1994) 'Do you or your customer need a loyalty scheme?', *Journal of Targeting, Measurement and Analysis*, **2** (4), 335–50.

Wetsch, L.R. (2003) 'Trust, satisfaction and loyalty in customer relationship management: an application of justice theory', *Relationship Marketing Colloquium 2003*, University of Gloucestershire.

Woodall, P. (2000) 'Untangling e-conomics: a survey of the new economy (Part 1)', e-businessforum.com, *The Economist*, 27 September.

Zablah, A.R., Bellenger, D.N. and Johnson, W.J. (2003) 'Customer relationship management: an explanation of its domain and avenues for further inquiry', in Kleinaltenkamp, M. and Ehret, M. (eds) *Relationship Marketing, Customer Relationship Management and Marketing Management: Co-operation, Competition and Co-Evolution*, Berlin: Freie University Berlin, pp. 115–24.

Zineldin, M. (2000) 'Beyond relationship marketing: technologicalship marketing', *Marketing Intelligence and Planning*, **18** (1), 9–23.

Notes

1 A good example of this was the first generation 'Internet linked' (WAP) mobile telephones, which were difficult to use, with benefits that could more easily be satisfied by simpler technologies.

2 Enterprise resource planning (ERP), according to Price-Waterhouse Coopers, is a systems software package designed to increase efficiency, identify shortcomings in your business processes and resolve complex problems. For further details see <www.pwcglobal.com/ca/eng/about/svcs/techs_erp.html?.

12 Relationship management

Key issues

- The management of relationships
- The marketing plan
- High/low involvement management
- Managing personal information
- Criticism of RM

Introduction

How do you manage relationships of the type discussed in previous chapters? Perhaps the idea of managing relationships is itself illusory as it implies controlling, or attempting to control, a notoriously fickle and increasingly independent customer base. Evans (2003, p. 263) has described the phrase relationship management as an oxymoron in that it represents two reactionary and opposing elements. According to O'Toole and Donaldson (2003, p. 208), the application of a planning framework to relationship marketing is 'taking a managerial perspective to something that cannot be managed'. This should not mean the equivalent of commercial anarchy. Management planning and decision-making are necessary to coordinate the direction and resource allocation of any organisation and important factors in creating the organisational climate in which relationships can flourish. Simply overlaying RM onto an existing organisational structure and systems, however, without any consideration of how relationships are pursued and developed, will cause problems (O'Malley, 2003, p. 142). But how can this be orchestrated? What RM management does not imply is a formulaic or prescriptive solution that can guarantee success. Both the decision to apply relational strategies and the ways in which these are designed and implemented are, if they are to be successful, situation specific.

Little has been provided by way of practical recommendation as to how to implement RM or what that implementation entails (Too *et al.*, 2001, p. 290). Predictably this lack of specific guidelines has led to criticism. RM has been accused of failure to be systematic and relationship marketers as 'happy-clappy, touchy-feely, weepy-creepy, born-again zealots without any underpinning process' (McDonald, 2000, p. 8). This criticism is perhaps partly dependent upon whether you view marketing as an art or a science. A scientific view of marketing demands systematic solutions and has little room for the subjective. The view of marketing as an art, however, suggests creating the 'best-fit' and perhaps unique solution to an individual situation that may not be replicated elsewhere. There is little point, therefore, duplicating a strategy simply because it worked elsewhere. The science versus art debate has continued for some time with little hope of resolution. Many marketing researchers agree with Tapp (2004, p. 582) when he suggests that 'marketing as a science is now so seriously in doubt that even the most die-hard positivist would struggle to dismiss the need for mixed philosophies'. Perhaps the worst outcome is when polarisation of opinion takes place and marketers reject alternative perspectives and (at the extreme) claim that success is only achievable by adopting their particular prescriptive solution. There is room for alternate opinions and approaches of both a scientific and artistic nature. To paraphrase Voltaire, those who are certain they are right should be certified.

Advocates of direct marketing, database marketing and customer relationship management, in particular, are prone to advance generalised solutions, often with too little consideration as to appropriateness to particular situations. Not that all RM supporters are innocent of such overstatement. Relationship marketing, whatever its faults, is conceptually distinct from direct marketing, database marketing, customer relationship management, loyalty marketing, etc., in so much as these are tactical methodologies, by definition short term, although they might contribute in various ways to longer-term relational development.

There is no claim (at least in this text) that RM is right for every, or even the majority of, situations (see Chapter 13); further, that one particular standpoint has no credible right to be dominant or superior (Littler, 1998, p. 1) over any other. As Micklethwait and Wooldridge (1996, p. 22) somewhat sarcastically note:

> Dig into virtually any area of management theory and you will find, eventually, a coherent position of sorts. The problem is that in order to extract that nugget you have to dig through an enormous amount of waffle.

The application of relational strategies should be a response to a need and implies an element of flexibility and cunning. Neither are relational strategies mutually exclusive. Rather than single, narrow, one-concept strategies, companies need a 'portfolio of strategy types' (see Chapter 5) of which relational strategies can play an important part. Ideas ebb and flow, concepts come and go. Industrial priorities change, which calls for adaptable strategies. What is right for one generation may have no place in the next. Indeed, the uniqueness of relationships makes the mechanical transfer of successful practices among different companies dubious at best (Håkansson and Snehota, 2000, p. 83). After all, isn't differentiation at the heart of marketing? If so, why are marketers peddling generalisable solutions?

The company needs to examine the ideas and adopt or reject as appropriate. After all, observation of 'real world' marketing practice suggests that a hybrid managerial approach is the most appropriate response to prevailing marketing circumstances (Chaston, 1998, p. 273). It is even possible to envisage a company using a relational approach for some customers who need or require this, or in situations where it is profitable for the company. Other customers may not seek such services, or may contribute nothing to profit. There are dangers in such tactics. As noted in the Chapter 11 case study, HSBC has recently attracted negative comment for its decision to use UK call centres for top clients whilst diverting less valuable ones to its call centres overseas. The skill (or art) of the marketer is not in the application of RM or TM strategies per se but in applying the strategies most appropriate to its customers in any given situation.

Relationship management

None of the foregoing should suggest that management has no role. Neither is there any pretence that managing relational strategies is easy. Indeed, making RM work in practice, by means of a system within the company, is one of the most difficult of marketing tasks (Ryals, 2000, p. 231). What should be avoided is 'throwing the baby out with the bath water'. In our headlong rush for instant results (prompted by prophets of doom) there is the danger of applying inappropriate relational strategies to a given situation. The biggest risk of all is creating relationships without considering how value will be created (Ballantyne, 2000, p. 4). Ballantyne calls this the 'lobsterpot approach' to RM, characterised by an over-enthusiastic rush into the unknown. If we accept (as it is suggested) that every customer is uniquely individual, we must accept that every company is unique too. So beware of following the herd too far and too fast. As Damarest (1997, p. 375) notes, not 'what is right' but 'what works' or even 'what works better'.

Marketing, perhaps more than any other discipline, is prone to the 'new broom' syndrome (Mazur, 2000, p. 33). Attempting to restructure everything overnight is more than chancing fate. Flexible adaptation over time is the key. Using a scalpel, not a hatchet (Micklethwait and Wooldridge, 1996, p. 21), is the appropriate metaphor; reviewing and adapting current strategies the most appropriate solution. According to Grönroos (2000, p. 11):

> We know too little about how relationship marketing should be best integrated into the planning of a company. The only way to find out is through trial and error in our companies and through research. Under these circumstances it seems reasonable to start by adding RM dimensions to the marketing plan in use, retaining its basic format.

The advantage of using the 'current format' and 'adding RM dimensions' is direct comparability: the ability to establish what works and why. Although most marketing plans tend towards being overly systematic and to be applied prescriptively, it is better to adapt than replace one system for another, as yet untried. There is, however, a downside. The language of strategy, tactics, power and intelligence gathering coexists rather uncomfortably with that of trust, harmony and commitment (O'Malley and Tynan, 1999, p. 595). Where practical, 'new' language might be adopted that recognises the value of cooperation over confrontation and competition.

The marketing plan

The traditional marketing plan usually follows the pattern of analysis, design, implementation and control. Various formats exist so no generic form is proposed as necessarily better than any other. The plan presented in Figure 12.1, for example, is represented by the acronym SOSTAC (Situation, Objectives, Strategies, Tactics, Action, Control) and follows, approximately, the 'standard' format. One difference from most is that, rather than a linear approach, the model recognises that marketing plans are not 'one-off' but need to be continually revisited. Rather than a list, the model is seen as a continuous circle of activities.

Alternatively, other, perhaps more traditional, marketing plan formats exist. In Figure 12.2, for example, Brassington and Pettitt's (1997, p. 882) 'stages in the planning process' and McDonald's (1999) '10-step strategic marketing planning' model are shown for comparison. The similarities may be noted although different authors give different prominence to different parts of the plan. In any marketing plan, although they appear sequential, several stages may happen simultaneously and information is being constantly updated. As systematic as they appear, flexibility is again the key. Decisions are rarely made in neat stages and planning happens in 'an evolutionary, organic way emerging from organisations and their interaction over time' (O'Toole and Donaldson, 2002, p. 199).

Figure 12.1
Basic SOSTAC
planning model

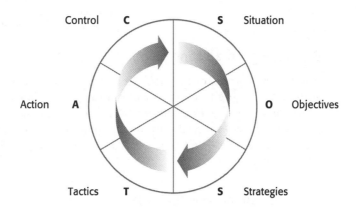

Figure 12.2
Alternative
marketing plans

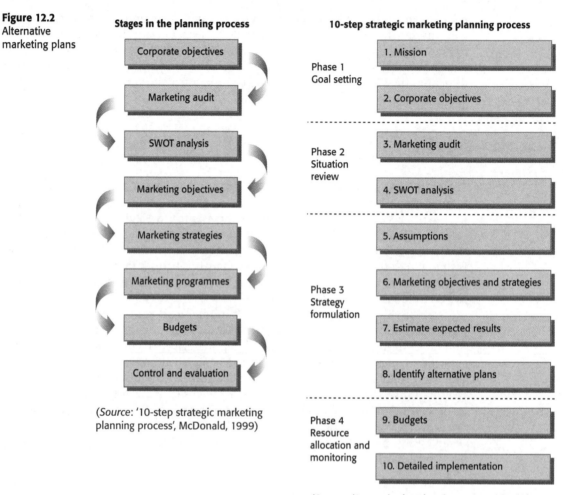

Stages in the planning process

Corporate objectives

Marketing audit

SWOT analysis

Marketing objectives

Marketing strategies

Marketing programmes

Budgets

Control and evaluation

(*Source*: '10-step strategic marketing
planning process', McDonald, 1999)

10-step strategic marketing planning process

Phase 1
Goal setting

1. Mission

2. Corporate objectives

Phase 2
Situation
review

3. Marketing audit

4. SWOT analysis

5. Assumptions

Phase 3
Strategy
formulation

6. Marketing objectives and strategies

7. Estimate expected results

8. Identify alternative plans

Phase 4
Resource
allocation and
monitoring

9. Budgets

10. Detailed implementation

(*Source*: 'Stages in the planning process', based on
Brassington and Pettitt, 1987, p. 822)

Developing a marketing plan

It is not the purpose of this book to go into the minutiae of a marketing plan. Other
authors (including those represented in Figure 12.2) have covered this extensively.
What follows is a series of observations concerning the development of a marketing
plan particularly as it relates to the incorporation of relational strategy development.
The structure is based on the SOSTAC model in Figure 12.1 but might well apply to
any chosen plan.

Situation (situational analysis)

The old adage rings true: how can you know which direction to go when you do not
know where you are coming from? Most companies begin (or resume) the planning

process by establishing (or reiterating or adapting) their mission and scope. The mission and scope relate to the 'attitudes and expectations within the organisation with regard to the business that the organisation is in, how the organisation rates against competition and how it fits into its environment' (O'Malley *et al.*, 1999, p. 37). Corporate and/or business objectives need to be known so that the priorities (often financial) of the organisation can be attended to and incorporated into the plan.

The situational analysis, upon which decisions will be based, is a comprehensive assessment of the organisation and its competitive and macroenvironment. Analysts have commonly used versions (both simple and complex) of **PEST(L)**, **SWOT** and competitive market models to develop such analyses.[1] As RM emphasises the importance of customer retention and the existing customer base, a 'customer analysis' is considered vital. Buyer–seller relationships rarely exist in pure types. Conceptualising where the company and the individual customer types are on the strategy continuum could provide useful insight. Review of the drivers towards relational and/or traditional marketing could help in this process. Understanding when to utilise RM strategies requires distinguishing between the discrete transaction, which has a distinct beginning, short duration and sharp ending, and relational exchange, which traces back to previous agreements and is longer in duration, reflecting an ongoing process (Morgan and Hunt, 1994, p. 21). In addition, the consequences of other relationships require consideration as to how they affect the strategic direction of the company.

Although much has been said about the advantages of the 'segment-of-one', current capabilities are such that aggregation of customer types is likely to still be the most practical in all but a very few industries. The identification and profiling of target markets is, therefore, important. For 'customer acquisition' purposes this may still require the use of sociodemographic, geodemographic and/or life style (including propensity to buy) data, whether exercised through rented 'lists' or communications media audience classifications. The Internet holds out the potential of tracking actual behaviour (see Chapter 11) that may revolutionise customer profiling over time. Not all customers are equal and part of the 'skill' of the relational marketer is targeting the 'right' customer, not necessarily the easiest to attract or the most profitable in the short term (Reichheld, 1993, p. 65).

From the customer retention and development perspective the company database will be of considerable importance as it should indicate customer preferences and profitability. Direct marketers, for example, use recency, frequency and monetary value (RFV) models that incorporate data on a customer's most recent purchases and the frequency and value of previous purchases to target offerings (including 'cross-selling' and 'up-selling'). In addition to establishing customer traits, an RM perspective implies segmentation by type of relationship that can profitably be engaged (Smith and Higgins, 2000, p. 87).

Objectives

Objectives are what drive an organisation. They are the 'where we want to be' of any business. They should be **SMART** (strategic, measurable, actionable, realistic and timely), communicable and aspirational. Traditionally, marketing objectives are derived (or cascade down from) business objectives. The development of technologies that can interrogate databases and establish objectives from this information has led to the incorporation of this 'bottom-up' approach to objective setting into the existing model.

To ensure that everyone in the company is working to the same agenda, there is a need to ensure that all employees are aware of top-level and marketing objectives. The RM approach further suggests that this information should be available to all other core relationship partners. This is seen as a particular failing with many CRM implementations.

Strategies

If the objectives are 'where we want to be', then the strategies are 'how we are going to get there'. Marketing strategies may include sub-strategies (e.g. media strategy, creative strategy). Box 12.1 indicates a number of different strategic options that may prove useful in strategy development, dependent on whether the aim is transactional or relational. They should, however, be recognised as a range of indicators rather than as a prescription for either TM or RM. Keep the customer at the core of the planning and avoid strategies that promote behaviours positive for the bottom line but destructive to customer relationships (Young, 2006, p. 116), or what Reichheld has called 'bad profits' (Schulz and Levy, 2006, p. 1).

Box 12.1 Transactional versus relationship marketing

Transactional marketing	**Relationship marketing**
■ Do the deal and disappear	■ Negotiate a 'win–win' sale situation and stay around being a resource for better results
■ Push price	■ Promote value
■ Short-term thinking and acting	■ Long-term thinking and acting
■ Build the business on deals	■ Build the business on relationships
■ Getting new customers	■ Keeping customers
■ No structure for ongoing business	■ Structure created to support relationships
■ Selling focused	■ Relationship focused
■ Short-term empathy	■ Long-term empathy and rapport
■ Incentive for 'doing the deal'	■ Incentive for long-term relationship and revenue
■ Foundation of sale telling and selling	■ Foundation of revenue trust
■ After-sales service at additional cost	■ After-sales service as investment in relationship
■ Product service focused	■ People expectations and perception focused
■ Rewards incentives for 'doing deals'	■ Rewards incentives for maintaining and growing relationships and revenue
■ The deal is the end	■ The sale is the beginning

(*Source*: Adapted from Thomas, 2000, p. 531)

Tactics

Tactics are the operational element and, by necessity, short term. The choice may be between different media (including the Internet) or techniques (e.g. direct marketing). The danger here is confusing the tactical with the strategic. For all its influence on business habits in general, the Internet is a tactical tool. It is part (certainly not all) of a company's armoury. It may promote different approaches but it is, in strict terms, another media channel. In the same way, database marketing, direct marketing and CRM are, within a RM strategy, tactical responses rather than strategic approaches to company development.

Action

Action plans provide the means by which the organisation's ideas are turned into reality by being given a structure and format through which they can be implemented (O'Malley *et al.*, 1999, p. 59). The action plan is the blueprint through which the objectives are realised. As with the objectives, there is a need to disseminate information to employees and, increasingly, to suppliers, customers and strategic partners.

Control

The control element involves setting clear evaluation criteria (e.g. target response levels). It may also involve testing prior to full execution. Testing differs from research in that it is actual response (albeit on a smaller scale) as opposed to forecast response. In this regard technology has a considerable part to play in the control element of any marketing plan.

Managing relationships

When an RM dimension is incorporated into a company's marketing plan this should be done in the knowledge that certain additional factors will need to be incorporated and subsequently managed.

Handling relationships

While there is nothing new in the desire of businesses to develop ongoing relationships with their customers, recent developments in information technology offer new opportunities for creating individual relationships between a seller and each of its customers (Bejou and Palmer, 1998, p. 7). Ultimately it may lead to a greater ability to attend to individual customer's concerns (or one-to-one marketing). If, as many RM authors suggest, each customer is an individual regardless of the number of customers to be addressed (Kunoe, 1998, p. 1125), then 'one-to-one marketing' is the ultimate aim. It emphasises that every customer requires a different form of communication and (in an ideal world) individual attention. The danger of replacing personal contact with technology is a real one. Such a decision must be taken in the knowledge that it may do harm.

The management of customer relationships will differ from industry to industry. In 'low involvement' consumer markets the relationship with the customer is likely to be managed through technologies such as a database and/or the World Wide Web (O'Malley and Tynan, 1999, p. 589). Databases can be used to target customers with customers having little or no knowledge of the company in question or the existence of the database (Barnes and Howlett, 1998, p. 15). This database view of RM, according to Copulsky and Wolf (1990, pp. 16–17), incorporates three key elements:

■ identifying and building a database of current and potential customers;

■ delivering differentiated messages;

■ tracking each relationship.

The 'low involvement' customer may be quite happy with technology-based RM where technology substitutes for physical proximity (Zineldin, 2000, p. 16). This may contrast with the 'high involvement' consumer who may need a more personal, less mechanised and individually tailored approach that technology (currently) finds difficult to duplicate.

The management of relationships is prone to pitfalls. The problem is that many marketers take their eye off the ball. Rather than viewing a database as simply an 'enabling technology' too many firms have focused their energies on 'database building' rather than 'relationship building' (O'Malley *et al.*, 1997, p. 553). In addition, now that it is possible to manipulate a database in such a way that relationship development is feasible does not mean that all customers want or need such a relationship. Contacting customers on too regular a basis can be worse than not contacting them at all. As Pels (1999, p. 33) points out, this 'technology-allows-me-to-do' approach has more in common with a production type orientation than a marketing orientation.

Managing personal information

The management of customer information through advanced technology can create doubts over privacy, and privacy concerns tend to erode buyer–seller relationships (Prabhaker, 2000, p. 160). Although these concerns are not peculiar to RM, CRM, DbM etc. – medical records being another example – what differs is the depth and variety of information that is collected and used (Smith and Higgins, 2000, p. 83). The three major concerns would appear to be that:

■ The handing over or collection of personal information is an infringement of personal liberty.

■ The handing over of information will result in unwanted attention being paid to that customer.

■ If companies are permitted to hold such information then they should utilise the information wisely.

Infringement of personal liberty

The commercial incentive to collect, merge, warehouse and sell customer information is enormous while the safeguards tend to be weak and easily ignored (ibid., p. 158). In the UK, which has data protection legislation, there is continued pressure from the regulator for tighter control. There is little doubt that the European legislation will get tougher and already many markets have introduced rules that require customers to opt-in (rather than opt-out) if they wish customers to use their data. Practitioners have developed techniques for encouraging customers to 'opt in' or 'join' them. This may include the provision of information or services (e.g. online news) in exchange for data. This range of customer-authorised data collection strategies has been called 'permission marketing'.

There is also some suggestion that customers react badly when they believe their personal details are being indiscriminately passed on. The covert acquisition of information, rather than representing a phase in relationship building, may actually undermine the relationship building process (O'Malley *et al.*, 1997, p. 552). On the other side of the coin there is the irony that strictly regulating the collection of personal information could ultimately limit the quality and level of service that a business can deliver (Prabhaker, 2000, p. 160).

Nowhere is this privacy debate more pertinent than with the Internet.[2] As Prabhaker (p. 159) notes:

> Every time an individual interacts with the web she leaves behind a trail of extraordinary detailed information about who she is, her buying habits, financial status, maybe her medical records and other intimate personal details. She has very little control over who can have access to this information and what they will do with it. It is unrealistic to expect profit driven businesses not to infringe on consumer privacy in an environment that makes it increasingly profitable and a technology that makes it easier than ever to collect and share personal information.

Undoubtedly what some marketers imagine as a means of developing the relationship through information exchange some customers will see as intrusion into their private lives. Finding an acceptable balance may become marketing's greatest challenge.

Unwanted attention

O'Malley *et al.* (1997, p. 553) quote one respondent in their research into consumer's views on data management as commenting that 'handing over personal details just means more rubbish coming through the letterbox'. Fournier *et al.* (1998, p. 43) report that a woman interviewed concerning the number of approaches made to her every day stated 'it's overkill . . . one is more meaningless than the next'. These are not isolated perceptions and it is easy to see why. Direct mail, for example, while being described as a more targeted and flexible medium, has a response rate of around 4 per cent, a return generally seen as satisfactory in the industry. This means that for every one customer evidently interested enough in the offer to respond 24 are not. The cost of sending emails is so low that unrestricted and unwanted emails have quickly become a source of 'Internet pollution' (Hanson, 2000, p. 67). Although many consumers will, as a consequence of modern life, take this in their stride, a percentage will be annoyed about what they regard as untargeted junk mail. Whether the direct marketing industry likes it or not, the ever-growing number of postal and electronic mailshots will ensure that this will become an even greater cause for concern in the future.

Utilising information

The poor utilisation of information is surprisingly commonplace. Another customer in the O'Malley *et al.* (1997, p. 551) study showed her frustration with companies that have the information (they suppose) but do not use it (see also Box 6.3). She explains:

> I go overdrawn at the end of every month and have trouble making the repayments but my bank are constantly making me loan offers. They should know that I can't afford to take out another loan. They, of all people, should know because they have all my details and I often deal with them person-to-person.

Fournier *et al.* (1998, p. 47) note what they call 'the forgotten rule': that intimacy and vulnerability are intertwined. If a company routinely asks its customers for sensitive information, but does not put that information to good use, it should stop asking those questions. Marketers must use the information they already have more effectively and develop appropriate processes to initiate and maintain meaningful dialogue with customers (O'Malley *et al.*, 1997, p. 553). Today's 'interactive age customers' are accustomed to having their needs met immediately, conveniently and inexpensively (Peppers and Rogers, 2000, p. 243) by companies utilising the information they already have at their disposal. Nothing can be more frustrating than having to repeat the details of problems over and over again to assorted customer service personnel. Studies support this. Participants in the O'Malley *et al.* (1997, p. 551) research believed that, if companies used the data they already had more effectively, it would reduce the quantity of irrelevant communications they received.

Appropriateness

Used appropriately, technology can help the company learn from every customer interaction and deepen the relationship by advancing ideas and solutions likely to suit the customer (Gordon, 1998, p. 168). Used inappropriately, the backlash is likely to ensure restrictive controls. Ultimately the evolution of any technical advances in information gathering is dependent on its acceptance by the public (Prabhaker, 2000, p. 161). The compromise is likely to settle around what is becoming known as 'permission marketing' (Chaffey *et al.*, 2000, p. 233) where consumers actively cooperate in the supply of data.

Criticism of RM

An important aspect of management is knowledge of the (actual or perceived) weaknesses of any strategy. Although this book chronicles and generally supports the development of relational strategies in marketing, it would be inappropriate to ignore any perceived weaknesses or criticism of the RM concept or indeed the dangers inherent in the introduction of any new management ideas. Although some of these criticisms have emerged earlier in the text it may be valuable, at this stage, to consolidate them. It is only by acknowledging the weaknesses that the strengths of relational strategies can be fully appreciated.

Management fads

Is RM a fad? Will companies ten years from now regret adopting RM strategies, as has happened with other fads in the past (see Micklethwait and Wooldridge, 1996, for an excellent discussion of this phenomenon)? In their introduction to a collection of writings on RM, Payne *et al.* (1995, p. vii) include this warning:

> There is a tendency when new ideas in management emerge to embrace them keenly for a while and to see them as the ultimate solution to whatever problems we currently perceive to exist. Equally there is a tendency to put them aside after the initial novelty has worn off, and they are found to be not quite the panacea that we once thought. Marketing particularly has been prone to this 'flavour of the month' syndrome . . . Already there are some who would claim that 'relationship marketing' is another of these short-lifecycle management phenomena.

Dholakia (2001, p. 1), talking about CRM in financial services, might as well have been talking about RM or indeed any of the managerial developments of the last one hundred years when noting:

> Ideas that become buzzwords typically begin as clever, useful concepts of great practical value. Then others add bells and whistles to make them more marketable and profitable. As more and more people get acquainted with the concept and become convinced of its value, the 'bandwagon' effect results in certain aspects of the concept getting emphasised, while others remain overlooked.

Brennan (1997, p. 768) too has noted that fashionable management expressions are prone to over-use, abuse and consequently devaluation. RM has not proved immune to this effect.

RM, like all successful ideas, has initial intuitive appeal (Blois, 1997, p. 53) and there have been a number of successful interpretations that have helped to promote the concept. It would, however, also be true to suggest that, with the rapid development of RM, the boundaries have often been stretched and claims made which could never be universally justified. As East (2000, p. 1) notes, some of these propositions have little evidence to support them and/or rest on invalid or over-simplified reasoning. As is often the case with radical change, there is a tendency to over-correct (Baker, 1999, p. 212) and consequently over-hype a concept. Care should be taken, therefore, when implementing relational strategies, to clarify that the concept is right for particular industries or individual situations. This involves seeing through the rhetoric to the core of what RM purports to be all about.

RM as a new marketing concept

Is RM a totally new phenomenon? Haven't RM objectives always been important to marketing? If the answer is yes to either or both of these questions, then how is RM different (Sheth and Parvatiyar, 2000, p. 123)? The question frequently asked is whether RM is a 'new' concept or simply an old concept given a new lease of life by marketing's spin doctors: a new paradigm or an old idea in new clothes (Palmer, 1998, p. 106); possibly 'the emperor's new clothes' (Gummesson, 1997, p. 53). Brown (1998, p. 173) is particularly scathing. RM, he suggests is not new and was already anticipated as part of the original marketing concept. His view is that to regard RM as something novel is 'arrant nonsense'. There is certainly a justifiable criticism regarding RM's novelty. The emergence of RM in the 1980s was not so much a discovery as a rediscovery of long-held and successful strategies (Payne, 2000, p. 41), a return to practices of a pre-industrial era when producers and consumers dealt directly with each other and 'a potential for emotional bonding that transcends economic exchange' (Sheth and Parvatiyar, 2000, p. 123). The concept of 'relationships in marketing' is, indeed, not new as traders have been practising it for centuries. Cynics might suggest, therefore, that RM is nothing but a marketing makeover, the latter-day version of changing the sign on the departmental door from 'sales' to 'marketing' (Brown, 1998, p. 173).

In RM's favour, it is frequently suggested that its biggest achievement is that it has brought back 'relationships' into the mainstream of marketing. That it is really a rebirth of marketing practices of the pre-industrial age (Sheth and Parvatiyar, 1995, p. 399). This may be largely true; however, while relationships may have been 'rediscovered in western corporate markets' they have remained a fundamental part of exchange in many eastern cultures (Palmer, 1996, p. 19). Perhaps, even in our own culture, the concept may have also been kept alive in 'less sophisticated' village and suburban communities or small companies previously largely ignored by marketing academics. According to Gummesson (1999, p. 6):

> The renewed interest in RM may imply that marketing theorists are getting closer to reality; that we are beginning to discern the marketing content of Japanese *Keiretsus*, Chinese *Quanxies*, global ethnic networks, the British school tie, trade between friends, loyalty to the local pub and so on. Marketing has not invented these phenomena, practice has!

In these terms RM is merely re-emphasising certain neglected areas of marketing (Brown, 1998, pp. 173–4) rather than creating something wholly new – the equivalent of 'going back (or forward) to basics' (Gummesson, 1999, p. 13). RM's biggest benefit is that it has caused marketers to question the process-led 4Ps (or 7Ps) approach of the traditional marketing paradigm and to consider the importance of the core firm and its relationships.

Selective research

Another valid criticism of RM is that the universal success implied in case studies is frequently based on selective organisations in a limited number of industries. These claims are usually implied rather than directly stated when, in promoting RM (or indeed DM, DbM or CRM) strategies, writers frequently omit industries where relational strategies may be of marginal, if any, importance. A potential hazard is where this selective research leads to a polarisation of opinions. This in turn causes some marketers to reject alternative perspectives and, at the extreme, begin to claim that firms can only succeed by adapting their particular prescriptive solutions (Chaston, 1998, p. 277).

These prescriptive solutions are of particular concern when it comes to dealing with consultant agencies that promote the RM (or any other) concept. Any search of the Internet using the phrase 'relationship marketing' (or more recently 'customer relationship management') will produce a host of these consultants each extolling the virtues of their vision. As Mitchell (1997, p. 37) cynically notes, consultants 'peddling relationship marketing solutions' are growing at a rate of 30–40 per cent per year, whereas their clients are growing at a more modest 3–4 per cent. Marketers should, therefore, take care, when examining the evidence supporting RM that the factors which led to its successful implementation in one industry or in other contexts are comparable to their own.

O'Malley and Tynan (2000, p. 12) also point out that, although marketers have appropriated the technology, it remains unclear whether they have internalised the philosophy, particularly in consumer markets. They note that, in many markets, all that is apparent is a resource shift from above (i.e. advertising) to below the line (other marketing communications tools; e.g. sales promotion), indicating that RM may, on occasion, be more rhetoric than reality.

One-sided communication

It is suggested that, despite claims to co-produce value, the voice of the customer is often missing from much of RM (Buttle, 1996, p. 13), most particularly in consumer goods marketing. Caught up in the enthusiasm for the rapid increase in information gathering techniques and for the benefits that long-term engagement with customers may hold, many companies that claim to have adopted RM techniques and concepts have forgotten that relationships take two (Fournier *et al.*, 1998, p. 42). The term 'relationship' has often been used by practitioners to underpin a supplier's marketing activities without the customer necessarily being conscious that they are even participating in an RM campaign (Blois, 1997, p. 53).

This viewpoint raises the question (discussed in Chapter 3) of whether it is legitimate to use the term 'relationship' for the interaction between the consumer and a company. Perhaps predictably, much RM research is designed not for the benefit of the consumer but in the interest of the selling firm (Mattsson, 1997, pp. 43–4). This has meant a focus on suppliers' needs regardless of whether or not the buyer wants to develop an ongoing relationship (Palmer, 1998, p. 118). There is also concern over pseudo-relationships (Barnes, 1994, p. 565), where what passes for a relationship is one-sided, with customers locked in, effectively kept in the relationship against their will, because the costs of leaving the relationship are seen to be too high.

Corruption

Social bonds (particularly in business-to-business situations) can, without doubt, become pervasive to the point where they allow economic inefficiencies to develop. In extreme cases networks of corrupt buyers and sellers may acquire sufficient market power to result in an overall loss of economic welfare (Palmer, 1998, p. 118). In addition many of the basic tenets of cooperative marketing would appear to be contrary to competitive philosophy (Palmer, 2001, p. 762). Indeed, anti-competitive legislation has been introduced in most developed markets of which some cooperating companies have, or may in the future, fall foul. Gummesson's (1999, p. 6) reference to the 'British school tie' and 'trade between friends' also raises possible moral issues into cooperative trade. There is indeed a fine line between cooperative behaviour and collusion (Sheth and Sisodia, 1999, p. 84).

Outmoded marketing

It has been said that marketing in general is going through a 'mid-life crisis'. Perhaps it is just that it has not yet matured. Certainly the heat generated by the RM debate suggests less rationality than juvenile pride. Micklethwait and Wooldridge (1996, pp. 15–17) in their critique of management theory list four grounds which link to a description of a management discipline as adolescent:

- it is constitutionally incapable of self-criticism;
- its terminology usually confuses rather than educates;
- it hardly rises above basic common sense;
- it is faddish and bedevilled by contradiction that would not be allowed in more rigorous disciplines.

RM could be accused of all four – but again so could many of the alternative theories, many of which are put forward as solutions. It is hoped that this text has avoided all four!

Postscript

Whereas many would argue that the 'classical approach' to marketing is coming to an end and that we are in the process of an orderly transition to a 'new marketing paradigm', there are powerful voices that suggest that marketing is in a state of chaos and going nowhere (Brookes and Little, 1997, p. 96) and should be given 'the dignified burial it deserves' (Holbrook and Hulbert 2002, p. 726). Indeed, it may also be said of RM, with some justification, that, although it is powerful in theory, it may be decidedly troubled in practice (Fournier *et al.*, 1998, p. 42). On this basis it has some way to go before fully justifying the faith and resources that academics and practitioners have put behind it.

While none of the criticisms or potential dangers noted earlier can be ignored or swept under the carpet, they should not be allowed to wholly devalue RM as a valuable marketing concept. Without doubt, overly simple arguments have been put forward under the guise of RM that ignore the full complexity of relationships and have the potential to mislead. Even simple arguments, such as those put forward for RM, by the originators of a theory, give no guarantee against misuse (Holland, 1990, p. 24). The role of true marketing scholars is to eliminate, as far as possible, misuse and abuse, uncover myths and present reality in innovative ways, thus providing improved road maps (Gummesson, 1997, p. 58). Most of all, marketers must learn that, if we are to prevent the premature death of RM, we must separate the rhetoric from the reality (Fournier *et al.*, 1998, p. 42).

Summary

This chapter looked at the management of RM. It noted the criticism that RM was not systematic enough for some although this may be more to do with whether marketing is viewed as an art or a science. The chapter suggested 'using a scalpel not a hatchet' by introducing RM strategies into an existing marketing plan. This allows for comparability with existing strategies. A number of aspects, specific to RM, were discussed within the context of the marketing plan.

The chapter looked specifically at how relationships might be managed, particularly in relation to available technology. It reviewed the concerns relating to information handling, notably the infringement of personal liberty, unwanted attention and poor utilisation of information.

The chapter concluded with a review of some of the criticisms of RM as it was proposed that knowledge of RM's actual or perceived failings may contribute to the development of successful relational strategies. Specifically, it challenged and clarified claims that RM is a 'management fad', a reworked (and therefore not new) concept, based on selective research and one-sided communication, and prone to corruption.

In a postscript it was proposed that, while none of the criticisms or potential dangers could be ignored, they should not be allowed to wholly devalue RM as a valuable marketing concept. Most importantly, marketers must distinguish the rhetoric from the reality.

Discussion questions
1 What factors distinguish a marketing plan that incorporates relational strategies from a more traditional plan?
2 Why might the management of customer information become even more important in the future?
3 What, in your judgement, are the most sustainable and least sustainable criticisms of RM?

Case study   A decisive edge

Your company is in a crisis. Its pole position as the producer of a best-selling consumer brand is under attack from a long-term rival. The competitor's new marketing campaign has focused consumer attention on a particular characteristic of its otherwise identical brand – an aspect you had considered unassailable. Your company is desperate to win this highly public battle. In a tense board meeting, it's suddenly your turn to speak. The company's future rests on the board's decision. What do you suggest?

Coca-Cola found itself in this predicament in the 1980s, when its arch-rival launched the Pepsi Challenge taste tests. Faced with a fight on the one area they'd never worried about before – taste – Coca-Cola ran focus groups that seemed to confirm it as the issue. Yet the company made a primary error – it failed to look for contradictory evidence before settling on a solution. It did everything else by the book – including reformulating the Coca-Cola recipe (at great expense). But the result, New Coke, was an embarrassing flop. Changing the flavour was the wrong decision.

Coke's case illustrates the truism that a great team, a fast brain and a lot of data don't guarantee a good decision. For a manager, decision-making skills are essential to continued success. Get a decision like this right and you're likely to be congratulated. Get it wrong and you'll be sidelined by your boss and lose the confidence of your team. A bad decision can stall a promising career.

The quest is on, then, for smarter decision-making. Academic research divides this subject roughly into three areas: structures, styles and thinking errors. Knowing how to use the structure is of course helpful, but it's an awareness of decision-making styles and avoidance of common errors in thinking that can turn a bright individual into a reliable decision-maker. 'Structures allow a perspective on the problem and on the risks,' says Derek Bunn, professor of decision sciences at the London Business School. 'They also enable you to make decisions that are defensible, credible and that you can easily communicate.'

But structures are only as good as the person using them. 'There's no panacea,' explains Bunn. 'You can't automate decision-making. All that structures can do is provide an extra level of analytic capability. No one believes that you can delegate an intuitive decision to a quantitative model anymore.'

What Bunn is driving at is that a bad decision is less likely to be a result of the decision-making process than of the mindset of the decision-maker. Different decision styles include those of the snap decision-maker, who boasts of 'gut instinct'; the fence-sitter, who keeps the options open; the democratic decider, who canvasses colleagues' opinions; and the uncertain manager, who's easily led.

Says Professor Nigel Nicholson of the London Business School, author of *Managing the Human Animal* (Texere): 'Styles vary across cultures, over time, with maturity and experience, and with background. There is a bias towards one of two models. Model 1 is the collegial first-among-equals style: high in involvement and low in power. Model 2 is the lead-from-a-distance style: top-down, goal-setting, sometimes visionary, often empowering (by leaving people to their own devices), yet driving for action and results.'

Both styles can work, and it's possible for one person to switch between them. 'Model 1 suits situations where you have to constantly adjust to change and work together,' explains Nicholson. 'And you can be very successful in model 2 if you have highly skilled, self-managing professionals reporting to you.'

High-flyers know that once you've found your style, you don't stop there. Talented managers adapt their decision-making as their career progresses. Kenneth Brousseau, CEO of US software house Decision Dynamics, and Gary Hourihan at Korn/Ferry International have identified the decision-making patterns that permeate an individual's career (*Harvard Businesss Review*, February 2006). Junior managers favour a 'decisive' style that focuses on choosing and implementing one option, with an emphasis on speed and simplicity. But as managers progress, the most successful adopt a flexible and integrative style, which enables them to solicit, choose from and adapt solutions as the situation changes.

This more participative and responsive style is clearly evident across the highest-performing 20 per cent of managers studied by Brousseau and Hourihan. Failure to evolve, they say, 'can be fatal to your career'. As evidence, they point to the lowest-performing managers, whose styles do not develop over time.

What about those who find it hard to make decisions? According to LBS's Nicholson, it's rare for hopeless prevaricators to get into positions of leadership – one good reason to brush up on your decision-making skills. Yet some leaders are accused of inconsistency because they can see everyone's point of view. Says Nicholson: 'If you're lost in a forest, you need a compass. The compass for decision-making is an overarching concept of the company's vision and purpose, and of your own identity. If you don't have this, you need to spend time digging down into yourself and thinking about what sort of leader you want to be.' In other words, to become better at decisions, look at the bigger picture – the company's aims and your own career objectives – and use that as your decision frame.

Of course, not all decisions are entirely your own. Some you inherit, others are partially or wholly dictated by a boss, the context, a competitor's actions or your predecessor's choices. Says Ralph Keeney, a research professor at the Fuqua School of Business at Duke University, North Carolina: 'There are three things that unambiguously frame your decisions: what is the problem, what are the objectives, and what are the alternatives? It's after this that the decision-making takes off. Too often, that initial framing is left to someone else. The fundamental thing is to recognise that this occurs and try to put it right. You need to ask the right questions. Don't just decide what your objectives are by reacting to the moves of others – whether competitors, colleagues or bosses.'

But your mind can trip you up even when you've developed your decision-making style, such is the faulty psychology underpinning many of our decisions. Social scientists recognise the tricks our minds play on us, such as discounting important information, misremembering facts and acting on our biases - all while we think we're doing no such thing.

According to Max Bazerman, professor of business administration at Harvard Business School, such flaws are rife, even among seasoned decision-makers. 'While there is plenty of good advice available, most people do not follow it. Why not? Because we fall victim to a variety of predictable errors that not only destroy our intuition but also hinder our tendency to implement good advice.'

Imagine you're choosing a new software package to process sales data and bring you up to the speed of your competitors. A consumer report lists a particular package as the best, but a friend who has just installed the system says it's nothing but trouble. The friend represents one isolated, unrepresentative incident, whereas the consumer report has tested thousands of software packages and is far more accurate. Yet you're now very unlikely to buy that particular software.

Bazerman calls this the 'availability trap'. The more salient, memorable or recent information is, the more we rely on it to make our decision. An anecdote is far more available, and therefore persuasive, than dry data – but that doesn't make it the right information on which to base a decision. Instead, examine data, information and statistics carefully and don't let colourful information or anecdotes influence you. The availability trap is one of several decision-making errors we're prone to, particularly under pressure. Faced with cognitive overload, our minds use shortcuts-known as heuristics – to see us through. These rely on a combination of received wisdom, previous experience, habit and emotion – all of which can go against rational calculation.

For some theorists, heuristics is enjoying a resurgence over old-fashioned deliberative decision-making. Author and New Yorker journalist Malcolm Gladwell recently devoted a whole book, *Blink* (Allen Lane), to instinct, or 'thinking without thinking'. Research from decision-making experts in the Netherlands suggests that 'unconscious thought' (akin to 'sleeping on it') leads to better decisions than the slow, analytical approach. And business leaders like Jack Welch have popularised the 'from the gut' leadership style so that many now see instinctive decisions as the hallmark of a great leader. As *Harvard Business Review* suggested in January 2006: 'Pragmatists act on evidence. Heroes act on guts.'

And, indeed, most of the time heuristics works. Imagine if, when you got up in the morning, you stopped to consider which side of the bed to get out of or whether to put on your right or left sock first. If you deliberated over each decision, colleagues might soon call, wondering why you weren't at work. Heuristics avoids this problem as it enables you to make decisions fast, but largely unconsciously.

Think back to this morning. Why did you put your socks on in that particular order? It's unlikely you'll have a reasoned answer. This highlights two main problems with heuristics: we use it all the time, but we're not always aware that we're doing so; and it may conceal basic flaws in our thinking and judgment.

Keeney has compiled common pitfalls in his book, *Smart Choices: A Practical Guide to Making Better Decisions* (HBS Press), co-written by John Hammond and Howard Raiffa. A common error he picks out is our tendency to seek confirming evidence. We often subconsciously decide we do or don't like a particular solution or decision and then look for evidence to confirm our hunch. This might explain the New Coke debacle. Coca-Cola went about its decision-making the right way – carefully analysing and weighing evidence. But Pepsi's campaign lured it into chasing the wrong information and falsely confirming taste as an issue.

To avoid this, Keeney recommends being honest about your motives in making a decision. Are you really scrutinising data with a view to making a smart choice, or looking for evidence that supports your favourite option? If you are decision-making with your team, don't ask leading questions – encourage team members to play devil's advocate rather than yes-men.

Another common pitfall is anchoring. As an example, ask yourself the following: Are there more than 150 nations in the UN? Got an answer? Now try this: What's your best guess of how many nations belong to the UN? For most of us, the number 150 influences our answer to the second question. If the first had said 'are there more than 50 nations in the UN?', our answer to the second would have been much lower. Our minds seize on initial impressions, data or estimates and use them to anchor subsequent thoughts and judgments.

Even the way a problem is presented can serve as an anchor. If your manager highlights an issue – say, poor sales – and suggests spending more on advertising, you and your team are more likely to focus on this solution than to explore new, unrelated avenues. Your boss's comments, however throwaway, have become your anchor. To get round the problem, Keeney suggests approaching decisions from different angles, deliberately abandoning your first line of thought, and not taking the first thing you hear as gospel. Push yourself to seek fresh perspectives.

We're also biased in favour of the status quo. Maintaining it means we avoid sticking our necks out. Faced with a plethora of options, choosing the status quo is easier – which is why so many of us fail to switch mortgage lenders when the honeymoon period of low rates expires; we just can't face the choice and look for reasons to stick with what we know.

Keeney suggests asking yourself: 'Would I consider the status quo as a good option if it wasn't already the status quo?' Don't dramatise the difficulty of changing the old order. And if there are many possible options, force yourself to choose rather than default to what you know.

Even once we're aware of these pitfalls, we will inevitably still make poor decisions at times. What then? First, admit your mistake – to yourself if no one else. It's tempting to keep metaphorically throwing good money after bad – persisting with that dying project, hanging on to the underperforming member of staff you hired. To do otherwise would be to admit your mistake – particularly hard if your company doesn't tolerate errors of judgment. But it's imperative to cut your losses and start afresh. Imagine you are approaching the situation as an outsider – what would you change? Don't waste time on recriminations, instead, start the search for new solutions.

We can be our own worst enemy. Even if we know which decision-making strategy to use, we can trip ourselves up with our unconscious biases, lazy thinking and failure to seek out as many options as possible. Because taking mental shortcuts is pretty much bar-coded into our brains, it requires constant attention to adjust our decision-making. As Keeney points out: 'The best defence is always awareness.'

Be prepared to evolve your style, to spot the tricks your mind plays on you, and to guard against them, and you're well on the way to being an excellent decision-maker.

(*Source*: Rebecca Alexander, *Management Today*, May 2007)

Case study questions

1 What makes a good decision-maker?
2 What part does intuition play in decision-making?
3 Explain the 'availability trap' and 'anchoring'.

References

Baker, M.J. (1999) 'Editorial', *Journal of Marketing Management*, **15**, 211–14.

Ballantyne, D. (2000) 'Interaction, dialogue and knowledge generation: three key concepts in relationship marketing', in 2nd WWW Conference on Relationship Marketing, 15 November 1999 to 15 February 2000, Paper 7 <www.mcb.co.uk/services/conferen/nov99/rm>.

Barnes, J.G. (1994) 'Close to the customer: but is it really a relationship?', *Journal of Marketing Management*, **10**, 561–70.

Barnes, J.G. and Howlett, D.M. (1998) 'Predictors of equity in relationships between service providers and retail customers', *International Journal of Bank Marketing*, **16** (1), 5–23.

Bejou, D. and Palmer, A. (1998) 'Service failure and loyalty: an exploratory empirical study of airline customers', *Journal of Services Marketing*, **12** (1), 7–22.

Blois, K.J. (1997) 'When is a relationship a relationship?', in Gemünden, H.G., Rittert, T. and Walter, A. (eds) *Relationships and Networks in International Markets*, Oxford: Elsevier, pp. 53–64.

Brassington, F. and Pettitt, S. (1997) *The Principles of Marketing*, London: Pitman.

Brennan, R. (1997) 'Buyer/supplier partnering in British industry: the automotive and telecommunications sectors', *Journal of Marketing Management*, **13** (8), 758–76.

Brookes, R. and Little, V. (1997) 'The new marketing: what does "customer focus" mean?', *Marketing and Research Today*, May, 96–105.

Brown, S. (1998) *Postmodern Marketing II*. London: International Thomson Business Press.

Buttle, F.B. (1996) *Relationship Marketing Theory and Practice*, London: Paul Chapman.

Chaffey, D. (2006) *Internet Marketing: Strategy, Implementation and Practice*, 3rd edn, Harlow: Pearson Education.

Chaffey, D., Mayer, R., Johnston, K. and Ellis-Chadwick, F. (2000) *Internet Marketing*, Harlow: Pearson Education.

Chaston, I. (1998) 'Evolving "new marketing" philosophies by merging existing concepts: application of process within small high-technology firms', *Journal of Marketing Management*, **14**, 273–91.

Copulsky, J.R. and Wolf, M.J. (1990) 'Relationship marketing: positioning for the future', *Journal of Business Strategy*, **11** (4), 16–20.

Damerest, M. (1997) 'Understanding knowledge management', *Long Range Planning*, **30** (3), 374–84.

Dholakia, P. (2001) 'Customer relationship management: the three myths of financial services CRM', *Financial Services Marketing*, **3** (2), 40–1.

East, R. (2000) 'Fact and fallacy in retention marketing', *Professorial Inaugural Lecture*, 1 March, Kingston University Business School, UK.

Evans, M. (2003) 'Marketing communications changes', in Hart, S. (ed.) *Marketing Changes*, London: International Thomson Business Press, pp. 257–72.

Fournier, S., Dobscha, S. and Mick, D.G. (1998) 'Preventing the premature death of relationship marketing', *Harvard Business Review*, January/February, 42–9.

Gordon, I.H. (1998) *Relationship Marketing*, Etobicoke, Ontario: John Wiley & Sons.

Grönroos, C. (2000) 'The relationship marketing process: interaction, communication, dialogue, value', in 2nd WWW Conference on Relationship Marketing, 15 November 1999 to 15 February 2000, Paper 2 <www.mcb.co.uk/services/conferen/nov99/rm>.

Gummesson, E. (1997) 'Relationship marketing: the emperor's new clothes or a paradigm shift?', *Marketing and Research Today*, February, 53–60.

Gummesson, E. (1999) *Total Relationship Marketing: Rethinking Marketing Management from 4Ps to 30Rs*, Oxford: Butterworth Heinemann.

Håkansson, H. and Snehota, I (1989) 'No business is an island: the network concept of business strategy', *Scandinavian Journal of Management*, **4** (3), 187–200.

Håkansson, H. and Snehota, I.J. (2000) 'The IMP perspective: assets and liabilities of business relationships', in Sheth, J.N. and Paryatiyar, A. (eds) *Handbook of Relationship Marketing*, Thousand Oaks, CA: Sage, pp. 69–93.

Hanson, W. (2000) *Principles of Internet Marketing*, Cincinnati, OH: South-Western College Publishing.

Holbrook, M.B. and Hulbert, J.M. (2002) 'Elegy on the death of marketing: never send to know why we have come to bury marketing but ask what you can do for your country churchyard', *European Journal of Marketing*, **36**, (5/6), 706–32.

Holland, R. (1990) 'The paradigm plague: prevention, cure and inoculation', *Tavistock Institute of Human Relations*, **43** (1), 23–48.

Kunøe, G. (1998) 'On the ability of ad agencies to assist in developing one-to-one communication: measuring "the core of dialogue"', *European Journal of Marketing*, **32** (11/12), 1124–37.

Littler, D. (1998) 'Editorial: perspective on consumer behaviour', *Journal of Marketing Management*, **14**, 1–2.

McDonald, M. (1999) 'Strategic marketing planning: theory and practice', in Baker, M. (ed.) *The CIM Marketing Book*, 4th edn, Oxford: Butterworth Heinemann, pp. 50–77.

McDonald, M. (2000) 'On the right track', *Marketing Business*, April, 28–31, 28.

Mattsson, L.G. (1997) 'Relationships in a network perspective', in Gemünden, H.G., Rittert, T. and Walter, A. (eds) *Relationships and Networks in International Markets*, Oxford: Elsevier, pp. 37–47.

Mazur, L. (2000) 'A difficult age', *Marketing Business*, December 1999/January 2000, 33.

Micklethwait, J. and Wooldridge, A. (1996) *The Witch Doctors: What the Management Gurus are Saying*, London: Heinemann.

Mitchell, A. (1997) 'Evolution', *Marketing Business*, June, 37.

Morgan, R.M. and Hunt, S.D. (1994) 'The commitment–trust theory of relationship marketing', *Journal of Marketing*, **58** (3), 20–38.

O'Malley, L. (2003) 'Relationship marketing', in Hart, S. (ed.) *Marketing Changes*, London: International Thomson Business Press, pp. 125–45.

O'Malley, L. and Tynan, C. (1999) 'The utility of the relationship metaphor in consumer markets: a critical evaluation', *Journal of Marketing Management*, **15**, 587–602.

O'Malley, L. and Tynan, C. (2000) 'Relationship marketing in consumer markets: rhetoric or reality?', *European Journal of Marketing*, **34** (7).

O'Malley, L., Patterson, M. and Evans, M. (1997) 'Intimacy or intrusion? The privacy dilemma for relationship marketing in consumer markets', *Journal of Marketing Management*, **13** (6), 541–59.

O'Malley, L., Patterson, M. and Evans, M. (1999) *Exploring Direct Marketing*, London: International Thomson Business Press.

O'Toole, T. and Donaldson, W. (2003) 'The strategy to implementation cycle of relationship marketing planning', *Marketing Theory*, **3** (2), 195–209.

Palmer, A.J. (1996) 'Relationship marketing: a universal paradigm or management fad?', *The Learning Organisation*, **3** (3), 18–25.

Palmer, A.J. (1998) *Principles of Services Marketing*, London: Kogan Page.

Palmer, A.J. (2001) 'Co-operation and collusion: making the distinction in marketing relationships', *Journal of Marketing Management*, **17** (7/8), 761–84.

Payne, A. (2000) 'Relationship marketing: the UK perspective', in Sheth, J.N. and Parvatiyar, A. (eds) *Handbook of Relationship Marketing*, Thousand Oaks, CA: Sage, pp. 39–67.

Payne, A., Christopher, M. and Peck, H. (eds) (1995) *Relationship Marketing for Competitive Advantage: Winning and Keeping Customers*, Oxford: Butterworth Heinemann.

Pels, J. (1999) 'Exchange relationships in consumer markets?', *European Journal of Marketing*, **33** (1/2), 19–37.

Peppers, D. and Rogers, M. (2000) 'Build a one-to-one learning relationship with your customers', *Interactive Marketing*, **1** (3), 243–50.

Prabhaker, P.R. (2000) 'Who owns the on-line consumer?', *Journal of Consumer Marketing*, **17** (2), 158–71.

Reichheld, F.F. (1993) 'Loyalty based management', *Harvard Business Review*, March/April, 64–73.

Ryals, L. (2000) 'Planning for relationship marketing', in Cranfield School of Management, *Marketing Management: A Relationship Marketing Perspective*, Basingstoke: Macmillan, pp. 231–48.

Schultz, R. and Levy, R.H. (2006) 'Reichheld's new metric: the net promoter score', *Chief Marketer*, 22 February, <http://chiefmarketer.com/crm_loop/roi/new-metric/022206/index.html>.

Sheth, J.N. and Parvatiyar, A. (1995) 'The evolution of relationship marketing', *International Business Review*, **4** (4), 397–418.

Sheth, J.N. and Parvatiyar, A. (2000) 'The evolution of relationship marketing', in Sheth, J.N. and Parvatiyar, A. (eds) *Handbook of Relationship Marketing*, Thousand Oaks, CA: Sage, pp. 119–45.

Sheth, J.N. and Sisodia, R.S. (1999) 'Revisiting marketing's lawlike generalizations', *Journal of the Academy of Marketing Sciences*, **17** (1), 71–87.

Smith, W. and Higgins, M. (2000) 'Reconsidering the relationship analogy', *Journal of Marketing Management*, **16**, 81–94.

Tapp, A. (2004) 'A call to arms for applied marketing academics', *Marketing Intelligence and Planning*, **22** (5), 579–90.

Thomas, M.J. (2000) 'Commentary: princely thoughts on Machiavelli, marketing and management', *European Journal of Marketing*, **34** (5/6), 524–37.

Too, L.H.Y., Souchon, A.L. and Thirkell, P.C. (2001) 'Relationship marketing and customer loyalty in a retail setting: a dynamic exploration', *Journal of Marketing Management*, **17** (3–4), 287–319.

Young, L. (2006) 'Trust: looking forward and back', *Journal of Business and Industrial Marketing*, **21** (7), 92–3.

Zineldin, M. (2000) 'Beyond relationship marketing: technologicalship marketing', *Marketing Intelligence and Planning*, **18** (1), 9–23.

Notes

1 PEST (or STEP) stands for elements of the macroenvironment: political, economic, sociological and technological, to which legal is frequently added; SWOT stands for strengths, weaknesses, opportunities and threats.

2 It is not within the scope of this chapter to distinguish between terms such as World Wide Web, Internet, intranet etc. For a full explanation, see Chaffey, 2006.

13 Back to the future

Key issues

■ The relationship marketing divide
■ Focused and diffuse relationship marketing
■ Implications for RM research

Introduction

The first edition of this text was published at a time of turmoil for RM. This additional chapter was added to the second edition and was designed to bring the relationship marketing (RM) debate up to date. In this third edition the ideas discussed are revisited. To put the debate in context, the chapter looks again, briefly, at the origins of RM's broad-church approach and the development of relational theory during the last decades of the twentieth century. It notes the re-emergence of the theoretically narrow view of relationship marketing and speculates on the implications for researchers in the future.

RM research

The end of the twentieth century was a watershed for RM. Certainly the clarity (and to some extent the certainty) surrounding relational concepts in the 1990s was not as evident in the new millennium. Whereas there had always been differences in tactical emphasis and a lack of a precise definition (or definitions), researchers in the past appeared willing to accept, or at least acknowledge, a range of broad principles associated with relationship marketing. This 'broad church' approach has now been challenged. There appears to be a significant rift developing between those who maintain a holistic view of diverse organisational relationships and those who wish to de-emphasise all relationships except that of the customer–supplier dyad.

From the earliest discussions on relationship marketing, a diversity of influences have led to a surfeit of academic perspectives from which RM theory (or more correctly theories) were to develop. With so many doubts concerning relationship marketing's origins and the development of regional schools of thought (see Chapter 2), it is no wonder that different perspectives were to appear. Relationship marketing covered a fragmented set of ideas and theoretical frameworks held together by a faith (largely untested) in the value of relationships within and without the organisation. This faith promoted the accusation that its discussion was characterised more by rhetoric than vigorous examination of what the concept actually means (Möller and Halinnen, 2000).

The new century also brought with it a push for greater marketing accountability led in the USA by the Marketing Science Institute[1] and in the UK by the Chartered Institute of Marketing.[2] This movement sought to justify, through measurement, marketing's place in the organisational framework. With 'marketing metrics' becoming more important on the mainstream marketing agenda, any theories built upon humanistic concepts (as opposed to process doctrine) was open to the charge that its processes were too subjective for the accountability that marketers believed they required.

Between the extremes ran a continuum along which most researchers travelled without being particularly argumentative about their views and accepting, in a reasonable manner, that there are diverse ways of thinking (Levy, 2002). Although broad variations created difficulties, this was accepted as part of RM's broad appeal. There was a problem with the diversity in operational approaches employed such that it was 'impossible to delimit the (RM) domain' as the boundaries were 'completely permeable and elastic' and this did result in 'difficulties in identifying appropriate contexts for empirical research and exacerbated conceptual problems within the emerging discipline' (O'Malley and Tynan, 2000, p. 809). Despite this the broad 'school of RM' was holding together largely because the 'philosophy of relationships' was still a developing theme and RM research did appear to be extending the theoretical boundaries of marketing (e.g. through internal marketing).

On the shoulders of giants

To get an overview of the developing RM themes there is a need to track back. A feature of older definitions and writings on the subject of relationship marketing was that it focused wholly on the supplier–customer relationship (the 'supplier–customer dyad'). Berry (1983, p. 25), for example, suggested that the 'new' relationship marketing approach should be defined as 'attracting, maintaining and . . . enhancing customer relationships'. The concentration here was both on acquiring and, perhaps more importantly, retaining customers. Customer service was central to this philosophy and although definitions of what this service included were various, what they had in common was that it was concerned with relationships at the buyer–seller interface (Clark, 2000).

Later contributions to the relationship marketing debate, however, were seen to widen RM's scope (Buttle, 1996). According to Gummesson (1999), marketing was more than just the dyadic relationship between the buyer and the seller; rather it represented the whole series of 'relationships, networks and interactions' that the company (or more strictly the company's employees or representatives) undertook as part of their commercial dealings. RM thinking, therefore, developed away from the strictly 'two-way dialogue' between the supplier and the customer towards the synonymous development of other company relationships. Business-to-business research (largely through the work of the IMP[3] group) and services marketing research in particular promoted these conceptions and it was these areas that were viewed as most likely to benefit from relational strategies. Among the relationships (the simple dyad as well as the complex networks) the parties were seen in active contact with each other. Thus RM was seen to represent all marketing activities directed towards establishing, developing and maintaining successful relational exchanges (Morgan and Hunt, 1994).

These concepts, ideas and developments are present in Grönroos's (1994, p. 9) widely quoted definition of relationship marketing (quoted in full on page 37) in which he suggests that RM involves 'relationships with customers *and other stakeholders*'. Although there was no single model encapsulating these ideas there appeared to be a consensus that, in addition to a customer focus, a company should be considering a range of partnerships with suppliers, internal customers, institutions and intermediaries (Clarkson *et al.*, 1997). Indeed the scope of RM was at the core of its philosophy (Veloutsou *et al.*, 2002). These 'network' or extended relationship theories, ideas and concepts were advanced by a number of eminent marketing writers including Christopher *et al.* (1991, 1994), Kotler (1992), Millman (1993), Hunt and Morgan (1994), Doyle (1995), Peck (1996), Buttle (1996) and Gummesson (1996) (see Part II). The common theme promoted by these researchers was that firms should compete through the development of relatively long-term relationships with all its stakeholders (Reichheld 1996; Hunt, 1997). The common ground between these concepts was 'the core firm and its partnerships' (Doyle, 1995). While the centrality of customer markets was never in doubt, the move to RM was, therefore, seen as a move from a single dyadic relationship to a multi-faceted series of interrelationships important to, influenced through, but not necessarily dominated exclusively by, the supplier–customer interaction. Despite the broad, seemingly unending, range of tactical approaches associated with RM, there appeared to be widespread agreement that what has particularly distinguished it, strategically, from traditional marketing was this multiplicity in conceptualising markets (Dean and Croft, 2001).

Brave new world

As we entered the new century, this largely agreed multi-relationship approach appeared to be under challenge. Although 'breadth of domain' has always been an issue, arguments appear to be coalescing around two, perhaps irreconcilable, camps of researchers. A schism appears to have developed between those who conceive marketing from a broad and pluralistic orientation and those who take a narrower functional marketing perspective. In effect ideas are polarising between those researchers who continue to support the holistic, multi-relationship, definition of relationship marketing and those whose focus is solely concerned with the 'customer–supplier dyad' (Payne, 2000). Among this latter group the suggestion is that non-customer relationships are 'outside the domain of marketing' and that their inclusion in the marketing research agenda 'risks diluting the value and contribution of the marketing discipline in directing relationship marketing practice and research and theory development' (Parvatiyar and Sheth, 2000).

In effect the divide is between those researchers who see RM as a wide range of relationships, albeit that its benefits appear limited to certain industries and situations (e.g. Grönroos, 1994; Barnes, 1994; Palmer, 1996), and those whose definition is restricted but who choose to apply relational thinking across the industrial board. In essence, it is between a broad definition of RM with a narrow application (that could be termed 'focused') and a narrower viewpoint with a distinctly broader application (that might be called 'diffuse') (see Figure 13.1).

It would appear, therefore, that many of the academics and practitioners who wholeheartedly in the past embraced the philosophy of multifarious relationships have 'moved-on' (or is it back?) to concepts that claim to focus on the fundamentalism of customer relationships. This view is supported by the 'marketing metrics' evangelism associated with the scientific view of marketing in general and, perhaps, customer relationship management (CRM) in particular.

It would seem that the driving force behind the diffuse approach may be the belief that only by adapting RM in such a way that it can be embraced across the board can it have the potential to become the dominant paradigm and orientation of marketing (Parvatiyar and Sheth, 2000). A feature of this is the extension of the term 'relationships' to the non-personal, i.e. technology-driven contact associated with direct marketing and, latterly, CRM. A secondary feature of this divide appears to be that between the non-American (principally Nordic and Anglo-Australian approaches) and American researchers. Although it is always dangerous to generalise,[4] North American researchers (e.g. Evans and Laskin, 1994; Smith and Higgins, 2000; Parvatiyar and Sheth, 2000) appear to be adopting the narrower (i.e. focused) form ahead of their European and southern hemisphere colleagues. Perhaps this is in part due to what one academic (Tapp, 2002) has described as 'the American dominated view that marketing as a science has driven an academic culture that demands de-personalisation, objectivity and cold emotional analysis'. Gummesson (2003, p. 168) too reflects this view when he notes that 'in the dominating US version of RM, the content of the phenomenon is locked in a box of simplistic one-to-one customer supplier relationships – an approach touted especially in CRM'.

A possible lack of cross-fertilisation and coordination may account for the apparent geographical differences in RM research emphasis. It is rare, for example, for non-American writers to make it to the pages of North American journals. This may be because, being generally less encumbered by the conformist doctrine of US journal reviewers, non-American papers are rarely accepted for publication.

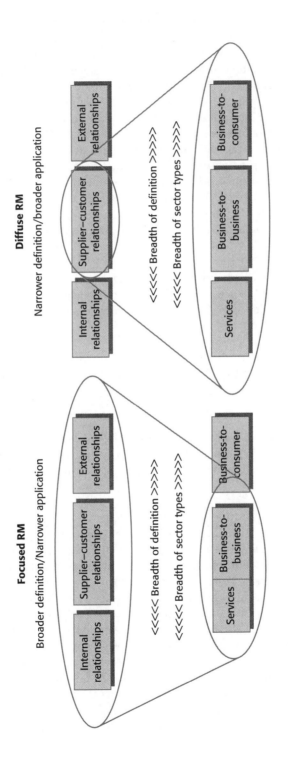

Figure 13.1 Focused and diffuse relationship marketing

The 'diffuse' (or North American) approach emphasises the relationship between the buyer and the seller in the context of the organisational environment (Payne, 2000). Evans and Laskin (1994, p. 440), for example, define RM as 'a customer centred approach by which firms seek long-term business relationships with prospective and existing customers'. Parvatiyar and Sheth (2000, pp. 7/8) too see RM as 'the on-going process of engaging in co-operative and collaborative activities and programmes' not with a broad range of stakeholders but 'with [the] immediate and end-user customers to create and enhance mutual economic value'. These authors distinguish between 'relationship marketing' and 'marketing relationships' and suggest that RM should not be concerned with all aspects of the latter, concentrating instead on 'developing closer relationships with . . . customers and turning them into loyal ones'. The same authors (p. 7) explicitly criticise writers such as Morgan and Hunt (1994) for including other 'partnerships' within the remit of RM. They argue strongly against the 'focused' approach and suggest that researchers should 'delimit the domain of RM', arguing that:

> many of the partnerships have been constructed as being outside the domain of marketing and hence their inclusion risks diluting the value and contribution of the marketing discipline in directing relationship marketing practice and research and theory development.

By suggesting RM should not stray 'outside the domain of marketing' they are explicitly challenging the RM view of marketing as an orientation rather than a function. While acknowledging other relationships exist, Parvatiyar and Sheth (2000, p. 8) insist that:

> other aspects of organisational relationships, such as supplier relationships, internal relationships and lateral relationships are aspects that are attended [to] by such disciplines as purchasing and logistics management, human resource management and strategic management.

This 'diffuse' positioning refutes that tenet of RM that suggests that 'functional silos' decrease the efficiency with which the body of knowledge grows (Hunt and Lambe, 2000) and many of the concepts (e.g. empowerment) associated with internal relationships and 'internal marketing' (e.g. Reynoso and Moores, 1996) (see Chapter 8). It further sidelines, from a marketing perspective, those strategic external relationships that appear so important in modern business (see Chapters 9 and 10).

Payne (2000) is one author who recognises and accepts the growing divide. He argues for the necessity to adopt agreed-upon terminology to differentiate between the broad and narrow approaches. He suggests the term 'customer relationship marketing' for the narrow (diffuse) view, leaving RM as a theoretically broader, but more focused, term. The closeness of 'customer relationship marketing' to the widely utilised phrase 'customer relationship management' (CRM) should not be lost in this discussion as it too remains firmly focused on the customer–supplier dyad with the added twist of technology-managed relationships.

Implications

This 'breadth of domain' is not a new issue, as Coviello *et al.* (1997) have pointed out earlier. Whereas previously these viewpoints were accommodated within RM's broad church it is now becoming not just one of the central issues in relational research (Payne, 2000) but one likely to lead to divisions in the relationships marketing research community. It may be hypothesised that this theoretically narrow, diffuse, view fits closer with the needs of the mass market. This is despite there being little to support the fact that mass marketing has moved significantly away from transactional marketing towards relationships other than those quasi-relationships enabled through technology. As O'Malley and Tynan (1999, pp. 595) note, marketers have:

> ignored the fact that RM was intended as an alternative approach to marketing in contexts which differ significantly from mass marketing situations and where high interpersonal interaction occurs. Despite this the assumption that RM is relevant in mass marketing situations has not been challenged or tested in any meaningful way. Rather the limitations of RM in this context has been camouflaged by the possibilities attended to by Direct Marketing . . .

and, one supposes, CRM. The drive toward a form of marketing that will exist comfortably in all situations and in all industries and, most importantly, as Robert Shaw (quoted in Bartram, 2002) puts it, enables marketing 'to shed its smoke and mirrors reputation . . . [and] gain credibility in the boardroom', means settling for the lowest common denominator. The Holy Grail of 'one-size-fits-all' seems to be the aim. This directly contradicts the 'focused' approach that acknowledges RM has limitations and must co-exist with more traditional forms of marketing (Brodie *et al.*, 1997). As Coviello and Brodie (2001, p. 396) note:

> it is important to understand both similarities and differences in marketing practice across contexts, including when and why different approaches to marketing are being practised, how multiple approaches can be practised simultaneously, and how these practices might be influenced by other firms, market or managerial characteristics.

Summary

While recognising (in the fashion of any 'broad church') that all views are equally valid, the theoretically narrow 'diffuse' view appears to manipulate the central tenets of RM. The attempt to 'force-fit' relational strategies in markets where interpersonal interaction is low promotes the use of technology (specifically that associated with CRM) as a supposed substitute for personal closeness. That the marketing impact of these strategies is measurable (and, therefore, reportable) too encourages this development. There is nothing inherently wrong in this approach except when companies start to believe there is more to their relationship than is in fact the case. For example, the growth of call centres (a central platform of CRM) no doubt adds to marketing effectiveness on the basis of cost reduction. Whether this creates or defends customer value or could potentially harm customer relationships (both near impossible to measure) are not part of these calculations.

It is evident that the language of RM misleads some organisations into assuming that all customer–supplier contacts are capable of closeness when many are not much more than personal exchanges. Perhaps this explains the 70–80 per cent failure rate of CRM projects reported by KPMG (Sussex and Cox, 2002). According to Mitchell (2001), 'corporate disillusionment and downright hostility to the whole CRM bandwagon is reaching fever pitch'.

Why should this schism concern marketers? After all, as Sheth and Sisodia (1999) note, we should always bear in mind that marketing is context driven, that the context has changed, is changing and will no doubt change in the future. Marketers should continuously question and challenge what these authors call the well-accepted 'law-like generalisations' that have grown up around marketing, including relationship marketing. In addition, might not the break-up into two constituent parts (focused and diffuse) be expected to add structure and clarity to the debate? More probably, however, the argument will develop between the two positions with each claiming to be the true faith. As the diffuse viewpoint is likely to be (at least superficially) measurable and, to a large extent, sustains the traditional, functionalist, marketing viewpoint, it is likely to dominate. The wider relationships associated with the focused perspective may gradually fade from the marketing research agenda. Potential heresies, such as the breaking down of functional barriers and strategy portfolios, would become discussions of the past.

On a more positive note it may be reasonably argued that RM's broad church has contributed to the diversity of marketing debate and has helped integrate other aspects of management (Brodie *et al.*, 2002). As Brown (2002) notes, ongoing debate over definitions, domains and the nature of the discipline itself is a sign of a healthy and imaginative marketing environment. From the perspective of the researcher the 'one-size-fits-all' diffuse approach to marketing narrows potential research areas, in particular those that may be considered cross-functional. Whereas the broad, focused definition of RM encourages researchers to investigate or even engage in other disciplines (e.g. human resource management, strategic management) the diffuse, functionalist, viewpoint once more restricts the domain. Perhaps the constriction of viewpoints is manifesting itself in a paucity of new ideas.

In limiting argument to a functional agenda, marketers are potentially excluded from the 'top-table' strategic decision-making of the future. If we are to prevent this schism narrowing the research agenda then there must be some agreement on the boundaries of relationship thinking (a potentially fruitful area for further research). If this is impossible (as may indeed be the case), then Payne (2000) recommends there is a necessity to adopt agreed-upon terminology to differentiate between the theoretically broad, focused perspective and the narrow diffuse approach.

Discussion questions
1 What are the features associated with a focused and diffuse view of RM?
2 What dangers does the chapter describe?
3 What are the advantages of a broad research agenda?

Case study   Keep your customers cool

Most businesses will probably never face a customer as angry as William Foster, the character played by Michael Douglas in the film *Falling Down* (1993). After being told in a fast-food restaurant that he cannot order a breakfast meal because he's missed the cut-off point by three minutes, Foster pulls out a machine gun and threatens the staff until the manager relents. In the end, Foster proves a fickle customer: he changes his mind and decides he wants to order from the lunch menu instead, only to lose his temper again when his flaccid-looking Double Whammy Burger with Cheese fails to live up its glossy representation on the printed menu.

While most people would not condone Foster's behaviour, many would sympathise with his frustration: arbitrary rules and misleading advertising are among the biggest complaints of consumers across the world. It's just that most of them don't have an AK-47 to hand to help them make their point. But although the law-abiding and sane are much less visible than the obviously disturbed Foster, their quieter frustration is more of a serious problem for businesses. Once loyalty is lost, it can be very difficult to retrieve, which can lead to serious financial repercussions.

Much has been written about how to handle angry customers and most businesses realise how much difference the good management of complaints can make. Winning back unhappy customers can increase repurchases by 50 per cent and generate 20 times more positive referrals by word-of-mouth than by advertising, thus potentially responsible for 20–70 per cent of new customers. Retaining customers is 5–7 per cent cheaper than finding new ones, but if customer defections go down by just 5 per cent, profits will rise by 25–85 per cent. Conversely, a company's sales can go down by as much as 15 per cent if it does not handle complaints well.

Computer giant Dell discovered this to its cost. Last year, American journalist Jeff Jarvis purchased a Dell computer, encouraged by a discount coupon. He was unhappy with the product and even unhappier with Dell's customer service. He posted an online diary about the experience, which attracted hundreds of sympathisers, who reported equally bad experiences with the company. Shortly after this he wrote a 'Dear Mr Dell' letter online in which he claimed the product was a 'lemon' and that the customer service was 'appalling'.

The response surprised Jarvis. He says it amazed him 'how other consumers coalesced around the original email'. In the end, thousands of 'Dell-Hellers', as they are known, posted their own tales of woe. Jarvis followed up in August with an article published in the *Guardian* newspaper in the UK: 'I updated my audience with my latest tales of trans-oceanic frustration: I'd paid for home service, but couldn't get it; Dell replaced half my machine, but it still wouldn't work; my email-entreaties went unnoticed . . . and so did my blog posts.' Jarvis believes that a new breed of consumer has arrived. 'We spit back,' he wrote. Market researchers concluded that Dell had 'sustained long-term damage to its brand image'.

Dell's experiences prove that companies need to think carefully about how they manage angry customers. Ignoring the problem or getting it wrong can weaken the brand, hit sales and reduce customer loyalty. While most companies understand the importance of managing complaints well, in many cases they are not ready for the difficulties and complexities it involves.

A large part of the problem is that most corporate processes are geared to finding short-term solutions to the problem of a frustrated customer. This is perhaps understandable: unhappy customers invariably want a quick response, and in the majority of cases they can be dealt with through short-term actions, such as refunds, compensation or apologies. But companies that respond to customer frustration only in this way do nothing to help gain a deeper understanding of what went wrong.

Ideally, companies will respond to every customer's complaint on an individual basis. Complaints may seem similar on the surface, but each complainant will have their own views about what went wrong and what would be a fair response. Responding in the same way to all complaints may work with some, but not others. Customers need to know that your interest in them extends to when they are unhappy with the service or product and is not just limited to when they are buying it. But most of the time, companies rely on standard language and inflexible policies. They deny the customer's claims, get lost in protracted arguments, blame third parties or simply pay out. The short-term nature of these responses often fails to calm the customer down. Sometimes, they just make things worse.

And the power of word-of-mouth means that this can be disastrous. Last Christmas consultant Verde Group, which specialises in helping North American firms measure and overcome customer dissatisfaction, conducted a survey of 1,200 US consumers. It showed that for every 100 shoppers, 64 will be told about a store's poor products or services. Nearly a third of all US retail customers who have a bad shopping experience will tell four people in such a way that those four people will have a more negative impression than the person who initially had the problem. Paula Courtney, Verde Group's chief executive, says: 'A lot of companies actively try to generate positive word-of-mouth, but very few understand the power of negative word-of-mouth. They just don't get how much collateral damage can be done by unhappy customers.'

You cannot avoid angry customers and you can't afford to ignore them, so there is little choice but to listen. After all, they are trying to maintain the relationship with your company. They may be pointing to a bigger problem that you can fix to the benefit of other customers. Patrick Barwise, professor of management and marketing at London Business School, and co-author of *Simply Better: Winning and Keeping Customers by Delivering What Matters Most* (2004), says: 'There are two things that valuable brands have in common: brand awareness and trust, and trust does not come from the brand saying "trust me". It comes from experience. When a well-managed company such as Carphone Warehouse gets it wrong and tries to solve the problem, customers are more forgiving.'

Developing a fast and efficient response system might increase the number of complaints coming through, but it will also reduce the number of horror stories spread between consumers. Time is undoubtedly an issue. Customers want to be able to ask a question quickly, so it is critical that your company is accessible and ready to listen to them straight away. But many customers will be prepared to wait for an answer so long as they can see that this is likely to be to their benefit. They want to be able to communicate. Once they have done so, they do not want an unreasonable delay and they don't want to see any broken deadlines.

It is crucial to insist on a good two-way conversation to make sure negotiation takes root. This requires skill and a carefully managed process. First, companies should acknowledge the customer's emotions without justifying or evaluating them. For example, you might say: 'I can see you are frustrated about the loss of your bag and concerned about having something to wear for your meetings.' Second, you should paraphrase the customer's concerns to test your understanding and show the customer you are trying to see things from their point of view. You may, for example, say: 'If I understand you correctly, you either need your bag or an early warning before lunch-time, so you can at least buy a suit to be able to meet with an important client.' Finally, confirm that you understand and clarify any vague details.

Even if you have to disappoint the customer with a negative answer, they will appreciate the effort you have made. You should show that you are trying to be flexible and creative, and you should show commitment to help them, but not necessarily to give them something. Most customers understand that not all cases can be solved, but they definitely want to see you try to deal with them.

Apologising is a powerful tool, but also a risky one. It is probably true in most, if not all, cases that the company's product or service contributed to the customer's distress, even when it was the customer's fault. Many customers seek an apology and delivering it can calm them down to a point. But there may be a temptation to apologise too quickly, with the result that you appease the customer too early. You have gone some way to accepting blame for the problem and therefore taken responsibility for fixing it, yet you do not know the source of the problem yet.

At the first, most emotionally charged phase, the company's goals are usually to regain the customer's trust and calm them down, reassure them that the complaint will be handled and that the company is committed to building a good relationship. The temptation is to try to solve the customer's complaint straight away. It is far better, however, to wait until you can discuss the issue in a calm and rational manner.

If it is established that the company has been at fault, compensation can then be negotiated. There are four ways to compensate angry customers: fix it, replace it, provide a partial rebate or refund the whole amount. Each will generate different reactions from the customer, but are still preferable to no compensation at all. What is fair compensation? There is no easy answer to this. Compare the delay on the delivery of a book to a delay on the arrival of food and drink to a wedding. In the former case, you have a minor irritation. In the latter, you have hundreds of angry guests.

Many companies attempt to be fair to customers at a reasonable cost. One example is Air France's limit of €100 for a baggage delay of more than 24 hours. Perceptions of fairness are usually bound up with a sense of equity, equality or need. It is clear that Air France's policy is based on equality, but not equity or need. Business travellers may need to buy a new suit or miss an important meeting on that same day; holiday travellers may need to buy toiletries, but they will not really lose out on anything. The compensation actually gives them more money than they need.

Air France's policy attempts to be fair through the principle of equality. The problem is that this enables it to view every occurrence of delayed luggage as essentially the same problem, when the consequences it has for an individual vary enormously and can be worth a lot more – or less – than €100. Standard guidelines make it easier for staff to handle complaints, but equality can be a very crude measure of fairness and, perversely, create lasting feelings of unfairness. This type of policy also risks sending the wrong message to the consumer by suggesting that the company is not interested in individual cases. A compensation policy intended to be scrupulously fair can therefore actually reduce customer loyalty.

A potentially better policy would be to find out what the customer feels would be fair compensation. Companies can try to discover this during the negotiation: if the first phase has worked, the anger has been dissipated and the customer is more likely to be reasonable about compensation. Perhaps, then, several compensation cases will be solved by the principle of equality, as long it is clear that the problems and their consequences are the same or at least similar. If individual customers' cases are different, however, it may be necessary to move the conversation up a level to someone more senior. Air France could, for example, reduce the €100 compensation fee for most complaints, but increase it to €500 for a few customers. In doing so, it will be satisfying more customers in the long term and delivering a consistent message that the company treats its customers fairly.

If a company negotiates with each individual, it may find a more practical and efficient solution. Air France might tell a customer that the missing luggage will arrive in two hours' time and that it will deliver it to their hotel. However, the business traveller may need to go to a meeting directly from the airport and may suggest waiting in the business lounge until the luggage arrives. In this case, Air France will save money by not having to courier the luggage to the hotel. A negotiated fair compensation deal can be managed with minimal costs and result in greater satisfaction.

However, there will always be some people who are still dissatisfied with the process, no matter what the company does to compensate them or win back their trust. These customers present companies with a difficult problem. In an intensely competitive global market, customers are bombarded with choices and can easily switch to another firm. Even if you handle complaints well, some of your former customers will remember that they were angry with you in the past and may not want to run the risk of getting angry, frustrated and dissatisfied again.

Some companies react to this by offering a discount on future purchases as a way of keeping the customer. In so doing, they reward the complaint, but do not necessarily build a strong relationship. It is likely that the customer will use the discount and then walk away because the underlying issue of their lack of trust has not been resolved. Verde's Courtney says: 'A big mistake companies make is to link the compensation to their product – say, a discount or a month's free service. But this is so obviously designed to keep the customer in a relationship with the company that it often backfires. A much better way would be to offer a gift unrelated to the company – vouchers for a restaurant, for example, or tickets to a show.'

It is important to remember that there are two aims in any negotiation with angry customers. First, ensure the customer feels that the process is inclusive and that they have had every chance to influence the outcome. Second, understand the customer's decision-making process in the future to guarantee that they repurchase from the company again. The first objective is reinforced by a good relationship and substantive negotiations. The second has to be explicitly covered at the end of the process. The question is simple: 'What can we do to guarantee that you will do business with us in the future?'

Here, many customers may be tempted to ask for money or discounts. But these will not guarantee future purchases and are therefore of dubious value. If a senior representative manages to convince a customer that the problem will not be repeated, that customer will be much more inclined to repurchase. Certainly, they are unlikely to get the same guarantee from the competition. Sticking with the current company becomes a better and safer choice.

Courtney says: 'One of the most powerful things a company can do is for a senior manager to deliver a written promise that everything will be done to prevent the problem from recurring. It should be signed and include the direct phone line of that manager should any further difficulties arise.'

Encouraging a positive attitude towards angry customers among front-line staff is difficult but necessary. When one company renamed its customer complaint form a 'consultant's report', it found that managers paid closer attention to the advice given. The valuable knowledge gained from angry customers should be passed on to the marketing and sales departments. Customer repurchases can be traced back to the employee who dealt with the complaint and they can then be rewarded accordingly.

A month after Jarvis's blog, Dell's senior vice-president for the US consumer business, John Hamlin, said the company was opening more call centres and improving training for phone representatives. The company had also started to scan the web for blog complaints and make contact with them: 'We will now go wherever they are and get involved in their conversations, where we try to resolve the issues.'

Dell has introduced a new service called Dell Connect, where technicians can access customers' computers remotely to solve their problems. But despite such measures, Dell's efforts to deal with its angry customers has fallen short. Although it has put a lot of effort into improving its complaints procedures, it did not take the crucial step of addressing Jarvis's (and other customers') perception of future risk. Because it did not work hard enough to convince him that he could have the confidence to buy its products in future, Dell failed to make the final, necessary, move in dealing with the complaint. This is one angry customer who has not been won back.

(*Source*: Horacio Falão, *World Business*, November/December 2006)

Case study questions

1 What are the advantages of problem recovery?
2 What are the effects of negative word-of-mouth?
3 Could a 'fair compensation' policy work?

References

Barnes, J.G. (1994) 'Close to the customer: but is it really a relationship?', *Journal of Marketing Management*, **10**, 561–70.

Bartram, P. (2002) 'Measure it, prove it', *Marketing Business*, May, 18–20.

Berry, L.L. (1983) 'Relationship marketing', in Berry, L.L., Shostack, G.L. and Upsay, G.D. (eds) *Emerging Perspectives on Service Marketing*, Chicago: American Marketing Association, pp. 25–28.

Brodie, R.J., Coviello, N.E., Brookes, R.W. and Little, V. (1997) 'Toward a paradigm shift in marketing: an examination of current marketing practice', *Journal of Marketing Management*, **13** (5), 383–406.

Brodie, R.J., Glynn, M.S. and Van Durme, J. (2002) 'Toward a theory of marketplace equity: integrating branding and relationship thinking with financial thinking', *Marketing Theory*, **2** (1), 5–28.

Brown, S. (2002) 'Vote, vote, vote for Philip Kotler', *European Journal of Marketing*, **36** (3), 313–24.

Buttle, F.B. (1996) *Relationship Marketing Theory and Practice*, London: Paul Chapman Publishing.

Christopher, M., Payner, A. and Ballantyne, D. (1991) *Relationship Marketing*, Oxford: Butterworth Heinemann.

Christopher, M., Payne, A. and Ballantyne, D. (1994) *Relationship Marketing*, London: Butterworth Heinemann.

Clark, M. (2000) 'Customer service, people and processes', in Cranfield School of Management, *Marketing Management: A Relationship Marketing Perspective*, Basingstoke: Macmillan, pp. 110–24.

Clarkson, R.M., Clarke-Hill, C. and Robinson, T. (1997) 'Towards a general framework for relationship marketing? a literature review', paper presented at the Academy of Marketing Conference, Manchester, UK.

Coviello, N.E. and Brodie, R.J. (2001) 'Contemporary marketing practices of consumer and business-to-business firms: how different are they?', *Journal of Business and Industrial Marketing*, **16** (5), 382–400.

Coviello, N.E., Brodie, R.J. and Monro, H.J. (1997) 'Understanding contemporary marketing: development of a classification scheme', *Journal of Marketing Management*, **13** (6), 501–22.

Day, G.S. and Montgomery, D.B. (1999) 'Charting new directions for marketing', *Journal of Marketing*, **63**, 3–13.

Dean, D. and Croft, R. (2001) 'Friends and relations: long term approaches to political campaigning', *European Journal of Marketing*, **35** (11/12), 1197–216.

Doyle, P. (1995) 'Marketing in the new millennium', *European Journal of Marketing*, **29** (12), 23–41.

Evans, J.R. and Laskin, R.L. (1994) 'The relationship marketing process: a conceptualisation and application', *Industrial Marketing Management*, **23** (5), 439–52.

Grönroos, C. (1994) 'From marketing mix to relationship marketing: towards a paradigm shift in marketing', *Management Decisions*, **32** (2), 4–20.

Gummesson, E. (1996) 'Why relationship marketing is a paradigm shift: some conclusions from the 30R approach', presented at 1st Management and Decision Internet Conference on Relationship Marketing, MCB Publishing.

Gummesson, E. (1999) *Total Relationship Marketing: Rethinking Marketing Management from 4Ps to 30Rs*, Oxford: Butterworth Heinemann.

Gummesson, E. (2003) 'Relationship marketing: it all happens here and now!', *Marketing Theory*, **3** (1), 167–9.

Hunt, S.D. (1997) 'Competing through relationships: grounding relationship marketing in resource-advantage theory', *Journal of Marketing Management*, **13** (5), 431–45.

Hunt, S.D. and Lambe, C.J. (2000) 'Marketing's contribution to business strategy: market orientation, relationship marketing and resource-advantage theory', *International Journal of Management Reviews*, **2** (1), 17–43.

Hunt, S.D. and Morgan, R.M. (1994) 'Relationship marketing in the era of network competition, *Journal of Marketing Management*, **5** (5), 18–28.

Kotler, P. (1992) 'Total marketing', *Business Week*, Advance Executive Brief No. 2.

Levy, S.J. (2002) 'Revisiting the marketing domain', *European Journal of Marketing*, **36** (3), 299–304.

Millman, A.F. (1993) 'The emerging concept of relationship marketing', Proceedings of the 9th Annual IMP Conference, Bath, 23/25 September.

Mitchell, A. (2001) 'Playing cat and mouse games with marketing', *Precision Marketing*, 16 March, 14.

Möller, K. and Halinnen, A. (2000) 'Relationship marketing theory: its roots and directions', *Journal of Marketing Management*, **16**, 29–54.

Morgan, R.M. and Hunt, S.D. (1994) 'The commitment–trust theory of relationship marketing', *Journal of Marketing*, **58** (3), 20–38.

O'Malley, L. and Tynan, C. (1999) 'The utility of the relationship metaphor in consumer markets: a critical evaluation', *Journal of Marketing Management*, **15**, 587–602.

O'Malley, L and Tynan, C. (2000) 'Relationship marketing in consumer markets: rhetoric or reality?', *European Journal of Marketing*, **34** (7), 797–815.

Palmer, A.J. (1996) 'Relationship marketing: a universal paradigm or management fad?', *The Learning Organisation*, **3** (3), 18–25.

Parvatiyar, A. and Sheth, J.N. (2000) 'The domain and conceptual foundations of relationship marketing', in Sheth, J.N. and Parvatiyar, A. (eds) *Handbook of Relationship Marketing*, Thousand Oaks, CA: Sage, pp. 3–38.

Payne, A. (2000) 'Relationship marketing: the UK perspective', in Sheth, J.N. and Parvatiyar, A. (eds) *Handbook of Relationship Marketing*, Thousand Oaks, CA: Sage, pp. 39–67.

Peck, H. (1996) 'Towards a framework for relationship marketing: the six markets model revisited and revised', Marketing Education Group (MEG) Conference, University of Strathclyde.

Reichheld, F.F. (1996) *The Loyalty Effect: The Hidden Force behind Growth, Profits and Lasting Value*, Boston: Harvard Business School Publications.

Reynoso, J.F. and Moores, B. (1996) 'Internal relationships', in Buttle, F.B. (ed.) *Relationship Marketing Theory and Practice*, London: Paul Chapman Publishing, pp. 55–73.

Sheth, J.N. and Sisodia, R.S. (1999) 'Revisiting marketing's lawlike generalizations', *Journal of the Academy of Marketing Sciences*, **17** (1), 71–87.

Smith, W. and Higgins, M. (2000) 'Reconsidering the relationship analogy', *Journal of Marketing Management*, **16**, 81–94.

Sussex, P. and Cox, J. (2002) 'Next generation customer relationship management: strategic CRM', Chartered Institute of Marketing Special Interest Group presentation, March.

Tapp, A.J. (2002) 'The changing face of marketing academia: what can we learn from commercial market research?', *Competitive Paper, Academy of Marketing Conference*, Nottingham University.

Veloutsou, C., Saren, M. and Tzokas, N. (2002) 'Relationship marketing: what if?', *European Journal of Marketing*, **36** (4), 433–49.

Notes

1 As one of the Institute's 1998–2000 research priorities (Day and Montgomery, 1999).

2 Under the heading of a campaign for marketing effectiveness.

3 Industrial Marketing and Purchasing Group (see Chapter 2).

4 For example, Hunt, Morgan and Lambe are prominent American RM researchers who should be excluded from this generalisation. There are also a number of non-American writers, particularly those associated with CRM and/or marketing metrics (e.g. Stone, Shaw, Ambler), who enrich this viewpoint.

Glossary

4Cs model of marketing A variation of the 4Ps model considered from the customer perspective thus price becomes cost to customer, place becomes convenience, product becomes customer wants and needs and promotion becomes communication.

4Ps model of marketing The marketing Mix consisting of Price, Product, Promotion and Placement

abductive research Reasoning for the purposes of discovery as opposed to the justification of scientific hypotheses or theories.

acquisition/retention cost ratios The ratio between the cost of acquiring a new customer and the cost of retaining one.

affinity partnering/packages A strategy in which the primary goal is to leverage the affinity, goodwill or brand name strength of a partner so as to enhance relational market behaviour. The programmes are known variously as affinity packages, cause-related marketing and other terms

alliances Where a group or groups of competitors (as opposed to the whole industry) collaborate to achieve cost and efficiency objectives.

Barriers to exit (see switching costs)

BCG matrix The Boston Consulting Group Matrix based on market share and market growth

bilateral relationships Bilateral relationships are those in which both parties are motivated highly enough to invest in a relationship.

bonds The (often invisible) constraints which hold individuals or groups together.

brand image A term used to describe the unique, emotional personality of a brand.

brand management model Marketing theory based on the management of the brand through the manipulation of the marketing mix.

branding The act of differentiating products and services by a name, symbol, trade mark or other characteristic.

business process reengineering (BPR) A management approach that aims at improvements through the increased efficiency and effectiveness of organisational processes.

B2B marketing business-to-business or industrial marketing

B2C marketing business-to-consumer marketing

buyer-maintained relationships Relationships maintained by the buyer who is usually dominant in a relationship.

campaign analysis The measurement of the effectiveness of individual campaigns and media.

cause-related marketing A partnership between an organisation and a charity or cause where the commercial organisation gains positive publicity and the partner gains usually monetarily (also see affinity partnering/packages).

client conversion rate the rate at which prospects are converted into customers

co-branding A partnership between two distinct brands for mutual benefit.

collaborations The (usually formal) relationships between organizations that they are recognised externally as well as on a company-wide basis.

commitment The implicit or explicit pledge of continuity between relationship partners.

commodity approach An early 20th century school of thought that focused on those marketing actions involved in a particular product category

conjoint analysis The determination of what combination of a limited number of attributes is most influential on respondent choice or decision making.

Cooptition simultaneous competition and collaboration

corporate social responsibility (CSR) A management concept where organizations consider the interests of society by taking responsibility for the impact of their activities on customers, employees, shareholders, communities and the environment in all aspects of their operations.

cost per thousand The cost of reaching 1000 target readers, viewers or listeners in a particular media.

critical episode an episode (or incident) that is of great importance to a relationship and upon which the continuation of that relationship is dependent

cross-selling The encouragement to purchase additional products or services.

customer contact analysis The analysis of any individual customer's contact history.

customer exit When a customer severs the relationship with an organisation

customer profile analysis An analysis which enables the organisation to distinguish, from the mass of customer data, the individuals as well as the micro-segments.

customer relationship management (CRM) A continuous performance initiative designed to increase a company's knowledge of its customers, to support access across all communications channels and to cut costs.

database marketing (DbM) The use of a database to hold and analyse customer information, thereby helping develop strategic information for marketing.

De-commodifying Differentiating your brand from the competition.

deductive research Argument from general principles to particular conclusions, thus analytical and certain. Deduced, or capable of being deduced, from premises. Deductive research is associated with a 'scientific' view of research.

demarketing Marketing designed to change behaviour (e.g. smoking) that is seen to be harmful either to the individual, the community or the environment.

demographic profiling The profiling of individuals on the basis of their demographic (e.g. age) profile.

direct marketing (DM) Direct marketing (DM) focuses on using a database to communicate (and sometimes distribute) directly to customers so as to attract a direct and measurable response.

discrete exchanges Individual exchanges (i.e. purchases) that are made without reference to any other exchange in the past or on any purchase in the future.

dissolution The termination of a relationship.

distribution management The function associated with distributing products directly or indirectly to the customer.

economic benefit The benefit, in financial terms, of an action or exchange.

economic value See economic benefit

elasticity of demand The flexibility in supply or demand in response to variations in other factors.

empowerment The freedom to make decisions. It looks to the performer of the tasks for solutions to problems, and to these employees to suggest new services and products and to solve problems creatively and effectively.

episode configuration The episode types and number of each type that occur over time in the relationship between a provider and a customer.

FMCG Fast-moving consumer goods

functional approach An approach to marketing that focuses on the marketing functions (e.g. communication) in isolation from other functions (e.g. human resources) rather than as an overarching organisational philosophy. See functional silos.

functional silos Where barriers exist between functions (e.g. Marketing and HRM) and little if any coordination exists between them. See functional approach

horizontal relationships The relationship between organizations that are at the same point in the channel of distribution (including competitors) who seek to cooperate and collaborate for mutual benefit.

inductive research Making empirical generalisations (i.e. founded on experience and observation and not theory) by observing particular instances. The conclusions go beyond the facts so they can never be more than strong possibilities. Inductive research is associated with qualitative research methods.

Inertia The inclination to do nothing to change the status quo unless provoked.

inseparability Products may be produced in one location and sold in another. The production and consumption are, therefore, said to be separable. This is not the case for services, which are produced and consumed at one time and place. This inseparability occurs whether the producer is human (e.g. a doctor) or machine (e.g. an ATM machine).

institutional approach An early approach to marketing that focused on describing the operations of a specialized type of marketing agency, such as a wholesaler or a broker.

intangibility The intangible process characteristics that define services include such factors as reliability, personal care, attentiveness, friendliness etc.. These can only be verified once a service has been purchased and 'consumed'.

interdependance The reliance of two companies upon each other.

internal marketing Any activity within an organisation that focuses staff attention on the internal activities that need to be changed in order to enhance the external marketplace performance and that improve internal communication and customer consciousness among employees.

internal partnerships/relationships The relationship between employees and the organisation.

knowledge management The effective management of the sharing and retention of information in an organization and the use of management techniques to optimize the acquisition, dissemination, and use of that knowledge.

lifestyle analysis The profiling of customers on the basis of their lifestyles.

lifetime value The value of customers' purchasing over the lifetime of a relationship.

loyalty A definition of loyalty in *behavioural* terms, is based on the number of purchases and measured by monitoring the frequency of such purchases and any brand switching. A definition of loyalty in *attitudinal* terms, incorporates consumer preferences and disposition towards brands to determine levels of loyalty.

loyalty marketing A marketing strategy which seeks to encourage repeat behaviour and retain customers.

loyalty schemes A scheme designed to establish a higher level of customer retention in profitable segments by providing increased satisfaction and value to certain customers

macromarketing school In the 1970s the Macromarketing School examined the impact of marketing practices on society and society on marketing.

market price The economic value of a product or service on the open market.

market segmentation Identifying specific markets and developing different products and/or services for each segment.

marketing Traditionally seen as that management process responsible for identifying, anticipating and satisfying customer's profitably. In philosophical terms a holistic approach by an organisation to the needs and wants of the customer and other stakeholders.

marketing orientation Where a business sees the needs of customers and consumers as vital and where they develop and market products or services to meet those demands

mass customisation Relates to the notion that, by leveraging certain technologies, companies can provide customised products while retaining the economic advantages of mass production.

mass-marketing The broadcasting of messages that will reach the largest number of people possible usually through mediums such as radio, television, newspapers, etc.

mission The attitudes and expectations within an organisation with regard to the business that the organisation is in.

monopoly A long-lasting situation where there is only one provider of a product or service in a particular market.

network marketing Marketing through a network of contacts.

network-interaction marketing all activities undertaken by the firm to build, maintain and develop customer relationships.

networks A series of formal or informal contacts.

non-price competition Competition based upon differential advantages and not price.

not-for-profit marketing Marketing in the not-for-profit (e.g. charities) sector.

oligopoly A market form in which a market or industry is dominated by a small number of suppliers.

one-to-one marketing One-to-one marketing (sometimes written as 1:1 marketing) is a strategy that emphasises personalised interactions with customers.

organisational climate The deep-seated, unwritten system of shared values and norms within an organization.

organisational culture The policies and practices that characterise an organisation.

partnering B2B partnerships with suppliers and/or customers.

part-time marketers (PTM) All of those employees (excluding full-time marketers) who, in any way, influence customer relations, customer satisfaction and customer perceived quality.

patronage concentration The share of a customer's cash-flow in a certain industry in which the customer chooses to concentrate on one provider.

perceived sacrifice Perceived sacrifices (e.g. price, physical effort etc.) across all service episodes in the relationship compared with some explicit or implicit comparison standard.

perceived service quality Customer's cognitive evaluation of the service across episodes compared with some explicit or implicit comparison standard.

perceived value Service quality compared with perceived sacrifice or cost.

perishability A characteristic of services are they are perishable (i.e. they cannot be stored for sale in the future).

PEST(L) A pneumonic representing the analysis of political, economic, sociological, technological and sometimes legal factors influencing the organisation.

problem recovery The recovery from a critical situation or incident.

process management perspective (PMP) A PMP approach would see department boundaries broken down and the work-flow (including sales and marketing activities, productive, administrative and distributive activities and a host of 'part-time' marketing activities) organised and managed as a value-creation process.

product life cycle The concept that products have a series of life-stages including the introduction, growth, maturity and decline (or reinvention).

production-led economies Economies dominated by product manufacturing (as opposed to services).

profitability analysis A key CRM application that involves measuring and analysing the many different dimensions of profitability.

prospects Potential customers.

psychological benefit A non-financial, personal benefit (e.g. status).

recency, frequency and monetary value (RFV) model A model used in the direct marketing industry to calculate the value of individual customers.

relationship costs The cost involved in setting up and maintaining relationships.

relationship drivers Those factors which suggest that relationship strategies would benefit the business.

relationship marketing (RM) May be defined as the means by which organisations can 'identify and establish, maintain and enhance and, when necessary, terminate relationships with customers and other stakeholders, at a profit so that the objectives of all parties involved are met; and this is done by mutual exchange and fulfilment of promises.' (Grönroos 1994: 9)

relationship profitability The value outcome from the development of relationships.

relationship revenue The total revenue generated from a customer relationship during a fiscal year.

relationship strength The outcome measured using purchase behaviour and communication behaviour (word of mouth, complaints). The bonds between the customer and the service supplier also affect the behaviour.

resource dependence theory The theory that suggests that few organisations are self-sufficient in critical resources.

retention strategies Strategies that promote the retention of customers.

return on customer See relationship profitability.

return on investment (ROI) The percentage return on any investment.

return on relationships (ROR) See relationship profitability.

risk the perceived probability of making a loss as interpreted by the decision-maker

sales analysis The analysis of sales for specific periods and across time.

salience The level of importance or prominence associated with an exchange (i.e. purchase).

scientific marketing management An early (1923) proposal which offered guidance to companies who wish to understand marketing. Used more recently to describe marketing's preoccupation with the manipulation of quantitative data.

scope Associated with an organisation's mission statement scope relates to the attitudes and expectations within the organisation, how the organisation rates against competition and how it fits into its environment.

segmentation A group of brands or organizations sharing one or more characteristics that cause them to have similar needs.

seller-maintained relationships Relationships that rely on the seller to sustain them.

service bureaucrats A derogatory term for managers interested simply in systems maintenance, and routine adherence to uniform operating guidelines and procedures.

service encounter In the short-term they are the social occasion of economic exchange in where society allows strangers to interact. In the longer-term they provide the social occasions in which buyer and seller can negotiate and nurture their relationship.

service industries Those businesses where the greater part of the company's central offerings are intangible.

service-led economies Economies dominated by services (as opposed to manufacturing).

services marketing Strategies aimed at the specific needs of service markets.

SMART objectives A pneumonic which reminds us that objectives should be strategic, measurable, actionable, realistic and timely.

societal marketing Marketing that specifically acknowledges that organisations must respect the community and the environment.

STEP A variation of PEST (L) excluding legal aspects.

sticky demand curve An inelastic (i.e. low response to price change) demand curve.

strategic planning school In the 1970s the Strategic Planning School explored the relationship between environmental change and change within the organisation.

supplier withdrawal Where a supplier terminates the relationship with its customer.

supplier–customer dyad The understanding that only the supplier/customer relationship is of value to marketers.

switching costs Those costs involved in changing from one supplier or partner to another (e.g. search costs)

SWOT analysis The analysis of the strengths, weaknesses, opportunities and threats of and to an organisation.

toolbox approach The application (and perhaps the simplification) of marketing using models such as the 4Ps

total quality management (TQM) A management strategy aimed at ensuring awareness of quality in all organizational processes

transactional marketing (TM) A traditional viewpoint that sees marketing as a decision-making activity designed to satisfy the customer, at a profit, by targeting and making optimal decisions on the various elements of the marketing mix.

trust The confidence in the reliability and integrity of an individual or group.

value theory An area of economic and philosophical thought built upon by early marketers. Value theorists investigated how people value things (positively or negatively), the reasons why they make such evaluations and use consumer choice as evidence of intrinsic value.

variability In relation to services there are two dimensions to variability. The amount the production varies from the norm and the extent it needs to be varied to suit the individual customer's needs.

vertical relationships Vertical relationships represent those relationships that integrate all or part of the supply chain through component suppliers, manufacturers and intermediaries.

white and brown goods White goods are large kitchen appliances. Brown goods are typically small household electrical entertainment appliances such as DVD players and televisions

zone of tolerance (ZOT) That range of service performance where small increases or decreases in performance quality do not lead to any (positive or negative) action.

Index

Terms in **bold** indicate glossary entries.